THE ZHIVAGO AFFAIR

Peter Finn is national security editor for *The Washington Post* and previously served as the *Post*'s bureau chief in Moscow.

Petra Couvée is a writer and translator, and teaches at Saint Petersburg State University.

PETER FINN AND PETRA COUVÉE

The Zhivago Affair

THE KREMLIN, THE CIA, AND THE BATTLE OVER A FORBIDDEN BOOK

VINTAGE

2 4 6 8 10 9 7 5 3 1

Vintage
20 Vauxhall Bridge Road,
London SW1V 2SA

Vintage is part of the Penguin Random House group of companies whose addresses can be found at global.penguinrandomhouse.com

First published in Vintage in 2015

First published in Great Britain in 2014 by Harvill Secker

Grateful acknowledgment is made to the following for the permission to reprint previously published material:

Doubleday: "Autumn," "The Earth," and "Lieutenant Schmidt" from *A Captive of Time* by Olga Ivinskaya, translated by Max Hayward, copyright © 1978 by Doubleday & Company, Inc. Reprinted by permission of Doubleday, a division of Random House LLC. All rights reserved. Houghton Mifflin Harcourt Publishing Company: Excerpt from *Feltrinelli: A Story of Riches, Revolution and Violent Death* by Carlo Feltrinelli, translated by Alastair McEwen. Copyright © 1999 by Giangiacomo Feltrinelli. Translation copyright © 2001 by Alastair McEwen. Excerpt from *Meetings with Pasternak: A Memoir* by Alexander Gladkov, translated by Max Hayward. Copyright © 1977 by Alexander Gladkov. Translation copyright © 1978 by Max Hayward. Reprinted by permission of Houghton Mifflin Harcourt Publishing Company. All rights reserved.

Pantheon Books: "August" and "Winter Night" from *Doctor Zhivago* by Boris Pasternak, translated by Richard Pevear and Larissa Volokhonsky, translation copyright © 2010 by Richard Pevear and Larissa Volokhonsky. "Hamlet" from *Doctor Zhivago* by Boris Pasternak, translated by Max Hayward and Manya Harari, translation copyright © 1958 by William Collins Sons and Co. Ltd., copyright © 1958 by Pantheon Books Inc. Reprinted by permission of Pantheon Books, an imprint of the Knopf Doubleday Publishing Group, a division of Random House LLC. Underlying rights to *Doctor Zhivago* by Boris Pasternak, copyright © 1957 by Giangiacomo Feltrinelli Editore, Milano, Italy, copyright © The Heirs of Boris Pasternak, granted by Feltrinelli and the agents for the Estate of Pasternak. Reprinted by permission of the heirs of Boris Pasternak and Giangiacomo Feltrinelli Editore, Milan. All rights reserved.

Random House Group Limited: Excerpts from *Boris Pasternak: The Tragic Years, 1930–1960* by Evgeny Pasternak, translated by M. Duncan. Reprinted by permission of The Random House Group Limited. Simon & Schuster, Inc.: Excerpt from *Hope Against Hope: A Memoir* by Nadezha Mandelstam, translated from the Russian by Max Hayward. Copyright © 1970 by Atheneum Publishers. Reprinted by permission of Scribner Publishing Group. All rights reserved.

www.vintage-books.co.uk

A CIP catalogue record for this book is available from the British Library

ISBN 9780099581345

Printed and bound by CPI Group (UK) Ltd, Croydon CR0 4YY

For Nora FitzGerald, and our children, Rachel, Liam, David, and Ria
and
For Koos Couvée and Paula van Rossen

Contents

The Zhivago Affair

Prologue

"This is *Doctor Zhivago*. May it make its way around the world."

On May 20, 1956, two men took the suburban electric train from Moscow's Kiev station to the village of Peredelkino, a thirty-minute ride southwest of the city. It was a blue-sky Sunday morning. Spring had pushed the last of the snow away just the previous month, and the air was sweet with the scent of blooming lilac. Vladlen Vladimirsky, easily the bigger of the two, had bright blond hair and wore the billowing pants and double-breasted jacket favored by most Soviet officials. His slender companion was clearly a foreigner—Russians teased the man that he was a *stilyaga,* or "style maven," because of his Western clothing. Sergio D'Angelo also had the kind of quick smile that was uncommon in a country where circumspection was ingrained. The Italian was in Peredelkino to charm a poet.

The previous month D'Angelo, an Italian Communist working at Radio Moscow, read a brief cultural news item noting the imminent publication of a first novel by the Russian poet Boris Pasternak. The two-sentence bulletin told him little except that Pasternak's book promised to be another Russian epic. The novel was called *Doctor Zhivago*.

Before leaving Italy, D'Angelo had agreed to scout out new Soviet literature for a young publishing house in Milan that had been established by a party loyalist, Giangiacomo Feltrinelli. Getting the rights to a first novel by one of Russia's best-known poets would be a major coup both for himself and the new publishing concern. He wrote a letter to an editor in Milan in late April, and before receiving a reply asked Vladimirsky, a colleague at Radio Moscow, to set up a meeting with Pasternak.

Peredelkino was a writers' colony built on the former estate of a Russian nobleman. Set down amid virgin pine, lime trees, cedars, and larches, it was created in 1934 to reward the Soviet Union's most prominent authors with a retreat that provided escape from their apartments in the city. About fifty country homes, or dachas, were built on large lots on 250 acres. Writers shared the village with peasants who lived in wooden huts—the women wore kerchiefs and men rode on horse-drawn sleds.

Some of the biggest names in Soviet letters lived in Peredelkino—the novelists Konstantin Fedin and Vsevolod Ivanov lived on either side of Pasternak. Kornei Chukovsky, the Soviet Union's most beloved children's-book writer, lived a couple of streets away as did the literary critic Viktor Shklovsky. As idyllic as it looked, the village was haunted by its dead, those executed by the state during the Great Terror of the late 1930s—the writers Isaak Babel and Boris Pilnyak were both arrested at their dachas in Peredelkino. Their homes were handed off to other writers.

According to village lore, Soviet leader Joseph Stalin had asked Maxim Gorky, the father of Soviet literature and one of the founders of the socialist-realist school of writing, how his counterparts in the West lived. When Gorky said they lived in villas, Peredelkino was ordered up by Stalin. Legend or not, writers were a privileged caste. They were organized into the nearly four-thousand–strong Union of Soviet Writers, and lavished with perks unimaginable for ordinary Soviet citizens, who often lived in tiny spaces and suffered through long lines for basic goods. "Entrapping writers within a cocoon of comforts, surrounding them with a network of spies" was how Chukovsky described the system.

Novels, plays, and poems were seen as critical instruments of mass propaganda that would help lead the masses to socialism. Stalin expected his authors to produce fictional or poetic celebrations of the Communist state, the story lines full of muscular progress in the factories and the fields. In 1932, during a meeting with writers at Gorky's home, Stalin launched the new literature with a toast: "The production of souls is more important than the production of tanks. . . . Here someone correctly said that a writer must not sit still, that a writer must know the life of a country. And that is correct. Man is remade by life itself. But you, too, will assist in remaking his soul. This is important, the production of souls. And that is why I raise my glass to you, writers, the engineers of the human soul."

After leaving the train station, D'Angelo and Vladimirsky passed the walled summer residence of the patriarch of the Russian Orthodox Church. They crossed a stream by a graveyard and walked along roads that were still a little muddy before turning onto Pavlenko Street, the narrow lane at the edge of the village where Pasternak lived. D'Angelo was unsure what to expect. He knew from his research that Pasternak was esteemed as a supremely gifted poet and was praised by scholars in the West as someone who stood out brightly in the stolid world of Soviet letters. But D'Angelo had never actually read anything by him. Within the Soviet establishment, recognition of Pasternak's talent was tempered by doubts about his political commitment, and for long periods original work by the poet was not published. He earned a living as a translator of foreign literature, becoming one of the premier Russian interpreters of Shakespeare's plays and Goethe's *Faust*.

Pasternak's dacha, emerging from stands of fir and birch, was a chocolate-brown, two-story building with bay windows and a veranda; it reminded some visitors of an American timber-frame house. As D'Angelo arrived at the wooden gate, the sixty-six-year-old writer, in Wellington boots and homespun pants and jacket, was working in his front garden, where the family had a vegetable patch among the fruit trees, bushes, and flowers. Pasternak was a physically arresting man, remarkably youthful, with an elongated face that seemed sculpted from stone, full sensuous lips, and lively chestnut eyes. The poet Marina Tsvetaeva said he looked like an Arab *and* his horse. A visitor to Peredelkino noted that he could pause at certain moments as if recognizing the impact "of his own extraordinary face . . . half closing his slanted brown eyes, turning his head away, reminiscent of a horse balking."

Pasternak greeted his visitors with firm handshakes. His smile was exuberant, almost childlike. Pasternak enjoyed the company of foreigners, a distinct pleasure in the Soviet Union, which only began to open up to outsiders after the death of Stalin in 1953. Another Western visitor to Peredelkino that summer, the Oxford don Isaiah Berlin, said the experience of conversing with writers there was "like speaking to the victims of shipwreck on a desert island, cut off for decades from civilization—all they heard they received as new, exciting and delightful."

The three men sat outside on two wooden benches set at right angles in the garden, and Pasternak took some delight in Sergio's last name, stretching it out in his low droning voice with its slightly nasal timbre. He asked about the name's origin. Byzantine, said D'Angelo, but very common in Italy. The poet talked at length about his one trip to Italy when he was a twenty-two-year-old philosophy student at the University of Marburg in Germany in the summer of 1912. Traveling in a fourth-class train carriage, he had visited Venice and Florence but had run out of money before he could get to Rome. He had written memorably of Italy in an autobiographical sketch, including a sleepy half-day in Milan just after he arrived. He remembered approaching the city's cathedral, seeing it from various angles as he came closer, and "like a melting glacier it grew up again and again on the deep blue perpendicular of the August heat and seemed to nourish the innumerable Milan cafes with ice and water. When at last a narrow platform placed me at its foot and I craned my head, it slid into me with the whole choral murmur of its pillars and turrets, like a plug of snow down the jointed column of a drainpipe."

Forty-five years later, Pasternak would become bound to Milan. Just a short distance away from the cathedral, through the glass-vaulted Galleria Vittorio Emanuele II and past La Scala, was Via Andegari. At number 6 was the office of Feltrinelli, the man who would defy the Soviet Union and first publish *Doctor Zhivago*.

Conversations with Pasternak could become soliloquies. Once engaged, he talked in long, seemingly chaotic paragraphs, full of coltish enthusiasm, words and ideas hurtling ahead before he alighted on some original point. Isaiah Berlin said, "He always spoke with his peculiar brand of vitality, and flights of imaginative genius." D'Angelo was enthralled, happy to be an audience, when Pasternak apologized for talking on and asked his visitor why he wanted to see him.

D'Angelo explained that his posting in Moscow was sponsored by the Italian Communist Party, which encouraged its leading activists to experience life in the Soviet Union. D'Angelo worked as an Italian-language producer and reporter for Radio Moscow, the Soviet Union's official international broadcaster, which was housed in two buildings behind Pushkin Square in central Moscow. Before coming to the Soviet Union, he had been the manager of the Libreria Rinascita, the Italian Communist Party bookstore in Rome. D'Angelo was a committed activist from an anti-Fascist family who joined the party in 1944, but some of his Italian comrades felt he was a little too bookish and lacked sufficient zeal. They hoped a spell in Moscow would stoke some fire. The party leadership arranged a two-year assignment in the Soviet capital. He had been in the Soviet Union since March.

D'Angelo, who spoke Russian well and only occasionally had to ask Vladimirsky to help him with a word, told Pasternak that he also acted as a part-time agent for the publisher Feltrinelli. Not only was Feltrinelli a committed party member, D'Angelo said, he was a very rich man, the young multimillionaire scion of an Italian business dynasty, who had been radicalized during the war. Feltrinelli had recently started a publishing venture, and he especially wanted contemporary literature from the Soviet Union. D'Angelo said he had recently heard about *Doctor Zhivago,* and it seemed an ideal book for Feltrinelli's new house.

Pasternak interrupted the Italian's pitch with a wave of his hand. "In the USSR," he said, "the novel will not come out. It doesn't conform to official cultural guidelines."

D'Angelo protested that the book's publication had already been announced and since the death of Stalin there had been a marked relaxation within Soviet society, a development that got its name—"the thaw"—from the title of a novel by Ilya Ehrenburg. The horizons of literature seemed to broaden as old dogmas were challenged. Fiction that was somewhat critical of the system, reflected on the recent Soviet past, and contained complex, flawed characters had begun to be published.

The Italian said he had a proposal. Pasternak should give him a copy of *Doctor Zhivago* so that Feltrinelli could have it translated, although he would of course wait until publication in the Soviet Union before bringing it out in Italy. And Pasternak could trust Feltrinelli because he was a Communist Party loyalist. This all sounded reasonable to the eager D'Angelo, anxious as he was to secure the manuscript and justify the stipend he was receiving from Feltrinelli.

D'Angelo had no sense of the risk Pasternak would be taking by placing his manuscript in foreign hands. Pasternak was all too aware that the unsanctioned publication in the West of a work that had not first appeared in the Soviet Union could lead to charges of disloyalty and endanger the author and his family. In a letter to his sisters in England in December 1948, he warned them against any printing of some early chapters he had sent them: "Publication abroad would expose me to the most catastrophic, not to mention fatal, dangers."

Pilnyak, Pasternak's former next-door neighbor in Peredelkino (the side gate between their gardens was never closed), was executed with a single bullet to the back of the head in April 1938. Pilnyak was skeptical of the Soviet project, tackled themes such as incest in his fiction, and described Stalin's and Gorky's literary commands as the castration of art. Pilnyak's fate may well have been foreordained as early as 1929 when he was accused, falsely, of orchestrating publication abroad of his short novel *Mahogany* by anti-Soviet elements. Set in a postrevolutionary provincial town, the novel includes a sympathetically drawn character who is a supporter of Leon Trotsky—Stalin's bitter rival. Pilnyak was subjected to a public campaign of abuse in the press. "To me a finished literary work is like a weapon," wrote Vladimir Mayakovsky, the brash and militant Bolshevik poet, in a review of Pilnyak's work that noted, without blushes, he had not actually read *Mahogany*. "Even if that weapon were above the class struggle—such a thing does not exist (though, perhaps, Pilnyak thinks of it like that)—handing it over to the White press strengthens the arsenals of our enemies. At the present time of darkening storm clouds this is the same as treachery at the front."

Pilnyak tried to win his way back into the party's good graces with some kowtowing pronouncements about Stalin's greatness, but he couldn't save himself. The charge of disloyalty was memorialized in a file. With the Great Terror at its height, he was tormented by the fear of imminent arrest. The country was in the grip of a mad, murderous purging of the ranks of the party, the bureaucracy, and the military as well as the intelligentsia and whole ethnic groups. Hundreds of thousands were killed or died in detention between 1936 and 1939; hundreds of writers were among the victims. Pasternak remembered Pilnyak constantly looking out the window. Acquaintances he ran into expressed amazement that he hadn't already been picked up. "Is it really you?" they asked. And on October 28, 1937, the secret police came. Pasternak and his wife were at their neighbor's house; it was the birthday of Pilnyak's three-year-old son, also named Boris. That evening, a car pulled up and several men in uniform got out. It was all very polite. Pilnyak was needed on urgent business, said one officer.

He was charged with belonging to "anti-Soviet, Trotskyist, subversive and terrorist organizations," preparing to assassinate Stalin, and spying for Japan; he had traveled to Japan and China in 1927 and written about his journey. He had also spent six months in the United States in 1931 with Stalin's permission, traveling cross-country in a Ford and working briefly in Hollywood as a screenwriter for MGM. His travelogue novel *Okay* offered a harsh view of American life.

Pilnyak "confessed" to everything, but in a final word to a military tribunal he said he would like "to have paper" in front of him on which he "could write something of use to the Soviet people." After a fifteen-minute trial, from 5:45 to 6:00 p.m. on April 20, 1938, Pilnyak was found guilty and sentenced to the "ultimate penalty," which was carried out the next day—in the sinister language of the bureaucracy—by the "head of 1st special section's 12th department." Pilnyak's wife spent nineteen years in the Gulag, and his child was raised in the Soviet republic of Georgia by a grandmother. All of Pilnyak's works were withdrawn from libraries and bookstores, and destroyed. In 1938–39, according to a report by the state censor, 24,138,799 copies of "politically damaging" works or titles of "absolutely no value to the Soviet reader" were pulped.

In the wake of the arrest of Pilnyak and others, the Pasternaks, like many in the village, lived with fear. "It was awful," said Pasternak's wife, Zinaida, pregnant at the time with their first son. "Every minute we expected that Borya would be arrested."

Even after the death of Stalin, no Soviet writer could entertain the idea of publication abroad without considering Pilnyak's fate. And since 1929 no one had broken the unwritten but iron rule that unapproved foreign publication was forbidden.

As he continued his patter, D'Angelo suddenly realized that Pasternak was lost in thought. Chukovsky, Pasternak's neighbor, thought he had a "somnambulistic quality"—"he listens but does not hear" while away in the world of his own thoughts and calculations. Pasternak had an uncompromising certainty about his writing, its genius, and his need to have it read by as wide an audience as possible. The writer was convinced that *Doctor Zhivago* was the culmination of his life's work, a deeply authentic expression of his vision, and superior to all of the celebrated poetry he had produced over many decades. "My final happiness and madness," he called it.

Both epic and autobiographical, the novel revolves around the doctor-poet Yuri Zhivago, his art, loves, and losses in the decades surrounding the 1917 Russian Revolution. After the death of his parents, Zhivago is adopted into a family of the bourgeois Moscow intelligentsia. In this genteel and enlightened setting, he discovers his talents for poetry and healing. He finishes medical school and marries Tonya, the daughter of his foster parents. During World War I, while serving in a field hospital in southern Russia, he meets the nurse Lara Antipova and falls in love with her.

Upon his return to his family in 1917, Zhivago finds a changed city. Controlled by the Reds, Moscow is wracked by the chaos of revolution and its citizens are starving. The old world of art, leisure, and intellectual contemplation has been erased. Zhivago's initial enthusiasm for the Bolsheviks soon fades. Fleeing typhus, Zhivago and his family travel to Varykino, their estate in the Urals. Nearby, in the town of Yuryatin, Zhivago and Lara meet again. Lara's husband is away with the Red Army. Zhivago's desire for her is rekindled, but he is troubled by his infidelity.

Captured by a band of peasant soldiers who press-gang him into serving as a field doctor, Zhivago witnesses the atrocities of the Russian Civil War, committed by both the Red Army and its enemy, a coalition of anti-Bolshevik forces known as the Whites. Zhivago eventually "deserts" the revolutionary fight and returns home to find that his family, believing him dead, has fled the country. He moves in with Lara. As the war draws near, they take refuge in the country house in Varykino. For a brief moment, the world is shut out, and Zhivago's muse returns to inspire a burst of poetry writing. The howling of the wolves outside is a portent of the relationship's doom. With the end of the war, and the consolidation of Bolshevik power, fate forces the couple apart forever. Lara leaves for the Russian Far East. Zhivago returns to Moscow and dies there in 1929. He leaves behind a collection of poetry, which forms the novel's last chapter and serves as Zhivago's artistic legacy and life credo.

Zhivago is Pasternak's sometime alter ego. Both character and writer are from a lost past, the cultured milieu of the Moscow intelligentsia. In Soviet letters, this was a world to be disdained, if summoned at all. Pasternak knew that the Soviet publishing world would recoil from *Doctor Zhivago*'s alien tone, its overt religiosity, its sprawling indifference to the demands of socialist realism and the obligation to genuflect before the October Revolution. The novel's heresies were manifold and undisguised, and for the Soviet faithful, particular sentences and thoughts carried the shock of an unexpected slap. A "zoological apostasy" was the reaction in an early official critique of the novel. The revolution was not shown as "the cake with cream on top," Pasternak acknowledged, as the writing neared completion. The manuscript "should be given to anyone who asks for it," he said, "because I do not believe it will ever appear in print."

Pasternak had not considered Western publication, but by the time D'Angelo arrived at his gate, he had endured five months of complete silence from Goslitizdat, the state literary publisher, to which he had submitted the novel. Two leading journals, *Zna-*

mya (The Banner) and *Novy Mir* (New World), which he hoped might excerpt parts of *Doctor Zhivago,* had also not responded. For D'Angelo, the timing of his pitch was the height of good fortune; Pasternak, when presented with this unexpected offer, was ready to act. In a totalitarian society he had long displayed an unusual fearlessness—visiting and giving money to the relatives of people who had been sent to the Gulag when the fear of taint scared so many others away; intervening with the authorities to ask for mercy for those accused of political crimes; and refusing to sign drummed-up petitions demanding execution for named enemies of the state. He recoiled from the group-think of many of his fellow writers. "Don't yell at me," he said to his peers at one public meeting, where he was heckled for asserting that writers should not be given orders. "But if you must yell, at least don't do it in unison." Pasternak felt no need to tailor his art to the political demands of the state; to sacrifice his novel, he believed, would be a sin against his own genius.

"Let's not worry about whether or not the Soviet edition will eventually come out," he said to D'Angelo. "I am willing to give you the novel so long as Feltrinelli promises to send a copy of it, shall we say in the next few months, to other publishers from important countries, first and foremost France and England. What do you think? Can you ask Milan?" D'Angelo replied that it was not only possible but inevitable because Feltrinelli would surely want to sell the foreign rights to the book.

Pasternak paused again for a moment before excusing himself and going into his house, where he worked in a Spartan study on the second floor. In winter it looked out over "a vast white expanse dominated by a little cemetery on a hill, like a bit of background out of a Chagall painting." Pasternak emerged from the dacha a short time later with a large package wrapped in a covering of newspaper. The manuscript was nearly 800 closely typed pages divided into five parts. Each part, bound in soft paper or cardboard, was held together by twine that was threaded through rough holes in the pages and then knotted. The first section was dated 1948, and the work was still littered with Pasternak's handwritten corrections.

"This is *Doctor Zhivago*," Pasternak said. "May it make its way around the world."

With all that was to come, Pasternak never wavered from that wish.

D'Angelo explained that he would be able to get the manuscript to Feltrinelli within a matter of days because he was planning a trip to the West. It was just before noon, and the men chatted for a few more minutes.

As they stood at the garden gate saying their good-byes, the novel under D'Angelo's arm, Pasternak had an odd expression—wry, ironic—playing on his face. He said to the Italian: "You are hereby invited to my execution."

The publication of *Doctor Zhivago* in the West in 1957 and the award of the Nobel Prize in Literature to Boris Pasternak the following year triggered one of the great cultural storms of the Cold War. Because of the enduring appeal of the novel, and the 1965 David Lean film based on it, *Doctor Zhivago* remains a landmark piece of fiction. Yet few readers know the trials of its birth and how the novel galvanized a world largely divided between the competing ideologies of two superpowers.

Doctor Zhivago was banned in the Soviet Union, and the Kremlin attempted to use the Italian Communist Party to suppress the first publication of the novel in translation in Italy. Officials in Moscow and leading Italian Communists threatened both Pasternak and his Milan publisher, Giangiacomo Feltrinelli. The two men, who never met, resisted the pressure and forged one of the greatest partnerships in the history of publishing. Their secret correspondence, carried in and out of the Soviet Union by trusted couriers, is its own manifesto on artistic freedom.

The Soviet Union's widely reported hostility to *Doctor Zhivago* ensured that a novel that might otherwise have had a small elite readership became an international best seller. *Doctor Zhivago*'s astonishing sales increased even more when Pasternak was honored by the Swedish Academy with the 1958 Nobel Prize in Literature. The writer had been nominated several times before in acknowledgment of his poetry, but the appearance of the novel made Pasternak an almost inevitable choice. The Kremlin dismissed Pasternak's Nobel Prize as an anti-Soviet provocation and orchestrated a relentless internal campaign to vilify the writer as a traitor. Pasternak was driven to the point of suicide. The scale and viciousness of the assault on the elderly writer shocked people around the world, including many writers sympathetic to the Soviet Union. Figures as diverse as Ernest Hemingway and the Indian prime minister, Jawaharlal Nehru, rose to Pasternak's defense.

Pasternak lived in a society where novels, poems, and plays were hugely significant forms of communication and entertainment. The themes, aesthetics, and political role of literature were the subjects of fierce ideological disputes, and sometimes the losers in these debates paid with their lives. After 1917, nearly 1,500 writers in the Soviet Union were executed or died in labor camps for various alleged infractions. Writers were to be either marshaled in the creation of a new "Soviet man" or isolated, and in some cases crushed; literature could either serve the revolution or the enemies of the state.

The Soviet leadership wrote extensively about revolutionary art; gave hours-long speeches about the purpose of fiction and poetry; and summoned writers to the Kremlin to lecture them about their responsibilities. The men in the Kremlin cared about writing all the more because they had experienced its capacity to transform. The revolutionary Vladimir Lenin was radicalized by a novel, Nikolai Chernyshevsky's *What Is to Be Done?* "Art belongs to the people," Lenin said. "It should be understood and loved by the masses. It must unite and elevate their feelings, thoughts and will. It must stir them to activity and develop the artistic instincts within them. Should we serve exquisite sweet cake to a small minority while the worker and peasant masses are in need of black bread?"

As Stalin consolidated power in the early 1930s, he brought the country's literary life under strict control. Literature was no longer the party's ally, but its servant. The artistic vitality of the 1920s withered. Stalin, a poet in his youth, was a voracious reader of fiction, sometimes devouring hundreds of pages in a day. He red-lined passages that displeased him. He weighed in on what plays should be staged. He once telephoned Pasternak to discuss whether a particular poet, Osip Mandelstam, was a master of his art—a conversation that was really about Mandelstam's fate. He decided which writers should receive the country's premier literary award, inevitably named the Stalin Prize.

The Soviet public longed for great writing with a desire that was rarely sated. The country's shelves groaned under the dry, formulaic dreck produced to order. Isaiah Berlin found it all "irretrievably second-rate." Those writers who held on to their individual voices—Pasternak and the poet Anna Akhmatova, among a few others—were rewarded with near adulation. Their readings could fill concert halls and their words, even when banned, found a way to their public's lips. In the Obozerka forced-labor camp near the White Sea, some inmates amused and bolstered each other by trying to see who could recite the most Pasternak. The Russian émigré critic Victor Frank, explaining Pasternak's appeal, said that in his poetry "the skies were deeper, the stars more radiant, the rains louder and the sun more savage. . . . No other poet in Russian literature—and, perhaps, in the world at large—is capable of charging with the same magic the humdrum objects of our humdrum lives as he. Nothing is too small, too insignificant for his piercing eye, the eye of a child, the eye of the first man on a new planet: rain puddles, window-sills, mirror stands, aprons, doors of railway carriages, the little hairlets standing off a wet overcoat—all this flotsam and jetsam of daily life is transformed by him into a joy for ever."

The poet had a deeply ambivalent relationship with the Communist Party, its leaders, and the Soviet Union's literary establishment. Before the Great Terror of the late 1930s, Pasternak had written poetry in praise of Lenin and Stalin, and he was for a time transfixed by Stalin's guile and authority. But as the bloodletting of the purges swept the country, he became profoundly disillusioned with the Soviet state. That he survived the Terror when so many others were swallowed by its relentless, blind maw has no single explanation. The Terror could be bizarrely random—mowing down the loyal and leaving some of the suspect alive.

Pasternak was protected by luck, by his international status, and, perhaps most critically, by Stalin's interested observation of the poet's unique and sometimes eccentric talent.

Pasternak did not seek to confront the authorities but lived in the purposeful isolation of his creativity and his country life. He began to write *Doctor Zhivago* in 1945 and it took him ten years to complete. The writing was slowed by periods of illness; by the need to set it aside to make money from commissioned translations of foreign works; and by Pasternak's growing ambition and wonder at what was flowing from his pen.

It was, effectively, a first novel, and Pasternak was sixty-five when he finished it. He channeled much of his own experience and opinions into its pages. *Doctor Zhivago* was not a polemic, or an attack on the Soviet Union, or a defense of any other political system. Its power lay in its individual spirit, Pasternak's wish to find some communion with the earth, some truth in life, some love. Like Dostoevsky, he wanted to settle with the past and express this period of Russia's history through "fidelity to poetic truth."

As the story evolved, Pasternak realized that *Doctor Zhivago* stood as a rebuke to the short history of the Soviet state. The plot, the characters, the atmosphere embodied much that was alien to Soviet literature. There was in its pages a disdain for the "deadening and merciless" ideology that animated so many of his contemporaries. *Doctor Zhivago* was Pasternak's final testament, a salute to an age and a sensibility he cherished but that had been destroyed. He was obsessively determined to get it published—unlike some of his generation who wrote in secret for the "drawer."

Doctor Zhivago appeared in succession in Italian, French, German, and English, among numerous languages—but not, at first, in Russian.

In September 1958, at the World's Fair in Brussels, a Russian-language edition of *Doctor Zhivago,* handsomely bound in a blue linen hardcover, was handed out from the Vatican Pavilion to Soviet visitors. Rumors about the genesis of this mysterious edition began almost immediately; the CIA was first mentioned by name as its secret publisher in November 1958. Until now, the CIA has never acknowledged its role.

Over the years, a series of apocryphal stories have appeared about how the CIA obtained an original manuscript of *Doctor Zhivago* and its motivation in printing the novel in Russian. It was said that British intelligence had forced down a plane in Malta that was carrying Feltrinelli from Moscow and secretly photographed the novel, which they removed from his suitcase in the plane's hold. It never happened. Some of Pasternak's French friends believed, incorrectly, that an original-language printing of *Doctor Zhivago* was necessary to qualify for the Nobel Prize—a theory that has periodically resurfaced. The Nobel Prize was not a CIA goal, and an internal accounting of the agency's distribution of the book shows that no copies were sent to Stockholm; the CIA simply wanted to get copies of *Doctor Zhivago* into the Soviet Union and into the hands of Soviet citizens.

It has also been argued that the printing was the work of Russian émigrés in Europe and the agency's involvement was marginal—no more than that of the financier of émigré front organizations. The CIA was in fact deeply involved. The operation to print and distribute *Doctor Zhivago* was run by the CIA's Soviet Russia Division, monitored by CIA director Allen Dulles, and sanctioned by President Eisenhower's Operations Coordinating Board, which reported to the National Security Council at the White House. The agency arranged the printing of a hardcover edition in 1958 in the Netherlands and printed a miniature paperback edition of the novel at its headquarters in Washington, D.C., in 1959.

A weapon in the ideological battles between East and West—this, too, is part of *Doctor Zhivago*'s extraordinary life.

Chapter 1

"The roof over the whole of Russia has been torn off."

Bullets cracked against the facade of the Pasternak family's apartment building on Volkhonka Street in central Moscow, pierced the windows, and whistled into the plaster ceilings. The gunfire, which began with a few isolated skirmishes, escalated into all-out street fighting in the surrounding neighborhood, and drove the family into the back rooms of the spacious second-floor flat. That, too, seemed perilous when shrapnel from an artillery barrage struck the back of the building. Those few civilians who ventured out on Volkhonka crab-ran from hiding spot to hiding spot. One of the Pasternaks' neighbors was shot and killed when he crossed in front of one of his windows.

On October 25, 1917, in a largely bloodless coup, the Bolsheviks seized power in Petrograd, the Russian capital, which had been called Saint Petersburg until World War I broke out and a Germanic name became intolerable. Other major centers did not fall so easily as militants loyal to the revolutionary leader Vladimir Lenin battled the Provisional Government that had been in power since March. There was more than a week of fighting in Moscow, the country's commercial center and second city, and the Pasternaks found themselves in the middle of it. The family's apartment building was on a street that crested a hill. The flat's nine street-side windows offered a panoramic view of the Moscow River and the monumental golden dome of Christ the Savior Cathedral. The Kremlin was just a few hundred meters to the northeast along the bend of the river. Pasternak, who rented a room in the Arbat neighborhood, had happened over to his parents' place on the day the fighting began and found himself stuck there, eventually huddling with his parents and younger, twenty-four-year-old brother, Alexander, in the downstairs apartment of a neighbor. The telephone and lights were out, and water only occasionally, and then briefly, trickled out of the taps. Boris's two sisters—Josephine and Lydia—were caught in similarly miserable conditions at the nearby home of their cousin. They had gone out for a stroll on an unseasonably mild evening when, suddenly, armored cars began to careen through streets that quickly emptied. The sisters had just made it to the shelter of their cousin's home when a man across the street was felled by a shot. For days, the constant crackle of machine-gun fire and the thud of exploding shells were punctuated by "the scream of wheeling swifts and swallows." And then as quickly as it started "the air drained clear, and a terrifying silence fell." Moscow had fallen to the Soviets.

Russia's year of revolution had begun the previous February when women protesting bread shortages in Petrograd were joined by tens of thousands of striking workers and the national war weariness swelled into a sea of demonstrators against the exhausted autocracy. Two million Russians would die in the carnage at the Eastern Front and another 1.5 million civilians died from disease and military action. The economy of the vast, backward Russian empire was collapsing. When troops loyal to the czar fired on the crowds, killing hundreds, the capital was in open revolt. On March 3, having been abandoned by the army, Nicholas II abdicated, and the three-hundred-year-old Romanov dynasty was at an end.

Pasternak, who had been assigned to a chemical factory in the Urals to support the war effort, hurried back to Moscow. He traveled part of the journey on a *kibitka,* a covered wagon on runners, and warded off the cold with sheepskin coats and hay. Pasternak and his siblings welcomed the fall of the monarchy, the emergence a new Provisional Government, and, above all, the prospect of a constitutional political order. Subjects became citizens, and they reveled in the transformation. "Just imagine when an ocean of blood and filth begins to give out light," Pasternak told one friend. His sister Josephine described him as "overwhelmed" and "intoxicated" by the charisma of Alexander Kerensky, a leading political figure, and his effect on a crowd outside the Bolshoi Theatre that spring. The Provisional Government abolished censorship and introduced freedom of assembly.

Pasternak would later channel the sense of euphoria into his novel. The hero of *Doctor Zhivago* was spellbound by the public discourse, which was brilliantly alive, almost magical. "I watched a meeting last night. An astounding spectacle," said Yuri Zhivago, in a passage where the character describes the first months after the fall of the czar. "Mother Russia has begun to move, she won't stay put, she walks and never tires of walking, she talks and can't talk enough. And it's not as if only people are talking. Stars and trees come together and converse, night flowers philosophize, and stone buildings hold meetings. Something gospel-like, isn't it? As in the time of the apostles. Remember, in Paul? 'Speak in tongues and prophesy. Pray for the gift of interpretation.' "

It seemed to Zhivago that "the roof over the whole of Russia has been torn off." The political ferment also enfeebled the Provisional Government, which was unable to establish its writ. It was overwhelmed above all by the widely hated decision to keep fighting in the world war. The Bolsheviks, earning popular support with the promise of "Bread, Peace and Land," and driven by Lenin's calculation that power was for the taking, launched their insurrection and a second revolution in October. "What magnificent surgery," Pasternak wrote in *Doctor Zhivago*. "To take and at one stroke artistically cut out the old, stinking sores!"

The Bolsheviks, in their constitution, promised Utopia—"the abolition of all exploitation of man by man, the complete elimination of the division of society into classes, the ruthless suppression of the exploiters, the establishment of a socialist organization of society, and the victory of socialism in all countries."

Yuri Zhivago quickly is disillusioned by the convulsions of the new order: "First, the ideas of general improvement, as they've been understood since October, don't set me on fire. Second, it's all still so far from realization, while the mere talk about it has been paid for with such seas of blood that I don't think the ends justify the means. Third, and this is the main thing, when I hear about the remaking of life, I lose control of myself and fall into despair."

The word *remaking* was the same one Stalin used when toasting his writers and demanding engineers of the soul. Zhivago tells his interlocutor, a guerrilla commander: "I grant you're all bright lights and liberators of Russia, that without you she would perish, drowned in poverty and ignorance, and nevertheless I can't be bothered with you, and I spit on you, I don't like you, and you can all go to the devil."

These are the judgments of a much older Pasternak, writing more than three decades after the revolution and looking back in sorrow and disgust. At the time, when Pasternak was twenty-seven, he was a man in love, writing poetry, and swept along in the "greatness of the moment."

The Pasternaks were a prominent family within Moscow's artistic intelligentsia, who looked to the West, and were disposed to support the political reform of an autocratic, sclerotic system. Boris's father, Leonid, was a well-known impressionist painter and a professor at the Moscow School of Painting, Sculpture and Architecture. He was born to a Jewish innkeeper in the Black Sea city of Odessa, a multi-ethnic and dynamic center within the Pale of Settlement where most of Russia's Jews were forced to reside. Odessa had a rich cultural life and Alexander Pushkin, who lived there in the early part of the nineteenth century, wrote "the air is filled with all Europe." Leonid first moved to Moscow in 1881, to study medicine at Moscow University. By the fall of 1882, queasy about working with cadavers, he abandoned medicine and enrolled at the Bavarian Royal Academy of Art in Munich. His daughter Lydia described him as "a man of a dreamy, gentle disposition . . . slow and uncertain in anything but his work."

After obligatory military service, Leonid returned to Moscow in 1888, and his first sale—a painting entitled *Letter from Home*—was to Pavel Tretyakov, a collector whose purchases denoted a kind of arrival for favored artists. Leonid also established a reputation as a skilled illustrator, and he contributed to an edition of Leo Tolstoy's *War and Peace* in 1892. The following year, Leonid and Tolstoy met and became friends. Over the years, Leonid sketched the Russian writer numerous times, including in death at the Astapovo train station in 1910. Leonid brought Boris on the overnight train to pay respects to Tolstoy, and Boris recalled that the grand old man seemed tiny and wizened, no longer a mountain, just "one of those he had described and scattered over his pages by the dozen."

Tolstoy visited the Pasternak apartment in Moscow, as did the composers Sergei Rachmaninov and Alexander Scriabin, among other cultural figures of the day, many of whom were painted by Leonid. The children viewed the visiting dignitaries as a fact of home life. "I have observed art and important people from my earliest days, and I have become accustomed to treating the sublime and exclusive as something natural, as a norm of life," wrote Pasternak, recalling the luminaries who graced his parents' parlor and his father's studio.

Pasternak's childhood was also filled with music. His mother, née Rozalia Kaufman, was an extraordinarily precocious child who, as a five-year-old coming to the piano for the first time, perfectly reproduced pieces played by her cousin simply from having watched him. Roza, as she was called, was the daughter of a wealthy soda-water manufacturer in Odessa. She gave her first recital at age eight, by eleven was drawing glowing reviews in the local press, and two years later toured southern Russia. She performed in Saint Petersburg, studied in Vienna, and was appointed a professor of music at the Odessa conservatory before she was twenty. "Mother was music," her daughter Lydia wrote. "There may be a greater virtuoso, a more brilliant performer but no-one with greater penetration, something indefinable, which makes you burst out in tears at the first chord, at each movement in sheer joy and ecstasy." Roza's potential as a major pianist of her age was curtailed, however, by anxiety, heart problems, and marriage. She met Leonid Pasternak in 1886 in Odessa, and they were married in February 1889 in Moscow. Boris was born the following year. His brother, Alexander, was born in 1893, Josephine in 1900, and Lydia in 1902.

By twelve, Boris was imagining a career as a pianist and composer. The "craving for improvisation and composition flared up in me and grew into a passion." He quit when he realized that his skills at the piano lacked the brilliance and natural flair of some of the composers he idolized, such as Scriabin. Pasternak could not tolerate the possibility that he would not achieve greatness. As a boy, he was used to being the best and the first, and he had an inner arrogance about his own skills. He had equal measures of physical and intellectual confidence. After watching local peasant girls ride horses one summer in the countryside, Boris convinced himself that he, too, could ride bareback. It became an obsession to test himself. When he finally persuaded a girl to let him ride her mount, the twelve-year-old boy was thrown by a panicking filly while jumping a stream, and broke his right thighbone. When it healed, his right leg was slightly shorter, and the resulting lameness, although disguised for much of his life, kept him out of military service in the First World War. Pasternak's brother said that his natural talents "confirmed in him a strong faith in his own powers, in his abilities and in his destiny." Second-best was something to be cast aside in a fit of pique, and forgotten. "I despised everything uncreative, any kind of hack work, being conceited enough to imagine I was a judge in these matters," Pasternak wrote many years later. "In *real* life, I thought, everything must be a miracle, everything must be predestined from above, nothing must be deliberately designed or planned, nothing must be done to follow one's own fancies." The piano abandoned, he turned toward poetry.

While he was a student at Moscow University, where he studied law and then philosophy and graduated with a first-class honors degree, Pasternak attended a salon of young authors, musicians, and poets—a "tipsy society" that mixed artistic experimentation and discovery with rum-laced tea. Moscow was full of overlapping and feuding salons built around competing philosophies of art, and Pasternak was an ardent if little-known participant. "They did not suspect that there before them was a great poet, and meanwhile treated him as an intriguing curiosity without ascribing any serious importance to him," said his friend Konstantin Loks. One observer at a reading said he "spoke in a toneless voice and forgot nearly all the lines. . . . There was an impression of painful concentration, one wanted to give him a push, like a carriage that won't go—'Get a move on!'—and as not a single word came across (just mutterings like some bear waking up), one kept thinking impatiently: 'Lord, why does he torment himself and us like this.'" His cousin Olga Freidenberg thought Pasternak was "not of this world," that he was absent-minded and self-absorbed: "Borya did all the talking as usual," Olga exclaimed to her diary after a long walk.

Pasternak was prone to unrequited infatuations, a spur for his poetry but dispiriting for the young man. While at the University of Marburg, where he studied philosophy in the summer of 1912, he was rebuffed by a woman, Ida Vysotskaya, the daughter of a rich Moscow tea merchant, to whom he professed his love. "Just try to live normally," Ida told him. "You've been led astray by your way of life. Anyone who hasn't lunched and is short of sleep discovers lots of wild and incredible ideas in himself." Ida's rejection led to a burst of poetry writing on the day he was supposed to be turning in a paper for his philosophy class. He ultimately decided against staying at the German university to pursue a doctorate in philosophy. "God, how successful my trip to Marburg is. But I am giving up everything—art it is, and nothing else." Pasternak tended to talk at his wished-for lovers, interspersing rhapsodies of affection with philosophical treatises. Another woman, who balked at something more intimate than friendship, complained their "meetings were rather monologues on his part." These amorous failings left Pasternak emotionally shattered, and they prompted some intense periods of writing.

His first stand-alone publication appeared in December 1913 after a productive summer where he "wrote poetry not as a rare exception but often and continuously, as one paints or composes music." The resulting collection, called *Twin in the Storm Clouds,* drew little attention or enthusiasm and an older Pasternak later dismissed these efforts as painfully pretentious. A second volume, *Over the Barriers,* appeared in early 1917. Some of the poems were cut—grievously—by the czarist censor, the book was littered with misprints, and it, too, received little attention from the critics. Still, for *Over the Barriers,* Pasternak got paid for the first time—150 rubles, a memorable moment for any writer. The Russian writer Andrei Sinyavsky described Pasternak's first two volumes as "a tuning-up," and said it was "part of the search for a voice of his own, for his own view of life, for his own place amid the diversity of literary currents."

In the summer of 1917 Pasternak was in love with Yelena Vinograd, a young war widow, student, and enthusiastic supporter of the revolution. She took the poet to demonstrations and political meetings, enjoyed his company, but was not sexually attracted to him. "The relationship remained platonic, unphysical and unconsummated emotionally, and it was thus an intensely tormenting one for Pasternak," wrote one scholar. The fuel of passion and frustration, all playing out against the backdrop of a society that was being utterly transformed, led to a cycle of poems that would vault Pasternak into the front ranks of Russian literature. The collection was called *My Sister Life* and came with the subtitle *Summer 1917*. At first, only handwritten copies of the poems circulated and the work gained a popularity "no poet since Pushkin achieved on the basis of manuscript copies."

Because of the upheaval of revolution, and the subsequent privation of the civil war, when much literary publishing ground to a halt because of a lack of paper, the book did not appear until 1922—long after Vinograd had departed and Pasternak had finally found love with Yevgenia Lurye, an artist.

They first met at a birthday party where Yevgenia, striking in a green dress, drew the attention of a number of young men. Pasternak recited his poetry, but the young woman was distracted and didn't pay attention. "Right you are, why listen to such nonsense?" said Pasternak.

She wanted to see him again and was responsive to his expressions of ardor. "Ah, it were better I never lose this feeling," he wrote her, describing how much he missed her when she visited her parents before their marriage. "It is like a conversation with you, murmuring profoundly, dripping mutely, secretly—and true. . . . What am I to do, what am I to call this magnetism and saturation with the melody of you other than the distraction you compel, and which I would dispel—like one lost in the woods."

They married in 1922. Pasternak had the gold medal he won as his high school's best student melted in order to make wedding rings, which he engraved roughly himself: "Zhenya and Borya."

Their son Yevgeni—named after his mother—was born in 1923. They lived in a small section of the Pasternak family's old apartment now divided among six families. "Hemmed in on all sides by noise, can only concentrate for periods at a time by dint of extreme sublimated desperation, akin to self-oblivion," he complained to the All-Russian Union of Writers. Often he could only work at night when silence fell over the house, staying awake with cigarettes and hot tea.

Both Pasternak and Yevgenia had their own artistic ambitions, and the marriage was marked by their competing struggle to assert themselves creatively and an inability to make concessions. There was also the unavoidable and looming fact that Pasternak was "a man with inarguably more talent," their son later wrote.

Pasternak's relations with women continued to be fraught. The marriage was buffeted by the heat of some of his correspondence with the poet Marina Tsvetaeva, which greatly irritated his wife. In the summer of 1930, he found himself increasingly attracted to Zinaida Neigauz, the wife of his best friend, the pianist Genrikh Neigauz, with whom the Pasternaks vacationed in Ukraine. Zinaida was born in Saint Petersburg in 1897, the daughter of a Russian factory owner and a mother who was half Italian. When she was fifteen, she became involved with a cousin, a man in his forties and married with two children, an affair that informed some of the early experience of the young Lara in *Doctor Zhivago*. In 1917, Zinaida moved to Yelisavetgrad where she met and married her piano teacher, Neigauz.

Before he was even sure of Zinaida's feeling, Pasternak told his wife he was in love. He then immediately proceeded to announce his passion to Genrikh. Pasternak and Genrikh wept, but Zinaida, for the moment, remained with her husband. By early the next year, the two were sleeping together, and Zinaida confessed the affair in a letter to her husband, who was on a concert tour in Siberia. He left a recital in tears and returned to Moscow.

Pasternak, with more than a measure of narcissism, argued that he could maintain his marriage, continue his affair, and sustain his friendship, all the while remaining above reproach. "I've shown myself unworthy of [Genrikh], whom I still love and always will," said Pasternak in a letter to his parents. "I've caused prolonged, terrible, and as yet undiminished suffering to [Yevgenia]—and yet I'm purer and more innocent than before I entered this life."

The complicated ménage continued for some time. Yevgenia went to Germany with her young son, leaving Boris and Zinaida free to consort together. In a poem, he encouraged Yevgenia to make a fresh start without him:

Do not fret, do not cry, do not tax
Your last strength, and your heart do not torture.
You're alive, you're inside me, intact,
As a buttress, a friend, an adventure.

I've no fear of standing exposed
As a fraud in my faith in the future.
It's not life, not a union of souls
We are breaking off, but a hoax mutual.

Many years later, he remembered the marriage as unhappy and lacking passion. He said that "beauty is the mark of true feelings, the sign of its strength and sincerity." And he thought it unfair that his son bore the trace of his failure to love in his "ugly face" with its reddish complexion and freckles.

Yevgenia's eventual return to Moscow in early 1932 left Boris and Zinaida without a place to live in a city where flats were a very precious commodity. Zinaida, feeling "painfully awkward," returned to Genrikh and asked him to take her back as "a nanny for the children" and "to help him do the housekeeping." Pasternak returned to Yevgenia—for three days. "I begged her to understand—that I worship [Zinaida]—that it would be despicable to fight against this feeling." When he met friends, he gave long, tearful accounts of his complicated family affairs.

Effectively homeless and in love, Pasternak began to despair. "It was around midnight—and freezing. A terrible, accelerating conviction of hopelessness tightened like a spring inside me. I suddenly saw the bankruptcy of my whole life." He ran through the streets to the Neigauzes' apartment. "Der spät kommende

Gast? [The late-arriving guest?]," said Genrikh laconically as he opened the door and promptly left. Inside, Pasternak pulled a bottle of iodine from a shelf and drank it in one gulp. "What are you chewing? Why does it smell so strong of iodine?" asked Zinaida, who began to scream. A doctor living in the building was summoned, and Pasternak was induced to vomit repeatedly and then put to bed, still very weak. "In this state of bliss, my pulse almost gone, I felt a wave of pure, virginal, totally untrammeled freedom. I actively, almost languidly, desired death—as you might want a cake. If there had been a revolver by my side, I would have reached out my hand like reaching for a sweet."

Genrikh, who at this point seemed quite happy to rid himself of Zinaida, said, "Well, are you satisfied? Has he proved his love for you?"

For Pasternak, Zinaida, to whom he was now married, was a homemaker who allowed him the physical and emotional space to work—something Yevgenia was less disposed to do.

Yevgenia "is much cleverer and more mature than [Zinaida] is, and perhaps better educated too," Pasternak told his parents. Yevgenia "is purer and weaker, and more childlike, but better armed with the noisy weapons of her quick temper, demanding stubbornness and insubstantial theorizing." Zinaida had "the hard-working, industrious core of her strong (but quiet and wordless) temperament."

Yevgenia, said her son, "continued loving my father for the rest of her life."

Pasternak's complicated relations with more than one woman were far from over. Nor was his impulse to surrender to providence. And fate may have repaid his trust with the poet's unlikely survival of Stalin's purges in the years to follow.

Chapter 2

"Pasternak, without realizing it, entered the personal life of Stalin."

The revolution was followed by a devastating and prolonged civil war between the Red Army and the anti-Bolshevik forces, the Whites. The winters were unusually severe. Food was scarce, and the Pasternak family was routinely undernourished. Boris sold books for bread, and traveled to the countryside to scrounge for apples, dry biscuits, honey, and fat from relatives and friends. He and his brother sawed wood from joints in the attic to keep fires burning at the Volkhonka apartment, where their living space was reduced by the authorities to two rooms; at night the brothers sometimes went out to steal fencing and other items that could be burned. Almost everyone's health declined, and in 1920 Leonid sought and obtained permission to take Roza to Germany for treatment after she suffered a heart attack. Their two daughters also moved to Germany, and the family was permanently divided. Pasternak's parents and sisters eventually settled in England before the outbreak of the Second World War.

Boris saw his parents only once more, during a visit to Berlin after he married his first wife, Yevgenia. That extended ten-month stay in Berlin, which had become the capital of émigré Russia, convinced Pasternak that his artistic future lay in his homeland, not amid the nostalgia and squabbling that marked the exile community. "Pasternak is uneasy in Berlin," wrote the literary theorist and critic Viktor Shklovsky, who also later returned to

Moscow. "It seems to me that he feels among us an absence of propulsion. . . . We are refugees. No, not refugees but fugitives—and now squatters. . . . Russian Berlin is going nowhere. It has no destiny." Pasternak was deeply wedded to Moscow and Russia. "Amidst Moscow streets, by-ways and courtyards he felt like a fish in water; here he was in his element and his tongue was purely Muscovite. . . . I recall how his colloquial speech shocked me and how it was organically linked to his whole Muscovite manner," observed Chukovsky.

Isaiah Berlin said Pasternak had "a passionate, almost obsessive desire to be thought a Russian writer with roots deep in Russian soil" and that this was "particularly evident in his negative feelings towards his Jewish origins . . . he wished the Jews to assimilate, to disappear as a people." In *Doctor Zhivago,* the character Misha Gordon articulates this point of view, demanding of the Jews: "Come to your senses. Enough. There's no need for more. Don't call yourselves by the old name. Don't cling together, disperse. Be with everyone. You are the first and best Christians in the world." When he was a child, Pasternak's nanny brought him to Orthodox churches in Moscow—services redolent with incense and watched over by walls of Byzantine iconography. But his sisters said he was untouched by Russian Orthodox theology before 1936, and Isaiah Berlin saw no sign of it in 1945, concluding that Pasternak's interest in Christianity was a "late accretion." As an older man, Pasternak was attached to his own version of Christianity, a faith influenced by the Orthodox Church but not formally part of it. "I was born a Jew," he told a journalist late in life. "My family was interested in music and art and paid little attention to religious practice. Because I felt an urgent need to find a channel of communication with the Creator, I was converted to Russian Orthodox Christianity. But try as I might I could not achieve a complete spiritual experience. Thus I am still a seeker."

By early 1921, the White forces who opposed the Bolsheviks were defeated, and literary life slowly rekindled in the ruined country. The first print run of *My Sister Life,* which also was published in Berlin, ran to about one thousand. It appeared in somewhat impecunious-looking khaki dustcovers—"the last gamble of some croaking publisher." *My Sister Life* drew euphoric, head-turning reviews that announced the entry of a giant.

"To read Pasternak's verse is to clear your throat, to fortify your breathing, to fill your lungs; surely such poetry could provide a cure for tuberculosis. No poetry is more healthful at the present moment! It is koumiss [fermented mare's milk] after evaporated milk," said the poet Osip Mandelstam.

"I was caught in it as in a downpour. . . . A downpour of light," swooned Tsvetaeva in a 1922 review. "Pasternak is all wide-open—eyes, nostrils, ears, lips, arms."

The collection barely seemed to touch on the actual events of 1917 beyond what Tsvetaeva called "the faintest hints." The only time the word *revolution* was employed was to describe a haystack. In "About these Poems," which appears at the beginning of the collection, the airy indifference to the political moment engendered some carping that Pasternak seemed a little too precious for the times:

The window-halves I'll throw apart,
In muffler from the cold to hide,
And call to children in the yard,
"What century is it outside?"

A "hothouse aristocrat of our society's private residences," sneered the Marxist critic Valerian Pravdukhin. Such criticism would eventually grow louder, but in 1922 whatever ideological shortcomings might be surmised were muted by the widely acknowledged poetic genius of his lines.

Pasternak had arrived, and it did not take the Soviet leadership long to notice. In June 1922, Pasternak was summoned to the Revolutionary Military Council for a meeting with Leon Trotsky, the head of the Red Army, a leading theoretician of the new Marxist state, and the best-known, behind Lenin, of the new leadership. Trotsky was the member of the Politburo most interested in culture, and he believed artists, and agitprop, had a critical role in the elevation of the working class, with the ultimate goal of creating what he called a "classless culture, the first that will be truly universal." In 1922, Trotsky began to familiarize himself with prominent and emerging writers, and the following year he would publish *Literature and Revolution*. "It is silly, absurd, stupid to the highest degree," he wrote in the introduction, "to pretend that art will remain indifferent to the convulsions of our epoch. . . . If nature, love or friendship had no connection with the social spirit of an epoch, lyric poetry would long ago have ceased to exist. A profound break in history, that is, a rearrangement of classes in society, shakes up individuality, establishes the perception of the fundamental problems of lyric poetry from a new angle, and so saves art from eternal repetition."

"Trotsky was no liberal in affairs of culture," wrote one of his biographers. "He felt that no one in Russia who challenged the Soviet order, even if only in novels or paintings, deserved official toleration. But he wanted a policy of flexible management within this stern framework. He aimed to win the sympathy of those intellectuals who were not the party's foes and might yet become its friends."

Trotsky wanted to find out if Pasternak was willing to commit his lyrical talent and subsume his individuality to a greater cause: the revolution. Pasternak was recovering from a night of drinking when the summons by telephone came. He and Yevgenia were about to embark on their trip to Germany to introduce her to his parents, and a farewell party at the Volkhonka apartment had left a number of people the worse for wear. Pasternak was sleeping late when the phone rang at noon. He was summoned to the Revolutionary Military Council for an audience with Trotsky in one hour. Pasternak quickly shaved, poured water over his throbbing head, and washed his mouth out with cold coffee before throwing on a starched white shirt and a freshly pressed blue jacket. An official motorbike with a sidecar picked him up.

The two men greeted each other formally with first name and patronymic.

Pasternak apologized: "Sorry, I have come to you after a farewell party with some heavy drinking."

"You're right," said Trotsky, "you really look haggard."

The two men chatted for more than half an hour, and Trotsky asked Pasternak why he "refrained" from reacting to social themes. Pasternak said his "answers and explanations amounted to a defense of true individualism, as a new social cell in a new social organism." Pasternak said Trotsky had "enraptured and quite captivated" him before confessing to a friend that he had monopolized the talk and prevented Trotsky from fully expressing his opinions. Indeed, the conversation seemed to achieve the remarkable feat of leaving Trotsky a little flabbergasted.

"Yesterday I began struggling through the dense shrubbery of your book," said Trotsky, referring to *My Sister Life*. "What were you trying to express in it?"

"That is something to ask the reader," replied Pasternak. "You decide for yourself."

"Oh well, in that case I'll carry on struggling. It's been nice to meet you, Boris Leonidovich."

Pasternak did not get a mention in *Literature and Revolution*—a fortunate snub given the emerging power struggle between Trotsky and Stalin, and Trotsky's ultimate fall. After Lenin's death in 1924, Stalin gradually outmaneuvered and crushed his rivals within the party.

There was a beguiling obliviousness to Pasternak's encounters with the powerful, which would continue to mark his relations with the Soviet state. He had a preternatural willingness to express his opinions in a society where people filtrated their words for ideological or other offenses. Pasternak was never openly hostile to Soviet power, and his attitude to the men in the Kremlin swung between fascination and loathing. No one engendered more of that strange ambivalence—allure and disgust—than Stalin, who also seemed a little transfixed by Pasternak's reputation as a poet-seer. Nadezhda Mandelstam, Osip's wife, wrote there was "one remarkable feature of our leaders: their boundless, almost superstitious respect for poetry." This was especially true of the relationship between Stalin and Pasternak. They never met, spoke only once on the phone, yet a mysterious, unknowable bond existed between the two. Pasternak, for a time, idealized the dictator. Stalin indulged the poet with his life.

On November 11, 1932, Pasternak stood at the window of his apartment on Volkhonka Street and watched the black funeral carriage, decorated with onion domes, which carried Stalin's dead wife to Novodevichy Cemetery. Pasternak was agitated, according to his son. And his public response to the death—published six days later—would forever stir speculation that he had earned an unlikely benediction from Stalin, a former seminarian.

Early in the morning of November 9, 1932, Nadya Alliluyeva, Stalin's thirty-one-year-old wife, killed herself. No one heard the shot. By the time a maid found her body, lying in a pool of blood on the floor of her bedroom in a Kremlin apartment, she was already cold; down a corridor, in another bedroom, her husband was sleeping off a boozy night. The previous evening, the ruling party's moguls had celebrated the fifteenth anniversary of the revolution at the home of the defense chief, Kliment Voroshilov; the leadership all lived in claustrophobic proximity inside the Kremlin's thick, redbrick walls. Their parties tended to be boisterous, alcohol-soaked affairs, and Stalin, whose lupine malice was never far from the surface, was particularly obnoxious that evening. His wife, stern and aloof, even with their two children, eleven-year-old Vasili and six-year-old Svetlana, was an austere Bolshevik who favored the dull look of the dutiful servant. She had married a forty-one-year-old Stalin when she was a girl, just eighteen. He was neglectful, and she was increasingly prone to severe migraines, bouts of hysteria, and exhaustion. One of Stalin's biographers said Alliluyeva "suffered from a serious mental illness, perhaps hereditary manic depression or borderline personality disorder."

For the evening at Voroshilov's, Alliluyeva stepped out a little. She wore a stylish black dress with embroidered red roses, which had been purchased in Berlin. Her husband, who arrived at the party separately, didn't notice, although he sat opposite her, at the middle of the dinner table. Instead, he flirted with a film actress, the wife of a Red Army commander, playfully tossing little pieces of bread at her. The meal was washed down with Georgian wine and punctuated with frequent vodka toasts. Stalin at one point raised his drink to call for the destruction of the enemies of the state; Alliluyeva pointedly ignored the raising of the glasses. "Hey, you!" shouted Stalin. "Have a drink." She screamed back, "Don't you dare 'hey me'!" According to some accounts, Stalin flicked a lit cigarette at her, and it went down her dress. Alliluyeva stormed off, followed by Polina Molotova, the wife of Vyacheslav Molotov, chairman of the Council of People's Commissars. She complained to Molotova about her husband's behavior and talked about her suspicion that Stalin was sleeping with other women, including a Kremlin hairdresser. When the two women separated, Alliluyeva appeared to have calmed down. Nikita Khrushchev in his memoirs said that Alliluyeva tried to reach her husband later that night and learned from a doltish guard that Stalin was at a nearby dacha with a woman. Nadya is said to have written Stalin a last letter—lost to history—that burned with personal and political condemnations. She shot herself in the heart.

The death certificate, signed by compliant doctors, said the cause of death was appendicitis. Suicide could not be acknowledged. Soviet ritual required collective expressions of grief from different professions. In a letter to the newspaper *Literaturnaya Gazeta* (Literary Gazette), a group of writers said Alliluyeva "gave all her strength to the cause of liberating millions of oppressed humanity, the cause that you yourself lead and for which we are ready to surrender our own lives as confirmation of the uncrushable vitality of this cause." There were thirty-three signatures, including Pilnyak, Shklovsky, and Ivanov, but Pasternak's was not among his colleagues'. Instead he somehow managed to append a separate, individual message. "I share in the feelings of my comrades," he wrote. "On the evening before I had for the first time thought about Stalin deeply and intensively as an artist. In the morning I read the news. I was shaken as if I had actually been there, living by his side, and seen everything."

Stalin's reaction to this bizarre message and its hint of clairvoyance is unrecorded. In the wake of the suicide, Stalin was deeply emotional, openly wept, and "said he didn't want to go on living either." Pasternak's words, amid all the chest-thumping and sterile pronouncements, may have been read by Stalin as the pronouncement of a *yurodivy,* or "holy fool"—an otherworldly man with a gift for prophecy. In the New York Russian-language newspaper *Novy Zhurnal,* the émigré scholar Mikhail Koryakov wrote, "From that moment onwards, 17 November 1932, it seems to me, Pasternak, without realizing it, entered the personal life of Stalin and became some part of his inner world." If the dictator, in response to the message, did extend a protective cloak to the poet when others were being slain, it was not something Pasternak could know; he, too, could feel the cold fear that Stalin engendered.

One evening in April 1934, Pasternak ran into Osip Mandelstam on Tverskoi Boulevard. The poet—passionate, opinionated, and a brilliant conversationalist—was someone Pasternak acknowledged as an equal, another master of his art. But he was also a dyspeptic and incautious critic of the regime. Right on the street, because "the walls have ears," he recited some new verse about Stalin. It read:

We live, deaf to the land beneath us,
Ten steps away no one hears our speeches.

But where there's so much as half a conversation
The Kremlin's mountaineer will get his mention.

His fingers are fat as grubs
And the words, final as lead weights, fall from his lips,

His cockroach whiskers leer
And his boot tops gleam.

Around him a rabble of thin-necked leaders—
Fawning half-men for him to play with.

They whinny, purr or whine
As he prates or points a finger,

One by one forging his laws, to be flung
Like horseshoes at the head, the eye or the groin.

And every killing is a treat
For the broad-chested Ossete.

In the version that came to the attention of the secret police, the poem included the phrase "the murderer and peasant slayer."

"I didn't hear this; you didn't recite it to me," said Pasternak, "because, you know, very dangerous things are happening now. They've begun to pick people up." He described the poem as an act of suicide, and implored Mandelstam not to recite it to anyone else. Mandelstam didn't listen, and inevitably he was betrayed. The secret police appeared at Mandelstam's apartment in the early morning of May 17. The poet Anna Akhmatova had arrived the previous evening and was staying with the Mandelstams. As the search commenced, the three sat in silent fear; it was so quiet they could hear a neighbor playing the ukulele. The spines of books were cut open to see if they hid a copy of the poem, but the agents failed to find one. Mandelstam had not committed it to paper. It was already light when the poet was taken to the cells at the Lubyanka, the massive security complex in central Moscow that housed the Joint State Political Directorate, or OGPU, a forerunner of what became known as the KGB. His interrogator presented him with a copy of the poem, one that must have been memorized by the informer. Mandelstam thought he was doomed.

Pasternak interceded with Nikolai Bukharin, the recently appointed editor of the daily newspaper *Izvestiya* and a man Lenin called the "darling of the Party"—one of the old Bolsheviks from the revolutionary leadership in 1917. Bukharin knew and admired the country's artistic elite, even those outside the reigning dogma, and he was a "persistent opponent of cultural regimentation," according to his biographer. "We serve up an astonishingly monotonous ideological food," Bukharin complained. As editor of *Izvestiya,* he had brightened up its pages with new subjects and writers. Pasternak had just contributed some translations of the Georgian poets Paolo Yashvili and Titsian Tabidze.

Bukharin was out when Pasternak came to see him, and the poet left a note asking him to intervene in the case. In a message he sent to Stalin in June 1934, Bukharin added a postscript: "Pasternak is completely bewildered by Mandelstam's arrest."

The entreaties worked, and Mandelstam, who could have been

accused of terrorism and sent to almost certain death at a forced-labor camp on the White Sea canal, was allowed to admit to the relatively mild offense of "composing and distributing counter-revolutionary works." Stalin issued a decisive and chilling command that was passed down the chain: "Isolate but preserve." On May 26, Mandelstam was sentenced to three years in internal exile in the town of Cherdyn, far to the northeast in the Urals. He was dispatched almost immediately, and his wife traveled with him.

In Cherdyn, Mandelstam threw himself out the second-floor window of a hospital. Fortunately he landed in a heap of earth that was intended for a flower bed, and only dislocated his shoulder. His wife sent a flurry of telegrams to Moscow to insist that he needed to be moved to a larger city to get psychiatric care. The OGPU was inclined to listen; Stalin had ordered him preserved. Moreover, the first Congress of Soviet Writers was soon to take place in Moscow, and the leadership did not want the death of a prominent writer to mar it. The writer's case again came to Stalin's attention, and he decided to speak to Pasternak directly.

By 1934, the building on Volkhonka had been turned into communal apartment housing where families each had a room to sleep, and shared a bathroom and kitchen. The phone was in the hallway. A call from Stalin was highly unusual, if not extraordinary, but Pasternak—as he did at first with everyone he spoke to on the phone—launched into a ritual complaint about the din around him because of noisy children.

Stalin addressed Pasternak with the familiar *you,* and told him that Mandelstam's case had been reviewed and "everything will be alright." He asked Pasternak why he hadn't petitioned the writers' organization on Mandelstam's behalf.

"If I were a poet and a poet friend of mine were in trouble, I would do anything to help him," said Stalin.

Pasternak told him that the writers' organization hadn't tried to help arrested members since 1927.

"If I hadn't tried to do something, you probably would never have heard about it," said Pasternak.

"But after all he is your friend," said Stalin.

Pasternak rambled on about the nature of his relationship with

Mandelstam and how poets, like women, are always jealous of one another.

Stalin interrupted him: "But he's a master, he's a master, isn't he?"

"But that's not the point," said Pasternak.

"What is, then?"

Pasternak sensed that Stalin actually wanted to find out if he knew about Mandelstam's poem. "Why do you keep on about Mandelstam?" asked Pasternak. "I have long wanted to meet you for a serious discussion."

"What about?" Stalin asked.

"About life and death."

Stalin hung up.

Pasternak redialed the number, but Stalin's secretary told him he was busy. (Perhaps, or just as likely exasperated.) The OGPU allowed Mandelstam to move to Voronezh, about three hundred miles south of the capital, but decreed that he was barred from living in Moscow, Leningrad, as Petrograd had been renamed, and ten other major cities. Word of Pasternak's conversation with Stalin raced through Moscow, and some thought Pasternak lost his nerve and didn't defend his fellow poet with sufficient zeal. But the Mandelstams, when they learned of the call, said they were happy with Pasternak. "He was quite right to say that whether I'm a master or not is beside the point," said Osip. "Why is Stalin so afraid of a master? It's like a superstition with him. He thinks we might put a spell on him like shamans." Pasternak continued to regret that he didn't get a meeting with Stalin.

"Like many other people in our country, Pasternak was morbidly curious about the recluse in the Kremlin," according to Nadezhda Mandelstam. "Pasternak still regarded Stalin as the embodiment of the age, of history and the future, and that he simply longed to see this living wonder at close quarters." And Pasternak felt that he, uniquely, had "something to say to the rulers of Russia, something of immense importance." Isaiah Berlin, to whom he confessed this sentiment, found it "dark and incoherent."

The First Congress of the Union of Soviet Writers opened on August 17, 1934, and ran through the end of the month with speeches, workshops, and pageantry. The gathering was broadly divided between those who favored strict party control of literary efforts, and liberals who argued for some artistic autonomy. The Soviet Union's artistic establishment was in almost constant debate over the form of literature, its relationship to the audience, and its duty to the state. These disputes often assumed the bitter character of religious schism—the conservative and heterodox in a running battle for supremacy. In a three-hour address, Bukharin spoke about "Poetry, Poetics, and the Tasks of Poetry Creativity in the USSR." Among those he singled out for praise was Pasternak. He acknowledged that Pasternak "is a poet remote from current affairs . . . from the din of battle, from the passions of the struggle." But he said he had not "only gemmed his work with a whole string of lyrical pearls, but . . . also given us a number of profoundly sincere revolutionary pieces." For the champions of populist, committed poetry, this was heresy. Alexei Surkov, a poet, song lyricist, and budding functionary, who would grow to hate Pasternak with all the bitterness of envy, responded in a speech that Pasternak's art was no model for emerging Soviet poets.

"The immense talent of B. L. Pasternak," Surkov said, "will never fully reveal itself until he has attached himself fully to the gigantic, rich, and radiant subject matter [offered by] the Revolution; and he will become a great poet only when he has organically absorbed the Revolution into himself."

Stalin eventually weighed in, declaring in December 1935 that Vladimir Mayakovsky, dead by his own hand since 1930, "was and remains the best and most talented poet of our epoch." The pronouncement led Pasternak to write to thank Stalin: "Your lines about him had a saving effect on me. Of late, under the influence of the West, [people] have been inflating [my significance] terribly and according [me] exaggerated significance (it even made me ill): they began suspecting serious artistic power in me. Now, since you have put Mayakovsky in first place, this suspicion has been lifted from me, and with a light heart I can live and work as before, in modest silence, with the surprises and mysteries without which I would not love life.

"In the name of this mysteriousness, fervently loving and devoted to you. B. Pasternak."

The Leader scribbled on it: "My archive. I Stalin."

As the literary scholar Grigori Vinokur, who knew Pasternak, said: "I am never sure where modesty ends and supreme self-esteem begins."

Pasternak would, in the New Year's Day 1936 edition of *Izvestiya,* publish two poems that lauded Stalin as the "Genius of Action," and he expressed a vague desire for some "mutual awareness." Pasternak later characterized these adulatory lines as "a sincere and one of the most intense of my endeavors—and the last in that period—to think the thoughts of the era, and to live in tune with it."

In 1936, Stalin began a series of show trials, macabre pieces of theater that would over the next two years mow down the old revolutionary leadership—among them Kamenev, Zinoviev, Rykov, and, in 1938, Bukharin. "Koba, why is my death necessary for you?" Bukharin asked Stalin in a last note. He was shot in a prison in Oryol on March 15, 1938. Across the Soviet Union, there were waves upon waves of arrests and executions in the ranks of the party, the military, the bureaucracy, and the intelligentsia. Close to a quarter of a million people were killed because they were members of national minorities deemed a threat to state security. The country was in the grip of a deranged, pitiless slaughter. With each torture session, the enemies of the state grew exponentially. In 1937 and 1938, Stalin personally signed lists of names for execution comprising 40,000 people, according to Robert Conquest, a historian of the Great Terror. He notes that on one day, on December 12, 1937, Stalin approved 3,167 death sentences. And Stalin only dealt with middle- and higher-ranking officials, and well-known individuals. Across the country, the system's lower tiers—the regional bosses—were engaged in their own paroxysms of execution to please Moscow. Feverish denunciation became an integral part of the political culture at all levels of society. Citizens felt compelled to name enemies, or be named.

In *Pravda,* on August 21, 1936, a letter appeared from sixteen writers under the headline "Wipe Them from the Face of the Earth." It called for the execution of sixteen defendants in the first major show trial, including Grigori Zinoviev, the former head of the Communist International, and Lev Kamenev, who was the acting chairman of the Politburo during Lenin's last days. Pasternak had refused to sign, but the writers' union added his name without informing him. He learned of the addition only at the last minute and came under heavy pressure to let it stand, which he did. His wife, Zinaida, backed his decision, regarding any other choice as suicidal. But Pasternak was ashamed of his failure to strike his name. All sixteen defendants were found guilty of being part of a Trotskyist conspiracy to assassinate Stalin, and they were shot in the bowels of the Lubyanka. Anatoli Tarasenkov, an editor of the journal *Znamya,* wrote Pasternak a letter about the incident, to which he didn't respond. When Tarasenkov confronted Pasternak, the poet was evasive, and relations between the two ruptured. In the future, Pasternak decided, he would not allow himself to be compromised.

The sense of choking fear was all-powerful. Ordinary things struck strange notes. Pasternak's cousin Olga Freidenberg recalled how "every evening radio broadcasts telling about the bloody and basely conceived trial would be followed by the playing of gay folk dances—the *kamarinskaya* or the *hopak.*"

"My soul has never recovered from the trauma of the prison-like knell of the Kremlin chimes striking the midnight hour," she wrote in her diary. "We had no radio, but from the neighbor's room it came booming forth, cudgeling my brains and bones. The midnight chimes sounded particularly sinister when they followed on the terrible words 'The sentence has been carried out.' "

Even though Pasternak's signature ended up on the letter to *Pravda,* his reluctance to append his name marked him as suspect, and he came under increasing ideological attack from the purveyors of a literary credo. Vladimir Stavsky, a writers' union official and enthusiastic denouncer, accused Pasternak of "slandering the Soviet people" in some poems about Georgia. Pasternak later wrote of his own disillusionment: "Everything snapped inside me, and my attempt to be at one with the age turned into opposition, which I did not conceal. I took refuge in translation. My own creative work came to an end."

In a series of defiant gestures, Pasternak put himself at great risk. When Bukharin was placed under house arrest in early 1937, Pasternak sent a note—sure to be read by others—to his Kremlin apartment to say, "No forces will convince me of your treachery." Bukharin, a dead man walking, wept at the expression of support, and said, "He has written this against himself." In the 1937 file of the poet Benedikt Livshits, who was summarily executed as an enemy of the people, Pasternak's name is on a list of writers who were possibly being considered as targets for arrest.

In June 1937, Pasternak was asked to sign a petition supporting the death penalty for a group of military defendants, including Marshal Mikhail Tukhachevsky. When an official arrived at his dacha in Peredelkino, he ran him off, shouting, "I know nothing about them, I don't give them life and I have no right to take it away!" The refusal was followed by further pressure from a delegation from the writers' union led by the odious Stavsky, who screamed at and threatened Pasternak. Zinaida, who was pregnant, beseeched him to sign. "She threw herself at my feet begging me not to destroy her and the child," Pasternak said. "But there was no arguing with me." He said he wrote to Stalin to say that he was brought up with "Tolstoyan convictions," adding, "I did not consider I was entitled to sit in judgment over the life and death of others." He then said he went to bed and fell into a blissful sleep: "This always happens after I have taken some irrevocable step." Stavsky was probably more concerned about his own failure to bring Pasternak to heel than about the poet's actual stance. When the letter of condemnation appeared the next day, Pasternak's signature had been affixed. He was furious but safe.

Pasternak could not explain his own survival. "In those awful bloody years, anyone could have been arrested," he recalled. "We were shuffled like a deck of cards." That he lived left him with a fear that some might believe he had somehow colluded to save himself. "He seemed afraid that his mere survival might be attributed to some unworthy effort to placate the authorities, some squalid compromise of his integrity to escape persecution.

He kept returning to this point, and went to absurd lengths to deny that he was capable of conduct of which no one who knew him could begin to conceive him to be guilty," wrote Isaiah Berlin. There was no apparent logic to the killing. Ilya Ehrenburg asked, "Why, for example, did Stalin spare Pasternak who took his own independent line, but destroy [the journalist Mikhail] Koltsov who honorably carried out every task entrusted to him?"

Around Pasternak people disappeared, their fates suspected but unconfirmed—Pilnyak, Babel, and Titsian Tabidze, a Georgian friend whose poetry Pasternak had translated. At a meeting of the Georgian Union of Soviet Writers, another Georgian friend, Paolo Yashvili, shot himself before the inquisitors closed in.

The only happiness was the birth of Pasternak's son, Leonid. The birth was noted in *Vechernyaya Moskva* (Evening Moscow) "The first baby born in 1938 is the son of Mrs. Z.N. Pasternak. He was born 00:00 hour January 1st."

Osip Mandelstam was arrested later that year to be "consumed in their flames," as Pasternak put it. He starved to death in a camp in the Far East in December 1938. "My health is very poor. I am emaciated in the extreme, I've become very thin, almost unrecognizable," he told his brother in a last letter. He asked him to send food and clothes because "I get terribly cold without any [warm] things." In 1939, his wife learned of his fate when a money order she had sent Mandelstam was returned because of the "death of the addressee."

"The only person who . . . visited me was Pasternak—he came to see me immediately on hearing of M's death," said Nadezhda Mandelstam. "Apart from him no one had dared to come and see me."

Chapter 3

"I have arranged to meet you in a novel."

Pasternak began to write *Doctor Zhivago* on a block of watermarked paper from the desk of a dead man. The paper was a gift from the widow of Titsian Tabidze, the Georgian poet who was arrested, tortured, and executed in 1937. Pasternak felt the weight of those empty pages, writing to Tabidze's widow, Nina, that he hoped his prose would be worthy of putting down on her husband's paper. Pasternak visited Georgia in October 1945 to mark the centenary of the death of the Georgian poet Nikoloz Baratashvili, whose work he had recently translated. He stipulated that 25 percent of the advance for translating Baratashvili should be paid to Nina Tabidze.

Through much of his life Pasternak assisted people imprisoned or impoverished by the regime, and his surviving papers included large numbers of receipts for money orders sent all over the Soviet Union, including to prison camps. Nina Tabidze had not appeared in public in eight years, quarantined from the artistic circles in the capital, Tbilisi, where her husband was once feted. Nina had no word of the fate of Titsian, who was arrested on manufactured treason charges, and she would not learn definitively that he had been executed until after Stalin's death in 1953. While Nina Tabidze held on to some small flicker of hope that her husband survived in some distant camp, Pasternak later said he had not believed in the possibility that the Georgian poet was alive: "He was too great, too exceptional a man, who shed light all around him, to be hidden—for the signs of existence not to have filtered through any bars." When Pasternak arrived in Tbilisi, he said he would only participate in the festivities if Nina Tabidze also attended. At public events he sat her next to him. When he was asked to recite some of his translations of the poems of Baratashvili at the Rustaveli Theatre he turned to look at Nina Tabidze and asked if she wanted him to read. It was a defiant signal to the audience that he was embracing this outcast. Nina Tabidze returned the politically risky demonstration of respect with the gift of writing paper for the novel Pasternak planned.

Although Pasternak's reputation rested almost exclusively on his poems, he had written prose, including some well-received short stories, a long autobiographical essay, and drafts of a novel. Ideas and characters from these writings, but more fully developed, would eventually find their way into *Doctor Zhivago,* as if Pasternak were on a lifelong journey toward his novel. He was burdened over many decades by the sense that he had yet to create something big and bold, and came to believe that such an achievement could only be earned through prose—"what it can be, real prose, what a magic art—bordering on alchemy!" Pasternak also believed that "major works of literature exist only in association with a large readership." As early as 1917, Pasternak wrote in one poem, "I shall bid goodbye to verse; my mania. I have arranged to meet you in a novel." He told Tsvetaeva that he wanted to write a novel "with a love intrigue and a heroine in it—like Balzac." The reader of an early draft dismissed the effort as "dreamy, boring and tendentiously virtuous." It was abandoned. Pasternak projected some of this failed ambition onto his ultimate hero, Yuri Zhivago: "Still in his high school years, he dreamed of prose, of a book of biographies, in which he could place, in the form of hidden explosive clusters, the most astonishing things of all he had managed to see and ponder. But he was too young for such a book, and so he made up for it by writing verses, as a painter might draw sketches all his life for a great painting he had in mind."

World War II heightened Pasternak's preoccupation with the need for some singular piece of work. His friend the playwright Alexander Gladkov said that "his usual sense of acute dissatisfaction with himself now found an outlet in an exaggerated feeling that he was doing too little when set by the side of the enormous exertions of the country as a whole." In October 1941, as Nazi forces approached Moscow, Pasternak along with other writers was evacuated to Chistopol, a small town of 25,000 people nearly six hundred miles east of Moscow. He subsisted there for nearly two years on thin cabbage soup, black bread, and readings in the dining room of the Literary Fund. It was a drab, cold existence.

Pasternak visited the front near Oryol in 1943 and read his poems to the wounded. General Alexander Gorbatov invited a group of writers to "a sober dinner" of potatoes, a little ham, one shot of vodka per person, and tea. The meal was marked by speeches. Unlike some of his colleagues who were dull and soporific, Pasternak gave a clear, patriotic address leavened with humor and poetic dashes. The officers listened in complete silence, pale and moved. The visit to the front inspired some war poems and two pieces of short prose, and some of the destruction he witnessed would appear in the epilogue to *Doctor Zhivago*.

Pasternak, however, was never among those writers, such as Konstantin Simonov, whose poems and dispatches, circulated by the millions, were woven into the country's bloody resilience. "I am reading Simonov. I want to understand the nature of his success," he said. He considered a novel in verse, and he contracted with theaters to write a play, but nothing ever came of these aspirations. Pasternak complained that he lived "with the constant, nagging sense of being an imposter" because he felt he was "esteemed for more than I have actually done." His poems were published in the newspapers, and small volumes of poetry appeared in 1943 and 1945. He continued to earn a living through his translations. "Shakespearc, the old man of Chistopol, is feeding me as before."

In 1944, Pasternak received some wrenching encouragement to continue to reach for a greater artistic achievement. Anna Akhmatova, who had been evacuated to Tashkent in the Soviet Republic of Uzbekistan, arrived in Moscow in 1944 carrying an old letter for Pasternak from Osip Mandelstam, written two years before he perished. Mandelstam's widow had found it. Mandelstam, who had once warned Pasternak that his translation work would overwhelm his original creations, said in the letter, "I want your poetry, by which we have all been spoiled and undeservedly gifted, to leap further out into the world, to the people, to children. Let me say to you at least once in life: thank you for everything, and for the fact that this 'everything' is still 'not everything.'" For Pasternak, the letter, even if it referred to poetry, was a bitter prompt that there was more to strive for. The following year, in May 1945, Pasternak's father, Leonid, died in Oxford. Pasternak felt he should "burn with shame" when his "own role is so monstrously inflated" and his father's talent hadn't gained "a hundredth of the recognition it deserves."

Guilt, grief, dissatisfaction with himself, the need for that "great painting," the desire finally to write a classic were all combining to produce what one friend called a "profound inner change" that would propel Pasternak toward *Doctor Zhivago*. The first recorded mention of the novel appears in a letter to Nadezhda Mandelstam in November 1945, when Pasternak told her that he had been doing some new writing, a novel that would span the whole of their lives. On New Year's Eve 1945, Pasternak bumped into Gladkov on Mokhovaya Street near the Kremlin. The two were jostled by revelers, but they managed to exchange a few words as they stood in light snow, which dusted Pasternak's collar and cap. Pasternak said he was working on a novel "about people who could be representative of my school—if I had one." He smiled sheepishly before moving off.

In an end-of-year letter to his sisters in England, he said that he was compelled to portray the great events of his country in clear, simple prose. "I have started on this, but it's all so remote from what's wanted from us here, and what people are used to seeing from us, that it's difficult to write regularly and assiduously."

Pasternak's mood became more buoyant as the writing accelerated. "I am in the same high spirits I enjoyed more than 30 years ago; it's almost embarrassing." It seemed to him that the days and weeks were whistling past his ears. "I wrote it with great ease. The circumstances were so definite, so fabulously terrible. All that I had to do was listen to their prompting with my whole soul and follow obediently their suggestions." Pasternak was also cheered that spring of 1946 by the enthusiastic reception he received from Muscovites at a series of literary evenings. At Moscow University, in April 1946, the audience called for him to continue to recite as he made to leave the stage. The following month, there was another series of encores at a solo recital at the Polytechnic Museum. Pasternak told his sisters that he was experiencing a kind of unexpected fairy tale in this romance with his audience. "You see it in the concert halls which sell out as soon as my name appears on a poster—and if I ever hesitate while reciting any of my poems, I'm prompted from three or four different directions." (One acquaintance suggested Pasternak, who prepared for recitals, faked some memory lapses to test his audience, and bind it to him.)

On April 3, 1946, at a reading by Moscow and Leningrad poets, Pasternak arrived late and the audience burst into applause as he tried to sneak onto the stage. The poet who was speaking was forced to halt his recital until Pasternak sat down. The man who was interrupted and no doubt irritated was Alexei Surkov, his old and future foe, the poet who said Pasternak needed to imbibe the revolution to achieve greatness. The disruption seemed more than coincidental when much the same thing happened nearly two years later when Surkov was speaking at "An Evening of Poetry on the Theme: Down with the Warmongers! For a Lasting Peace and People's Democracy" at the Polytechnic Museum. The venue was one of the largest in Moscow, and it was so packed that people were sitting in the aisles while the street outside was crowded with those who couldn't get in. Surkov was nearing the end of a versified condemnation of NATO, Winston Churchill, and sundry Western belligerents when the audience erupted in applause, which seemed out of key with that moment in his recital. Over his shoulder, it was Pasternak again, stealing a little thunder from his rival, and supposedly slipping onto the stage. He stretched out his arms to hush the crowd, and allow Surkov to continue. When he was eventually called to the microphone Pasternak remarked coyly, "Unfortunately, I have no poem on the theme of the evening, but will read you some things I wrote before the war." Each poem drew bursts of delighted enthusiasm from the crowds. Someone shouted, "Shestdeesiat shestoi davai!"

(Give us the Sixty-Sixth!), a call for Shakespeare's sonnet, which Pasternak had translated in 1940, in which the Bard declaims:

And art made tongue-tied by authority,
And folly, doctor-like, controlling skill,
And simple truth miscall'd simplicity
And captive good attending captain ill:
Tir'd with all these, from these would I be gone,
Save that, to die, I leave my love alone.

Pasternak was smart enough not to recite the politically charged lines. But the sustained applause had become a clapping, stomping public demonstration—a potentially dangerous display of affection for its recipient. (When Akhmatova was similarly received at a reading during the war, Stalin is reported to have said: "Who organized that standing ovation?") The chairman of the meeting tried to restore order by ringing his bell, and Pasternak sported a smile of satisfied triumph. A large group from the audience followed him on his walk home.

Surkov could only fume. He had made his reputation during the war with unsubtle, patriotic verse that proclaimed:

Death to Fascism! The Soviet
Calls the brave to battle
The bullet fears the brave,
The bayonet the courageous.

One Western reporter in Moscow described Surkov as "emphatically masculine." Rudely pink-faced and muscular, he spoke in a loud voice—sometimes at such a decibel that he appeared to be addressing a crowd, not conversing—and he walked in exaggerated strides, fast and long. Nine years younger than Pasternak, Surkov grew up the son of a peasant in a district northeast of Moscow and on reaching the capital was consumed with his status there; the Hungarian writer György Dalos, who attended college in Moscow and knew Surkov, described him as a special Soviet case of Molière's *bourgeois gentilhomme.* Dalos concluded that "in order to understand a figure like Surkov, good and evil must be regarded not as opposites but as parts of one inseparable whole." A Soviet defector to the West later testified before the U.S. Congress that Surkov was "a KGB man," meaning he was one of a number of trusted prominent figures who would do the bidding of the secret police when called upon.

Nadezhda Mandelstam noted that in conversation, Surkov always referred to a mysterious entity called "they." He often wished to extend a kindness, but was unable to act until he had sounded out some superior entity.

"'They,' as I noticed, were always thinking this, that or the other, or giving it as their view. Once I asked him outright: 'Who are they?' As far as I am concerned you are 'they.' He was quite bowled over by such a question. . . . Later I realized that in a world horizontally divided, as it were, into floors, 'they' were always those on the next floor." Mandelstam concluded that "like all his kind he stultifies language, stifles thought and life. In so doing, he also destroys himself."

Surkov nursed a particular hostility toward Pasternak, yet he showed genuine kindness to Akhmatova, mitigating the worst of her persecutions and bringing her flowers. However, "he worked heart and soul for a system that had a pathological fear of every unfettered word, and so especially of poetry." And no poet focused his animus more than Pasternak. One Pasternak intimate concluded simply that Surkov "hated him." Pasternak, on the other hand, was never angered by Surkov's hostility or criticism. After the war, he praised Surkov's verse as exemplary of a new realism and said he was among his favorite poets because of his rough-hewn, boisterous style. "Yes, really, don't be surprised. He writes what he thinks: he thinks 'Hurray!' and he writes 'Hurray!'"

The novel, which Pasternak initially entitled *Boys and Girls,* began to come into focus as he worked on it intensely in the winter months of 1945 and 1946, and his ambitions for it grew. "This is a very serious work. I am already old, I may soon die, and I must not perpetually put off giving free expression to my true thoughts." He called it an epic, and said it was "a sad, dismal story, worked out in fine detail, ideally, as in a Dickens or Dostoevsky novel." He became absorbed with the writing. "I could not go on living another year unless this novel, my alter ego, in which with almost physical concreteness certain of my spiritual qualities and part of my nervous structure have been implanted, went on living and growing, too." He promised to give his views on art, the Gospels, on the life of man in history. He said it would "square accounts with Judaism" and with all forms of nationalism. And he felt that his subjects and their varying colors were "arranging themselves so perfectly on the canvas."

Like many of his contemporaries, Pasternak believed, or at least strongly hoped, that the sacrifice of the people in war, the millions dead and the awful struggle to defeat Nazism, would preclude a return to repression. But Pasternak was also alert enough to observe that the seemingly relaxed postwar atmosphere was eroding as tensions with the Western powers grew into the Cold War. In June 1946, Pasternak told his sisters that he moved around "on a knife-edge. . . . It's interesting, exciting and probably dangerous."

The crackdown on the intelligentsia came in August 1946. The targets, initially, were the satirical writer Mikhail Zoshchenko and Akhmatova. Stalin opened the campaign when the editors of two Leningrad journals were summoned to Moscow and harangued for publishing "silly" material. Zoshchenko, Stalin railed, "writes all kind of cock and bull stories, nonsense that offers nothing for the mind or the heart. . . . That's not why we built the Soviet order, to teach people drivel." The party's Central Committee followed with a resolution that said Zoshchenko had specialized in writing "vapid, content-less and vulgar things, in the advocacy of rotten unprincipledness . . . calculated to disorient our young people and poison their minds." The resolution singled out a story, "The Adventures of a Monkey," which depicted an escaped monkey who returned to his cage in the zoo rather than deal with everyday life in Leningrad. The resolution described the story as a "hooliganish depiction of our reality." Akhmatova was also charged with causing damage to young people with her "bourgeois-aristocratic aestheticism and decadence—'art for art's sake.'"

That a new unforgiving period of cultural repression had begun was driven home in a shrill, vulgar speech by Andrei Zhdanov, a member of Stalin's inner circle since the 1930s, a colossal boozer, and the piano player when the Leader sang on drunken evenings. Zhdanov spoke in the Great Hall of the Smolny Institute in Leningrad before an invited audience of writers, journalists, publishers, and bureaucrats. The location was well chosen; Lenin announced the Soviet takeover of power in the same hall in 1917. One attendee later wrote that the meeting, which began at five p.m. and lasted almost until midnight, was marked by "sycophantic contributions from the floor and hysterical self-criticism from writers taking part."

"Anna Akhmatova's subject-matter is thoroughly individualistic," said Zhdanov. "The range of her poetry is pitifully limited—this is the poetry of a feral lady from the salons, moving between the boudoir and the prayer stool. It is based on erotic motifs linked with motifs of mourning, melancholy, death, mysticism and isolation . . . she is half nun, half whore, or rather both whore and nun, fornication and prayer being intermingled in her world."

Zhdanov's campaign for conformity, which was infused with a chauvinistic hostility to all things Western, spread to the theater, cinema, music, the university, and eventually the sciences. Pasternak's cousin Olga, who taught at Leningrad University, wrote in her diary that the new academic year began with the rector appearing before the faculty in a peasant shirt to symbolize a shift in ideology towards the "great Russian people." She rued that "anyone who in any way shows respect for European culture is dubbed a toady." New grounds for arrest included "Praising American Democracy" or "Abasement before the West."

It was inevitable that Pasternak would become a target, and the new head of the writers' union, Alexander Fadeyev, accused him of being out of touch with the people—"not one of us." When it was suggested that Pasternak should condemn Akhmatova in print, he refused and said he loved her too much; to help Akhmatova, who had been expelled from the Union of Soviet Writers and left with no way to earn a living, Pasternak would slip a thousand rubles under her pillow when she came to Moscow and stayed with mutual friends. Pasternak was removed from the board of the Union of Soviet Writers in August 1946 when he failed to attend a meeting called to denounce Akhmatova and Zoshchenko. Pasternak was warned that he was no less suspect as an aesthete than Akhmatova, but he replied with characteristic insouciance: "Yes, yes, [out of touch with] the people, modern times . . . you know, your Trotsky once told me the same thing."

On September 9, 1946, *Pravda* reported that the Union of Soviet Writers had passed a resolution stating that Pasternak was "an author lacking in ideology and remote from Soviet reality." On the same evening, Pasternak had scheduled one of his first readings of the early part of the novel at his home in Peredelkino. He didn't read the newspapers and his wife didn't tell him about the attack, so the reading went ahead. It was attended by his neighbor Chukovsky and his son Nikolai; the literary scholar Korneli Zelinsky, who would, in time, launch a vicious attack on Pasternak and *Doctor Zhivago*; and about ten or eleven other listeners.

Chukovsky found himself perplexed by *Doctor Zhivago*. "For all the charm of certain passages," he wrote in his diary, "it struck me as alien, confusing and removed from my life, and much of it failed to involve me." The novel bewildered others who were close to Pasternak and steeped in the lyrical beauty of his poetry. When Akhmatova first heard an excerpt at a reading in a flat in Moscow, she "was acutely unhappy with the novel." She told the physicist Mikhail Polivanov, a friend of Pasternak's, that "it is a failure of genius." When Polivanov protested that the novel captures "the spirit and people of that age," Akhmatova replied, "It is my time, my society, but I don't recognize it." His neighbor Vsevolod Ivanov complained after a reading that he had heard none of the exquisite craft he would expect from Pasternak and that the writing seemed hurried and rough.

Pasternak was unmoved by those who complained of the admixture of styles, the reliance on coincidence, slackened writing, and a torrent of characters even compared with the bounteous peopling of the standard Russian novel. Pasternak responded that every aspect of the novel, including its "failings," was, to him, conscious. Writing much later, in his idiosyncratic English to the poet Stephen Spender, he explained that there is "an effort in the novel to represent the whole sequence of facts and beings and happenings like some moving entireness, like a developing, passing by, rolling and rushing inspiration, as if reality itself had freedom and choice and was composing itself out of numberless variants and versions." He said he didn't so much delineate characters as efface them, and coincidence showed "the liberty of being, its verisimilitude touching, adjoining improbability." Pasternak was no longer interested in stylistic experiment but "understandability." He said he wanted the novel "gobbled down" by everyone, "even a seamstress or a dishwasher."

Other listeners were enthusiastic, and moved by the passages they heard. Emma Gerstein, who heard Pasternak read the first three chapters of the novel to a small audience in April 1947, came away feeling that she had "heard Russia," adding, "With my eyes, my ears and my nose I sensed the era." Pasternak's friend the Leningrad poet Sergei Spassky said, "A spring of pristine, creative energy has gushed forth from inside you."

Pasternak continued to read drafts to small gatherings at apartments in Moscow, and those evenings formed a kind of dialogue with his audience and led him to make some adjustments to the text. At a reading in May 1947, the audience included Genrikh Neigauz, the first husband of his wife and long since reconciled to Pasternak, and Leo Tolstoy's granddaughter, among others. Pasternak arrived with the pages rolled in his hand. He kissed the hand of his hostess and embraced and firmly kissed Neigauz before sitting behind a table and saying, without any ceremony, "Let's start." He told the audience he hadn't yet decided on a title and for now was simply subtitling the novel *Scenes of Half a Century of Daily Life*. The following year, with four chapters completed, he would settle on the title *Doctor Zhivago*. While sounding like a Siberian name, Zhivago was derived from an Orthodox prayer. Pasternak told the Gulag survivor and writer Varlam Shalamov, who was the son of a priest, that as a child while saying the prayer lines "Ty est' voistinu Khristos, Syn Boga zhivago" (You truly are the Christ, Son of the the living God), he used to pause after *Boga* (God) before saying *zhivago* (the living).

"I did not think of the living God, but of a new one, who was only accessible to me through the name Zhivago," Pasternak said. "It took me a whole life to make this childish sensation real by granting the hero of my novel this name. "

For Pasternakians, invitations to these literary evenings were cherished. On February 6, 1947, the home of the pianist Maria Yudina was packed despite the raging blizzard outside. Yudina told Pasternak that she and her friends were looking forward to the reading "as to a feast."

"They will all squeeze into my luxurious single-celled palazzo," she told the poet in a note. Pasternak almost didn't make it because he was uncertain of the address and snow drifts were making it increasingly difficult to maneuver the car carrying him and his companions to the event. Finally, a candle in a window drew the group to the right location. Yudina's house was stiflingly hot because of the number of people inside, and it reeked of kerosene from a vain attempt to kill bugs earlier in the day; they still visibly scuttled across the wall. Yudina was dressed in her best black velvet dress and moved among the guests passing out sandwiches and wine. She played Chopin for a long time. Pasternak seemed nervous, or perhaps he was just uncomfortable from the heat, wiping sweat off his face. He read about the young student Zhivago dancing with his fiancée, Tonya, and the Christmas tree lights at the Sventitskys' house. When he stopped reading he was bombarded with questions about how the story would unfold. As Pasternak left at first light, he told his mistress that the evening, almost lost because of the snow, had inspired a poem, which would become Yuri Zhivago's "A Winter Night":

It snowed, it snowed over all the world
From end to end.
A candle burned on the table,
A candle burned.

The gatherings were also attracting some unwelcome attention. The deputy editor of *Novy Mir* described them as the "underground readings of a counter-revolutionary novel." The secret police were also monitoring the soirees and noting the book's contents for the moment when they would strike.

The attacks on Pasternak continued into 1947. Among those who singled him out for criticism was Fadeyev, the head of the writers' union. But Fadeyev also embodied the establishment's duality toward Pasternak. Ilya Ehrenburg recalled meeting Fadeyev after he had publicly inveighed against the "aloofness from life" of writers like Pasternak. Fadeyev took Ehrenburg to a café where, after ordering brandy, he asked Ehrenburg if he would like to hear some real poetry. "And he began to recite from memory verses by Pasternak, going on and on, and only interrupting himself from time to time to say: 'Wonderful stuff, isn't it?' " Pasternak had once remarked that Fadeyev was "well-disposed to me personally but if he received orders to have me hung, drawn and quartered he would carry them out conscientiously and make his report without batting an eyelid—though the next time he got drunk he would say how sorry he was for me and what a splendid fellow I had been." Fadeyev shot himself in 1956. As Pasternak bowed before his open coffin in the Hall of Columns in the House of the Unions, he said in a loud voice, "Alexander Alexandrovich has rehabilitated himself."

Official criticism of Pasternak in 1947 reached a pitch in a virulent signed piece by Surkov in the newspaper *Kultura i Zhizn* (Culture and Life), a principal mouthpiece for enforcing Zhdanov's line and labeled the "Mass Grave" by some of the intelligentsia. Surkov charged that Pasternak had a "reactionary backward-looking ideology," that he "speaks with obvious hostility and even hatred about the Soviet Revolution," and that his poetry was a "direct slander" of Soviet reality. He also said that Pasternak had "meager spiritual resources," which were incapable of "giving birth to major poetry."

On the totem of denunciation, which had its own semiotics in the Soviet Union, this was a couple of notches below a call for Pasternak's isolation and ruin—because if the article was signed, it was less menacing. Gladkov, who had anticipated the official censure and feared for his friend, said he could breathe easily again after reading it. "With all its dishonesty and deliberate obtuseness it did not amount to a definite 'excommunication.' " An anonymous piece in a major newspaper would have signaled ruin. "At least they are not going to let me starve," quipped Pasternak after getting a commission to translate *Faust*.

The times, however, demanded some punishment. The journal *Novy Mir* rejected some of his poems. The publication of his translated Shakespeare compendium was put on hold. And 25,000 printed copies of his selected lyric poetry were destroyed "on orders from above," on the eve of distribution in the spring of 1948. The readings stopped and he noted that "public appearances by me are regarded as undesirable."

Pasternak was able to exact some sly revenge. In a revision of his translation of *Hamlet,* he introduced lines that bear little if any fidelity to the original. Even allowing for Pasternak's belief that a translation should never be an attempt at "literal exactitude," the lines from *Hamlet,* when translated back into English again, were a biting commentary on the politics of the hour. Where Shakespeare wrote of the "whips and scorns of time," Pasternak had Hamlet say: "Who would bear the phony greatness of the rulers, the ignorance of the bigwigs, the common hypocrisy, the impossibility to express oneself, the unrequited love and illusoriness of merits in the eyes of mediocrities."

The renewed sterility of cultural life after a flush of postwar optimism was both dismaying to Pasternak and a prompt to burrow further into his new project. "I started to work again on my novel when I saw that all our rosy expectations of the changes the end of the war was supposed to bring to Russia were not being fulfilled. The war itself was like a cleansing storm, like a breeze blowing through an unventilated room. Its sorrows and hardships were not as bad as the inhuman lie—they shook to its core the power of everything specious and unorganic to the nature of man and society, which has gained such a hold over us. But the dead weight of the past was too strong. The novel is absolutely essential for me as a way of expressing my feelings." His attitude to the state, which had fluctuated between ambivalence and cautious embrace, was now consistently if quietly hostile. He told his cousin that he was as cheerful as ever despite the changed atmosphere in Moscow. "I write no protests and say nothing when addressed. It's no use. I never try to justify myself or get involved in explanations." He had other reasons for ignoring the deadening hand of the authorities.

Pasternak had fallen in love.

Chapter 4

"You are aware of the anti-Soviet nature of the novel?"

When World War II ended, Pasternak's marriage to his second wife, Zinaida, had long since settled into an arid routine. Zinaida ran the household with stern efficiency, and he appreciated her for it. "My wife's passionate love of work, her skill in everything—in washing, cooking, cleaning, bringing up the children—has created domestic comfort, a garden, a way of life and daily routine, the calm and quiet needed for work." He told a friend he loved her for her "big hands." But there was an air of deep regret in the home—"a divided family, lacerated by suffering and constantly looking over our shoulders at that other family, the first ones." When Zinaida got pregnant in 1937, Pasternak wrote his parents that "her present condition is entirely unexpected, and if abortion weren't illegal, we'd have been dismayed by our insufficiently joyful response to the event, and she'd have had the pregnancy terminated." Zinaida later wrote that she very much wanted "Borya's child," but her raw fear that her husband could be arrested at any moment—this was the height of the Terror and he was refusing to sign petitions—made it hard to carry the pregnancy.

Zinaida had little interest in Pasternak's writing, confessing that she didn't understand his poetry. Her principal diversion was sitting at the kitchen table chain-smoking and playing cards or mah-jongg with her female friends. Hard-edged and frequently ill-humored, Zinaida was described by Akhmatova as "a dragon on eight feet." But she had earned her unhappiness. In 1937, Adrian, the older of her two sons with her first husband, Genrikh Neigauz, was diagnosed with tuberculosis of the bone, a discovery that began a long and agonizing decline in his health. In 1942, in an effort to arrest the spread of the disease, one of the boy's legs was amputated, above the knee, and the previously active seventeen-year-old was inconsolable. Adrian died in April 1945 from tubercular meningitis after being infected by the boy next to him in a sanatorium; his mother was by his side there. After his death, his body was held in the morgue for four days for research. When Zinaida saw him again he had been embalmed. She cradled Adrian's head and was horrified that it was light "as a matchbox." His brain had been removed. Zinaida remained haunted by the sensation of holding him. She was suicidal for days after the death, and Pasternak remained close, doing chores with her, to distract and comfort her. Adrian's ashes were buried in the garden in Peredelkino. Zinaida said she neglected her husband and felt old. Intimacy seemed a "curse" to her and she said she could not always "fulfill my duty as a wife."

On an October 1946 day, just as winter announced itself with a driving snow, Pasternak walked into *Novy Mir*'s cavernous reception area, a converted former ballroom where Pushkin had once danced, now painted the dark red of Soviet gaud. After he had crossed the long carpet to the back of the room where the junior editors sat, Pasternak encountered two women about to go to lunch. The older of the pair held out her hand to be kissed and said to Pasternak. "Boris Leonidovich, let me introduce one of your most ardent admirers." The devotee was Olga Ivinskaya, a blond, in an old squirrel-fur coat and an editor at *Novy Mir*. She was more than twenty years Pasternak's junior, and later was a source of inspiration for the character Lara in *Doctor Zhivago*. Pretty, voluptuous, and sexually self-confident despite the prudish mores of Soviet society, the thirty-four-year-old Ivinskaya immediately felt his lingering stare—"so much a man's appraising gaze that there could be no doubt about it." As he bowed and took Ivinskaya's hand, Pasternak inquired as to which of his books she possessed. Just the one, she confessed. Pasternak promised to return with some volumes. "How interesting that I still have admirers." The next day, five books appeared on Ivinskaya's desk.

Ivinskaya had recently attended a Pasternak recital at the Historical Museum. It was the first time she had seen him at such close range, and she described him as "tall and trim, extraordinarily youthful, with the strong neck of a young man, and he spoke in a deep low voice, conversing with the audience as one talks with an intimate friend." When she returned to her flat after midnight, her mother complained about having to get up to let her in. "Leave me alone," said Ivinskaya, "I've just been talking to God."

Pasternak was typically self-deprecating about his own charms and described the "few women who have had an affair with me" as "magnanimous martyrs so unbearable and uninteresting am I 'as a man.'" He adored and idealized women and described himself as forever stunned and stupefied by their beauty. Among his fellow writers, Pasternak was known for his flings; women were drawn to him. Zinaida said that after the war Pasternak was showered by notes and unexpected visits from young women she chased out of the yard. Pasternak called them "the ballerinas." One of them sent him a note that she wanted to give birth to a Christ fathered by Pasternak.

Ivinskaya was twice married and had, by her own account, many passing relationships. Her first husband hanged himself in 1940 when he was thirty-two, after she had an affair with the man who would become her second husband. "Poor Mama mourned," remarked Olga's daughter, Irina, but her sorrow did not last very long; the forty-day mourning period had scarcely passed when "a guy in a leather coat turned up at the doorstep." Ivinskaya's second husband died of an illness during the war but not before informing on his mother-in-law (possibly to get her out of the crowded apartment), who then spent three years in the Gulag for making a slanderous remark about Stalin.

In 1946, Ivinskaya lived with her mother and stepfather; her two children, eight-year-old Irina and five-year-old Dmitri, one by each husband; and her many beloved cats. The fifty-six-year-old

Pasternak offered a release from a cramped world and an entrée into Moscow's salons. "I longed for recognition and wanted people to envy me," said Ivinskaya. She was seductive and devoted, clingy and calculating. Pasternak was a very big catch.

Ivinskaya had read Pasternak's poems since she was a girl; she described herself as a fan meeting her idol. "The magician, who had first entered my life so long ago, when I was 16, had now come to me in person, living and real." Ivinskaya's daughter would later nickname Pasternak "Classoosha," an affectionate diminutive of the word *classic,* and one mother and daughter came to share when referring to the writer.

The romance began as an old-fashioned courtship. Because both Pasternak and Ivinskaya had family at home, the couple had no private retreat. Pasternak would show up at *Novy Mir* at the end of the workday, and he and Ivinskaya would meander through the streets, talking at great length, before he would bid her farewell at her apartment building.

"I'm in love," Pasternak told a friend, who asked how this would affect his life. "But what is life?" Pasternak responded. "What is life if not love? And she is so enchanting, such a radiant, golden person. And now this golden sun has come into my life, it is so wonderful, so wonderful. I never thought I would still know such joy." He hated growing old and treated his birthdays as days of mourning, disdaining any attempt to celebrate. This unexpected romance was a time-stopping elixir.

The ritual of walking and talking continued until April when Ivinskaya's family went out of the city for the day. "As newlyweds spend their first night together [Boris] and I now had our first day together. He was borne up and jubilant over this victory." That day, Pasternak inscribed a collection of his verse: "My life, my angel. I love you truly. April 4, 1947."

The early affair, punctuated by unkept promises to end the romance because of the obvious domestic complications, found its way into some of Zhivago's poetry:

Don't cry, don't purse your swollen lips.
Don't draw them together like that.

Moscow was soon chattering about the deliciously scandalous liaison, and Pasternak's female friends—some of whom had their own strong feelings for the poet—were less than enamored with Ivinskaya. Some would never trust her. The writer Lydia Chukovskaya, who worked with Ivinskaya at *Novy Mir,* remarked of one evening that the couple's "faces could be seen side by side. Her make-up was a dreadful sight next to his natural face. A "pretty but slightly fading blonde," commented the literary scholar Emma Gerstein, remarking on how, during one reading, she "hurriedly powdered her nose, hiding behind a cupboard." However, the young poet Yevgeni Yevtushenko who saw her at a Pasternak reading called her "a beauty."

Zinaida found out about the affair in the winter of 1948 when she found a note sent by Ivinskaya to Pasternak while cleaning his study. Initially she said she felt guilty and that it was all her fault. It also seemed to her that after the war, "in our village community, [the men] started to leave the old wives and replace them with younger ones." Zinaida confronted Ivinskaya in Moscow, telling her that she didn't give a damn about their love and she wasn't going to allow her family to be broken up. She gave Ivinskaya a letter from Pasternak announcing the end of the affair. Ivinskaya's children overheard conversations that "Mom had tried to poison herself," her daughter recalled.

Pasternak's sense of loyalty to Zinaida and their son became a strain as he vacillated between family and flame. The prospect of a second divorce, a third marriage, and all the potential excruciating chaos may have been more than Pasternak wished to endure. The couple huddled in doorways to argue. Ivinskaya returned home furious from these rows and took down Pasternak's picture. "Where's your pride, Mama?" asked her daughter after the picture had been put back up yet another time. Ivinskaya's mother harangued both her daughter and Pasternak about Olga's status as a mistress, not a wife. "I love your daughter more than my life," Pasternak told her, "but don't expect our life to change outwardly all at once." The affair, at one point, appeared to be over. In a letter to his cousin in August 1949, Pasternak confessed that he had "formed a deep new attachment," but, he wrote, "since my relationship with [Zinaida] is a genuine one, sooner or later I had to sacrifice the other. Strangely enough, so long as my life was filled with agony, ambivalence, pangs of conscience, even horror, I easily bore it and even took pleasure in things that now, when I have made peace with my conscience and my family, reduce me to a state of unmitigated dreariness: my aloneness, my precarious place in literature, the ultimate pointlessness of my literary efforts, the strange duality of my life 'here' and 'there.'" He imagined at one point that he could get Zinaida, Olga, and his first wife, Yevgenia, to sit together happily on the veranda of the dacha with him. "He never wanted to cause anyone grief, but he did," said a friend.

By 1949, Pasternak was already a figure of some international renown, even if he was banished to the edges of literary life in Moscow. Cecil Maurice Bowra, who held the Oxford Chair of Poetry, had nominated Pasternak for the Nobel Prize in Literature in 1946, an honor that was repeated in 1947 and 1949. Bowra had also included seventeen poems by Pasternak in *A Second Book of Russian Verse,* which he had edited and was published in London in 1948. An American edition of Pasternak's *Selected Writings* appeared in New York in 1949. One of the leading academics in the West called Pasternak "the greatest of Russian poets." And in July 1950, the International Conference of Professors of English wrote to the Soviet ambassador to Britain to invite Pasternak to Oxford and said, "It appears to us beyond all doubt that the most eminent man of letters . . . in the Soviet Union today is Boris Pasternak."

The Kremlin leadership, locked in a global ideological struggle with the West, was exquisitely sensitive to any foreign depiction of Soviet culture and expended great national energy on projecting the country's intellectual achievements. Simultaneously, the government was pressing an increasingly sinister campaign against "rootless cosmopolitans," a policy that had an ugly anti-Semitic complexion. There were persistent rumors that Pasternak would be picked up by the secret police; Akhmatova at one point phoned from Leningrad to check that he was safe. A senior investigator in the prosecutor's office in 1949 said there were plans to arrest Pasternak. When Stalin was informed, he started to recite "Heavenly color, color blue," one of the Baratashvili poems that Pasternak had translated and read in Tbilisi in 1945. And then Stalin said, "Leave him, he's a cloud dweller."

Ivinskaya enjoyed no such protection; she was a surrogate who could be used to strike directly at her lover. The same pitiless logic was applied to Akhmatova, whose husband and son were both arrested separately in the second half of 1949 while she was physically untouched. On October 9, 1949, the secret police burst into Ivinskaya's apartment. Nearly a dozen uniformed agents, working through the blue haze of their cigarette smoke, searched the apartment, setting aside for seizure any book, letter, document, or scrap of paper that mentioned Pasternak. Ivinskaya was taken almost immediately to secret-police headquarters—the fearsome Lubyanka building, where she was strip-searched, had her jewelry and bra taken from her, and was placed in a dark, stultifying isolation unit. She was left to stew in her own anxiety for three days before she was moved in with fourteen other female prisoners. The crowded cell was illuminated with harshly bright lamps to ensure that the women were sleep-deprived and disoriented in advance of nighttime interrogations. Ivinskaya recalled that "the prisoners began to feel that time had come to a halt and their world had collapsed about them. They ceased to be sure of their innocence, of what they had confessed to, and which other prisoners they had compromised apart from themselves. In consequence, they signed any raving nonsense put before them."

Among Ivinskaya's cellmates was Trotsky's twenty-six-year-old granddaughter, Alexandra, who had just finished her studies at the Institute of Geology and was accused of copying an illicit poem. Long after Alexandra had left, Ivinskaya continued to remember her desperate wailing as she was taken away to be sent to a camp in Kazakhstan. Another woman who befriended Ivinskaya was a doctor at the Kremlin hospital who had attended a party where incautious remarks were made about Stalin's mortality.

Two weeks after her arrest, the guards called Ivinskaya out of her cell and led her down several long corridors past closed doors from behind which muffled cries of distress escaped. She was finally placed inside a cupboardlike compartment that rotated and opened into an anteroom. A group of agents fell silent as she appeared, and stood aside as she was ushered into a large office. Behind a desk covered in green baize was Stalin's minister of state security, Viktor Abakumov, another of the Leader's violent henchmen. Abakumov led SMERSH, an acronym for "Death to Spies," during the war. The military counterintelligence unit, which set up blocking positions immediately behind the front lines, killed Soviet soldiers who attempted to retreat. The unit also hunted down deserters and brutally interrogated German prisoners of war. Before torturing his victims, Abakumov was known to unroll a bloodstained carpet to save the sheen on his office floor.

"Tell me now, is Boris anti-Soviet or not, do you think?" began Abakumov, dressed in a military tunic buttoned to the bulging neck.

Before Ivinskaya could reply, Abakumov continued, "Why are you so bitter? You've been worrying about him for some reason! Admit it now—we know everything."

At that moment, Ivinskaya still didn't realize who was questioning her, and she pushed back with none of the caution an encounter with a monster like Abakumov would demand.

"You always worry about a person you love. As regards whether Boris Leonidovich is anti-Soviet or not—there are too few colors on your palette, only black and white. There is a tragic lack of half-tones."

The books and materials seized from Ivinskaya's apartment were piled on the desk in front of Abakumov. The KGB's accounting of its haul from Ivinskaya's apartment included: poems by Pasternak, Akhmatova, and Lydia Chukovskaya (to my dear O.V. Ivinskaya); a diary (30 pages); various poems, (460 pages); a "pornographic" poem; various letters (157 pieces); photos of Ivinskaya; and some of her own poems. Among these items was the small red volume of poetry that Pasternak had inscribed after the couple first made love in 1947.

"I would suggest you think very carefully about this novel Pasternak is passing around to people at the moment—at a time when we have quite enough malcontents and enemies as it is," said Abakumov. "You are aware of the anti-Soviet nature of the novel?"

Ivinskaya protested and began to describe the completed part of the novel before she was interrupted.

"You will have plenty of time to think about these questions and how to answer them. But personally I would like you to appreciate that we know everything, and that your own as well as Pasternak's fate will depend on how truthful you are. I hope that next time we meet you will have nothing to conceal about Pasternak's anti-Soviet views."

Abakumov then looked to the guard. "Take her away."

The subsequent questioning was led by a much more junior official, Anatoli Semyonov, who, like his boss, did not employ physical violence with Ivinskaya. He charged that Ivinskaya was planning to escape abroad together with her lover. He said Pasternak was a British spy, had Anglophile attitudes, and repeatedly used the analogy that Pasternak had sat at the table with the British and Americans "but ate Russian bacon." For his inquisitors, the fact that Pasternak had family in England and had held several meetings with the British diplomat Isaiah Berlin in 1946 was evidence enough of his disloyalty. Interrogation now became a nightly ordeal, until it went on so many weeks, it became routine, "quite humdrum."

"How would you characterize Pasternak's political sentiments? What do you know about his hostile work, his pro-English sentiments, his intention to commit treason?"

"He does not belong to the category of people with anti-Soviet sentiments. He did not have any intention to commit treason. He always loved his country."

"But in your home we confiscated a book of Pasternak's works in English. How did it get there?"

"That book I got from Pasternak, that's true. It is a monograph on his father, the painter, that was published in London."

"How did Pasternak get it?"

"Simonov [the acclaimed war poet and editor of *Novy Mir*] brought it to him from a trip abroad."

"What more do you know about Pasternak's ties with England?"

"I think he once got a parcel from his sisters, who are living there."

"What sparked your relationship with Pasternak? He is, after all, a lot older than you."

"Love."

"No, you were joined together by your shared political views and treasonous intentions."

"We never had such intentions. I loved and love him as a man."

Ivinskaya was also accused of speaking ill of Surkov, although the transcript—which no doubt bowdlerized some of the language and threats of the KGB official—misspelled the loyal poet's name.

"Facts testified to by witnesses show that you systematically praised the works of Pasternak and contrasted it with the work of patriotic writers such as Surikov and Simonov, whereas the artistic methods of Pasternak in depicting Soviet reality are wrong."

"It is true that I speak highly of him, and hold him up as an example to all Soviet writers. His work is a great asset to Soviet literature, and his artistic methods are not wrong but just subjective."

"You suggested that Surikov does not have any literary skills and that his poetry is merely printed because it is in praise of the party."

"Yes, I think those mediocre poems compromise the idea. But Simonov I always considered a talented man."

Ivinskaya was told to write a summary of *Doctor Zhivago,* and when she began to describe it as the life of a physician and intellectual in the years between the revolutions of 1905 and 1917, her interrogator scoffed. "You must simply say that you have actually read this work and that it constitutes a slander on Soviet life." At one point, Semyonov expressed bewilderment at the poem "Mary Magdalene" and the possibility that it might refer to Ivinskaya. "What era does it refer to? And why have you never told Pasternak that you're a Soviet woman, not a Mary Magdalene, and that it's simply not right to give such a title to a poem about a woman he loves?" On another night, he questioned the romance itself. "What have you got in common? I can't believe that a Russian woman like you could ever really be in love with this old Jew." When one session was interrupted by some loud clanging in the distance, Semyonov smiled: "Hear that? It's Pasternak trying to get in here! Don't worry, he'll make it before long."

When Pasternak learned of Ivinskaya's arrest, he called a mutual friend, who found him sitting on a bench near the Palace of Soviets Metro station. He was crying. "Everything is finished now. They've taken her away from me and I'll never see her again. It's like death, even worse."

Several weeks into her detention, Ivinskaya said, it became obvious to her jailors that she was pregnant. Her treatment improved marginally. She was allowed to sleep longer, and salad and bread were added to her diet of porridge. The exhausting interrogations continued but to little avail for Semyonov—Ivinskaya did not break and refused to sign anything that would condemn Pasternak.

She probably became pregnant in late summer, when the couple reconciled after a long break. Pasternak wrote about the moment in the poem "Autumn":

You fling off your dress
As a coppice sheds its leaves.
In a dressing gown with a silk tassel
You fall into my arms.

(Akhmatova railed at these love poems: "About the gown with the tassels, how she falls in his arms, that's about Olga, I can't stand it. At 60, one should not write about these things.")

Ivinskaya was eventually told to prepare to meet her lover. She was torn between the fear that he was being abused in some nearby cell and joy that she might be able to exchange a few words with him, perhaps even embrace him. Ivinskaya was signed out of the Lubyanka, placed in a wagon with blacked-out windows, and driven to another secret-police facility just outside the city. She was led down into a basement, where she was abruptly pushed through a metal door that shut loudly behind her. It was hard to see. The smell was odd. Beneath her feet water pooled on the whitewashed floors. As Ivinskaya's eyes adjusted to the semidarkness she saw bodies on a series of tables, each covered with gray tarpaulin. "There was the unmistakable sweetish smell of a morgue. Could it be that one of these corpses was the man I loved?"

Ivinskaya was left locked inside the prison morgue for some time, but the effort to terrorize, or reduce her to some state of despair, failed. "I suddenly felt completely calm. For some reason, as though God had put it in my mind, it dawned on me that the whole thing was a monstrous hoax, and that Borya could not possibly be here."

Trembling from the cold damp of the morgue, she was led back to her interrogator. "Please forgive us," said Semyonov. "We made a mistake and took you to the wrong place altogether. It was the fault of the escort guards. But now prepare yourself: We are waiting for you."

Ivinskaya was next subjected to a ritual of Soviet interrogation: a staged confrontation with a witness who had been primed, almost certainly after torture, to offer evidence of her treachery. The man brought into the room was Sergei Nikiforov, her daughter Irina's elderly English teacher. Nikiforov had been arrested shortly before Ivinskaya. He looked vacant and unkempt.

"Do you confirm the evidence you gave yesterday that you were present at anti-Soviet conversations between Pasternak and Ivinskaya?"

"Yes, I do. I was present," Nikiforov said.

Ivinskaya started to object but was told to shut up.

"Now you told us that Ivinskaya informed you of her plan to escape abroad together with Pasternak, and that they tried to persuade an airman to take them out of the country in a plane. Do you confirm this?"

"Yes, that is so."

"Aren't you ashamed, Sergei Nikolayevich?" shouted Ivinskaya.

"But you've confirmed it all yourself, Olga Vsevolodovna," he replied.

It was clear then to Ivinskaya that Nikiforov had been induced to provide false evidence after he was told that she had already confessed. Years later, Nikiforov wrote to Ivinskaya: "I have pondered for a long time whether to write to you. In the end, the conscience of an honest man . . . prompts me to account for the situation in which I put you—believe me, against my will, given the conditions then existing. I know that these conditions were familiar to you, and that to some extent they were experienced by you as well. But they were of course applied to us men more forcefully and severely than to women. Before our meeting at that time, I had repudiated two documents, even though I had signed them. But how many people are able to go boldly, and uprightly, to the scaffold. Unfortunately, I do not belong to their number, because I am not alone. I had to think of my wife and shield her."

Ivinskaya was driven back to the Lubyanka in what she described as a state of nervous shock after the gruesome theater of the morgue and the draining confrontation with Nikiforov. She said she was suddenly racked with pain and taken to the prison hospital. She was in her fifth month. "Here Borya's and my child perished before it even had a chance to be born."

Ivinskaya said that her family had learned of her pregnancy from a cellmate who was released, and they, in turn, had told Pasternak. Word of the miscarriage, however, did not immediately reach them. In the spring of 1950, Pasternak was told to report to the prison by the secret police and he expected to be handed the baby.

"I have told [Zinaida] that we must take it in and care for it until Olya comes back," he told a friend, adding that his wife made "a terrible scene."

At the Lubyanka, Pasternak was given a bundle of books and letters. He at first refused to accept them and wrote a letter of protest to Abakumov. It did no good. On July 5, 1950, Ivinskaya was sentenced to five years in a hard-labor camp "for close contact with persons suspected of espionage."

Chapter 5

"Until it is finished, I am a fantastically, manically unfree man."

In October 1952, Pasternak suffered a serious heart attack and was rushed to Moscow's Botkin Hospital, where he spent his first night "with a miscellany of mortals at death's door." As he drifted in and out of consciousness, lying on a gurney in a corridor because the hospital was so crowded, he said, he whispered: "Lord, I thank you for having laid on the paints so thickly and for having made life and death the same as your language—majestic and musical, for having made me a creative artist, for having made creative work your school, and for having prepared me all my life for this night."

Death had brushed very close, and Pasternak, who was treated by some of the city's best cardiologists, spent a week in the emergency department and another two and a half months in a general ward. Before the hospitalization, Pasternak suffered constantly from toothache and boils on his gums. His heart condition was discovered when he fainted while coming home from the dentist. He also had dental surgery while in the hospital, and his uneven equine teeth were replaced with a gleaming set of American dentures, which, Akhmatova said, gave him a new "distinguished" look.

His doctors warned him to be careful. His heart problems had begun two years earlier, after Ivinskaya's arrest and his visit to the Lubyanka. As with so much else, he explored his condition through Yuri Zhivago, who was bestowed with similar cardiac problems: "It's the disease of our time. I think its causes are of a moral order. A constant, systematic dissembling is required of the vast majority of us. It's impossible, without its affecting your health, to show yourself day after day contrary to what you feel, to lay yourself out for what you don't love, to rejoice over what brings you misfortune. . . . Our soul takes up room in space and sits inside us like the teeth in our mouth. It cannot be endlessly violated with impunity."

Ivinskaya had been sent by train to Mordovia, about three hundred miles southeast of Moscow, sleeping on a luggage rack above the crush of prisoners. The rural camp was reached after a forced march from the train station. Prison life alternated between long, buggy summer days digging fields with a pick and the bitter cold of winter in bare barracks. Only immediate family were allowed to write to prisoners, so Pasternak, in his distinctive flowing script, sent postcards under the name of Ivinskaya's mother: "May 31, 1951. My dear Olya, my joy! You are quite right to be cross at us. Our letters to you should pour straight from the heart in floods of tenderness and sorrow. But it is not always possible to give way to this most natural impulse. Everything must be tempered with caution and concern. B. saw you in a dream the other day dressed in something long and white. He kept getting into all kinds of awkward situations but every time you appeared at his right side, light-hearted and encouraging. . . . God be with you, my darling. It is all like a dream. I kiss you endless times. Your Mama."

With Ivinskaya away, Pasternak continued to support her family, making arrangements for her mother to get direct payments from one publisher for his work. "Without him my children would not have survived," said Ivinskaya.

Pasternak alternated between paid translation commissions and *Doctor Zhivago.* "I am burying myself in work," he told his cousin. He had little expectation that his novel would be published. "When they print it, in ten months or fifty years, is unknown to me and just as immaterial."

Friends continued to encourage him. Lydia Chukovskaya wrote

to him in August 1952 after reading Part 3: "Already for a day I don't eat, sleep, exist, I am reading the novel. From beginning to end, and again from the end, and in parts. . . . I read your novel like a letter addressed to me. I feel like carrying it in my bag all the time so that at any moment I can take it out, convince myself it is still there, and reread my favorite passages."

Pasternak continued to read *Doctor Zhivago* to small groups, but his life was now largely confined to Peredelkino in summer, his apartment in Moscow in winter, and a small circle of trusted friends and young writers. At the dacha he read in his upstairs study to groups of up to twenty guests for a couple of hours on Sundays, and the gatherings formed an alternative to the events at the Union of Soviet Writers. Often attending were Boris Livanov, the great actor from the Moscow Art Theatre Company, and the young poet Andrei Voznesensky, slouching in his chair. The pianist Svyatoslav Richter, his eyes half-closed in contemplation, and his life partner, the soprano Nina Dorliak, were also regulars.

On some weekends, Yuri Krotkov was present. Krotkov, a playwright, had a room in the nearby House of Creative Artists in Peredelkino. He was a familiar face among some diplomats and journalists in the city. A card player, he had endeared himself to Zinaida, earning a seat at her table. He was also a KGB informer who had been involved in a number of stings, including setting up the French ambassador in a "honey-trap" operation with a Russian actress.

When the reading was over, everyone carried their chairs and stools back downstairs and crowded around the feast Zinaida had prepared: often wine and vodka and kvass, a homemade fermented drink, with caviar, marinated herring, and pickles, sometimes followed by a stew made of game. Pasternak sat at the head of the table, Livanov at the other end, a hint of rivalry in their exchanges, both players to the boisterous crowd.

"I have a question for Slava!" said Pasternak, looking at Richter. "Slava! Tell me, does art exist?"

"Let's drink to poetry!" shouted Livanov.

Some reactions to the novel continued to be mixed, but Pasternak was unshaken. "Of those who have read my novel the majority are dissatisfied. They say it is a failure, and they expected more from me, that it is colorless, that it is not worthy of me, but I, acknowledging all this, just grin as though this abuse and condemnation were praise."

The anti-Semitic character of the long campaign against "cosmopolitans" became hysterical and brutal in 1952 and 1953. All of the Soviet Union's leading Yiddish writers were shot in August 1952 after a secret trial on treason charges. In January 1953, *Pravda* announced a "Doctors' Plot" in which Jewish physicians were accused of the medical murder of prominent figures, including Zhdanov. The persecutor of Akhmatova and Zoshchenko had died in August 1948 from a heart attack brought on by his prodigious drinking. But his death was characterized as part of an American-Zionist conspiracy. Among those caught up in the purge and savagely tortured was Dr. Miron Vovsi, the former surgeon general of the Red Army and one of the cardiologists who had recently helped to save Pasternak. Vovsi confessed to being the inspiration for a terrorist group of Kremlin doctors. Prominent Jewish cultural figures, including the journalist Vasili Grossman and the violinist David Oistrakh, were forced to sign an appeal to Stalin asking him to resettle all Jews in the East to protect them from the "wrath of the people."

Pasternak was probably saved from the danger of refusing to sign this petition by his heart attack. After his release from the hospital he went to a sanatorium in Bolshevo, just northeast of the city, to continue his recovery and write. "I am now happy and free, in good health and cheerful spirits, and it is with a light heart that I sit down to work on Zhivago, that although of no use to anyone is an integral part of me." Pasternak was in Bolshevo on March 5, 1953, when Stalin's death was announced. Zinaida, who once said her sons loved Stalin before their mother, reacted like many Soviet citizens and mourned his death. She suggested Pasternak write a memorial poem. He refused, telling her that Stalin was the killer of the intelligentsia and drenched in blood.

On March 27, in the wake of Stalin's death, the new leadership announced a broad amnesty for prisoners, including women with children and those sentenced to five years or less. Ivinskaya, thinner and ruddily tanned from long days in the fields, returned to Moscow. Pasternak initially had qualms about rekindling the affair. Zinaida had nursed him back to health and he felt he owed her his life. He also was unable to tell Ivinskaya the relationship was over, and he blundered about like a child. He arranged to meet Ivinskaya's daughter Irina before her mother reached the capital. He asked the fifteen-year-old to tell her mother that while he still loved Olga, the relationship could not continue. Thinking it ridiculous that she should be his messenger, Irina said nothing to her mother. For Ivinskaya, informed of the conversation only years later, it revealed a "mixture of candor, guileless charm, and undeniable heartlessness." Her lover could be gauche and cruel.

The dacha in Peredelkino was winterized in 1953 and "turned into a palace" with a gas supply, running water, a bath, and three new rooms. Pasternak said he was ashamed of the grandeur of his large study and its parquet floor. His father's drawings were hung on the pink-washed walls, including some original illustrations for Tolstoy's *Resurrection*. He started to live year-round in the village, the wish of his doctors, who wanted him in more restful surroundings than Moscow. Pasternak kept some emotional distance from Ivinskaya for several months after her return to Moscow. But the affair had resumed by 1954, and that summer she was a frequent visitor to the village, especially when Zinaida and Leonid went on vacation to Yalta on the Black Sea. Ivinskaya became pregnant again, but in August, after a very bumpy ride in a small truck, she was taken ill. The child was stillborn in the ambulance on the way to the hospital. The following summer, in 1955, Ivinskaya rented part of a dacha on Izmalkovo Pond, across a wooden footbridge from Peredelkino. She put a large bed in a glassed–in veranda and some dark-blue chintz curtains to create some privacy. When summer ended Ivinskaya rented an insulated room in a nearby house so she could be near Pasternak year-round. He commuted between his wife in what he called the "Big House" and his lover's pad—a ritual of lunch and lazy afternoons with Ivinskaya before returning home for dinner. Mornings were reserved for writing.

Ivinskaya now began to act as Pasternak's agent, managing his affairs in Moscow so he rarely had to go into the city. The role brought renewed questions about Ivinskaya's trustworthiness, allegations that, in various forms, would continue to shadow her. Lydia Chukovskaya said she ended her friendship with Olga in 1949 because of "her debauchery, irresponsibility, her inability to do any sort of work, her greed that generates lies." After Ivinskaya's release, Chukovskaya nonetheless said she entrusted her with cash to buy and mail a monthly package of food, clothes, and books to Nadezhda Adolf-Nadezhdina, a mutual friend who was still held in a camp. Chukovskaya said Ivinskaya insisted on assuming responsibility for the mailings because of Lydia's heart condition; it was necessary to travel to a post office outside of Moscow to mail a package to the camps. No goods ever reached Nadezhdina, and Chukovskaya accused Ivinskaya of the unforgivable theft of gifts intended to help keep an inmate alive. Chukovskaya told Akhmatova and others about the betrayal, but said she never told Pasternak because she didn't want to upset him. "I've never heard of such a thing even among gangsters," said Akhmatova. Nadezhdina, however, strongly objected to Chukovskaya's account when she later read it, and said there was no proof that Ivinskaya stole gifts intended for her and there were other plausible explanations why she might not have received the packages.

Ivinskaya later wrote, "It pains me to think that even Lydia Chukovskaya took one of these slanders at its face value," but she said she followed Pasternak's advice to ignore "filthy insinuations."

"Those who know you will never believe you capable of theft or murder, or whatever it is," she wrote. "If some slander is going the rounds, say nothing. . . . And so I simply kept my peace."

The charge nonetheless deeply colored the attitude of some of Pasternak's closest friends toward Ivinskaya. And it led some to believe that Ivinskaya, already seen as demanding and manipulative, was capable of any kind of treachery, including selling out Pasternak himself.

There is some evidence she was not always faithful to him. Varlam Shalamov, a Gulag survivor and one of Pasternak's most ardent admirers, wrote a pair of passionate letters to Ivinskaya in 1956 and seemed to believe they had a future together. Shalamov, who spent sixteen years in the camps and was not allowed to live in Moscow when he was released in 1953, apparently did not know of Ivinskaya's relationship with Pasternak. He later recalled the whole episode as a "painful moral trauma."

"For Mrs. Ivinskaya, Pasternak was just the subject of the most cynical trade, a sale, which Pasternak of course knew," wrote Shalamov in a letter to Nadezhda Mandelstam. "Pasternak was her bet, a bet she used when she could."

Stalin's death led to some searing criticism of the ideological straitjacket suffocating artists and created the expectation of greater imaginative freedom. In the summer of 1953, the editor of *Novy Mir,* Alexander Tvardovsky, published a provocative poem that dwelled on the sad state of writing:

And everything looks real enough, everything resembles
That which is or which could be
But as a whole it is so indigestible
That you want to howl out in pain.

In the October issue of *Znamya,* Ilya Ehrenburg wrote a piece, "Concerning the Writer's Work," and argued that "a writer is not an apparatus mechanically recording events" but writes "to tell people something he personally feels, because he has 'begun to ache' from his book." There were calls for "sincerity" in literature. Shouting over the fence at Chukovsky that month, Pasternak declared, "A new age is beginning: they want to publish *me*!"

In early 1954, Pasternak's translation of *Hamlet* was performed at the Pushkin Theatre in Leningrad. In April, *Znamya* published ten poems from the set planned for the end of *Doctor Zhivago*—the first publication of original material by Pasternak since the war. The more religious verse from among the poems was excluded, but Pasternak was allowed to write an introductory note describing *Doctor Zhivago:* "It is anticipated that the novel will be completed by the summer. It covers the period from 1903 to 1929, with an epilogue relating to the Great Patriotic War. Its hero, Yuri Andreyevich Zhivago, a doctor, a thinker, a seeker after truth with a creative and artistic cast of mind, dies in 1929. After his death there remain his notebooks and, among other papers written in his youth, poems in finished form, part of which are presented here and which, taken all together, form the last, concluding chapter of the novel."

Pasternak was elated: "The words 'Doctor Zhivago' have made their appearance on a contemporary page—like a hideous blot!" He told his cousin that "I have to and want to finish the novel, and until it is finished I am a fantastically, manically unfree man."

The guardians of ideological rigidity may have been staggered by the changes, but they were not in retreat. As new, unsettling fiction and poetry began to appear, Surkov took to the pages of *Pravda* to warn against such experiments and instruct writers where their duty lay. "The party has always reminded Soviet writers that the strength of literature lies in intimacy with the life of the people, from which it cannot be estranged. . . . We have fought against succumbing to literary influences that are not ours, or are no longer ours—against bourgeois nationalism, against great power chauvinism, against the anti-patriotic activity of the cosmopolitans." The following month, another conservative critic singled out Pasternak's poem "The Wedding Party" as representative of this pervasive and false sincerity. Others continued to act as if Pasternak were irrelevant. Boris Polevoi, the head of the foreign branch of the Union of Soviet Writers, said on a visit to New York that he had never heard of any novel by Pasternak. And an accompanying Soviet journalist said Pasternak was unable to finish the novel because he had become "rich and indolent" from translation work.

Pasternak spent much of the winter of 1954 in Peredelkino working intensively on the novel's last chapters. His study looked out on the garden and across a broad meadow to the small church that the poet occasionally attended. He wrote in a room with a cot, a wardrobe, two desks, including one to stand at, and a narrow, dark-stained bookshelf that included a large Russian-English dictionary and a Russian Bible among a small collection of books. "I personally do not keep heirlooms, archives, collections of any kind, including books and furniture. I do not save letters or draft copies of my work. Nothing piles up in my room; it is easier to clean than a hotel room. My life resembles a student's."

He was a man of routine. He rose early and washed outside at a pump, even on harsh winter mornings, steam rising off his face and chest. When he was younger he regularly bathed in the river, and he still dipped his head in its waters when the ice broke in the spring. Each day, he liked a long, briskly taken walk, and he always took candy for children he might meet around the village.

Pasternak wrote in his upstairs study, and Zinaida was protective of his privacy, refusing to allow visitors to disturb him. She was particularly watchful that winter, having learned that her husband had rekindled relations with Ivinskaya. Akhmatova described Pasternak as half ill, half detained and noted that Zinaida was rude to him. A visitor described "her lips pursed in an injured Cupid's bow." Pasternak himself was occasionally irritated by distractions from his rush to get *Zhivago* finished. He reluctantly translated the speech of the German poet Bertolt Brecht, who was in Moscow to receive the Stalin Prize, but when the Union of Soviet Writers suggested he translate some of Brecht's poems he was openly irritated: "Surely Brecht realizes that engaging in translations is a disgrace. I am busy with important work, for which the time has not yet come—unlike Brecht's old junk." He refused to go into Moscow for the reception for the visiting German.

Through the summer of 1955, Pasternak continued to edit the manuscript as it neared completion. After reading a newly typed version, he said that several "heavy and complicated passages will have to be simplified and lightened." Even amid the relative relaxation of the "thaw," he was not optimistic about publication. As Pasternak and Ivinskaya walked over the footbridge across Izmalkovo Pond one evening that fall, he said: "You mark my words—they will not publish this novel for anything in the world. I don't believe they will ever publish it. I have come to the conclusion that I should pass it around to be read by all and sundry."

A final revision took place in November, and on December 10, 1955, he said the novel was complete: "You cannot imagine what

I have achieved! I have found and given names to all this sorcery that has been the cause of suffering, bafflement, amazement, and dispute for several decades. Everything is named in simple, transparent, and sad words. I also once again renewed and redefined the dearest and most important things: land and sky, great passion, creative spirit, life and death."

Chapter 6

"Not to publish a novel like this would constitute a crime against culture."

The publisher Giangiacomo Feltrinelli was an unlikely Communist. His entrepreneurial ancestors, stretching back to the mid-nineteenth century, had over several generations built a great fortune. These businessmen, with multinational interests across numerous sectors, had made Feltrinelli one of those names—like Agnelli, Motta, and Pirelli—synonymous with the industrial development of northern Italy. Feltrinelli was born on June 19, 1926, into a cocooned life of nannies and tutors that shifted, depending on the season, between various villas and hotels—Lake Como, Lake Garda, the Baur au Lac in Zurich, and the Excelsior at the Venice Lido. The family, much like some of Italy's other great industrial concerns, coexisted—sometimes uneasily, sometimes profitably—with Mussolini's Fascist government, which had come to power in 1922. Feltrinelli's father, Carlo, died in 1935 of a heart attack while in the middle of a financial dispute with the regime over assets held abroad by his mother. He was fifty-four. The parenting of Giangiacomo and his sister Antonella now fell to his mother, Giannalisa, insofar as she devoted time to it. She "would punish and then repent. She would mortify and then shower them with kisses and hugs." Feltrinelli was enrolled by his mother in the Gioventù Italiana del Littorio, the Italian Fascist youth movement. A substantial check from

Giannalisa also induced Mussolini to bestow the title Marquess of Gargnano on the boy.

Feltrinelli later described himself as a teenage mass of contradictions, urging on the Fascist armies but also opposing the Germans while listening to Radio London, as some called the BBC World Service during the war. Ignored at home, he befriended the workers and farmhands who took care of his mother's property, and they opened up a previously invisible world of hard labor and injustice. The allied bombing raids and the arrival of the Germans in Italy to prop up Mussolini added to the radicalization of a young man who was searching for a set of ideas to cling to.

Feltrinelli was a man of great enthusiasms, whether for politics or literature. He didn't hold his loyalties and ideas lightly, but when they clashed, as they would over *Doctor Zhivago,* he followed his conscience, not a party line. A friend said his passion was easily aroused and he was devoted to his principles, "but he was just as prepared to abandon a cause, without standing on ceremony, if he felt it was outdated or did not serve his way of thinking." By 1944, after the liberation of Rome, and still only eighteen, Feltrinelli was reading *The Communist Manifesto* and Lenin's *State and Revolution.* That November, he enlisted with the Legnano combat unit which fought with the American Fifth Army, and he saw some action near Bologna.

Feltrinelli joined the Communist Party in March 1945. His mother, a royalist, was appalled. When Italy held a referendum in June 1946 on whether to keep the monarchy or adopt a republican form of government, Giannalisa Feltrinelli handed out leaflets in support of the House of Savoy in the streets of Rome—through the window of her Rolls-Royce. Feltrinelli had already skipped town after intelligence he gathered about pro-royalty meetings in his mother's home ended up in the pages of *L'Unità,* the Communist newspaper. To wit: "On the basis of information received from an excellent source we are able to provide news of an important meeting held in the home of a family of big industrial sharks, the Feltrinellis."

Between the fall of Mussolini (who briefly commandeered the Villa Feltrinelli on Lake Garda, where he was surrounded by a protective guard of crack Nazi troops) and the first postwar election, the Italian Communist Party was transformed from a small underground organization of fewer than 10,000 activists to a mass movement of 1.7 million members. The party benefited, above all, from its vanguard role in the Resistance, where two-thirds of all partisan bands were inspired by communism. After the war, under the leadership of the pragmatic Palmiro Togliatti, the party advocated "progressive democracy" and appeared more anti-Fascist than anti-capitalist. The Communists seemed open to innovation in the arts, literature, and the social sciences. They were allied with or controlled some of the most progressive forces in the country, from the feminist Unione Donne Italiane to the Movement for the Rebirth of the South to the Union for Popular Sport. The party had a glamorous air. And it attracted a couple of generations of intellectuals and idealists—those who had survived the long years of fascism and young people such as Feltrinelli who were seeking a political movement to champion their desire for social change. The party was the natural home for what the writer Italo Calvino called the "little big world" of anti-Fascists, that passionate, postwar swell of believers who yearned for a new Italy. Feltrinelli was a disciplined and earnest young recruit. "I learned to control, at least in part, my impulsiveness and my impetuosity; I learned method in debate, in the work of persuasion and clarification that I had to carry out among the comrades."

At the age of twenty-one, Feltrinelli came into his inheritance, including substantial holdings in construction, lumber, and banking, and he became a significant financial supporter of the Italian Communist Party. One activist recalled, "We had dreams. . . . Giangiacomo could make them come true, and it seemed miraculous to have him on our side." The house at Lake Garda was used as a summer camp for young party members. Feltrinelli drove around in his smoky-blue Buick convertible to put up party posters. At home with his new wife—dubbed the "Muscovite Pasionaria" by her mother-in-law—he hung a portrait of Stalin among the old masters on the wall.

In the late 1940s, Feltrinelli began his formal entry into the world of books. He and Giuseppe Del Bo, a Marxist academic and writer, began to create a library devoted to a history of the working classes and social movements. The Italian police called it a "little university of Marxism," but with Feltrinelli's wealth and his passion for the pursuit of rare books and materials across Europe, it became a treasure house holding tens of thousands of pieces of radical literature—-a first edition of *The Communist Manifesto,* original working notes of both Marx and Engels, a first edition of Jean-Jacques Rousseau's *Social Contract,* Victor Hugo's letters to Garibaldi, and a rare copy of Thomas More's *Utopia.* The collection brought Feltrinelli to the attention of the Soviet Union. In 1953, he was invited to Moscow to discuss cooperation between the Biblioteca Giangiacomo Feltrinelli in Milan and the Institute of Marxism-Leninism. Little came of the meeting; it would be his only visit to Moscow.

Feltrinelli also ran his businesses, proving himself an able, sometimes hard-nosed, manager and capitalist. The party drew on his financial acumen as well as his cash. In 1950, Feltrinelli became involved in a publishing house tied to the Communist Party and brought some management systems and financial controls to the floundering entity. Eventually, in 1955, the house was dissolved, and it gave way to a new business, Feltrinelli Editore.

The twenty-nine-year-old was now an independent Milanese publisher, and he looked the part: hair already slightly receding, a wingspan moustache, dark horn-rimmed glasses, and an arched, feline quality to his face. He was nicknamed "the Jaguar." Feltrinelli Editore's first two books came off the presses in June 1955—*An Autobiography: Jawaharlal Nehru* and *The Scourge of the Swastika* by Lord Russell of Liverpool. The publisher wanted books that were fresh, progressive, dissonant, and influential. He wanted intellectual excitement, discoveries.

On February 25, 1956, at a secret session of the Twentieth Congress of the Soviet Union, Khrushchev launched an astonishing and devastating attack on Stalin entitled "On the Cult of Personality and Its Consequences." He said the former, hallowed Leader was guilty of the gravest abuse of power, and that during Stalin's rule "mass arrests and deportation of thousands and thousands of people, executions without trial or normal investigations, created insecurity, fear and desperation." Khrushchev spoke of torture, even of former members of the Politburo. He said Lenin wanted to fire Stalin as general secretary of the party. He said Stalin was confused and essentially missing in action when the Nazis invaded. The delegates in the Great Hall of the Kremlin sat in stupefied silence.

The CIA, which obtained a copy of what became known as the "Secret Speech," leaked it to *The New York Times*. For all the shock among many Communists worldwide, there was also a desire for renewal, as if the movement had passed from one age into another. The sense of change was short-lived; it would die with the Soviet invasion of Hungary. But it was in this brief clearing that Feltrinelli received *Doctor Zhivago*. Cooperation with Soviet writers and publishers seemed particularly opportune now that reform was gusting through the Kremlin. Feltrinelli had no sense yet that his possession of the novel would infuriate the Soviet leadership.

The week after he left Pasternak's dacha in Peredelkino in May 1956, D'Angelo flew to Berlin. He wasn't searched as he left Moscow, probably because he was a fraternal comrade, and he also had no thought that there was anything untoward about carrying the novel out. He landed in Berlin, a city not yet divided by the wall, and went from Schönefeld Airport in the East to a hotel just off West Berlin's showcase shopping avenue, the Kurfürstendamm. D'Angelo called Milan, and Feltrinelli decided to fly to Berlin himself to pick up the manuscript. It was passed the following day from one suitcase to another at a small hotel on Joachimstaler Strasse. *Doctor Zhivago* had found a publisher.

Feltrinelli didn't read Russian, so after he returned from Berlin with the manuscript, he sent it to Pietro Zveteremich, an Italian Slavist, for review. Judgment was swift: "Not to publish a novel like this would constitute a crime against culture."

Pasternak seemed quite pleased with himself after giving the book to D'Angelo, but he also realized that those close to him might think him reckless. When he informed his stepson and daughter-in-law that Sunday in May, Pasternak asked them not to tell his wife. At a dinner with friends that week, Pasternak brought up the subject anyway. "What kind of nonsense is that?" scoffed Zinaida. The table fell silent.

Ivinskaya was in Moscow when Pasternak met with D'Angelo, and returned to Peredelkino only later that evening. Pasternak met her on the road near his dacha, and told her he had had a visit from two charming young people, an Italian Communist and an official in the Soviet embassy in Rome. D'Angelo's companion was no diplomat, and Pasternak was dissembling to cushion the fact that he had handed over his manuscript to strangers, one of them a foreigner. Ivinskaya was furious; she realized that no post-Stalinist glow would shield a writer who defied the system by consorting with Westerners.

Ivinskaya was returning from negotiations with the state publishing house on a one-volume collection of poetry, which was being overseen by a sympathetic young editor, Nikolai Bannikov. "This may put an end to the poetry volume!" she shouted. She was also afraid for her own safety. "I've been in prison once, remember, and already then, in the Lubyanka, they questioned me endlessly about what the novel would say. . . . I'm really amazed you could do this."

Pasternak was a little sheepish, but unapologetic. "Really, now, Olya, you're overstating things, it's nothing at all. Just let them read it. If they like it, let them do what they want with it—I said I didn't mind." To assuage his lover, Pasternak said Ivinskaya could try to get it back from the Italian if she was so upset. Or perhaps, he suggested, she could sound out any official reaction to what he had done.

Ivinskaya turned on her heels and went back to Moscow to see Bannikov. The poetry editor was familiar with the novel. The manuscript had been gathering dust at the state publishing house for several months, and Pasternak had referred to it in the introductory essay for his collections of poems: "Quite recently I have completed my main and most important work, the only one of which I am not ashamed and for which I answer without a qualm—a novel in prose with additions in verse, *Doctor Zhivago.* The poems assembled in this book, which are scattered across all the years of my life, constitute preparatory stages to the novel. Indeed, I view their republication as a preparation for the novel."

The state publisher had been notably silent about Pasternak's manuscript—almost certainly because the senior editors viewed the novel as objectionable. Bannikov was frightened by Ivinskaya's news. After she left, he wrote her a note, which was delivered to her apartment on Potapov Street: "How can anyone love his country so little? One may have one's differences with it, but what he has done is treachery—how can he fail to understand what he is bringing on himself and us as well?"

Feltrinelli moved quickly to secure his rights. In mid-June, he wrote to Pasternak to thank him for the opportunity to publish *Doctor Zhivago,* which he described as a work of enormous literary importance. He then got down to business, discussing royalties and foreign rights. Feltrinelli had a trusted courier hand-deliver the letter and two copies of an enclosed contract. If Pasternak had any real desire to get the novel back, this was the moment. But he had no second thoughts. A couple of weeks after meeting D'Angelo, Pasternak was visited by the Italian scholar Ettore Lo Gatto and told him he was willing to face "any kind of trouble" as long as the novel was published. After consulting with his sons, Pasternak decided to sign the contract with Feltrinelli. In a letter to the publisher at the end of June, Pasternak told him that, while he wasn't completely uninterested in money, he realized that geography and politics could make it impossible to receive his royalties. The writer made Feltrinelli aware of the risks to Pasternak of first publication in the West but did not bar him from bringing the novel out: "If its publication here, promised by several of our magazines, were to be delayed and your version were to come before it, I would find myself in a tragically difficult situation. But this is not your concern. In the name of God, feel free to go with the translation and the printing of the book, and good luck! Ideas are not born to be hidden or smothered at birth, but to be communicated to others."

The Kremlin leadership quickly learned about Pasternak's contact with Feltrinelli. On August 24, 1956, KGB general Ivan Serov, the head of the secret police and a longtime enforcer of the Kremlin's will, including in Eastern Europe, wrote to the Politburo, the country's small ruling group. The Politburo, led by the general secretary, Nikita Khrushchev, oversaw the Central Committee of the Communist Party of the Soviet Union and its various departments, including culture. In a long memo, Serov informed the Communist leadership of the manuscript's delivery to Feltrinelli and how Pasternak had requested the rights be assigned to publishers in England and France. After noting that permission to publish *Doctor Zhivago* in the Soviet Union had not been granted, Serov quoted from a note Pasternak had recently mailed with an essay to a French journalist, Daniil Reznikov, in Paris. The parcel was intercepted by the KGB: "I realize perfectly well that [the novel] cannot be published now, and that this is how it is going to be for some time, perhaps forever," Pasternak wrote. Noting the likelihood of foreign publication, Pasternak continued: "Now they will tear me limb from limb: I have this foreboding, and you shall be a distant and sorrowful witness to this event." Pasternak, however, seemed willing to countenance even more danger: He included a biographical essay that he had written for the state literary publishing house, which was planning to bring out a collection of his poems. Pasternak told Reznikov, who had visited him earlier in the year, to do as he wished with the essay.

Serov noted that Pasternak was a Jew and did not have a party card, and said his work was typified by "estrangement from Soviet life."

A week later, the Central Committee's culture department prepared a detailed report on *Doctor Zhivago* for the leadership with a series of tendentious but damning quotations from the novel. The book was described as a hostile attack on the October Revolution and a malicious libel of the Bolshevik revolutionaries by an author who was labeled a "bourgeois individualist." Publication of this novel is impossible, the report concluded. In an accompanying note, the deputy foreign minister of the Soviet Union said officials would use their contacts with the Italian Communist Party to prevent publication abroad. Feltrinelli, after all, was a Communist.

It is unclear exactly how the KGB learned the details of Pasternak's communications with Feltrinelli, including his wish to assign the rights to English and French publishers. That fact must have come directly from an account of Pasternak's meeting with D'Angelo. Both the Italian scout and his companion, Vladimirsky, talked openly at their workplace in Radio Moscow about getting the manuscript and delivering it to Feltrinelli.

Ivinskaya's contacts with various editors about Pasternak's involvement with an Italian publisher and how to salvage the situation also raised an alarm within the system. A senior editor at the state literary publishing house told her that she would show the novel to Vyacheslav Molotov, a senior Politburo member, and seek his advice on how to proceed. The editor of *Znamya,* the magazine that had published some of Pasternak's *Zhivago* poems, said he would inform an official at the Central Committee.

For the next two years, Ivinskaya became the authorities' favored conduit to the writer. It was a difficult and controversial role. The author's well-being, Ivinskaya's fears for her own safety, and the state's interests were tangled up in her sometimes-frantic mediation efforts. "She relieves me from the vexing negotiations with the authorities, she takes the blows of such conflicts on herself," Pasternak told his sister. She was his chosen emissary, but her contacts with the bureaucrats were watched with suspicion by some of Pasternak's circle. She was in a hopeless position. Ivinskaya was not the informer some would label her many decades later. In a contemporaneous judgment in a top-secret memo, the chairman of the KGB labeled her "very anti-Soviet." She tried to please the officials she dealt with, and they tried to make her their semi-witting instrument but, in the end, her influence on Pasternak was limited. Pasternak was a self-aware and intuitive actor in the unfolding drama, and the key decisions in the matter, from the day he handed the manuscript to D'Angelo, remained his.

Ivinskaya was soon summoned to meet Dmitri Polikarpov, the head of the Central Committee's culture department. The haggard, bleary-eyed Polikarpov said it was imperative that Ivinskaya get the novel back from D'Angelo. Ivinskaya suggested that the Italians might not be willing to return the manuscript and the ideal solution would be to publish *Doctor Zhivago* in the Soviet Union as quickly as possible, preempting any foreign edition.

"No," said Polikarpov, "we must get the manuscript back, because it will be very awkward if we cut out some chapters and they print them."

Polikarpov was known in the literary community as *dyadya* Mitya—"Uncle Mitya"—an unapologetic enforcer of orthodoxy who confronted writers about their errors. Polikarpov once told the deputy editor of *Literaturnaya Gazeta:* "Your newspaper I read with a pencil in my hand." The poet Yevgeni Yevtushenko said that "for him the Party came before everything, before people, including himself."

Polikarpov, in front of Ivinskaya, phoned the director of the state literary publishing house, Anatoli Kotov, to tell him to draw up a contract with Pasternak and appoint an editor. "The editor should think about passages to change or cut out, and what can be left unchanged." Pasternak was unimpressed with Ivinskaya's efforts: "I am by no means intent on the novel being published at the moment when it cannot be brought out in its original form." He nonetheless agreed to meet Kotov, who assured him *Doctor Zhivago* was a magnificent work but said that "we will have to shorten a few things, and perhaps add some." Pasternak thought Kotov's proposal was absurd.

The writer Varlam Shalamov wrote to Pasternak to tell him that "without any doubt, this great [publication] battle will be won by you." He told Pasternak that he was "the conscience of our age like Lev Tolstoy was of his" and that "our time will only be justified because you lived in it."

Pasternak continued that summer to hand over copies of the manuscript to various foreign visitors to Peredelkino, including the French scholar Hélène Peltier, who would work on the French translation of *Doctor Zhivago*. The daughter of a French diplomat, she had studied Russian literature at Moscow University in 1947—a remarkable opportunity just as the Cold War was intensifying and the regime was intent on preventing any spontaneous contact between foreigners and ordinary Russians. She returned to Moscow in 1956 and got to know Pasternak, who gave her a copy of his manuscript to read. During a visit to Peredelkino that September or another trip to the village at the end of the year, Pasternak entrusted Peltier with a note for Feltrinelli. It was undated and typed on a narrow strip of paper torn from some copybook: "If ever you receive a letter in any language other than French, you absolutely must not do what is requested of you—the only valid letters shall be those written in French." This would prove to be a prescient and critical security measure that would allow Feltrinelli to distinguish between coerced messages and freely written ones from a writer who would soon feel the intense displeasure of the state.

Isaiah Berlin, the Oxford don who first met Pasternak in late 1945, also returned to Russia that summer of 1956, another in a long line of scholars enjoying the liberal, post-Stalin visa regime. Berlin traveled out to Peredelkino with Neigauz, the first husband of Pasternak's wife. Neigauz told the Briton of his concern for Pasternak's safety because the writer was so fixed on getting his novel published. Neigauz said if Berlin got a chance he should urge Pasternak to halt or at least delay foreign publication. Neigauz said that "it was important—more than important—perhaps a matter of life and death." Berlin agreed that "Pasternak probably did need to be physically protected from himself." Berlin was especially cautious because he feared that his meeting with Akhmatova in 1946 was a major factor in her persecution.

Pasternak took Berlin to his study and pressed a thick envelope into his hands. "My book, it is all there. It is my last word. Please read it." Berlin plunged into the novel as soon as he returned to Moscow, and finished it the next day. "Unlike some of its readers in both the Soviet Union and the West, I thought it was a work of genius. It seemed—and seems—to me to convey an entire range of human experience, and to create a world, even if it contains only one genuine inhabitant, in language of unexampled imaginative power." Berlin saw Pasternak a few days later, and the writer told him he had assigned world rights to Feltrinelli. Pasternak "wished his work to travel over the entire world," and he quoted Pushkin to hope that it would "lay waste with fire the hearts of men."

When she got a chance, Zinaida pulled Berlin aside and, weeping, she begged him to ask Pasternak not to have the novel published abroad without official permission. She told Berlin she did not want her children to suffer. Zinaida believed that their son Leonid was deliberately failed on the exam for entry to the Higher Technical Institute simply because he was Pasternak's son. In May 1950, during Stalin's anti-Semitic campaign, Pasternak's eldest son, Yevgeni, was prevented from finishing his postgraduate studies at the Moscow Military Academy and sent to Ukraine and then near the border with Mongolia for his compulsory military service. Berlin asked Pasternak to consider the consequences of defying the authorities. He assured Pasternak that his novel would endure and that he would have microfilms of it made and buried in all four corners of the globe so that *Doctor Zhivago* would survive even nuclear war. Pasternak was incensed and, with a dash of sarcasm, thanked Berlin for his concern. He said he had spoken to his sons and "they were prepared to suffer." He told Berlin not to mention the matter again. Surely, Pasternak said, Berlin realized that the dissemination of *Doctor Zhivago* was paramount. Berlin said he was shamed into silence. He later concluded that Pasternak "chose open-eyed" to pursue publication "fully realizing the danger to himself and his family." When he returned to Britain, Berlin brought back a manuscript for Pasternak's sisters in Oxford. And he included the first letter Pasternak had sent his English relatives since 1948. He told them about the novel with his usual preamble of caveats: "You may not even like it, finding its philosophy tedious and alien, some passages boring and long-drawn-out, the first book diffuse, and the transitional passages grey, pallid and ineffectual. And yet—it's an important work, a book of enormous, universal importance, whose destiny cannot be subordinated to my own destiny, or to any question of my well-being." He told them that he had asked Berlin to make up to twelve copies of the manuscript and circulate them among the leading Russians in Britain. And he asked his sisters to ensure that the book found a very good translator—"an Englishman who is a gifted writer with a perfect command of Russian."

Pasternak was visited in mid-September by another Oxford professor, George Katkov, a Moscow-born émigré, philosopher, and historian. An "original," according to a friend, he was a "tall, mustachioed, hugely impressive *ancient regime* Russian *intelligent*." The KGB referred to him contemptuously as a "White émigré." Katkov was a friend of the Pasternak sisters and a colleague of Berlin's. He was much more enthusiastic about publication. Pasternak also gave a manuscript to Katkov and asked him as well to ensure its translation and publication in England. Katkov said that the *Zhivago* cycle of poems would present a special challenge for a translator. He suggested the novelist Vladimir Nabokov to handle the verse. "That won't work; he's too jealous of my position in this country to do it properly," said Pasternak. As early as 1927, Nabokov had expressed his deep irritation with Pasternak's style. "His verse is convex, goitrous and goggle-eyed, as though his muse suffered from Basedow's disease. He is crazy about clumsy imagery, sonorous but literal rhymes, and clattering metre." When he finally read *Doctor Zhivago,* Nabokov was no less derisive, not least because Pasternak's novel would knock *Lolita* off the top of the best-seller list—"*Doctor Zhivago* is a sorry thing, clumsy, trite and melodramatic, with stock situations, voluptuous lawyers, unbelievable girls, romantic robbers and trite coincidences." Nabokov said Pasternak's mistress must have written it.

Katkov promised Pasternak with a kiss that *Doctor Zhivago* would be well-translated into English. He eventually settled on his protégé Max Hayward, a research fellow at St. Antony's College, Oxford, and a gifted linguist who famously taught himself Hungarian in six weeks. Russians who met Hayward insisted that he must be a native speaker, or at least the son of émigrés. He was neither. Hayward was a Londoner, the son of a mechanic, who sometimes called himself a Cockney. In the interests of speed, Hayward was joined in the translation effort by Manya Harari, the cofounder of the small publishing house the Harvill Press, a division of Collins in London. An émigré, from a wealthy Saint Petersburg family, Harari had moved to England with her family during World War I. The pair alternated chapters and then checked each other's work. Katkov supervised both of them, "going over everything for accuracy and nuance."

Katkov and Berlin would clash bitterly over the novel in 1958. Berlin continued to be concerned about Pasternak's safety and was skeptical of any push for swift publication. "That's all nonsense," Berlin said. "It's an interesting novel, but whether it's published now, or fifteen years from now, doesn't matter." Katkov took a very different view. He advocated for the widest possible dissemination and later argued that, since Pasternak "obviously wished to be a martyr," he "had to be sacrificed to the 'cause.'" The cause was the Cold War struggle against the Soviet Union.

First, however, Feltrinelli had to help *Doctor Zhivago* make its way around the world, and to do so, he had to face down his comrades—Russian and Italian.

Chapter 7

"If this is freedom seen through Western eyes, well,
I must say we have a different view of it."

In mid-September, the editorial board of *Novy Mir* formally rejected *Doctor Zhivago* in a long, detailed review. The critique was written mostly by Konstantin Simonov, the celebrated wartime poet. Four other board members, including Pasternak's next-door neighbor, Konstantin Fedin, offered editorial suggestions and additions. All five men signed the document.

The letter, along with the manuscript, was hand-delivered to Pasternak, who barely acknowledged its contents: "The thing that has disturbed us about your novel is something that neither the editors nor the author can change by cuts or alterations. We are referring to the spirit of the novel, its general tenor, the author's view on life. . . . The spirit of your novel is one of non-acceptance of the socialist revolution. The general tenor of your novel is that the October Revolution, the Civil War and the social transformation involved did not give the people anything but suffering, and destroyed the Russian intelligentsia, either physically or morally." The writers continued with a scene-by-scene dissection of the novel's ideological failings, the "viciousness" of its hero's conclusions about the revolution, and Yuri Zhivago's "hypertrophied individualism"—code for Pasternak's fundamental personal flaw.

After a backhanded compliment, they attacked the novel's

artistry: "There are quite a few first-rate pages, especially where you describe Russian natural scenery with remarkable truth and poetic power. There are many clearly inferior pages, lifeless and didactically dry. They are especially rife in the second half of the novel." Fedin, in particular, smarted from Zhivago's judgment of his contemporaries, seeing Pasternak's sentiments in Zhivago's words, and all the arrogance of the supremely talented: "Dear friends, oh, how hopelessly ordinary you and the circle you represent, and the brilliance and art of your favorite names and authorities, all are. The only live and bright thing in you is that you lived at the same time as me and knew me."

One of Pasternak's biographers noted that the authors of the letter either missed or did not articulate the novel's "most heretical insinuation: by artistically conflating the Stalinist period with early revolutionary history, Pasternak implied (many years before Solzhenitsyn's *Gulag Archipelago*) that the tyranny of the last twenty-five years was a direct outcome of Bolshevism." For Pasternak, Stalinism and the purges were not a terrible aberration—the accepted Soviet explanation under Khrushchev—but a natural outgrowth of the system created by Lenin. This was an idea that could not be broached even in a rejection letter.

Fedin's signature was particularly difficult for Pasternak to accept, as he regarded his neighbor as a friend. Only two weeks earlier, Fedin, pacing the room and waving his arms in enthusiasm, had told Chukovsky that the novel was "brilliant, extremely egocentric, satanically arrogant, elegantly simple yet literary through and through." He may have spoken before he had read the entire novel and was bruised by the implication of Zhivago's words. Or duty may have led him to bury his actual assessment of the work.

Pasternak held no open grudge, and may even have understood the hopelessness of his colleagues' position. He invited Fedin to Sunday lunch a week after getting the letter and told some other guests, "I have also asked Konstantin Aleksandrovich—as wholeheartedly and unreservedly as in previous years—so don't be surprised." He asked Fedin not to mention the rejection and when he arrived the two men embraced. At dinner, Pasternak was in good spirits.

Pasternak didn't bring himself to read the long letter carefully until a week later. He told a neighbor that the critique was "composed very courteously and gently, painstakingly thought out from a viewpoint that has become traditional and seemingly irrefutable." He said, with perhaps a touch of irony, that he was "pained and regretful at having caused my comrades such work."

There was now little reason to believe that even an unexpurgated *Doctor Zhivago* would be published in the Soviet Union; Simonov and the others had pronounced it irredeemably flawed. Still, Pasternak told Katkov that Western publication might yet prompt a Soviet edition, and said he might countenance some changes to make the novel palatable for the Soviet audience. This was his own private logic. The Soviet authorities did not want the book published—anywhere.

In August, a group of senior Italian Communists, including the party's vice secretary, Pietro Secchia, were guests at the exclusive Barvikha sanatorium just west of Moscow. D'Angelo and his wife visited two old friends there—Ambrogio Donini, a university professor, and Paolo Robotti, an old-school Communist activist.

International Communists in the Soviet Union were also targeted during the purges. Robotti's faith in the cause had survived his arrest and torture by Stalin's secret police when he was living in exile in Moscow before the war; when D'Angelo mentioned that he had handed the manuscript of a Russian novel to Feltrinelli, Robotti was visibly upset. He said the transfer was probably illegal under Soviet law. Secchia and Robotti were subsequently visited by an official from the Central Committee's section on relations with foreign Communist parties. They were told of the Kremlin's concerns about an Italian edition. Secchia and Robotti assured the official they would get the novel back from Feltrinelli. On October 24, the Central Committee was informed through the Soviet embassy in Rome that Robotti had reported, "The issue with Pasternak's manuscript has been settled and it will be returned to you in the nearest future." Robotti was mistaken. The pressure divided editors at the publishing house. Zveteremich was asked to return the manuscript, and the translation was interrupted for several months, while Feltrinelli, undecided about how to proceed, considered his options. He had not, however, abandoned publication.

The diplomatic note from Rome came just a day after several hundred thousand people flowed onto the streets of Budapest to demand reform, and the Hungarian Revolution began. The popular revolt was eventually crushed by a large Soviet invasion force and some twenty thousand Hungarians lost their lives in often brutal street fighting—as the West, impotent and paralyzed, watched helplessly. The Kremlin and the conservative bureaucracy seized on the events in Budapest to reverse the "thaw" in Moscow. The liberal *Literaturnaya Moskva* (Literary Moscow), which had only recently published Pasternak's "Notes on Translations of Shakespeare's Dramas," was closed; editors were fired across the major literary journals; and young, daring poets such as Andrei Voznesensky and Yevgeni Yevtushenko came under attack. Khrushchev would eventually argue that "bourgeois" tendencies among Hungarian intellectuals had sparked insurrection.

The bloody suppression of the Hungarian revolution was also deeply traumatic for many Italian Communists. Most of the leadership of the party supported the Soviet invasion, but a quarter of a million rank-and-file members abandoned the movement, including significant numbers of artists, academics, and journalists. Even before the worst of the bloodshed in Budapest, Feltrinelli, along with a number of his colleagues at the Feltrinelli library and institute in Milan, signed a letter to the party leadership asserting that in the "fundamental nature of the Hungarian movement" there is "a strong plea for socialist democracy." Feltrinelli watched with dismay the exodus of intellectuals from the party and bristled at the leadership's attempt to argue that "the loss of small fringe groups of intellectuals is not an important phenomenon."

"These comrades," Feltrinelli replied, "have not only brought luster to the party, the working class and the socialist movement but they have enabled us, since the fall of Fascism, to undertake a wealth of politico-cultural projects." Feltrinelli did not immediately turn in his party card, but his willingness to act as a financier began to fade. His desire to proceed with Pasternak's book was only strengthened.

By January 1957, officials in the Central Committee's departments on culture and relations with foreign Communist parties were wringing their hands. Despite the promise of the Italian comrades back in October, there was still no sign of the manuscript. Instead of hoping that Feltrinelli would bow to instructions from his party leadership, it was decided to use Pasternak himself to get the novel back. First, though, such a tactic had to be credible. On January 7, 1957, Pasternak signed a contract with Goslitizdat, the state literary publishing house. "I shall make this into something that will reflect the glory on the Russian people," said his editor, Anatoli Starostin. He was a genuine admirer of Pasternak, but Starostin was no more than a pawn, and the contract a ruse. The document would simply give greater legal weight to the effort to compel Feltrinelli to return the novel.

The following month, Feltrinelli received a telegram from Pasternak. It was in Italian: "Per request from goslitizdat . . . please hold Italian publication of *Doctor Zhivago* for half year until September 1957 and the coming out of Soviet edition of novel send reply telegram to Goslitizdat—Pasternak." But before he sent the telegram, Pasternak wrote a letter—in French—to his publisher in Milan. He explained that he sent the telegram under pressure and that the state was planning a modified version of *Doctor Zhivago*. He suggested that Feltrinelli agree to a six-month delay of the Italian edition. And then he pleaded with his publisher: "But the sorrow that, naturally, is caused me by the imminent alteration of my text would be far greater if I thought that you intended to base the Italian translation on it, despite my enduring desire that your edition be strictly faithful to the authentic manuscript."

Feltrinelli, at this point, had no reason to doubt a Soviet edition was coming in September. He wrote to Pasternak to say he would agree to the delay and he urged Zveteremich, his translator, to hurry up so an Italian edition could go on sale immediately afterward. Under international publishing law, Feltrinelli needed to publish within thirty days after the appearance of the Soviet edition to establish his rights in the West.

In April, in a letter to one of his Soviet editors, Pasternak asked for an advance against an upcoming volume of his poetry, his translation of *Faust*, or even *Doctor Zhivago*—although he admitted he was unlikely to get any money for the novel, since everything surrounding it was pure "phantasmagoria."

Feltrinelli met D'Angelo in Milan in May. Feltrinelli told him that Zveteremich was almost finished, and the poet Mario Socrate was polishing the last of the verse at the end of *Doctor Zhivago*. It seemed to D'Angelo that Feltrinelli was both satisfied and relieved. "He assures me that while he is still a man of the left, he will always fight for freedom and as a publisher, he will fight for freedom of thought and culture."

In June, Feltrinelli wrote to Goslitizdat. He agreed not to publish *Doctor Zhivago* until September. He also offered his "dear comrades" his opinion of Pasternak's novel, an assessment that while it invoked Soviet aesthetics no doubt caused some heartburn in Moscow. "His is a perfect portrayal of the nature, soul and history of Russia: characters, objects and events are rendered clearly and concretely in the finest spirit of realism, a realism that ceases to be merely fashion, and becomes art." Feltrinelli noted that the book might give rise to some controversy, but that after the Twentieth Congress, and the exposure of Stalin's crimes, "the revealing of certain facts no longer surprises or perturbs.

"Besides, Western readers will for the first time hear the voice of a great artist, a great poet who has made, in an artistic form, a detailed analysis of the October Revolution, the harbinger of a new epoch in which socialism became the only natural form of social life. For the Western public, the fact that this is a voice of a man alien to all political activity is a guarantee of the sincerity of his discourse, thus making him worthy of trust. Our readers cannot fail to appreciate this magnificent panorama of events from the history of the Russian people which transcends all ideological dogmatism, nor will they overlook its importance, or the positive outlook deriving from it. The conviction will thus grow that the path taken by your people has been for them a progressive one, that the history of capitalism is coming to an end, and that a new era has begun."

Feltrinelli concluded by saying whatever suspicions might exist in Moscow, it was never his intention "to lend this publication a sensational character."

Pasternak thanked Feltrinelli for agreeing to the delay but let him know that September publication in Moscow was a lie: "Here in Russia, the novel will never appear," he wrote in a letter to Feltrinelli at the end of June. "The troubles and misfortunes that will perhaps befall me in the event of foreign publication, that is to say without an analogous publication in the Soviet Union, are matters that must not concern us, either me or you. The important thing is that the work sees the light of day. Do not withhold your help from me."

Pasternak also wrote to Andrei Sinyavsky, another writer who was part of his trusted circle, that although others believed the "thaw" under Khrushchev would lead to more books being published, he "seldom, periodically and only faintly shared that belief." The publication of *Doctor Zhivago,* he added, was "out of the question."

The atmosphere in Moscow was becoming more hostile for writers and other artists. In May 1957, the party leadership, including Khrushchev, met with the board of the Union of Soviet Writers. Khrushchev spoke for nearly two hours. He described Vladimir Dudintsev's recently published novel, *Not by Bread Alone,* as "false at its base." The novel, which castigated the bureaucracy, had been read by its admirers as an audacious break with the past. The journal *Literaturnaya Moskva* was full of "ideologically fallacious" work, Khrushchev said. And the general secretary said that some writers seemed to have adopted an "indiscriminate rejection of the positive role of J. V. Stalin in the life of our party and country."

In June, the state literary publishing house announced that the publication of the volume of Pasternak's collected poems had been cancelled. That summer, the new Polish journal *Opinie* (Opinions) printed a thirty-five-page excerpt from *Doctor Zhivago*. Pasternak had given the manuscript to a Polish friend and translator shortly after D'Angelo had visited him in Peredelkino. The July/September issue of *Opinie,* which was devoted to Polish-Soviet friendship, introduced the excerpt with a note that said the novel was "a broad intricate story about the fate of the Russian intelligentsia and their ideological transformation which was frequently accompanied by tragic conflicts."

A note on the magazine that was prepared for the Central Committee in Moscow said the "choice of stories in the first issue shows that this magazine has a hostile attitude towards us." The Central Committee's culture department said it was "necessary to authorize the Soviet ambassador to draw the attention of Polish comrades to the unfriendly character of the magazine." The Soviet weekly *Literaturnaya Gazeta* was also instructed to attack the Polish magazine, but not in a manner that would "arouse an unhealthy interest abroad in Pasternak's evil plot." The Polish translators were summoned to Moscow and reprimanded. *Opinie* never appeared again. The authorities were also infuriated by the printing of some of Pasternak's more spiritual *Zhivago* poems in the émigré magazine *Grani* (Borders), an organ of the militant National Alliance of Russian Solidarists (NTS), which was published in West Germany. Pasternak had not sanctioned this publication, and his name was not attached to the poems, but it was clear that they were his work.

Officials complained in memos that Pasternak had agreed to revise *Doctor Zhivago* based on the *Novy Mir* critique of the novel, but, one of the bureaucrats wrote, he "has done nothing in terms of editing his novel or making proper changes." For much of the spring and early summer of 1957, Pasternak was hospitalized and in great pain with an inflamed meniscus in his right knee. (Zinaida visited him every day but was upset on one occasion when asked who she was. When she produced her identification, a hospital employee said there was a blonde in an hour before who had said she was the wife.)

The Central Committee official suggested another effort should be made to obtain the manuscript through the Italian Communists, since a delegation was in town for a World Youth Festival. The Italians were berated. Khrushchev himself complained to Velio Spano, the head of the Italian Communist Party's foreign affairs section, that D'Angelo, supposedly a friend and guest, had created all this turmoil over Pasternak's novel. Khrushchev had apparently been shown "a selection of the most unacceptable parts of the novel."

Pasternak was also sending messages to Italy. In July, he wrote to Pietro Zveteremich, the Italian translator, to tell him that he wanted all the Western publishers to proceed regardless of "the consequences it could have on me.

"I wrote the novel to be published and read, and that remains my only wish."

By August, Pasternak was under close watch. Letters to his sister Lydia in England were intercepted by the KGB and never reached her. That month, Pasternak was summoned to a meeting with the writers' union leadership. Pasternak gave Ivinskaya a note to represent him at the meeting. She was accompanied by Starostin, the editor handling the purported Soviet edition of *Doctor Zhivago*. The meeting was chaired by Surkov, who had risen to become first secretary of the writers' union. Surkov first met privately with Ivinskaya and asked her politely how the novel had ended up abroad. Ivinskaya said that Pasternak genuinely thought "with the spontaneity of a child" and he believed that in the case of art, borders were irrelevant.

"Yes, yes," said Surkov. "It was quite in character. But it was so untimely. You should have prevented him—he does, after all, have a good angel like you."

When the open session began, Surkov's placid demeanor vanished as he became more and more worked up about Pasternak's "treachery." He accused Pasternak of being driven by greed, and said he was negotiating to get money from abroad. Ivinskaya tried to speak but was rudely told not to interrupt. The novelist and member of the board Valentin Katayev shouted at her: "There really is no point in your being here. Who do you think you're representing? A poet or a traitor? Or doesn't it bother you that he's a traitor to his country?" When Starostin was introduced as the editor of the novel, Katayev continued, "Just fancy that—the editor, if you please. How can something like *this* be edited!"

Starostin was dejected and under no illusion about what the tongue-lashing augured for the novel. "We all left beaten, knowing that the road to publication of *Doctor Zhivago* was closed."

Pasternak later described the event as a "'37 type of meeting, with infuriated yelling about this being an unprecedented occurrence, and demands for retribution." The following day, Ivinskaya arranged for Pasternak to meet Polikarpov from the Central Committee. In advance of the meeting, Pasternak had Ivinskaya give him a letter. It seemed scripted to infuriate the bureaucrat: "People who are morally scrupulous are never happy with themselves; there are a lot of things they regret, a lot of things of which they repent. The only thing in my life for which I have no cause for repentance is the novel. I wrote what I think and to this day my thoughts remain the same. It may be a mistake not to have concealed it from others. I assure you I would have hidden it away had it been feebly written. But it proved to have more strength to it than I had dreamed possible—strength comes from on high, and thus its further fate was out of my hands."

Polikarpov was so incensed he demanded that Ivinskaya tear up the note in front of him. He insisted on seeing Pasternak. Both Polikarpov and Surkov met with Pasternak in the following days. The conversations were strained but civil, and both men told Pasternak that he had to send a telegram to Feltrinelli demanding the return of the book. Pasternak was warned that failure to act could lead to "very unpleasant consequences." The two men drew up a telegram for Feltrinelli and Pasternak was expected to send it: "I have started rewriting the manuscript of my novel *Doctor Zhivago,* and I am now convinced that the extant version can in no way be considered a finished work. The copy of the manuscript in your possession is a preliminary draft requiring thorough revision. In my view it is not possible to publish the book in its current form. This would go against my rule, which is that only the definitive draft of my work may be published. Please be so kind as to return, to my Moscow address, the manuscript of my novel *Doctor Zhivago,* which is indispensable for my work."

Pasternak refused to send it. Ivinskaya asked D'Angelo to speak to Pasternak and persuade him otherwise. The Italian was unable to get a word out before an angry Pasternak spoke. "If you're here to advise me to capitulate you should know that your charitable mission shows a lack of respect for me personally. You're treating me like a man who has no dignity. The publication of *Doctor Zhivago* has become the most important thing in my life, and I don't intend to do anything to prevent it. What would Feltrinelli think if he received a telegram that contradicted everything I have written and rewritten to him up to now? Would he take me for a crazy man, or a coward?"

D'Angelo recounted for Pasternak his conversation with Feltrinelli in Milan. Publication was inevitable. Moreover, numerous other Western publishers already had the manuscript and would go ahead on their own even if Feltrinelli were to follow the instructions in an obviously extorted telegram. D'Angelo told Pasternak there was no reason to resist this useless gesture, and it could save Pasternak and his loved ones. The Italian declared that the Soviet state had lost its ridiculous war against *Doctor Zhivago*.

The telegram—in Russian—was sent on August 21, 1957. Immediately, Polikarpov informed the Central Committee and suggested that they arm the Italian Communist Party with a copy so they could use it to add to the pressure on Feltrinelli. Mario Alicata, a literary critic and a senior figure in the party, was assigned to meet with Feltrinelli at the Milan office of the Communist Party. He angrily waved Pasternak's telegram in Feltrinelli's face, but the publisher would not relent.

Pasternak, meanwhile, was attempting to get messages to Feltrinelli and others lest the telegram be taken seriously. He told the Harvard scholar Miriam Berlin and her husband, who came to visit him in Peredelkino, that he certainly wanted the novel published outside the Soviet Union. Berlin had been asked by Pasternak's sister Josephine to confirm his intentions. Pasternak told Berlin that he had been forced to write the telegram and it should be ignored. "It does not matter what might happen to me. My life is finished. The book is my last word to the civilized world." When the Italian scholar Vittorio Strada came to see him, he whispered to him as he left, "Vittorio, tell Feltrinelli that I want my book to come out at all costs."

Despite all the intrigue and intimidation, Pasternak appeared remarkably unruffled to his visitors. Yevgeni Yevtushenko saw Pasternak that September when he brought yet another Italian professor, Angelo Rippelino, to visit him. "I'm very fond of Italians," said Pasternak. He invited them in for dinner. Yevtushenko remarked: "To look at him, Pasternak might have been forty-seven or forty-eight. His whole appearance had an amazing, sparkling freshness like a newly cut bunch of lilacs with the morning dew still on their leaves. It seemed as if there was a play of light all over him, from the flashing gestures of hands to the surprisingly childlike smile which constantly lit up his mobile face." Pasternak and Yevtushenko drank and talked late into the night long after Rippelino had left. Zinaida admonished the twenty-three-year-old Yevtushenko. "You're killing my husband," she said.

Yevtushenko read *Doctor Zhivago* a short time later and was "disappointed." He said the young writers of the post-Stalin period were attracted by the masculine prose of Hemingway, and the work of writers such as J. D. Salinger and Erich Maria Remarque. *Doctor Zhivago,* in comparison, seemed old-fashioned, even a little boring, the work of an earlier generation. He didn't finish reading it.

The September deadline for a Soviet edition passed, and officials in Moscow were becoming desperate. Soviet trade representatives in Paris and London attempted without success to get the publishers Gallimard and Harvill Press to return the manuscript. The Soviet embassy in London also insisted that, if publication was inevitable, Harvill Press ought to include an introduction stating that Pasternak himself had not wished his book to be published. The Foreign Office, which discouraged Harvill Press from sending a copy of the English translation to Pasternak for his corrections, suggested that instead of a note about Pasternak's purported objections, the publishers simply say, "Banned in the Soviet Union." "That might only be of advantage from the propaganda point of view but would perhaps serve as a slight protection to Pasternak himself," wrote Philip de Zulueta, the Foreign Office representative at No. 10 Downing Street. The remark may have been somewhat facetious, as it's unclear how noting that the book was banned would help Pasternak, although it would certainly boost sales.

Pietro Zveteremich was in Moscow in October and found that "the atmosphere created around the book" was "very ugly." Almost as soon as he arrived in the city, as part of an Italian delegation hosted by the Union of Soviet Writers, Zveteremich was told that publication of *Doctor Zhivago* would be an affront to both Pasternak and the Soviet Union. Zveteremich was handed a typewritten letter purportedly signed by Pasternak; it repeated some of what was in the February telegram and complained that Feltrinelli never replied. In a meeting with officials from the writers' union, Zveteremich said publication of *Doctor Zhivago* could not be stopped. "A brawl, I can truly say, broke out," he recalled. Pasternak felt it unsafe to meet with the translator, but Zveteremich was able to see Ivinskaya, who gave him a note from Pasternak for Feltrinelli, and it reflected the author's true sentiments. In a letter to Feltrinelli, Zveteremich wrote that "P. asks you not to pay any heed to this and cannot wait for the book to come out even though they have threatened to reduce him to starvation." Zveteremich's experience in Moscow led him to leave the Communist Party. "I became convinced that there was no socialism in the USSR, but rather just Asian theocratic despotism," he later wrote. In his short note to Feltrinelli, Pasternak wrote, "Forgive me for the injustices that have befallen you and for those perhaps yet to come caused by my wretched faith. May our distant future, the faith that helps me live, protect you."

Feltrinelli replied to Pasternak's telegram on October 10. The letter, although addressed to Pasternak, was clearly written for Soviet officialdom and was designed to protect Pasternak by shifting blame away from the author and onto the publisher. Feltrinelli began by saying that he saw none of the shortcomings described in the telegram: that the work was unfinished and needed thorough revision. Feltrinelli reminded his readers that he had agreed to delay publication until September and there was nothing now standing in the way of publication.

And he pretended to lecture his obstreperous author. "In order to avoid any further tension in Western literary circles, created as a result of your wholly regrettable telegram . . . we advise you to make no further attempts to hold up publication of the book, something that, far from preventing it, would lend the entire affair a tone of political scandal that we have never sought nor wish to create."

Surkov traveled to Italy in October as part of a Soviet delegation of poets, but his real mission was to confront Feltrinelli. With a translator in tow, he stormed into the publisher's offices on Via Andegari. His bellowing in Russian could be heard down on the street. Surkov, much like Alicata, waved Pasternak's telegram in the publisher's face. "I know how such letters are written," said Feltrinelli, a photo of Pasternak hanging on the wall over his shoulder. Surkov pressed his case for three hours, but left with nothing. Feltrinelli said he was a "free publisher in a free country," and he told Surkov that by publishing the novel he was paying tribute to a great narrative work of Soviet literature. The work was a testament to the truth, he said, even if the cultural bureaucrats in Moscow didn't get it. After the meeting, Feltrinelli said seeing Surkov was like encountering "a hyena dipped in syrup."

Surkov was not ready to quit, and he introduced the most menacing note to date in the affair. He gave an interview to *L'Unità,* the Communist party newspaper for which Feltrinelli had acted as a stringer eleven years earlier. In the first public comments by a Soviet official on *Doctor Zhivago,* he said he offered the facts, "in all sincerity": Pasternak's novel was rejected by his comrades because it cast doubt on the validity of the October Revolution. Pasternak accepted these criticisms and asked for the manuscript to be returned by his Italian publisher so he could revise it. But despite all this, the novel, according to press reports, will appear in Italy against the will of its author.

"The Cold War is beginning to involve literature," intoned Surkov. "If this is freedom seen through Western eyes, well, I must say we have a different view of it." The reporter noted that he spoke "to make clear how terrible he felt all of this was." Surkov continued: "Thus it is for the second time, for the second time in our literary history, after *Mahogany* by Boris Pilnyak, a book by a Russian will be first published abroad."

The invocation of Pilnyak, Pasternak's executed neighbor, was a direct threat. Surkov was comfortable with the exigencies of state violence. The previous year he told a Yugoslav newspaper, "I have seen my friends, writers, disappear before my eyes but at the time I believed it necessary, demanded by the Revolution." Feltrinelli told Kurt Wolff, Pasternak's American publisher, that Surkov's words should be quoted as widely as possible and "*Time* and *Newsweek* should get on the move."

At the end of October, Pasternak was compelled to send one more message to Feltrinelli. He told him he was "stunned" at Feltrinelli's failure to reply to his telegram, and said that "decency demands that you respect the wishes of an author."

With publication imminent, Pasternak followed up the final October 25 telegram with a private note to Feltrinelli. It was dated November 2:

> Dear Sir,
>
> I can find no words with which to express my gratitude. The future will reward us, you and me, for the vile humiliations, we have suffered. Oh, how happy I am that neither you, nor Gallimard, nor Collins have been fooled by those idiotic and brutal appeals accompanied by my signature (!), a signature all but false and counterfeit, insofar as it was extorted from me by a blend of fraud and violence. The unheard-of arrogance to wax indignant over the "violence" employed by you against my "literary freedom," when exactly the same violence was being used against me, covertly. And that this vandalism should be disguised as concern for me, for the sacred rights of the artist! But we shall soon have an Italian Zhivago, French, English and German Zhivagos—and one day perhaps a geographically distant but Russian Zhivago! And this is a great deal, a very great deal, so let's do our best and what will be will be.

The first edition of *Doctor Zhivago* in translation in Italian was printed on November 15, 1957, followed by a second run of three thousand copies five days later. The novel appeared in bookstores on November 23 following its launch the previous evening at the Hotel Continental in Milan. The book was an immediate best seller.

One of the first reviews appeared in the *Corriere della Sera* under the headline "You look for a political libel and find a work of art." "Pasternak does not require any political judgments from us, the first readers of his novel in the West," the review concluded. "Perhaps in the loneliness of his village, the old writer wants to know whether we heard his poetic voice in the story, whether we found proof of his artistic beliefs. And the answer is: yes, we did."

The novel had begun a long journey. But to get back home to Russia, *Zhivago* would have a secret ally.

Chapter 8

"We tore a big hole in the Iron Curtain."

The Russian-language manuscript of *Doctor Zhivago* arrived at CIA headquarters in Washington, D.C., in early January 1958 in the form of two rolls of film. British intelligence provided this copy of the novel. Inside the agency, the novel was the source of some excitement. In a memo to Frank Wisner, who oversaw clandestine operations for the CIA, the head of the agency's Soviet Russia Division described *Doctor Zhivago* as "the most heretical literary work by a Soviet author since Stalin's death."

"Pasternak's humanistic message—that every person is entitled to a private life and deserves respect as a human being, irrespective of the extent of his political loyalty or contribution to the state—poses a fundamental challenge to the Soviet ethic of sacrifice of the individual to the Communist system," wrote John Maury, the Soviet Russia Division chief. "There is no call to revolt against the regime in the novel, but the heresy which Dr. Zhivago preaches—political passivity—is fundamental. Pasternak suggests that the small unimportant people who remain passive to the regime's demands for active participation and emotional involvement in official campaigns are superior to the political 'activists' favored by the system. Further, he dares hint that society might function better without these fanatics."

Maury was a fluent Russian speaker who had been an assistant naval attaché in Moscow when Hitler invaded the Soviet Union. During the war, he served in Murmansk as part of the Lend-Lease program by which the United States delivered over $11 billion worth of supplies to the Soviet Union. Maury, however, had no affection for the former ally. He subscribed to the belief that Soviet action could best be understood through the prism of Russian history. "He considered the Soviet regime a continuation of imperial Russia, and thought the KGB had been founded by Ivan the Terrible," said one of his officers.

The CIA's Soviet Russia Division was stocked with first- and second-generation Russian-Americans whose families, in many cases, had fled the Bolsheviks. The division prided itself on its vodka-soaked parties with a lot of Russian singing. "Our specialty was the *charochka,* the ceremonial drinking song with its chorus of *pey do dna* [bottoms up!]," recalled one officer who served in the 1950s.

The American and British intelligence services agreed that *Doctor Zhivago* should be published in Russian, but the British "asked that it not be done in the U.S." This approach became policy for the CIA, which calculated that a Russian-language edition produced in the United States would be more easily dismissed by the Soviet Union as propaganda in a way that publication in a small European country would not. Moreover, they feared, overt American involvement could be used by the authorities in Moscow to persecute Pasternak.

In an internal memo shortly after the appearance of the novel in Italy, agency staff also recommended that *Doctor Zhivago* "should be published in a maximum number of foreign editions, for maximum free world distribution and acclaim and consideration for such honor as the Nobel prize." While the CIA hoped Pasternak's novel would draw global attention, including from the Swedish Academy, there was no indication that the agency considered printing a Russian-language edition to help Pasternak win the prize.

The CIA's role in operations involving *Doctor Zhivago* was backed at the highest level of government. The Eisenhower White House, through its Operations Coordinating Board (OCB), which oversaw covert activities, gave the CIA exclusive control over the novel's "exploitation." The rationale behind this decision was "the sensitivity of the operation, and that the hand of the United States government should not be shown in any manner." Instead of having the State Department or the United States Information Agency trumpet the novel publicly, secrecy was employed to prevent "the possibility of personal reprisal against Pasternak or his family." The OCB issued verbal guidelines to the agency and told the CIA to promote the book "as literature, not as cold-war propaganda."

The CIA, as it happened, loved literature—novels, short stories, poems. Joyce, Hemingway, Eliot. Dostoevsky, Tolstoy, Nabokov. Books were weapons. If a piece of literature was unavailable or banned in the USSR or Eastern Europe, and the work might challenge or contrast with Soviet reality, the agency wanted it in the hands of citizens in the Eastern Bloc. The Cold War was twelve years old in 1958, and whatever illusions might have existed about liberating the "captive peoples" of the East were shattered by the bloodshed in Budapest and the inability of the Western powers, and in particular of the United States, to do much more than peer through the barbed wire. The United States was unable to help the striking East Germans in 1953 or the Poles who also revolted in 1956. Communism would not be rolled back for the simple reason that no one could countenance an intervention that could escalate into war between superpowers armed with atomic weapons.

In the 1950s, the CIA was engaged in relentless global political warfare with the Kremlin. This effort was intended to shore up support for the Atlantic Alliance (NATO) in Western Europe, counter Soviet propaganda, and challenge Soviet influence in the world. The CIA believed the power of ideas—in news, art, music, and literature—could slowly corrode the authority of the Soviet state with its own people and in the satellite states of Eastern Europe. The agency was in a long game. Cord Meyer, the head of the CIA's International Organizations Division, which oversaw much of the agency's covert propaganda operations, wrote that exposure to Western ideas "could incrementally over time improve the chances for gradual change toward more open societies."

To further its objectives, the CIA, using a host of front organizations and phony foundations, spent untold millions to fund concert tours, art exhibitions, highbrow magazines, academic research, student activism, news organizations—and book publishing. In Western Europe, the CIA channeled money to the non-Communist left, which it regarded as the principal bulwark against its Communist foe. The alliance between Cold War anticommunism and liberal idealism "appeared natural and right" and would not break down until the 1960s. "Our help went mainly to the democratic parties of the left and of the center," said Meyer. "The right wing and the conservative forces had their own financial resources: the real competition with the communists for votes and influence lay on the left of the political spectrum, where the allegiance of the working class and the intelligentsia was to be decided."

In 1950s America, during and long after the poisonous anti-Communist crusade of Senator Joseph McCarthy, it would have been impossible to get Congress to appropriate money for the State Department or any other part of the government to openly fund left-wing organizations and the promotion of the arts in Europe. Even for direct operations against the Communist Bloc, Congress would have struggled to support activities as seemingly effete as book publishing. The CIA budget was black, and perfect for the job. The agency believed with genuine fervor that the Cold War was also cultural. There was a realization that this funding—millions of dollars annually—would support activities that would "manifest diversity and differences of view and be infused by the concept of free inquiry. Thus views expressed by representatives and members of the U.S. supported organizations in many cases were not shared by their sponsors. . . . It took a fairly sophisticated point of view to understand that the public exhibition of unorthodox views was a potent weapon against monolithic Communist uniformity of action." Thus the CIA "became one of the world's largest grant-making institutions," rivaling the Ford, Rockefeller, and Carnegie foundations.

President Harry Truman didn't like the idea of a peacetime American intelligence service. Newspapers and some congressmen worried aloud about an American gestapo. And immediately after World War II, a part of the establishment felt queasy about putting down a stake in the underworld of covert operations. But as tensions with the Soviet Union grew, the need for some "centralized snooping," as Truman called it, seemed unavoidable. The CIA was created in 1947, and, as well as authorizing intelligence gathering, Congress vested the spy agency with power to perform "other functions and duties related to intelligence affecting the national security." This vague authority would provide the legal justification for covert action, operations that cannot be traced to the CIA and can be denied by the U.S. government, although at first the CIA's general counsel was uncertain if the agency could undertake "black propaganda" without specific congressional authorization. In the first years of the Cold War, various government departments, including State and Defense, continued to debate how to institute a permanent and effective capability to run missions, which ranged from propaganda efforts to paramilitary operations such as arming émigré groups and inserting them back inside the Eastern Bloc to commit acts of sabotage.

The intellectual author of U.S. covert action was George Kennan, the influential diplomat and policy planner, who argued that the United States had to mobilize all its resources and cunning to contain the Soviet Union's atavistic expansionism. The United States was also facing a foe that, since the 1920s, had mastered the creation of the front organization—idealistic-sounding, international entities that promoted noncommunist ideas such as peace and democracy but were secretly controlled by the Kremlin and its surrogates. Washington needed a capability to "do things that very much needed to be done, but for which the government couldn't take official responsibility." In May 1948, the State Department's Policy Planning Staff, which Kennan headed, wrote a memo entitled "The Inauguration of Organized Political Warfare." The memo noted that "the Kremlin's conduct of political warfare was the most refined and effective of any in history" and argued that the United States, in response, "cannot afford to leave unmobilized our resources for covert political warfare." It laid down a series of recommendations to support and cultivate resistance within the Soviet Bloc and support the Soviet Union's émigré and ideological foes in the West.

The following month, the National Security Council created the Office of Special Projects, which was housed at the CIA although at first it was an independent office. The new group was soon renamed the equally anodyne Office of Policy Coordination (OPC). It was led by Frank Wisner, a veteran of the wartime intelligence service, the Office of Strategic Services (OSS). He had served for six months in Bucharest in 1944 and 1945 and watched in despair and fury as Russian troops put 70,000 Romanians of German descent onto boxcars destined for the Soviet Union, where they were to be used as slave labor. "The OSS operative was 'brutally shocked' by the spectacle of raw Soviet power at the same time that Russians were toasting a new era of Allied cooperation." The experience marked Wisner. He was suffused with an evangelical, anti-Communist zeal to take the fight to the enemy.

Wisner divided his planned clandestine activity into five areas—psychological warfare, political warfare, economic warfare, preventive direct action, and miscellaneous. He wanted the ability to do just about anything, from proselytizing against the Soviet Union to using émigré proxies to launch violent attacks and create some kind of anti-Communist resistance. The organization's powers continued to expand under new National Security directives, as did its personnel and resources. There were 302 CIA staffers involved in covert operations in 1949. Three years later, there were 2,812, with another 3,142 overseas contractors. These spies and officers were located at forty-seven locations worldwide; the budget for their operations in the same three-year period grew from $4.7 million to $82 million. In 1952, OPC was merged with the Office of Special Operations to create the Directorate of Plans.

One young recruit, the future CIA director William Colby, said Wisner instilled his organization with "the atmosphere of an order of Knights Templar, to save Western freedom from Communist darkness." Wisner was also "boyishly charming, cool but coiled, a low hurdler from Mississippi." He wanted people with that "added dimension"; war veterans like himself, athletic and smart but not bookish, from the best schools, and especially Yale.

Attracted by the sense of epic struggle and feeling certain about the moral clarity of the moment, writers and poets enlisted with the CIA. James Jesus Angelton, the CIA's counterintelligence chief, was an editor at *The Yale Literary Magazine* and cofounded the literary magazine *Furioso*. He counted Ezra Pound among his closest friends. Cord Meyer Jr., another alumnus of the *Yale Literary,* had published fiction in *The Atlantic Monthly* and continued to hanker for the writing life when he was running the agency's propaganda operations. When one of Meyer's recruits, Robie Macauley, formerly of *The Kenyon Review,* left the agency to become the fiction editor of *Playboy,* Meyer told him, "I might even send you a story under an appropriate pseudonym." John Thompson was another hire from *The Kenyon Review*. John Hunt was recruited around the time his novel *Generations of Men* appeared. Peter Matthiessen, a cofounder and editor of the *Paris Review,* wrote his novel *Partisans* while working for the agency.

"I went down to Washington in the spring of 1951 to enlist in a struggle that was less violent but more complex and ambiguous than the war I had volunteered to join ten years before," said Meyer, a combat veteran who was wounded on Guam and lost one of his eyes.

To funnel its money to the causes it wanted to bankroll, the CIA created a series of private, high-minded organizations. Prominent Americans were recruited to serve on their boards and create the illusion that these entities were stocked with the kind of wealthy benefactors whose involvement would explain away streams of cash. Among the first was the National Committee for a Free Europe, incorporated in 1949 with offices in New York. Members included Dwight D. Eisenhower, soon to be president; film moguls Cecil B. DeMille and Darryl Zanuck; Henry Ford II, the president of Ford Motor Company; Cardinal Francis Spellman, the archbishop of New York; and Allen Dulles, the new organization's executive secretary. Dulles would join the CIA in 1951 and become director in 1953. Most of these volunteers were made aware of or deduced CIA involvement. The Free Europe Committee, as it was renamed, purported to be self-financing through a national fund-raising campaign called the Crusade for Freedom. In fact, only about 12 percent of the FEC budget came from fund-raising, most of that corporate largesse. The bulk of the cash came via a weekly check that the CIA routed through a Wall Street bank.

The Free Europe Committee's principal project was Radio Free Europe, which began broadcasting in Czech, Slovak, and Romanian on July 4, 1950, followed soon after by programming in Polish, Hungarian, and Bulgarian. Radio Free Europe was followed in 1953 by a second station directed at the Soviet Union, Radio Liberation. This broadcaster, later and better known as Radio Liberty, was backed by another nonprofit front, the American Committee for Liberation. The committee, with offices in midtown Manhattan, had a less august board of Americans and was more secretive; at the first board meeting it was simply announced that the money to finance Radio Liberation would come from the "personal friends of the committee members." The agency decided to give Radio Liberation less obviously patrician backing because it was finding that it was sometimes difficult to command the large egos of the Free Europe Committee. Although both broadcasters were designed to further U.S. foreign policy and security interests, they enjoyed a good deal of autonomy if for no other reason than the CIA was unable to manage two large news organizations. After beginning as somewhat shrill mouthpieces, they settled down and became credible news organizations, particularly after 1956 when Radio Free Europe's role in encouraging the Hungarian revolutionaries, and creating the chimera of impending American intervention, was roundly criticized. Occasionally, secret messages were embedded in broadcasts and some officers used the radio stations as cover. But, for the most part, an American management team oversaw émigré editors with little direct interference from Washington, D.C. There was, in fact, no need to exercise stringent editorial control. The CIA saw the kind of message it wished to direct flow naturally from the routine judgments of the anti-Communist staffs. Radio Liberation acted as a surrogate domestic broadcaster largely focused on what was happening inside the Soviet Union, not around the world.

Radio Free Europe and Radio Liberation broadcast from Munich. The CIA, through the American Committee for Liberation, also established a number of related fronts in Munich such as the Institute for the Study of the Soviet Union and the Central Association of Post-War Émigrés, known by its Russian initials TsOPE. The agency's vast presence in Munich was an open secret.

One Radio Liberation employee doubted that there was "a single stoker or sweeper at [broadcast headquarters] who did not have some inkling of the true state of affairs." The KGB called Munich *diversionnyi tsentr*, the "center of subversion."

About one-third of the urban adult population in the Soviet Union listened to Western broadcasts. Aleksandr Solzhenitsyn called it "the mighty non-military force which resides in the airwaves and whose kindling power in the midst of communist darkness cannot even be grasped by the Western imagination." In 1958, the Soviet Union was spending more on jamming Western signals than it spent on its own domestic and international broadcasting combined.

The Free Europe Committee also established its own publishing unit, the Free Europe Press. It couldn't reach over the Iron Curtain via shortwave but it took to the air in its own way. On August 27, 1951, near the Czechoslovakian border in Bavaria, the FEC released balloons that were carried by the prevailing winds across the frontier. Dignitaries from the United States participated in a ceremony marking the first launch of balloons, including the chairman of the Crusade for Freedom, Harold Stassen; the newspaper columnist Drew Pearson; and C. D. Jackson, a former Time-Life executive, who would become one of Eisenhower's key advisers on psychological warfare. The balloons were designed to burst at 30,000 feet, scattering their cargo of thousands of propaganda leaflets on the land below. "A new wind is blowing. New hope is stirring. Friends of freedom in other lands have found a new way to reach you," read one of those first leaflets, prepared by the Free Europe Press. "There is no dungeon deep enough to hide truth, no wall high enough to keep out the message of freedom. Tyranny cannot control the winds, cannot enslave your hearts. Freedom will rise again."

"We tore a big hole in the Iron Curtain," Stassen told *Time* magazine.

Over the next five years, the FEC launched 600,000 balloons, dropping tens of millions of pieces of propaganda across Eastern Europe, including a letter-size magazine. The Czechoslovakian air force tried to shoot down the balloons. The United States put an end to the program in 1956 after the government of West Germany began to object to "an extremely worrisome violation of airspace sovereignty from the territory of the Federal Republic." The Czechoslovakian government falsely alleged that a balloon brought down an airplane. One balloon did cause a household fire in Austria. (A housewife overturned a cooking burner after she was startled by a balloon landing on her home.) The program was simply too random and crudely visible.

The agency turned to mailing books.

In April 1956, Samuel S. Walker Jr., the director of the Free Europe Press, called a meeting of the young Americans and Eastern Europeans who worked for him at their offices on West Fifty-seventh Street in Manhattan. On the agenda was a potential new project: mailing books across the Iron Curtain. The Eastern Europeans, who had experience sending packages to their relatives, believed it was plausible to mail propaganda. Others, including one of the Free Europe Committee's leading academic advisers, Hugh Seton-Watson of the University of London, feared that Communist censors would intercept books from the West. The final decision rested with Walker, still in his twenties, a former chairman of the *Yale Daily News* who had abandoned a career at *Time* for the intrigue of the Free Europe Press. "Let's do it," he said. The "friends down south," as the CIA was called, backed a plan that called for mailing books to specific individuals in official positions "to reduce the efficiency of the communist administration by weakening loyalty of the party and state cadres." That didn't work too well. The first mailings, mostly political articles, some translated, some not, were sent from New York and cities across Europe. Many packages never made it to their intended targets, or were turned in to the authorities. Through trial and error, the book program's developers learned that if they had books shipped directly from a publisher they often got through—even provocative titles such as Albert Camus's *The Rebel.* The Free Europe Press began to send lists of books to a wider audience of Eastern Europeans with an offer that if the recipient made a selection the titles would be mailed at no cost. Eventually, the head of the program, George Minden, a former Romanian refugee, told his staff to concentrate on "providing a minimum basis for spiritual understanding of Western values, which we hope to supply through psychology, literature, the theater and the visual arts. This will take the place of political and other directly antagonizing materials." An early planning memo in 1956 said, "There should be no total attacks on communism. . . . Our primary aims should be to demonstrate the superior achievements of the West."

The CIA entity purchased books and rights from major U.S. and European publishers, including Doubleday & Company, Harper & Brothers, Harvard University Press, Faber and Faber, Macmillan Publishing Company, Bertelsmann, and Hachette. All business and invoicing was run through the International Advisory Council, another CIA front with offices on East Sixty-fifth Street.

And some delighted responses found their way back to New York. "We are swallowing them passionately—strictly speaking they are being passed from hand to hand," wrote a student from Łódž in Poland who got copies of works by George Orwell, Milovan Đjilas, and Czesław Miłosz. "They are treated as greatest rarities—in other words, the best of bestsellers." A Polish scholar who received *Doctor Zhivago* wrote, "Your priceless publications will serve not only me but a large group of friends as well . . . and will be treated as [a] sensation!"

Shortly after the Free Europe Press began its mailings in 1956, the CIA, through the American Committee for Liberation, approved a book program for the Soviet Union. The agency funded the creation of the Bedford Publishing Company, another group in New York City, and its plan was to translate Western literary works and publish them in Russian. "The Soviet public, who had been subject to tedious Communist propaganda . . . was starved for Western books," wrote Isaac Patch, the first head of Bedford Publishing. "Through our book program we hoped to fill the void and open up the door to the fresh air of liberty and freedom." An initial CIA grant of $10,000 grew into an annual budget of $1 million. Bedford Publishing opened offices in London, Paris, Munich, and Rome, and in those days when money flowed freely, the staff held their annual meetings at places like Venice's San Giorgio Maggiore. Among the works translated were James Joyce's *Portrait of the Artist as a Young Man,* Vladimir Nabokov's *Pnin,* and George Orwell's *Animal Farm.*

Rather than mailing books, because the controls were stronger in the Soviet Union than in parts of Eastern Europe, Bedford Publishing concentrated on handing out books to Soviet visitors to the West or placing books with Westerners traveling to the Soviet Union so they could distribute them upon arrival. The company also stocked the U.S. embassy in Moscow with titles. Some miniature paperbacks, printed at CIA headquarters, were on the shelves at Stockmann, the famous Helsinki department store where Westerners stocked up on goods before or during stints in Moscow. Members of the Moscow Philharmonic, who were passed books while on tour in the West, hid them in their sheet music for the trip home. Books were also spirited home in food cans and Tampax boxes.

In its first fifteen years, Bedford distributed over one million books to Soviet readers. The program continued until the fall of the Soviet Union, and across the Eastern Bloc as many as 10 million books and magazines were disseminated. One KGB chief grumbled that Western books and other printed material are "the main wellspring of hostile sentiments" among Soviet students.

While the CIA's literary tastes were broad, they were not indiscriminate. The agency's publishing was guided by both the background of its officers and contractors and their understanding of the mission. The novelist Richard Elman complained that "the CIA has stood foursquare behind the Western Christian traditions of hierarchy, elitism, and antimillennial enlightenment of the benighted and has opposed revolutionary movements in literature as well as politics. It has been a staunch advocate of legitimacy, and it has carefully chosen to subsidize or disseminate the writings of literary artists such as V. S. Naipaul and Saul Bellow who were similarly inclined." This may be somewhat overstated given the breadth and numbers of books sent East, but a full analysis of the CIA aesthetics will remain impossible until it reveals all the titles it subsidized, translated, and disseminated—a list, if it exists, that remains classified.

The CIA chief of covert action boasted in 1961 that the agency could: "get books published or distributed abroad without revealing any U.S. influence, by covertly subsidizing foreign publications or booksellers; get books published which should not be 'contaminated' by any overt tie-in with the U.S. government, especially if the position of the author is 'delicate'; [and] get books published for operational reasons, regardless of commercial viability."

Indeed, the CIA commissioned its own works—as many as a thousand publications—because the "advantage of direct contact with the author is that we can acquaint him in great detail with our intentions; that we can provide him with whatever material we want to include and that we can check the manuscript at every stage." One example was a book by a student from the developing world about his experience studying in a communist country. A reviewer for CBS, who didn't know the book's provenance, said, "Our propaganda services could do worse than to flood [foreign] university towns with this volume." *The New York Times* reported in 1967 that a book purporting to be the journal of Soviet double agent Col. Oleg Penkovsky in the months before he was exposed and executed was an agency creation. *The Penkovsky Papers,* published by Doubleday, was ghostwritten from CIA files, including agency interviews with Penkovsky, by a *Chicago Daily News* reporter and a KGB defector who worked for the CIA. "Spies don't keep diaries," a former CIA official told *The Times,* backing assertions that the "journal" was at best a clever concoction.

"Books differ from all other propaganda media," wrote the CIA chief of covert action, "primarily because one single book can significantly change the reader's attitude and action to an extent unmatched by the impact of any other single medium . . . this is, of course, not true of all books at all times and with all readers—but it is true significantly often enough to make books the most important weapon of strategic (long-range) propaganda."

The remark was eerily reminiscent of Maxim Gorky's statement at the First Congress of Soviet Writers in 1934: "Books are the most important and most powerful weapons in socialist culture."

Chapter 9

"We'll do it black."

On March 6, 1958, George Katkov, the Oxford professor overseeing the English translation of *Doctor Zhivago,* visited the American consulate in Munich. He was in the city to give a series of lectures to the staff at Radio Liberation. Katkov told an American diplomat that he had information he wanted passed along to officials "on a high level" in Washington. He said one of the French translators of *Doctor Zhivago* had recently met Pasternak in Moscow, and the writer had told her he didn't want the Russian-language edition to be handled by any publishing firm connected to émigrés. Katkov continued that while Pasternak was "eager to see a Russian edition published abroad," he also didn't want it done in the United States or by U.S.–funded groups.

The consul-general sent a dispatch to the State Department about Katkov's visit: Pasternak "fears serious personal difficulties, however, if a Russian edition is first published in the United States or by some organization abroad which is generally known to have American backing, either official, commercial or private."

Katkov said there were no "anti-American implications" to Pasternak's request, only "considerations of personal safety." For the same reason, Katkov said, he would advise against a Russian-language publication in France or England. Katkov suggested Sweden as a neutral publishing venue. Alternatively, he noted that the academic branch of Mouton & Co., a distinguished publishing and printing house in the Netherlands, was already negotiating for the rights to a Russian edition; Pasternak had asked one of his French translators to manage a Russian-language edition and they had a meeting with the Dutch firm in December 1957. And Pasternak was enthusiastic about the possibility. "Don't let the opportunity pass, take it with both hands," he wrote the following month to Jacqueline de Proyart. Pasternak knew that Mouton was a house that specialized in Russian texts but was not connected to any émigré groups.

The consul also reported to Washington that after a preliminary check in Munich there was no indication of any plans by Russian émigrés, or similar groups, to bring out a Russian edition of *Doctor Zhivago*.

In Washington, the dispatch was forwarded to the CIA.

Inside the CIA, covert activities such as the radio stations in Munich and the book programs were normally managed by the International Organizations Division headed by Cord Meyer. But the Soviet Russia Division was also involved in getting books into the hands of Russians under a program code-named AEDINOSAUR, whose activities included the purchase of books to be given to tourists visiting the Soviet Union so that they could casually distribute a handful of copies. (The letters AE designated a Soviet Russia Division operation, and *DINOSAUR* was a randomly generated cryptonym.) After internal discussions, it was decided that the Soviet Russia Division would manage *Doctor Zhivago* under AEDINOSAUR.

The CIA had now received two warnings, from British intelligence and indirectly from Katkov, not to publish the novel in the United States or reveal any American involvement. That ruled out using émigré front organizations in Europe, as they were widely regarded as creatures of American foreign policy even if the CIA's specific role was hidden. The agency decided to use a New York publisher to prepare a Russian-language edition in the United States but take the proofs to Europe for printing so no American paper stock, which would be quickly identified as such in Moscow, would be used. If the European printer obtained the rights from Feltrinelli, all the better. If not, the CIA decided, "we'll do it black."

The CIA selected the 1958 Brussels World's Fair as its target for distributing *Doctor Zhivago.* The 1958 Brussels Universal and International Exposition, the first postwar World's Fair, was already shaping up as a Cold War political battleground. The fair opened on April 17 and would run until October 19, 1958; in all, about 18 million visitors came through the turnstiles. Forty-two nations and—for the first time—the Vatican were participating at the five-hundred-acre site just northwest of central Brussels. Both the United States and the Soviet Union built huge pavilions to showcase their competing ways of life. And what was especially interesting to the CIA: the fair offered one of those rare occasions when large numbers of Soviet citizens traveled to an event in the West. Belgium issued sixteen thousand visas to Soviet visitors.

"This book has great propaganda value," a memo to all branch chiefs of the CIA Soviet Russia Division stated, "not only for its intrinsic message and thought-provoking nature, but also for the circumstances of its publication: we have the opportunity to make Soviet citizens wonder what is wrong with their government, when a fine literary work by the man acknowledged to be the greatest living Russian writer is not even available in his own country in his own language for his own people to read."

To get *Doctor Zhivago* into the hands of Soviet tourists in Brussels, the agency would have to move quickly. And in its haste, the operation almost collapsed in farce. The CIA's publishing partner in New York—a civilian cleared by the agency's Office of Security for participation in a covert operation—nearly proved to be their undoing.

By 1958, Felix Morrow had made a very New York journey from Communist to Trotskyite to willing Cold Warrior for the CIA. The transformation of the fifty-two-year-old was representative of a larger intellectual migration from left to right among the city's radicals. Their disillusionment with the Soviet Union was first crystallized by the show trials of the old Bolsheviks. Stalin's treachery was confirmed by the Nazi-Soviet nonaggression pact. With the rise of the Cold War, they drifted, almost ineluctably, into the embrace of the new national security state, which found its ablest agitators among the disillusioned left. One loyal Trotskyite said the "loss of faith" among Morrow and others was caused by

"Stalinophobia—abhorrence at Stalinism to the point of seeing it as the principal evil force in the world." Within New York's intellectual life "organized anti-Communism had become . . . an industry," and the CIA was its lavish paymaster. One of the agency's largest front organizations, the American Committee for Cultural Freedom, which supported the Paris-based Congress for Cultural Freedom, was stocked with every shade of ex-Communist. Many years earlier, the American Committee's first chairman, Sidney Hook, had been Morrow's philosophy teacher at New York University; they became lifelong acquaintances. Hook, a former revolutionary Marxist, was a "contract consultant" for the CIA and negotiated directly with CIA director Allen Dulles for committee funding.

When Morrow was facing expulsion from the Trotskyite Socialist Workers Party in 1946, he experienced a moment of disbelief at his imminent apostasy. "You can't expel me; I'll live and die in the movement!" he shouted to the party delegates. Ten minutes later, the ousted Morrow found himself "tripping down the stairs of the convention hall with the greatest sense of glee and freedom."

Morrow was a charming, brilliant man, a former opera singer, and a natural storyteller. He had first worked as reporter for the *Brooklyn Daily Eagle* when he was sixteen and covered the Depression for the *Daily Worker*. His dispatches were translated into Russian and published in Moscow in 1933 as *Life in the United States in This Depression*.

After his break with the Trotskyite movement, Morrow entered publishing. With the help of Elliot Cohen, the editor of *Commentary,* who would later sit on the board of the American Committee for Cultural Freedom, Morrow got a job at Schocken Books, a well-regarded New York publisher. At Schocken, Morrow quickly rose to the position of vice president. In 1956, he branched out on his own, founding University Books, which specialized in the occult. Morrow was drawn to the subject when he was involved in the publication of the best seller *Flying Saucers Have Landed* in 1953.

Morrow formed contacts with those fighting the Cold War and occasionally lunched with CIA officers he had met through a friend who worked as a CIA consultant. A senior official in the agency's security division periodically visited Morrow at his house in Great Neck, Long Island, just outside the city, always arriving with a bottle of whiskey and a box of chocolates.

In early June 1958, Morrow was asked by a CIA officer if he was interested in preparing *Doctor Zhivago* for publication. The agency told Morrow that it planned to distribute the books in Brussels and asked him to also "make arrangements with anti-Stalinist trade unionists in Amsterdam and Brussels to distribute copies of the book at nominal cost to sailors" on ships bound for the Soviet Union. Morrow thought it "an astonishing and attractive task." And he believed he could get the printing done in Amsterdam, where, he said, the police chief, an ex-Trotskyite, was an old friend of his.

Morrow described himself as an "entrepreneur," and he bargained hard with the CIA for the maximum amount of money, including bonuses. The agency found Morrow's prices high but "probably warranted in view of the time factor." On June 23, 1958, Morrow signed a contract with a private lawyer acting for the CIA. Morrow was provided with a manuscript copy of *Doctor Zhivago* and was told that he would soon be provided with a publisher's note or preface to be included after the title page. The agency wanted a "major literary figure" to write a preface, but a staffer at the Soviet Russia Division also prepared a publisher's note as a backup. Initially, the agency was interested in printing 10,000 copies of the novel. Morrow was required to arrange the layout and design work to prepare the manuscript for typesetting; proofread the typeset copy; and produce two sets of photo-offset reproduction proofs. The contract said he would get an additional bonus for every day he came in before the July 31 deadline. The agency also said it would pay him to investigate where the novel could be printed in Europe and that there would be a separate, second contract for any printing in Europe.

There were signs of trouble from the beginning; Morrow either didn't understand or was unwilling to comply with the agency's demand for secrecy. Even before he signed a contract, he was discussing the operation with outsiders. At a meeting with a CIA officer on June 19, Morrow said he had already used his contacts to explore printing possibilities in the United States. Morrow had close ties to the University of Michigan Press, where his friend Fred Wieck was the director. Morrow was admonished by the CIA that he had no authority to contact any American publishing house.

Morrow also did not tell the agency that he had "credentialed Russian scholars check both the original and the repros"—an indiscretion that might account for rumors among émigrés in New York that a Russian-language edition was imminent. Moreover, the *Doctor Zhivago* reproductions for the CIA were prepared by Rausen Bros., a printing house in New York that was closely tied to the city's Russian community.

Once the European printing was complete, the CIA told Morrow that he could buy the rights to the Russian-language version of *Doctor Zhivago* from the agency—a deal that would have shocked and astonished Feltrinelli, who believed he had exclusive world rights to the novel, including in Russian, because the novel was not published in the Soviet Union. Morrow, however, was balking at the CIA's terms. In a July 7 letter, he said he couldn't secure a willing European publisher and get the printing done in eight weeks. Instead, he said, he could deliver the books with the imprint of an Amsterdam publisher, but he suggested that he would actually print them in the United States. Morrow also had a warning for the CIA: If the agency didn't back his plan and buy copies of the novel in bulk, he would simply commandeer the reproduction proofs and take them elsewhere. He informed the CIA that when the operation was over he planned to publish his own edition of *Doctor Zhivago* with the University of Michigan Press. "I can publish anywhere else I please," he told the agency.

The CIA's plans were unraveling. Two weeks later, to the consternation of its officers, the Soviet Russia Division was informed that the University of Michigan Press was planning to publish *Doctor Zhivago* in Russian. Not only that, officials in Washington received an inquiry from the academic press's offices in Ann Arbor about how many copies the government might be interested in purchasing. CIA officers were frantic and immediately wanted to know where and how the university press got its copy of the novel. They suspected that Morrow gave a copy of the manuscript to his friend Fred Wieck and the two had decided to publish the novel in some kind of joint venture.

A week later the CIA got even more of a jolt. The university press made a second inquiry about selling copies of the novel to the government and wanted to know about "the CIA's interest in the book and whether or not the agency was subsidizing the publishing of the book in Europe."

"It appears that [Morrow] in his dealings with [Michigan] has gone entirely too far and may well have committed one or more security violations," thundered the agency's Commercial Staff. The CIA decided it had to stop the University of Michigan Press, and its opening salvo was to have its lawyer in New York contact Ann Arbor and "bring out the fact that the Italian publisher is prepared to sue anyone publishing the book in Russian."

The academic publisher was unimpressed with the CIA's self-serving argument about Feltrinelli's rights. Lawyers for the University of Michigan had made a legal judgment that no one held the rights to the Russian-language edition of the novel for the United States because there was no treaty with the Soviet Union on copyright. The university publisher informed the CIA it was planning to bring out *Doctor Zhivago* in "five or six weeks or sooner" and refused to reveal the source of its manuscript.

At an internal CIA meeting, the Soviet Russia Division representative argued that the University of Michigan Press should not be allowed to publish "in advance of distribution of that edition being published in Europe under Agency sponsorship. Not only is there the question of reducing the effectiveness of the European edition, but there are also the important factors of protecting liaison services with other agencies involved."

On August 25, an officer from the Soviet Russia Division and a second CIA official flew to Michigan to meet with Harlan Hatcher, the president of the University of Michigan. The Soviet Russia Division officer had been given a series of talking points prepared at headquarters in Washington, a series of temporary buildings on the south side of the reflecting pool on the National Mall.

The CIA officer told Hatcher that the U.S. government had been "instrumental" in arranging the publication of *Doctor Zhivago* in

Russian. "It is felt," the CIA officer told Hatcher, "that to have the greatest psychological impact upon Soviet readers the Russian edition of this book should be published in Europe and not in the United States. To accomplish this, the U.S. government has made certain commitments to foreign governments."

The CIA officer also emphasized that "Pasternak specifically requested that the book not be published in the United States for his personal safety and other reasons. We have made every effort to honor the author's petition." The officer said that the CIA believed the University of Michigan Press got the proofs in "an unorthodox manner" and that they were, in fact, "the property of the U.S. government."

Hatcher was sympathetic and saw no reason why the publication of *Doctor Zhivago* couldn't be delayed at least until after it was published in Europe. The two officers met Wieck, the editorial director, the following day. They asked if they could examine the Michigan copy of *Doctor Zhivago* to compare it against the CIA's page proofs they had brought with them. The comparison was made with a magnifying glass and there was no dispute: they were identical. After some negotiation, the University of Michigan Press agreed to hold off on any announcement of its plans to publish *Doctor Zhivago* until the agency's edition appeared in Europe.

All that remained to tidy up was the mess with Morrow. The CIA agreed to a confidential settlement, but not before huffing about the publisher's duplicity. "It is our desire that it be made completely clear to [Morrow] that we are aware of his untrustworthy behavior during our relationship, and that we feel we are being most lenient in our final dealings with him."

When the CIA's difficulties with Morrow began, they prompted the agency to contact the Dutch intelligence service, the Binnenlandse Veiligheidsdienst (BVD). The CIA was already following reports of the possible publication of *Doctor Zhivago* in Russian by Mouton Publishers; a deal between the Dutch house and Feltrinelli appeared likely. Kurt Wolff, Pasternak's American publisher, had also heard rumors of a Mouton edition, and in May Feltrinelli confirmed a deal; Mouton offered to print three thousand copies at a cost of $4,160. The CIA wanted to know from their Dutch allies if it would be possible to obtain an early run of the book from Mouton.

The two intelligence agencies were close. CIA subsidies in 1958 paid for about 50 of the 691 staffers at the BVD, and new Dutch employees were trained in Washington. Joop van der Wilden, a BVD officer was dispatched to the U.S. embassy to discuss the issue with Walter Cini, a CIA officer stationed in The Hague. Cini told him it was a rush job and the agency was willing to pay well and in cash for a small print run of *Doctor Zhivago*—but again there should be no trace of American involvement or of any other intelligence agency.

The Dutch reported back to Washington that Mouton could complete the work, but would need to get started quickly to meet an early September deadline. The Soviet Russia Division decided around the end of July that it wanted to proceed "along this line provided the details [could] be suitably negotiated." On August 1, the reproduction proofs prepared by Morrow were sent to The Hague.

The BVD decided not to deal directly with Mouton but instead turned to Rudy van der Beek, a retired army major who ran the Dutch branch of an anti-Communist group, Paix et Liberté. Van der Beek's organization published a range of anti-Communist propaganda, including a recent attack on the Soviet pavilion in Brussels. A few days after the proofs arrived, Peter de Ridder, a Mouton Publishers executive, along with one of the company's printers, met with van der Beek in the large marble foyer of a grand town house on Prinsessegracht in the center of The Hague—probably number 27, the headquarters of the Dutch Red Cross, whose president served on the Dutch board of Paix et Liberté. The three men spoke for twenty minutes and van der Beek gave de Ridder the proofs of the novel and guaranteed to buy over a thousand copies.

"There was something mysterious about the encounter," said de Ridder, but he decided to take the deal. De Ridder was never clear about what motivated him. Later in 1958, he told a newspaper reporter for *Haagse Post* that van der Beek warned him that if he didn't print the book he would go elsewhere, and de Ridder feared that that would ruin the planned Mouton edition being negotiated with Feltrinelli. De Ridder said he tried to reach the Milanese publisher but was unsuccessful because he was on vacation in Scandinavia.

"I felt the book needed to be published," de Ridder said. He also thought he could get away with it. He calculated that a contract with Feltrinelli was about to be signed, and this was simply an early and lucrative sale that would draw no attention.

In the first week of September, the first Russian-language edition of *Doctor Zhivago* rolled off the printing press, bound in Mouton's signature blue-linen cover. The title page acknowledged the copyright of Feltrinelli with the words in Cyrillic, "G. Feltrinelli—Milan 1958." The name *Feltrinelli,* however, was not correctly transcribed in Russian, missing the soft sign after the *l* and before the *t*. The copyright note was de Ridder's last-minute decision, after a small number of early copies were printed without any acknowledgment of the Italian publisher. The use of Pasternak's full name, including the patronymic *Leonidovich* on the title page, also suggested that the book had been prepared by a non-native speaker; Russians would not use the patronymic on a title page. The book also had a short, unsigned preface, probably the one prepared for Morrow by a CIA staffer.

The books, wrapped up in brown paper and dated September 6, were packed into the back of a large American station wagon, and taken to the home of Walter Cini, the CIA officer in The Hague. Two hundred copies were sent to headquarters in Washington. Most of the remaining books were sent to CIA stations or assets in Western Europe—200 to Frankfurt; 100 to Berlin; 100 to Munich; 25 to London; and 10 to Paris. The largest package, 365 books, was sent to Brussels.

Visitors to the Soviet pavilion at the 1958 Brussels Universal and International Exposition first had to climb several flights of steps, as if approaching a great museum. Inside, two large statues of a male and a female worker in classic socialist-realist style greeted them. At the rear of the great central hall, which sprawled over nearly 120,000 square feet, stood a fifty-foot-tall bronze statue of Lenin. The revolutionary leader, his heavy coat draped over his shoulders, watched over Sputnik satellites, rows of agricultural machinery, models of Soviet jetliners, oil-drilling platforms, and coal mines, and exhibits on the collective farm and the typical Soviet kitchen.

The didactic message was clear. The Soviet Union was an industrial power to be reckoned with. After the launch the previous year of Sputnik 1, the first satellite in space, the Russians appeared ascendant. "Socialist economic principles will guarantee us victory" in the contest with capitalism, visitors to the Soviet pavilion were told.

Soviet brawn was also accompanied by a more seductive array of cultural offerings, from the Bolshoi Ballet to the Moscow circus, both at the fairgrounds and in the center of Brussels. The Soviets were going all out to awe and woo.

Hubert Humphrey, the Democratic senator from Minnesota, harrumphed that "from what we know about Soviet plans there will be scarcely a credible Soviet theater group, ballet artist, musician, singer, dancer or acrobat left in the Soviet Union if his services can be used in Brussels."

The United States was slower to recognize that the Brussels Exposition was a Cold War battlefield. Congress only reluctantly appropriated $13.4 million for an American pavilion, compared with the estimated $50 million the Soviet Union planned to spend. And the organizers were dogged by uncertainty about what to include, and whether the United States should also acknowledge the failings of American society, particularly the mob violence surrounding the desegregation of the public schools in Little Rock, Arkansas, the previous year. A small annex exhibition dealing, in part, with race relations was opened in Brussels but quickly closed after objections from southern congressmen.

The United States pavilion was a massive circular building with floor space to fit two football fields, and its creator, the architect Edward Stone, drew inspiration from the Roman Colosseum. With its translucent plastic roof, the structure was intended to be "very light and airy and crystalline." The organizers decided that America should be sold through "indirection," not "heavy, belabored and fatiguing propaganda." And the pavilion became a celebration of American consumerism and entertainment. There were several fashion shows every day, square dancing, and a Disney-produced film of American vistas on a 360-degree screen that took viewers from the New York City skyline to the Grand Canyon. There were hot dogs and abstract-expressionist art; a jukebox and copies of a 480-page Sunday *New York Times*. Eisenhower insisted on voting machines, and behind the curtains visitors could choose their favorite president, movie star, and musician.

When Anastas Mikoyan, the first deputy chairman of the Soviet Council of Ministers, visited the U.S. pavilion, he chose Abraham Lincoln, Kim Novak, and Louis Armstrong, although he first asked if he could choose Shostakovich for the last category. Another Soviet visitor, the writer Boris Agapov, a member of the board of *Novy Mir* who had signed the letter rejecting *Doctor Zhivago,* was unimpressed with the American pavilion. "These are all lies. . . . That is why the character, the general thrust of the American exhibition evokes bewilderment and yet another sentiment, which is shame. It is a disgrace that a talented, creative, and hard-working people is represented as a people of sybarites and thoughtless braggarts."

Doctor Zhivago could not be handed out at the American pavilion, but the CIA had an ally nearby. The Vatican pavilion was called "Civitas Dei," the "City of God." The modernist pavilion was crowned by a gleaming white belfry rising to 190 feet and topped by a large cross. Behind the belfry, the main building swooped toward the ground like a ski jump. Inside there was a church, six small chapels, and exhibition halls with displays on the papacy and the history of the church. The pavilion was nestled close to both the U.S. and Soviet buildings.

Vatican officials and local Roman Catholics began to prepare for Soviet visitors even before the fair opened. Irina Posnova, the founder of a religious publishing house in Belgium, saw an opportunity to proselytize. Born in Kiev in 1914, Posnova was the daughter of an exiled Orthodox theologian; she converted to Roman Catholicism while attending the Catholic University of Louvain. After World War II, Posnova founded Life with God, a Brussels-based organization that smuggled religious books in Russian into the Soviet Union. Posnova worked with the Vatican's organizing committee to set up a small library "somewhat hidden" behind a curtain just off the pavilion's Chapel of Silence—a place to reflect on the suppression of Christian communities around the world. With the help of Russian-speaking priests and lay volunteers, Life with God handed out religious literature, including bibles, prayer books, and some Russian literature. There was a steady stream of Soviet visitors to the Vatican pavilion, drawn, in part, by the presence of Rodin's sculpture *The Thinker,* which had been loaned by the Louvre for the duration of the fair.

Father Jan Joos, a Belgian priest and secretary-general of the Vatican organizing committee for the Brussels Expo, said three thousand Soviet tourists visited the Vatican pavilion over six months. He described them as from "the leading, privileged classes," such as members of the Academy of Sciences, scholars, writers, engineers, collective-farm directors, and city mayors.

Agapov also visited the Vatican pavilion and provided one of the few accounts of how Soviet visitors were greeted. He said he was first welcomed by a French-speaking priest who showed him Rodin's sculpture. As they talked, he said, the conversation was interrupted by a "sturdy, sloppily dressed woman" who spoke loudly in Russian and introduced him to another priest. This priest—"Father Pierre"—was about thirty-five, with a rosy complexion, a ginger beard, blue eyes, and breath that smelled of cigars and cognac. He spoke like a native Muscovite.

The priest told Agapov that modern man was confused, and only through the guidance of Christian principles could he find salvation. He led Agapov to the hidden library. Father Pierre explained, "We publish special bulletins, in which we state which movies, radio programs and books to watch and read, and which not to." Agapov noted with some satisfaction that he was reminded of the Index Librorum Prohibitorum, the Catholic Church's list of banned authors and books.

"Except for the gospels and prayer books," Agapov observed, "you can obtain all sorts of brochures and booklets in the 'City of God' in which you can find God knows what about our country, communism, Soviet power—despite the fact that this sort of propaganda is in violation of the Exposition's statute."

And, he continued, "Ladies with pointed noses are selling and distributing this with a 'blessed' smile."

In early September, these priests and ladies starting handing out copies of *Doctor Zhivago* in Russian. Finally, the CIA-sponsored edition of the novel was pressed into the hands of Soviet citizens. Soon the book's blue linen covers were found littering the fairgrounds. Some who got the novel were ripping off the cover, dividing the pages, and stuffing them in their pockets to make the book easier to hide.

A Russian weekly published in Germany by émigrés noted, "We Russians should be grateful to the organizers of the Vatican pavilion. Thanks to their efforts, the greatest contemporary work of Russian literature—Boris Pasternak's novel *Doctor Zhivago,* which is banned there—is able to find its way into the country. More than 500 copies were taken into Russia by common Russian people."

Word of the novel's appearance at the fair quickly reached Pasternak. He wrote in September to his friend Pyotr Suvchinsky in Paris, "Is it true that *Doctor Zhivago* appeared in the original? It seems that visitors to the exhibition in Brussels have seen it."

The CIA was quite pleased with itself. "This phase can be considered completed successfully," read a September 9 memo. And officials at the Soviet Russia Division noted that "as additional copies become available" they would be used "in contact and mailing operations and for travelers to take into the USSR." Walter Cini, the CIA officer in The Hague, sent a copy of the English-language edition of *Doctor Zhivago* as a gift to his BVD colleague Joop van der Wilden. He inscribed it and signed off with a code name: "In appreciation of your courage and relentless efforts to make the monster squeal in anguish. Voltaire."

There was only one problem: Mouton had never signed a contract with Feltrinelli. The Russian edition printed in The Hague was illegal. The Italian publisher was furious when he learned about the distribution of the novel in Brussels. In a letter to Manya Harari, one of the English translators, on September 18 he wrote, "I have just seen that somebody has printed and published somewhere in Holland under <u>my</u> name (!) an edition of DOCTOR

ZHIVAGO in Russian. I must say a rather extraordinary way of proceeding." Feltrinelli hired a detective and sent his lawyer to The Hague "to enquire on the matter and have hell broken out." He threatened to sue both Mouton and van der Beek, whose roles were quickly discovered.

For the CIA, the contretemps generated unwelcome publicity. *Der Spiegel* in Germany followed up on reporting in the Dutch press and identified one of the volunteers at the Vatican pavilion as "Count Vladimir Tolstoy" and said he was associated with the "militant American cultural and propaganda organization which goes under the name of Committee for a Free Europe."

Pasternak apparently read the *Spiegel* article and asked a friend if "one of the publishers of DZ in the original, C(ount) Vladimir Tolstoy," was one of Leo Tolstoy's grandsons. The article would also have alerted Pasternak to the intrigue surrounding its publication in Russian.

The American press picked up on the conspiracy. In early November, a *New York Times* books columnist wrote that "during the closing days of the Brussels Fair unknown parties stood before the Soviet pavilion giving copies of *Doctor Zhivago*—in Russian—to those interested. Origin of these copies? Classified."

Mouton held a press conference on November 2, and the company director Fred Eekhout mixed truth and lies to try to put an end to the speculation. He said de Ridder had first accepted delivery of the manuscript from some French person he believed was acting on behalf of Feltrinelli. This was nonsense. Mouton did not want to admit that it had dealt with a known Dutch anti-Communist agitator. The company eventually apologized in print, taking out ads in *The New York Times, Corriere della Sera, The Times, Le Figaro,* and the *Frankfurter Allgemeine Zeitung,* among others, to say that "only owing to a deplorable misunderstanding" had Mouton published *Doctor Zhivago* in Russian.

Posnova's organization was also baldly dissembling. At a press conference held at the Foyer Oriental in Brussels on November 10, Father Antoine Ilc said the organization was invited to a conference in Milan in August and was told by some unnamed professor there that Feltrinelli wanted to print *Doctor Zhivago* in

Russian as a gesture of gratitude to the author. Fifteen days later, the priest continued, "a gift of copies of *Doctor Zhivago* reached our residence." The books, he said, came with a note: "For Soviet tourists."

The spies in Washington watched the coverage with some dismay, and on November 15, 1958, the CIA was first linked by name to the printing by the *National Review Bulletin*, a newsletter supplement for subscribers to the *National Review*, the conservative magazine founded by William F. Buckley Jr. A writer using the pseudonym Quincy observed with approval that copies of *Doctor Zhivago* were quietly shipped to the Vatican pavilion in Brussels: "That quaint workshop of amateur subversion, the Central Intelligence Agency, may be exorbitantly expensive but from time to time it produces some noteworthy goodies. This summer, for instance, [the] CIA forgot its feud with some of our allies and turned on our enemies—and *mirabile dictu*, succeeded most nobly. . . . In Moscow these books were passed from hand to hand as avidly as a copy of *Fanny Hill* in a college dormitory. "

Mouton settled with Feltrinelli. The Dutch publishing house agreed to an "indemnity obligation" to print another five thousand copies for Feltrinelli. The Italian publisher imposed special controls on sales and said he would not permit the Dutch firm to fill any orders that might smell like exploitation of the book by intelligence operatives. Feltrinelli told journalists that he wanted only a small run of books in Russian "so that the 12 or 14 reviewers who are experts in Russian can appraise the literary quality of the work, which I feel is of the highest order."

Pasternak eventually saw a smuggled Russian-language edition of the novel—the Mouton edition printed for the CIA. He was sorely disappointed because it was based on an early uncorrected manuscript. "It abounds with errata," he told Feltrinelli. "This is almost another text, not the one I wrote," he complained to Jacqueline de Proyart, in a letter in March 1959. He asked her to make a "faithful edition."

Feltrinelli was anxious to end the dispute in the Netherlands because another had arisen in the United States. The University of Michigan announced in October—after the appearance of the

Dutch edition but before its agreed deadline with the CIA—that it was moving forward with its own edition. The Italian publisher fired off a letter to Ann Arbor saying, "It is our duty to inform you that Pasternak's *Doctor Zhivago* is protected by international copyright." He followed up with two telegrams before Fred Wieck, in a brusque reply, said, "We would be interested to know on what grounds you claim to hold copyright on the Russian text of this novel in the United States of America."

Kurt Wolff of Pantheon, Pasternak's American publisher for the English edition, sent an indignant letter to Hatcher, the president of the university. Noting the "frightful pressure," Pasternak was facing at home, he wrote, "we witness the amazing spectacle where only two institutions try to deny him his basic rights: the Soviet Writers Union which refuses to allow his book to be published in Russia . . . and the University of Michigan Press which is about to publish his work without his or his agent's permission."

Wolff asked the university "to right the wrong done to a man who cannot defend himself."

Wieck replied that the University believed it was extending a service to students and scholars by refusing to be bound by Feltrinelli's effort to "extend worldwide the censorship of the Soviet Writers' Union.

"You can see, therefore, why we resent your indictment of the University Press," Wieck continued, "and your placing of its procedures in the same category with those of the Soviet Writers Union." Wieck, however, said he was willing to compromise and suggested that Wolff use his influence to secure a license for Michigan from Feltrinelli to avoid having the matter settled in court. Agreement was reached and a University of Michigan edition appeared in January 1959 based on the CIA proof obtained from Morrow.

The CIA concluded that the printing was, in the end, "fully worth trouble in view obvious effect on Soviets," according to a cable sent by Allen Dulles, the agency director. By November 1958, according to a report in *Encounter,* a CIA-sponsored journal, "copies of an unexpurgated Russian edition of *Doctor Zhivago* (published in Holland) have already found their way to the U.S.S.R. Their reported price on the black market is 200–300 rubles."

That was almost a week's wages for a worker and a very steep price for a book in Moscow, but by then the Swedish Academy had awarded the Nobel Prize in Literature to Pasternak, and Muscovites were clamoring to get their hands on *Doctor Zhivago*.

Chapter 10

"He also looks the genius: raw nerves, misfortune, fatality."

On October 22, 1958, Max Frankel, Moscow correspondent for *The New York Times,* rushed out to Peredelkino to speak to Pasternak after the newspaper learned that the author of *Doctor Zhivago* seemed all but certain to win the Nobel Prize in Literature. The announcement was expected the following day. The dacha was crowded and Pasternak was surrounded by about a dozen friends. The gathering turned into a celebration with Frankel's news. There was a note of sedition in the air, and the reporter found himself running to the toilet to take furtive notes on some of the incendiary, alcohol-fueled remarks he was hearing. Buoyed by the atmosphere, Pasternak was forthright about the novel's genesis and message: "This book is the product of an incredible time. All around, you could not believe it, young men and women were being sacrificed up to the worship of this ox. . . . It was what I saw all around that I was forced to write. I was afraid only that I would not be able to complete it."

Pasternak's anticipation of the honor that Akhmatova believed he wanted "more than anything"—the Nobel Prize—was tinged with some trepidation—a shudder before the ordeal that was about to unfold. "You will think me immodest," he told Frankel. "But my thoughts are not on whether I deserve this honor. This will mean a new role, a heavy responsibility. All my life it has been this way for me. One moment after something happens to me it seems as though it had always been that way. Oh, of course, I am extremely happy, but you must understand that I will move immediately into this new lonely role as though it had always been that way."

The Nobel Prize in Literature is awarded by the Swedish Academy—a bequest of Alfred Nobel, the Swedish industrialist and inventor of dynamite, who said that the award should go to "the person who shall have produced in the field of literature the most outstanding work of an idealistic nature." The academy was founded in 1786 by King Gustav III as a small institute to promote the Swedish language and its literature—"to work for the purity, vigor and majesty of the Swedish Language, in the Sciences as well as in the Arts of Poetry and Oratory." It also supervises various linguistic working groups on orthography and grammar and projects such as the historical Swedish Academy dictionary of the Swedish language.

After some internal debate about the effect on its fundamentally parochial mission, the academy accepted Nobel's bequest and came to house the most prestigious international prize in literature. The eighteen members of the Swedish Academy appoint the Nobel Committee, a working group of four or five people from its own ranks. The committee solicits nominees from literary groups and academics around the world, evaluates nominees, and presents a shortlist to the full academy for a final vote. Along with its global prestige, the prize in 1958 carried the princely sum of 214,599.40 Swedish kronor, approximately $41,000.

Pasternak was first nominated in 1946, and he became a serious candidate in 1947 when the Nobel Committee asked the Swedish academic Anton Karlgren to write a detailed report on his work. Karlgren noted that Pasternak was the first Soviet writer to be considered by the academy; the émigré Russian writer Ivan Bunin had won the prize in 1933, but he spurned Moscow's offers to return home and embrace the Communist state. Largely focusing on Pasternak's poetry, Karlgren was not entirely positive and described the writer as often inaccessible to the ordinary reader. But Pasternak, he said, was regarded as the leading Russian poet by the most discerning Western critics. He added that in his prose

Pasternak demonstrated the ability to seize upon "the most secret movements of the spirit," and compared him to Proust.

Pasternak was considered every year for the Nobel Prize from 1946 to 1950. In 1954, the year Ernest Hemingway won, Pasternak believed he had been nominated again—although he was not. Pasternak said in a letter to his cousin that he was pleased "to be placed side by side, if only through a misunderstanding, with Hemingway." She replied that "never has dynamite led to such happy consequences as your candidacy for the throne of Apollo."

Pasternak was finally shortlisted in 1957, the year Albert Camus won the Nobel. In a lecture at the University of Uppsala on December 14, 1957, a few days after he accepted the prize, Camus spoke of the "great Pasternak" and opened a year of speculation that Pasternak's moment had now arrived. Although he yearned for the honor, Pasternak understood his candidacy was fraught with political peril. Four days after Camus spoke in Sweden, Pasternak wrote to his sister Lydia in Oxford. "If, as some people think, I'm awarded the Nobel Prize in spite of Soviet protests, then I'll probably be subjected to every kind of pressure here to refuse it. I think I have enough resolution to resist. But they may not allow me to travel to receive it."

By the February 1958 deadline, Pasternak was separately nominated by Renato Poggioli and Harry Levin, professors at Harvard, and Ernest Simmons of Columbia University. Poggioli was the only one of the three who had actually read *Doctor Zhivago*, and he said the novel was "modeled on *War and Peace*, and unquestionably is one of the greatest works written in the Soviet Union where it cannot appear for that reason."

Simmons wrote of Pasternak's "fresh, innovative, difficult style, notable for its extraordinary imagery, elliptical language and associative method. Feeling and thought are wonderfully blended in his verse that reveals a passionately intense but always personal vision of life. His prose likewise is highly poetic, perhaps the most brilliant prose to emerge in Soviet literature, and in fiction, as in his long short story, "Detstvo Lyuvers" [The Childhood of Luvers], he displays uncanny powers of psychological analysis. . . . One can characterize Pasternak's literary flavor by describing him as the T. S. Eliot of the Soviet Union."

Levin told the Swedish Academy, "In a world where great poetry is unquestionably increasingly rare, Mr. Pasternak seems to me one of the half-dozen first-rate poets of our own time. . . . Perhaps the most extraordinary fact about his career is that, under heavy pressures forcing writers to turn their words into ideological propaganda, he has firmly adhered to those esthetic values which his writing so richly exemplifies. He has thus set an example of artistic integrity well deserving of your distinguished recognition."

The publication of *Doctor Zhivago* in Milan gave new weight to Pasternak's standing in Stockholm. Anders Österling, the permanent secretary of the Swedish Academy, read the Italian edition and also compared the novel to *War and Peace*. On January 27, 1958, he wrote a review of *Doctor Zhivago* in the newspaper *Stockholms-Tidningen,* and his glowing assessment was an important if not decisive early endorsement: "A strong patriotic accent comes through but with no trace of empty propaganda. With its abundant documentation, its intense local color and its psychological frankness, this work bears convincing witness to the fact that the creative faculty in literature is in no sense extinct in Russia. It is hard to believe that the Soviet authorities might seriously envisage forbidding its publication in the land of its birth."

Doctor Zhivago had immediately generated headlines in Europe and the United States. The press focused on what they saw as its anti-Communist flavor and the efforts to suppress it by the Kremlin and the Italian Communist Party. *The New York Times,* in a piece on November 21, 1957, reproduced some of the more damning quotes uttered by characters about Marxism, collectivization, and the failure of the revolution to achieve its ideals. A few days later, *Le Monde* said the novel could have been another achievement for the Soviet Union if not for the country's inept censors. And *The Observer* in London wondered, "What are they afraid of?" The articles were translated for the Central Committee, but the Kremlin kept its silence on the publication of the novel, deciding that there was no advantage in any further statements after Surkov's failed mission to Italy. There was also some measure of self-deception. Polikarpov even suggested in one note to his colleagues, including the Politburo member Yekaterina Furtseva, that the novel didn't get a lot of attention in Italy and the efforts of those who wanted to organize an anti-Soviet sensation had failed.

Some of the continent's major writers as well as Russian scholars were weighing in on the book. They expressed some qualms about Pasternak's mastery of the novel as a form, but were still absorbed by its world, and the sensations it stimulated. In a long essay entitled "Pasternak and the Revolution," Italo Calvino wrote that "halfway through the twentieth century the great Russian nineteenth century novel has come back to haunt us, like King Hamlet's ghost." Calvino argued that Pasternak "is not interested in psychology, character, situations, but in something more general and direct: *life*. Pasternak's prose is simply a continuation of his verse." He wrote that Pasternak's "objections to Soviet communism seem . . . to move in two directions: against the barbarism, the ruthless cruelty unleashed by the civil war" and "against the theoretical and bureaucratic abstractions in which the revolutionary ideals become frozen."

In *The Dublin Review*, Victor Frank, the head of the Russian service at Radio Liberation and the son of the Russian philosopher Semyon Frank, who was expelled from the Soviet Union by Lenin, also concluded that Pasternak is "not really at home in prose." He still found the novel "a truly great and a truly modern piece of art.

"What makes the novel look as odd as an Aztec temple in a row of glum tenement blocks is its supreme indifference to all the official taboos and injunctions of modern Soviet literature. It is written as if the Communist Party line on art did not exist. It is written by a man who has preserved and deepened his freedom—freedom from all external restraints and all internal inhibitions."

Pasternak followed the novel's reception in the West, and the anti-Soviet complexion of some of the coverage. He argued that if the Soviet authorities would just issue the novel "in an openly censored form it would have a calming and soothing effect on the whole business. In the same way, Tolstoy's *Resurrection* and many other of our books published here and abroad before the revolution came out in two sharply different forms; and no one saw anything to be ashamed of and everyone slept peacefully in their beds, and the floor did not give way under them." The idea of publication was now anathema, and after the novel's appearance in Italy, Surkov, in a speech in Moscow, attacked efforts "to canonize" Pasternak's works.

Pyotr Suvchinsky, a Russian friend of Pasternak's living in Paris, wrote to him to tell him about the Italian translation. "The reviews were enthusiastic; they all agreed that this novel was of world significance. All of a sudden, a hidden Russia and Russian literature came back to life for everyone. I read your 'romanza' in Italian with a dictionary. So many questions came up!"

Noting the Cold War tone in some articles, Suvchinsky added: "It is, of course, annoying, unforgivable and stupid that the American blockheads are making a political case out of it. That makes no sense at all." Pasternak, too, was distressed by any reduction of his novel to something akin to a political pamphlet indicting his home country. "I deplore the fuss now being made about my book," he said in late 1957. "Everybody's writing about it but who in fact has read it? What do they quote from it? Always the same passages—three pages, perhaps, out of a book of 700 pages."

The year 1958 began badly for Pasternak. In late January, he developed a blockage in his bladder. He was running a high temperature and experiencing sometimes violent pain in his leg. His family was unable to get him the proper treatment; the previous year the writers' union had decreed that Pasternak was "unworthy of a bed in the Kremlin Hospital." His wife gave him mustard baths and a nurse fitted him with a catheter at home. Pasternak's neighbor Kornei Chukovsky visited him on February 3. Pasternak was exhausted, but seemed at first to be in good spirits. His neighbor noted that he was reading Henry James and listening to the radio. All at once, he seized Chukovsky's hand and kissed it. "There was terror in his eyes," recalled Chukovsky.

"I can feel the pain coming back. It makes me think how good it would be to . . . ," said Pasternak.

He didn't utter the word *die*.

"I've done everything I meant to in my life," Pasternak continued. "It would be so good."

Chukovsky was infuriated that "nobodies and lickspittles," as he called them, "scorned by one and all [could] command luxurious treatment at the drop of a hat, while Pasternak [lay] there lacking the most basic care."

Chukovsky traveled into Moscow and he and other friends pleaded with the authorities to have Pasternak hospitalized. A bed was eventually found in the Central Committee Clinic and an ambulance was dispatched to his dacha. Zinaida dressed her husband in his fur hat and coat. Some workers cleared the snow from the front door to the street, and Pasternak was carried on a stretcher to the waiting ambulance. He blew kisses as he passed his worried friends.

Pasternak spent a couple of months in treatment and convalescing. He was unable to work with any consistency and spent much of his time answering the admiring letters that began to arrive in increasing numbers from abroad. There was time to reflect on the achievement of having written *Doctor Zhivago*. "More and more does fate carry me off nobody knows where and even I have only a faint idea where it is," he wrote to a Georgian friend. "It is most probable that only many years after my death will it become clear what were the reasons, the great, the overwhelmingly great reasons that lay at the foundation of the activity of my last years, the air it breathed and drew sustenance from, what it served."

Pasternak came home in April and Lydia Chukovskaya saw him at her father's house. "My first impression was that he looked great: tanned, wide-eyed, youthful, grey, handsome. And possibly because he was so handsome and young, the mark of tragedy that had been on his face over the last years stood out even more. No weariness, no aging, but Tragedy, Fate, Doom." Her father concurred and thought Pasternak "cut a tragic figure: twisted lips, tieless . . . but he also looks the genius: raw nerves, misfortune, fatality."

Excitement about the novel continued to build abroad as translations into other languages neared completion. In February 1958, Kurt Wolff, the head of Pantheon Books, which was planning to publish *Doctor Zhivago* in the United States, wrote to Pasternak to introduce himself. He told Pasternak that he had only been able to read the novel in full in Italian as the English translation was still in progress. "It is the most important novel I have had the pleasure and honor of publishing in a long professional career," wrote Wolff. The German-born publisher reminisced about his time as a student in Marburg, a year before Pasternak attended in 1912. "It would be nice to chat about all this and more—perhaps there will be an opportunity in Stockholm toward the end of 1958." Pasternak replied, "What you write about Stockholm will never take place, since my government will never give permission for me to accept any kind of award."

The French edition of *Doctor Zhivago* was published in June 1958. When Pasternak saw a copy of it, he burst into tears. He wrote to de Proyart to say that "the publication of *Doctor Zhivago* in France, the remarkable personal letters, dizzying and breathtaking, which I have received from there—this is a whole novel in itself, a special kind of experience which creates a feeling of being in love."

Camus wrote to Pasternak that month, and enclosed a copy of his lecture in Uppsala. "I would be nothing without 19th century Russia," he said. "I re-discovered in you the Russia that nourished and fortified me."

Doctor Zhivago was published in Britain and the United States in September. In a long review in *The New York Times Book Review,* Marc Slonim was hugely enthusiastic: "To those who are familiar with Soviet novels of the last twenty-five years, Pasternak's book comes as a surprise. The delight of this literary discovery is mixed with a sense of wonder: that Pasternak, who spent all his life in the Soviet environment, could resist all the external pressures and strictures and could conceive and execute a work of utter independence, of broad feeling and of an unusual imaginative power, amounts almost to a miracle." Publication in Germany followed in early October, and in the *Frankfurter Allgemeine Zeitung,* the critic Friedrich Sieburg said, "this book has come to us like a refugee, or rather, like a pilgrim. There is no fear in it and no laughter, but certainty of the indestructability of human kind as long as it can love."

The notices were largely but not entirely positive. The daily reviewer for *The New York Times,* Orville Prescott, said the novel was merely "a respectable achievement."

If it were written by a Russian émigré, or by an American or

English author who had done a lot of conscientious research, *Doctor Zhivago* would be unlikely to cause much stir." Speaking on the BBC, E. M. Forster said he thought the novel was overrated. "It quite lacks the solidity of *War and Peace*. I don't think Pasternak is really very interested in people. The book seems to me to be most interesting for its epic quality."

Although the Kremlin had made no statements following the publication of the novel in Italy, official hostility toward Pasternak endured. When Surkov met the British journalist and politician R. H. S. Crossman in the summer, he defended the banning of the novel. "In your bourgeois society, so-called freedom is conceded not only to Shakespeare and to Graham Greene but to pornography. We see nothing immoral about forbidding publishers to print horror comics or damaging novels. Pasternak is a peculiar fellow. Some of his most distinguished colleagues tried to persuade him that the end of the novel was wrong, but he wouldn't accept their advice. Officially, he is a member of our union but spiritually he is anti-social, a lone wolf."

When Crossman remarked that many great writers were peculiar, including Nietzsche, Surkov shook his fist and shouted: "Yes, and we would have banned Nietzsche and in that way prevented the rise of Hitlerism."

Crossman noted that he was arguing about a novel he hadn't read.

"But *Doctor Zhivago* is notorious," Surkov angrily replied. "Everyone is talking about it."

"Everyone in Moscow?" replied Crossman with a little glee.

The attention Pasternak had received in the West not only brought fan mail, but letters from domestic critics. One writer from Vilnius, the capital of the Soviet Republic of Lithuania, told him, "When you hear the hired assassins from the Voice of America praise your novel, you ought to burn with shame." Fyodor Panfyorov, the editor of the literary journal *Oktyabr* (October), aggressively suggested to Ivinskaya that Pasternak go to Baku and write about the construction of oil rigs in an effort to redeem himself.

In April, Georgi Markov, a senior member of the writers' union, returned from an official trip to Sweden. He informed his colleagues that the Swedish intelligentsia and press were constantly discussing Pasternak and *Doctor Zhivago*. Markov passed along the rumor that potential candidates for the Nobel Prize included Pasternak, the Italian novelist Alberto Moravia, the American writer Ezra Pound, and Mikhail Sholokhov, the author of *And Quiet Flows the Don*. Sholokhov was Khrushchev's brother-in-law and a favored author of the Kremlin. His novel was held up as a model of socialist realism and was one of the most-read books in the Soviet Union. Moscow had pressed his nomination in previous years. Citing Swedish writers close to the academy, Markov said there was also some discussion about Pasternak and Sholokhov sharing the prize, and there was precedent for two writers winning the Nobel in the same year. "Wanting justice to be served and Sholokhov to win, our Swedish comrades believe that the struggle to support Sholokhov should be intensified," Markov wrote.

Dmitri Polikarpov, who along with Surkov had led the efforts to suppress the novel's publication in Italy the previous year, urged his comrades to go on the offensive to oppose Pasternak's candidacy. In a memo for the Central Committee, Polikarpov suggested that the newspapers *Pravda*, *Izvestiya*, and *Literaturnaya Gazeta* should immediately run articles about Sholokhov's writing, and his public activities. (Sholokhov was a member of the Supreme Soviet of the USSR, the country's highest legislative body.) Polikarpov said that the newspapers should also emphasize that Sholokhov, who had written nothing of note in years, had just completed the second volume of *Virgin Soil Upturned*. The first volume had come out in 1932.

Polikarpov also wanted the Soviet embassy in Stockholm to reach out to its contacts in the arts in Sweden and explain to them that selecting Pasternak would be "an unfriendly act." A few days later, the novelist and former war correspondent Boris Polevoi wrote to warn the Central Committee that the West might attempt to create an anti-Soviet "sensation" out of the Nobel Prize, and use it to stress the "lack of freedom of speech in the Soviet Union" and to claim there is "political pressure on certain authors." Polevoi recognized Pasternak's literary gifts but regarded him as alien to Soviet letters—"a man of immense talent; but he's a foreign body in our midst."

The Swedish Academy had experienced and rejected Soviet pressure before. In 1955, Dag Hammarskjöld, a member, wrote to a colleague, "I would vote against Sholokhov with a conviction based not only on artistic grounds and not only as an automatic response to attempts to pressure us, but also on the ground that a prize to a Soviet author today, involving as it would the kind of political motivations that would readily be alleged, is to me an idea with very little to recommend it."

Any efforts on Sholokhov's behalf failed again. The academy shortlisted three candidates for consideration: Pasternak; Alberto Moravia; and Karen Blixen (pen name Isak Dinesen), the Danish author who wrote *Out of Africa* in 1937.

By mid-September, Yekaterina Furtseva was requesting potential responses in the event that Pasternak won. Remarkably, Polevoi and Surkov said that *Doctor Zhivago* should be quickly published in a small edition of 5,000 to 10,000 copies that would not be sold to the general public but would be distributed to a select audience. They argued that such a printing would "make it impossible for the bourgeois media to make a scandal."

The proposal was rejected because the head of the Central Committee's culture department concluded that the Western press would make a scandal whether the book was published or not. Moreover, he feared, if the novel was published in the Soviet Union, it almost certainly would appear in other Eastern Bloc countries where it was also banned.

Instead, Polikarpov and other members of the Central Committee formulated a series of measures to be followed if the Swedish Academy took the "hostile act" of awarding the prize to Pasternak. Mikhail Suslov, the Kremlin's éminence grise and chief ideologist, signed off on the proposals.

The campaign to vilify the author began to take shape: The 1956 *Novy Mir* rejection letter should be published in *Literaturnaya Gazeta*. *Pravda* should run a "satirical article" denouncing the novel and "unveiling the true intentions of the bourgeois press's hostile campaign around the awarding of the Nobel Prize to Pasternak." A group of prominent Soviet writers should issue a joint statement that the award was an effort to ignite the Cold War. Finally, Pasternak should be told to refuse the Nobel, "since the award does not serve the interests of our Motherland."

In the summer, Pasternak was visited in Peredelkino by the Swedish critic Erik Mesterton, who was an expert for the academy. The two discussed the Nobel Prize and any risk the award might entail for Pasternak. Mesterton also met Surkov and when he returned to Sweden he told Österling that the prize could be awarded to Pasternak despite the political shadow over the author in Moscow. Pasternak mistakenly believed that the Swedish Academy would not make him the laureate without the approval of the Soviet authorities—and that, he thought, would never be forthcoming. He continued to meet other Swedish visitors and told them that he "would have no hesitation about receiving the prize." Pasternak continued to stress the eternal values in his work and his distance from the polemics of the Cold War. "In this era of world wars, in this atomic age . . . we have learned that we are the guests of existence, travellers between two stations," he told Nils Åke Nilsson, another Swedish academic close to the academy. "We must discover security within ourselves. During our short span of life we must find our own insights into our relationship with the existence in which we participate so briefly. Otherwise, we cannot live!"

Pasternak occasionally seemed hesitant about the growing speculation, telling his sister, "I wish this could happen in a year's time, not before. There will be so many undesirable complications." He sensed that the political threat to his position was only "temporarily eased" and that official silence masked seething hostility.

These concerns were mostly private. With the foreign visitors who alighted at his door, he was as voluble as ever, and he could appear supremely indifferent to the probability that he was being closely monitored. "He several times referred to the Soviet way of life with a grin and an airy wave in the direction of his windows as *vsyo eto:* 'all that,' " the British scholar Ronald Hingley recalled. When Hingley told Pasternak that he was nervous about a lecture he had to give at Moscow University, Pasternak dismissed his fears: "Never mind that; let them look at a free man." But when Hingley and Pasternak, who were chatting in the writer's upstairs study, saw a black sedan slowly and repeatedly pass the house, Pasternak stiffened.

Russian friends feared for him. Chukovsky warned Pasternak against attending a poetry evening at the Writers House because he feared that some of those in attendance "will turn the reading into a riot—just what Surkov wants." At an evening event of Italian poetry that fall, Surkov was asked why Pasternak was not present. Surkov told the audience that Pasternak had written "an anti-Soviet novel against the spirit of the Russian Revolution and had sent it abroad for publication."

In September, Österling argued before the academy that it should choose Pasternak, and not worry about any political fallout. "I strongly recommend this candidacy and think that if it gets the majority of the votes, the Academy can make its decision with a clear conscience—regardless of the temporary difficulty that Pasternak's novel, so far, cannot appear in the Soviet Union."

In a last-minute bid to postpone the award for at least a year, Pasternak's German friend the poet Renate Schweitzer wrote to the Swedish Academy on October 19 and enclosed a page from a letter Pasternak had sent her. In it, Pasternak said that "one step out of place—and the people closest to you will be condemned to suffer from all the jealousy, resentment, wounded pride, and disappointment of others, and old scars on the heart will be reopened." Schweitzer implored the committee to delay making an award to Pasternak for a year. Österling circulated the letter within the academy just before the final vote, but he told the members that the purported letter by Pasternak was not signed and, in any case, contradicted what Mesterton and Nilsson told him after they visited Pasternak during the summer.

The academy vote for Pasternak was unanimous. But in a nod to political sensitivities in Moscow, the citation that was agreed to did not mention *Doctor Zhivago*. The final language naming Pasternak said: "For his notable achievement in both contemporary poetry and the field of the great Russian narrative tradition." But *Doctor Zhivago* was singled out in Österling's official remarks: "It is indeed a great achievement to have been able to complete under difficult circumstance a work of such dignity, high above all political party frontiers and rather apolitical in its entirely human outlook."

At 3:20 p.m. on October 23, 1958, Österling entered the sitting room of the Nobel Library in Stockholm and announced to the waiting press: "It's Pasternak."

Chapter 11

"There would be no mercy, that was clear."

Wearing an overcoat and his old cap, Pasternak was walking in driving rain in the woods near his dacha on the afternoon of October 23 when a group of journalists who had come out from Moscow found him. The newsmen asked for his reaction to Österling's announcement, and his pleasure was obvious. "To receive this prize fills me with great joy, and also gives me great moral support. But my joy today is a lonely joy." He told the reporters there was little more he could say as he had yet to get any official notification of the Swedish Academy's decision. He seemed flushed and agitated. Pasternak told the correspondents that he did his best thinking while walking, and he needed to walk some more.

Pasternak got further confirmation that the prize was his when Zinaida came home from Moscow, where she and Nina Tabidze had been shopping. They had run into a friend of Tabidze's in the city who told them she had heard about the prize on the radio. Zinaida was shocked and upset, fearing a scandal.

That night, at around 11:00, Pasternak's neighbor, Tamara Ivanova, received a phone call from Maria Tikhonova, the wife of the secretary of the writers' union, who told her that Pasternak had won the prize. Ivanova was thrilled. Tikhonova, aware of the unease in official circles, said it was too early to get excited, but said Ivanova should alert Pasternak, who didn't have a phone. Ivanova roused her husband, Vsevolod, who got up and put on a housecoat and a winter coat over his pajamas, and the two of them padded over to Pasternak's house. Nina Tabidze let them in and a delighted Pasternak emerged from his study. While Tabidze opened some wine, Tamara Ivanova went to Zinaida's bedroom to tell her the news. Pasternak's wife refused to get up. She said she didn't expect anything good would come of the prize.

The first official Soviet reaction was muted and condescending. Nikolai Mikhailov, the Soviet minister of culture, said he was surprised by the award. "I know Pasternak as a true poet and excellent translator, but why should he get the prize now, dozens of years after his best poems were published?" He told a Swedish correspondent in Moscow that it would be up to the writers' union to decide if Pasternak would be allowed to receive the prize.

The Ivanovs got another call the following morning, Friday the twenty-fourth. They were told to tell Konstantin Fedin, Pasternak's other next-door neighbor, that Polikarpov was on his way out from Moscow. The Central Committee had earlier decided that Fedin had some influence with Pasternak and he should relay the Kremlin's decision that he must refuse the Nobel Prize. Polikarpov came directly to Fedin's house, gave him his instructions, and told him he would wait for him to return with Pasternak's response. From their window, the Ivanovs watched Fedin hurry up the path to Pasternak's door. When Fedin came in, Zinaida was baking. It was her name day, and her mood had improved over the previous night; she was now considering what she might wear in Stockholm at the awards ceremony. But Fedin ignored her and went directly up to Pasternak's study. He told Pasternak it was an official, not a friendly, call. "I'm not going to congratulate you because Polikarpov is at my place and he's demanding that you renounce the prize."

"Under no circumstances," said Pasternak.

They argued loudly for a few more minutes, and a report to the Kremlin stated that Pasternak was very aggressive and "even said, 'They can do whatever they want with me.'" Pasternak finally asked for some time to think things over, and Fedin gave him two hours. Polikarpov, infuriated by the delay, returned to Moscow.

Fedin sent a message to Polikarpov later to say that Pasternak never showed up with an answer. "That should be understood as his refusal to make a statement," Polikarpov told his superiors.

After Fedin left, Pasternak walked over to Vsevolod Ivanov's house to talk about Fedin's ultimatum. He appeared hurt and offended by the visit.

"Do what seems right to you; don't listen to anyone," his neighbor told him. "I told you yesterday and I say it again today: You're the best poet of the era. You deserve any prize."

"In that case I will send a telegram of thanks," Pasternak declared.

"Good for you!"

Kornei Chukovsky heard about the award from his secretary, who was "jumping for joy." Chukovsky grabbed his granddaughter Yelena and rushed over to congratulate Pasternak. "He was happy, thrilled with his conquest," Chukovsky recalled. "I threw my arms around him and smothered him with kisses." Chukovsky proposed a toast, a moment that was captured by some of the Western and Russian photographers who had already arrived at the dacha. (Fearful that his embrace of Pasternak could compromise him, Chukovsky, the victim of an earlier slander campaign that traumatized him, later prepared a note for the authorities explaining that he was "unaware that *Doctor Zhivago* contained attacks on the Soviet system.")

Pasternak showed Chukovsky some of the telegrams he had received—all from abroad. Several times, Zinaida said aloud that the Nobel Prize was not political and not for *Doctor Zhivago*, as if she could wish away her sense of danger. She also worried that she would not be allowed to travel to Sweden and whispered quietly to Chukovsky: "Kornei Ivanovich, what do you think? . . . After all, they have to invite the wife too."

When the photographers left, Pasternak went up to his study to compose a telegram for the Swedish Academy. Later in the afternoon, he sent it: "Immensely grateful, touched, proud, astonished, abashed. Pasternak."

When he was finished writing, he walked for a short while with Chukovsky and his granddaughter. He told them he wouldn't be taking Zinaida to Stockholm.

After leaving Pasternak, Chukovsky called on Fedin, who told him, "Pasternak will do us all great harm with all of this. They'll launch a fierce campaign against the intelligentsia now." In fact, Chukovsky was soon served with a notice to attend an emergency meeting of the writers' union the following day. A courier was going house to house in Peredelkino with summonses for the writers in the village—each understood the public indictment that was to come and felt again Stalin's shadow. After Vsevolod Ivanov received his notification, he collapsed and his housekeeper found him lying on the floor. He was diagnosed with a possible stroke and was bedridden for a month.

When the courier arrived at Pasternak's house, the writer's "face grew dark; he clutched at his heart and could barely climb the stairs to his room." He began to experience pain in his arm which felt as if it "had been amputated."

"There would be no mercy, that was clear," Chukovsky wrote in his diary. "They were out to pillory him. They would trample him to death just as they had Zoshchenko, Mandelstam, Zabolotsky, Mirsky and Benedikt Livshits."

Chukovsky proposed that Pasternak go see Yekaterina Furtseva, the only woman in the Politburo, and tell her that the novel had been taken to Italy against his wishes and that he was upset by all the "hullabaloo surrounding his name." Pasternak asked Tamara Ivanova whether he should write a letter to Furtseva. His neighbor thought it was a good idea. "Well, because, after all, she is a woman."

> Dear Yekaterina Alekseyevna,
>
> It always appeared to me that Soviet man can be something other than they want to let me believe, more alive, open to debate, free and daring. I do not want to abandon that idea and I am prepared to pay any price to stay true to it. I thought the joy of receiving the Nobel Prize would not be mine alone, but would be shared with the society which I am part of. I think the honor

> is granted not only to me, but to the literature to which I belong, Soviet literature, and to which, with my hand on my heart, I have contributed a thing or two.
>
> However great my differences with these times may be, I would not want them to be settled with an axe. Well then, if it seems right to you, I am willing to endure and accept everything. But I would not want that willingness to look like a provocation or impudence. Quite the contrary, it is an obligation of humility. I believe in the presence of higher forces on earth and in life, and heaven forbids me to be proud and presumptuous.
>
> B. Pasternak.

When he read it, Chukovsky was dismayed by the references to God and the heavens, and fled Pasternak's house in despair.

At some point in the afternoon, Pasternak also visited Ivinskaya at the "Little House." He probably brought over the letter to Furtseva, which was never sent and was found much later among Ivinskaya's papers. Like Chukovsky, she would have realized that this was not the act of contrition the authorities were looking for. Pasternak also told her about the telegram he had sent to Stockholm and was in an agitated state, turning over what Fedin had demanded. "What do you think, can I say I repudiate the novel?" He didn't really want an answer. Ivinskaya felt he was having a prolonged dialogue with himself.

The Kremlin regarded the reaction in the West to the award as entirely predictable. The despised Radio Liberation announced that it would immediately begin broadcasting the text of *Doctor Zhivago;* it was ultimately directed not to by the CIA for copyright reasons. In the American and European press, Pasternak was celebrated as a nonconformist facing down an oppressive system. In an official response to Österling, the Soviet Ministry of Foreign Affairs noted his remarks about *Doctor Zhivago* and wrote: "You and those who made this decision focused not on the novel's literary or artistic qualities, and this is clear since it does not have any, but on its political aspects since Pasternak's novel presents Soviet reality in a perverted way, libels the socialist revolution, socialism and the Soviet people." The ministry accused the academy of wanting to intensify the Cold War and international tension.

The full fury of the authorities was about to be unleashed, but in Pasternak's home the celebration continued as more friends came to toast him and celebrate Zinaida's name day. "No one foresaw the imminent catastrophe," Chukovsky wrote in his diary.

On Saturday morning, Muscovites snapped up copies of *Literaturnaya Gazeta* as word spread in the city about an extraordinary attack on Pasternak. The newspaper printed in full the 1956 rejection letter written by the editors of *Novy Mir,* and it was accompanied by a long editorial brimming with insults under the headline "A Provocative Sortie of International Reaction." For ordinary readers, many of whom were learning about *Doctor Zhivago* and the Nobel Prize for the first time, it was a feast of delicious detail about the novel's sins. Rarely were readers provided such unexpurgated descriptions and quotes from a piece of banned literature. By 6:00 a.m. people were lining up to buy copies of *Literaturnaya Gazeta*. The newspaper had a circulation of 880,000 and it sold out within a few hours.

The editorial read: "The internal emigrant Zhivago, faint-hearted and base in his small-mindedness, is alien to the Soviet people, as is the malicious literary snob Pasternak—he is their opponent, he is the ally of those who hate our country and our system."

Repeatedly, Pasternak was called a "Judas" who had betrayed his homeland for "thirty pieces of silver." The "Swedish litterateurs, and their inspirers from across the Atlantic," turned the novel into a Cold War weapon. After all, the readers of *Literaturnaya Gazeta* were told, Western critics didn't think much of *Doctor Zhivago*. Negative reviews from Germany, the Netherlands, and France were quoted to make the point that "many Western critics expressed themselves quite openly on its modest artistic merits." But when such an "arch-intriguer" as the owner of *The New York Times* extolled the novel for "spitting on the Russian people," *Doctor Zhivago* was guaranteed ovations from the enemies of the Soviet Union. The novel and "the personality of its author became a golden vein for the reactionary press."

"The honor conferred on Pasternak was not great," the editorial concluded. "He was rewarded because he voluntarily agreed to play the part of a bait on the rusty hook of anti-Soviet propaganda. But it is difficult to hold this 'position' for long. A piece of bait is changed as soon as it goes rotten. History shows that such changes take place very quickly. An ignominious end waits for this Judas who has risen again, for *Doctor Zhivago,* and for his creator, who is destined to be scorned by the people."

Around the city, bureaucrats took their cues from the newspaper and a drumbeat of condemnation began to dominate radio and television broadcasts. At the prestigious Gorky Literary Institute, the director told the students that they would have to attend a demonstration against Pasternak and sign a letter denouncing him that would be published in *Literaturnaya Gazeta*. He said their participation was a "litmus test." But despite the threats, many students balked at condemning Pasternak. As administrators went through the dorms, some hid in the toilets or the kitchen, or didn't answer their doors. Three students in Leningrad painted "Long Live Pasternak!" on the embankment of the river Neva. In Moscow, only 110 of about 300 Literary Institute students signed the letter, a remarkable act of defiance. Also, only a few dozen people from the student body attended the institute's "spontaneous demonstration," as administrators later described it. It was led by Vladimir Firsov, a budding poet, and Nikolai Sergovantsev, a critic. The group walked to the nearby Union of Soviet Writers building, and their handmade posters picked up on the anti-Semitic tone of the *Literaturnaya Gazeta* editorial. One placard depicted a caricature of Pasternak "reaching for a sack of dollars with crooked, grasping fingers." Another said: "Throw the Judas out of the USSR." They handed a letter to Konstantin Voronkov, a playwright and member of the union board, and said they planned to go to Peredelkino to continue the protest in front of Pasternak's house. Voronkov advised against it until an official decision was made to increase pressure on Pasternak.

Inside the union's palatial headquarters about forty-five writers who were also members of the Communist Party held a meeting about Pasternak. The comrades expressed their "wrath and indignation" and there was general agreement that Pasternak should be expelled from the Union of Soviet Writers—the ultimate sanction, as it would deprive him of the ability to earn a living and could also threaten his state-provided housing. A number of writers, including Sergei Mikhalkov, author of the lyrics to the Soviet national anthem, went further and said Pasternak should be expelled from the Soviet Union. There was also criticism of Surkov for allowing the situation to get out of control; at the time he was away at a sanitarium and didn't participate in any of the debates surrounding the Nobel Prize. A number of writers felt that Pasternak should have been expelled when it was learned he had given his manuscript to a foreigner. They deluded themselves into believing that if the *Novy Mir* rejection letter had been printed earlier it would have prevented Pasternak from winning the Nobel Prize, since "the progressive press all over the world would not have let it happen." A formal decision on expelling Pasternak was put on the agenda for a meeting of the union's executive on Monday.

Pasternak, as a matter of habit, didn't read the newspapers but the scale and vehemence of the campaign was inescapable. *Le Monde* correspondent Michel Tatu visited Pasternak with a couple of other journalists after the appearance of the harsh *Literaturnaya Gazeta* editorial. It had been raining for six days and they found Peredelkino desolate and melancholy. Pasternak, however, was in good spirits and they talked in the music room. Pasternak tried to speak French, not very well, but he enjoyed the effort. He told the reporters that the Nobel Prize was not only a joy but a "moral support." He added that it was a solitary joy.

Pravda, the official organ of the Communist Party, weighed in next with a long personal attack on Pasternak that was written by one of its more notorious journalists, David Zaslavsky. Both Lenin and Trotsky had dismissed Zaslavsky, an anti-Bolshevik before the revolution, as a hack. "Mr. Zaslavsky has acted only as a scandal monger," said Lenin. "We need to distinguish a slanderer and scandal monger from an unmasker, who demands the discovery of precisely identified facts." But under Stalin, the *Pravda* journalist was a favored hatchet man. Zaslavsky and Pasternak also had history. In May 1929, Zaslavsky began his career as a provocateur when he used the pages of *Literaturnaya Gazeta* to accuse Mandelstam of plagiarism. Pasternak, Pilnyak, Fedin, Zoshchenko, and others signed a letter defending Mandelstam and calling him "an outstanding poet, one of the most highly qualified of translators, and a literary master craftsman." The return of the seventy-eight-year-old Zaslavsky from semi-retirement to attack Pasternak gave the *Pravda* article "an especially sinister nuance."

The piece was headlined: "Reactionary Propaganda Uproar Over a Literary Weed."

"It is ridiculous, but *Doctor Zhivago,* this infuriated moral freak, is presented by Pasternak as the 'finest' representative of the old Russian intelligentsia. This slander of the leading intelligentsia is as absurd as it is devoid of talent," Zaslavsky wrote. "Pasternak's novel is low-grade reactionary hackwork."

The novel, he continued, "was taken up triumphantly by the most inveterate enemies of the Soviet Union—obscurantists of various shades, incendiaries of a new world war, provocateurs. Out of an ostensibly literary event they seek to make a political scandal, with the clear aim of aggravating international relations, adding fuel to the flames of the 'cold war,' sowing hostility towards the Soviet Union, blackening the Soviet public. Choking with delight, the anti-Soviet press has proclaimed the novel the 'best' work of the current year, while the obliging grovelers of the big bourgeoisie have crowned Pasternak with the Nobel Prize. . . .

"The inflated self-esteem of an offended and spiteful Philistine has left no trace of dignity and patriotism in Pasternak's soul," Zaslavsky concluded. "By all his activity, Pasternak confirms that in our socialist country, gripped by enthusiasm for the building of the radiant Communist society, he is a weed."

The state's giant propaganda machine was now working at full tilt, according to the Albanian writer Ismail Kadare, who was studying at the time in the Gorky Literary Institute. "The radio, from 5 in the morning until 12 at night, the television, the newspapers, the journals, magazines, even for children, were full of articles and attacks on the renegade writer."

Pasternak's friend Alexander Gladkov was in a barber shop on Arbat Square Sunday afternoon when Zaslavsky's article was read out over the radio. "Everybody listened in silence—a sullen kind of silence, I would say. Only one chirpy workman started talking about all the money Pasternak would get, but nobody encouraged him to go on. I knew that cheap tittle-tattle of this kind would be much harder for Pasternak to bear than all the official fulminations. I had felt very depressed all day, but this silence in the barber's shop cheered me up."

Pasternak tried to laugh some of it off but "it was in fact all very painful to him." On Sunday, Ivinskaya's daughter, Irina, visited Pasternak with two fellow students from the Literary Institute, the young poets Yuri Pankratov and Ivan Kharabarov. Pasternak wasn't happy to have visitors and made it clear he wanted to be alone. He said he was ready to "drink his cup of suffering to the end" as the three young people accompanied him along part of his walk. "One had the clear impression of his loneliness—a loneliness borne with great courage," recalled Ivinskaya's daughter. Pankratov recited some lines from one of Pasternak's poems:

That is the reason why in early Spring
My friends and I foregather,
Our evenings are farewells
Our revelries are testaments,
So that suffering's secret flow
Should warm the cold of being.

Pasternak was visibly moved, but the visit ended on a note of disappointment. Pankratov and Kharabarov explained that they were under pressure to sign the letter of denunciation at the Literary Institute and asked Pasternak what they should do. "Really now," said Pasternak, "what does it matter? It's an empty formality—sign it."

"When I looked out the window I saw them skipping with joy as they ran off hand in hand," Pasternak later told Yevtushenko, seeing their relief as a small betrayal. "How strange young people are now, what a strange generation! In our time, such things were not done."

Other former friends hurried to distance themselves. The poet Ilya Selvinsky, who had previously called Pasternak his teacher, and Pasternak's neighbor, the critic Viktor Shklovsky, sent telegrams of congratulations from the Crimea, where they were vacationing. But Selvinsky quickly followed it up with a letter when he read about the official reaction. "I now take it on myself to tell you that to ignore the view of the Party, even if you think it is wrong, is equivalent, in the international situation of the present moment, to deliver a blow at the country in which you live." Selvinsky and Shklovsky then wrote to a local newspaper in Yalta and accused Pasternak of "a low act of treachery."

"Why? The most terrible thing is I don't remember anymore," said Shklovsky many years later. "The times? Sure, but we're the time, I am, millions like me. One day everything will come to light: the records of those meetings, the letters from those years, the interrogation procedures, the denunciations—everything. And all that sewage will also dredge up the stench of fear."

The literary community was now "gripped by the sickening, clammy feeling of dread" and it led to a near-frenzy of condemnation. These inquisitorial feedings were an almost ritualistic part of the Soviet literary system that stretched back to Stalin. Error was followed by collective attack. The fallen writer was expected to respond with contrition and self-criticism before being welcomed back into the fold. Writers scurried to attack Pasternak. They were motivated by the need to survive within a system that could just as easily turn on them. Some despised Pasternak for his success and what they sensed or knew was his disdain for them. And others were true believers who were convinced that Pasternak was a traitor. The scale of the rhetorical assault and the global attention it drew was unprecedented. Moreover, Pasternak failed to follow the time-honored script.

The meeting of the executive of the writers' union was scheduled for noon on Monday. Pasternak went into town early with Vyacheslav "Koma" Ivanov, his neighbor's son. At Ivinskaya's apartment, Ivanov, with the support of Olga and Irina, argued that Pasternak should not go to the meeting, which was likely to be an "execution." Pasternak, who was pale and feeling ill, said he would instead send a letter to the meeting. It was written in pencil in a series of bullet points and Pasternak apologized in the text that it was "not as smooth and persuasive as [he] would like it to be." It was also not apologetic:

"I still believe even after all this noise and all those articles in the press that it was possible to write *Doctor Zhivago* as a Soviet citizen. It's just that I have a broader understanding of the rights and possibilities of a Soviet writer, and I don't think I disparage the dignity of Soviet writers in any way."

Pasternak described his attempts to have the book published in the Soviet Union, his requests to Feltrinelli to delay publication, and his unhappiness at the selective quotations from the book that had appeared in the Western press.

"I would not call myself a literary parasite," he told his colleagues. "Frankly, I believe that I have done something for literature.

"I thought that my joy and the cheerful feelings I had when the Nobel Prize was awarded to me would be shared by the society I've always believed I am a part of. I thought the honor bestowed on me, a writer who lives in Russia and hence a Soviet writer, is an honor for all of Soviet literature.

"As for the prize itself nothing would ever make me regard this honor as a sham and respond to it with rudeness."

He concluded by telling his colleagues that whatever punishment they might dole out would bring them neither happiness nor glory.

Ivanov rushed by taxi over to the writers' union and a young man "with the cold eyes of a dutiful clerk" took the letter from him. The vestibule of the old union building buzzed with the sound of voices as writers arrived for the meeting in the White Hall. All the seats were taken and writers lined up along the walls. Pasternak's letter was read, and greeted with "anger and indignation." Polikarpov's summary of the meeting for the Central Committee described the letter as "scandalous in its impudence and cynicism."

Twenty-nine writers spoke and the rhetoric became increasingly pitched. The novelist Galina Nikolayeva compared Pasternak to the World War II traitor Gen. Andrei Vlasov who collaborated with the Nazis. "For me it is not enough to expel him from the Writers' Union. This person should not live on Soviet soil."

Nikolayeva later wrote a letter to Pasternak declaring her love for his early poetry but adding that she would not hesitate to "put a bullet through a traitor's head."

"I am a woman who has known much sorrow and I am not a spiteful person, but for treachery such as this, I would not flinch from it," she wrote. Pasternak replied in a letter that said, "You are younger than I, and you will live to see a time when people take a different view of what has happened."

The novelist Vera Panova's speech was "harsh, very direct, hostile." When Gladkov asked her later why she was so vicious she said she panicked, felt like it was 1937 again, and had to protect her large family.

Nikolai Chukovsky, Kornei's son, also spoke at the meeting. "There is one good thing in this whole, shameful story—Pasternak has finally taken off his mask and openly acknowledged that he is our enemy. So let us deal with him as we always deal with our enemies."

Chukovsky's younger sister, Lydia, was appalled when she heard about his participation. She recalled in her diary that since her brother had tasted success with his novel *Baltic Skies* he increasingly had found his sister's outspokenness "sharp, ill-considered, or even dangerous for him." Nikolai wanted to protect his career in the Soviet literary bureaucracy; Chukovsky had recently set up the translators' section of the writers' union.

The meeting dragged on for hours and some writers slipped out to smoke and argue. Alexander Tvardovsky, known as a liberal editor at *Novy Mir,* was sitting under the painting entitled *Gorky Reading "The Girl and the Death" in the Presence of Stalin, Molotov and Voroshilov* when he was approached by Vadim Kozhevnikov, the editor-in-chief of the journal *Znamya.*

He teased Tvardovsky.

"Well, Sasha, tell me, didn't you want to publish that novel?"

"That was before my time," Tvardovsky replied. "But the former board did not want it either, and you know it. . . . Get out of here!"

"Why should I?"

"Because you lack conscience and honor."

"Why do I lack conscience and honor?"

"Go [to hell]."

A gloomy-faced Polikarpov also prowled the halls. He seemed uncertain if expulsion from the Union of Soviet Writers was the correct punishment. And a number of writers—Tvardovsky, Sergei Smirnov, and Konstantin Vanshenkin—told him they were opposed.

Both Smirnov and Nikolai Rylenkov would regret their dissent and would forcibly condemn Pasternak in the coming days.

The vote to expel Pasternak was "unanimous," according to the official record, and a long, formal resolution stated that "the novel *Doctor Zhivago,* around which a propaganda uproar has been centered, only reveals the author's immeasurable self-conceit coupled with a dearth of ideas; it is the cry of a frightened philistine, offended and terrified by the fact that history did not follow the crooked path that he would have liked to allot it. The idea of the novel is false and paltry, fished out of a rubbish heap. . . .

"Bearing in mind Pasternak's political and moral downfall, his betrayal of the Soviet Union, socialism, peace and progress, which was rewarded with the Nobel Prize for the sake of fanning the cold war, the presidium of the board of the Union of Writers . . . strip Boris Pasternak of the title of Soviet writer and expel him from the Union of Writers of the USSR."

Pasternak and Ivinskaya were now being followed by the KGB. The agents made no secret of their presence and harassed the couple—sometimes pretending to hold drunken parties outside Ivinskaya's apartment on Popatov Street. "Good day to you, microphone," said Pasternak when he entered Ivinskaya's room in Peredelkino. She recalled: "We spoke mostly in whispers, frightened of our own shadows, and constantly glancing sideways at the walls—even they seemed hostile to us." Pasternak took solace in small gestures of kindness like the postman who greeted him as always despite the secret policemen parked nearby.

On Tuesday morning, Lydia Chukovskaya went to see Pasternak. As she walked from her father's house, she saw four men sitting in a car, watching her. "To my shame, I have to say that fear already touched me." When she approached Pasternak's gate she expected to hear someone shout stop.

"Did they expel me?" asked Pasternak.

Chukovskaya nodded.

Pasternak took her inside and sat with her in the piano room.

"In the bright morning light, I saw his yellow face, with his shining eyes, and his old man's neck."

Pasternak began to talk with his usual fervor, jumping from subject to subject, and interrupting himself with questions.

"What do you think, will they also hurt Lyonya?" he asked, speaking of his son.

Pasternak told Chukovskaya that the Ivanovs had warned him to move into the city because they were afraid the dacha would be stoned by protesters.

He jumped up and stood in front of Chukovskaya. "But that's nonsense, isn't it? Their imagination has run away with them?"

"Right," said Chukovskaya, "pure nonsense. How is that possible?"

Chukovskaya, trying to change the subject, mentioned a recent poem by Pasternak.

"Poems are unimportant," he replied a little peevishly. "I don't understand why people busy themselves with my verses. I always feel awkward when your dad pays attention to this nonsense. The only thing worthwhile that I have done in my life is the novel. And it's not true that people only value the novel because of politics. That's a lie. They read it because they love it."

In his voice, she heard "something dry, something troubled, something more restless than in his usual impassioned speech."

Outside, in the quiet of the morning, Pasternak glanced around. "Strange," he said, "there is nobody there, yet it feels as though everybody is watching us."

Later that day, Pasternak went over to see Ivinskaya, who had come out from Moscow with her teenage son, Mitya. His mood had darkened and Pasternak spoke in a tremble. "I cannot stand this business anymore," he said to Olga and her son. "I think it's time to leave this life, it's too much."

Pasternak suggested that he and Olga take a fatal dose of Nembutal, a barbiturate.

"It will cost them very dearly," he said. "It will be a slap in the face."

Mitya went outside after listening to this plan to have his mother commit suicide. "Mitya, forgive me, don't think too badly of me, my precious child, for taking your mother with me, but we can't live, and it will be easier for you after our death."

The boy was pale with shock but obedient. "You are right, Boris Leonidovich. Mother must do what you do."

Ivinskaya, who had no desire to kill herself, told Pasternak that his death would suit the authorities.

"It shows we were weak and knew we were wrong, and they will gloat over us into the bargain," she said.

Ivinskaya asked him for time to see what the authorities wanted, and if there was no way out then, she said, "we'll put an end to it." Pasternak agreed. "Very well, go wherever it is today . . . and we'll decide then. I cannot stand up anymore to this hounding."

After Pasternak left, Ivinskaya and her son walked through a nasty sleet to Fedin's house. The roads were soft with slush, and by the time they reached their destination they were soaking wet and trailing mud. Initially, Fedin's daughter wouldn't let them beyond the hallway, but her father eventually appeared on the landing above and told Ivinskaya to come up to his study. She told him that Pasternak was contemplating suicide. "Tell me: what do they want from him? Do they really want him to commit suicide?"

Fedin walked over to the window, and Ivinskaya thought she saw tears in his eyes.

But when he turned around he had adopted his official manner: "Boris Leonidovich has dug such an abyss between himself and us that it cannot be crossed," he said.

"You have told me a terrible thing," he continued. "You realize, don't you, that you must restrain him. He must not inflict a second blow on his country."

Ivinskaya said she was looking for a way out and was "willing to write any letter to whomever, and convince Pasternak to sign it."

Fedin wrote a note to Polikarpov about Ivinskaya's visit. "I think you should be aware of the real or imaginary, serious or theatrical intention of Pasternak. You should know there is such a threat, or maybe it is an attempt to maneuver."

The following morning, Pasternak and Ivinskaya spoke by phone and argued. Ivinskaya accused him of being selfish. "Of course, they won't harm you," she said, "but I'll come off worse."

That same morning, Pasternak's brother drove him into the Central Telegraph Office near the Kremlin. He sent a second telegram, in French, to Stockholm: "Considering the meaning this award has been given in the society to which I belong, I must reject this undeserved prize which has been presented to me. Please do not receive my voluntary rejection with displeasure—Pasternak."

The Swedish Academy responded that it "has received your refusal with deep regret, sympathy and respect." It was only the third time a Nobel award had been rejected. Three German scientists had refused the prize on Hitler's orders. The German dictator had been infuriated when Carl von Ossietzky, who was in a concentration camp, was awarded the peace prize in 1935, and Hitler decreed that in the future no German could accept a Nobel Prize.

Pasternak sent a second telegram to the Central Committee informing the Kremlin of his decision and asking the authorities to allow Ivinskaya, who had been blackballed by official publishers, to work again.

Pasternak told a Western reporter: "I made the decision quite alone. I did not consult anybody. I have not even told my good friends."

The strain was now beginning to show. Pasternak's son Yevgeni was shocked when he saw his father later that day. Pasternak was "grey and disheveled," he later wrote.

"My father was unrecognizable."

Ivinskaya met Polikarpov and he told her that she had to stay by Pasternak's side and prevent him from getting any "silly ideas into his head." (The Central Committee also dispatched a nurse to Pasternak's dacha to keep watch over him; the nurse was told she was not wanted, but she refused to leave and was eventually set up with a cot in the drawing room.)

"This whole scandal must be settled—which we will be able to do with your help," Polikarpov told Ivinskaya. "You can help him find his way back to the people again. But if anything happens to him, the responsibility will be yours."

The decision to reject the Nobel Prize brought no respite, however. In fact, it was treated as an act of spite by a man who was expected to surrender and make no attempt to control events. "This is an even dirtier provocation," said Smirnov, reversing his support for Pasternak. The refusal of the prize, he said, "carries treachery still further."

Chapter 12

"Pasternak's name spells war."

The evening before Pasternak sent the telegram to Stockholm rejecting the prize, Vladimir Semichastny, the head of Komsomol, the youth wing of the Communist Party, was summoned to a meeting with Khrushchev at the Kremlin. The Soviet leader was waiting in his office with Mikhail Suslov, the party's enforcer of ideological purity.

Khrushchev remarked that Semichastny was making a major speech the following evening and told him he wanted to include a section on Pasternak. Semichastny said that something on the Nobel controversy might not be suited to the speech, which was supposed to celebrate the fortieth anniversary of the Komsomol organization.

"We'll find a place where it fits," said Khrushchev, who called in a stenographer. Khrushchev dictated several pages of notes, and goosed up the speech with a string of insults. He promised Semichastny that he would visibly applaud when he reached the passage about Pasternak. "Everyone will understand it," Khrushchev said. The following evening, on October 29, Semichastny spoke before twelve thousand young people at the Sports Palace in Moscow. The address was broadcast live on television and on the radio.

"As the Russian proverb goes, every flock has its mangy sheep," said Semichastny as Khrushchev beamed in the background. "We have such a mangy sheep in our socialist society in the person of Pasternak, who appeared with his slanderous work. . . . And this man has lived in our country and been better provided for than the average workman who worked, labored and fought. Now this man has gone and spat in the people's face. What can we call this? Sometimes, incidentally, we talk about a pig and say this, that or the other about it quite undeservedly. I must say this is a calumny on the pig. As everybody who has anything to do with this animal knows, one of the peculiarities of the pig is that it never makes a mess where it eats or sleeps. Therefore if we compare Pasternak with a pig, then we must say that a pig will never do what he has done. Pasternak, this man who considers himself amongst the best representatives of society, has fouled the spot where he ate and cast filth on those by whose labor he lives and breathes."

Semichastny was interrupted by repeated bursts of applause. He then issued the threat Pasternak feared most: "Why shouldn't this internal emigrant breathe the capitalist air which he so yearned for and which he spoke of in his book? I am sure our society would welcome that. Let him become a real emigrant and go to his capitalist paradise. I am sure that neither society nor the government would hinder him in any way—on the contrary, they would consider that his departure from our midst would clear the air."

The following morning, Pasternak read accounts of Semichastny's speech. He discussed the possibility of emigrating with his wife. She said that in order to live in peace he could go. Pasternak was surprised and asked, "With you and Lyonya?" referring to his son.

"Not in my life, but I wish you all the best and hope you'll spend your last years in honor and peace," said Zinaida. "Lyonya and I will have to denounce you, but you'll understand, that is just a formality."

"If you refuse to go abroad with me, I will not go, never," said Pasternak.

Pasternak also spoke to Ivinskaya, and wrote and tore up a note to the government requesting permission for Ivinskaya and her family to emigrate with him. Pasternak felt completely tied to Russia, and, in any case, he again found it impossible to choose between his two families. "I must have the work-a-day life I know here, the birch trees, the familiar troubles—even the familiar harassments."

Ivinskaya feared Pasternak might be given no choice. And she continued to try to wheedle some form of compromise. She went to see Grigori Khesin, who headed the "author's rights" section of the writers' union. He had always treated Ivinskaya well and had long declared his admiration for Pasternak. But his agreeability had vanished and he greeted his guest coldly.

"What are we to do?" asked Ivinskaya. "There is this dreadful speech by Semichastny. What are we to do?"

"Olga Vsevolodovna," replied Khesin, "there is now no further advice for us to give you. . . . There are certain things one cannot forgive—for the country's sake. No, I'm afraid I cannot give you any advice."

As Ivinskaya left, slamming the door behind her, she was approached by a young copyright lawyer, Isidor Gringolts, who said he would like to help. Gringolts described himself as an admirer of Pasternak: "For me, Boris Leonidovich is a saint!" Ivinskaya, desperate for any help, didn't question his gushing solicitousness. They agreed to meet two hours later at the apartment of Ivinskaya's mother. When Gringolts arrived he suggested that Pasternak write directly to Khrushchev to avoid being expelled from the country, and he offered to help draft a letter.

Ivinskaya called together her daughter, Irina, and some of Pasternak's close friends, and they debated the merits of a direct appeal to Khrushchev. The campaign seemed increasingly sinister—Pasternak was receiving threatening letters, and there were rumors that the house in Peredelkino would be sacked by a mob. One night a group of local thugs threw stones at the dacha and shouted anti-Semitic abuse. After Semichastny's speech, a demonstration of workers and young Communists outside Pasternak's home threatened to get out of hand, and police reinforcements were called to the scene.

Khesin of the writers' union had also informed Ivinskaya that unless Pasternak showed remorse he would be expelled from the country.

"It seemed clear to me that we had to give in," said Ivinskaya, who rejected her daughter Irina's defiant insistence that Pasternak should never apologize. Ivinskaya's stance was supported by the chain-smoking Ariadna Efron, the poet Tsvetaeva's daughter. Efron had just returned to Moscow after sixteen years in the camps and exile; she didn't think a letter would achieve much, but thought it couldn't hurt.

The group reworked the text prepared by Gringolts to make it sound more like Pasternak. A draft of the letter was brought to Pasternak in Peredelkino by Irina and Koma Ivanov. He met them at the gate of the dacha. "What do you think, with whom will I be expelled?" he asked. "My thought is: in Russian history, those who lived in exile meant a great deal more to the country: Herzen, Lenin."

The three walked down to the village post office, where Pasternak had a long telephone conversation with Ivinskaya. He agreed to review the letter and made only one change—adding that he was tied to Russia by birth, not to the Soviet Union. He signed a few blank pages in case his friends needed to make further revisions. His willingness to resist was draining away:

Dear Nikita Sergeyevich,

I am addressing you personally, the Central Committee of the Communist Party of the Soviet Union, and the Soviet Government.

From Comrade Semichastny's speech I learn that the government would not put any obstacles in the way of my departure from the USSR.

For me this is impossible. I am tied to Russia by birth, by life and by work.

I cannot conceive of my destiny separate from Russia, or outside it. Whatever my mistakes and failings, I could not imagine that I should find myself at the center of such a political campaign as has been worked up around my name in the West.

Once aware of this, I informed the Swedish Academy of my voluntary renunciation of the Nobel Prize.

Departure beyond the borders of my country would
for me be tantamount to death and I therefore request
you not to take this extreme measure against me.
With my hand on my heart, I can say that
I have done something for Soviet literature,
and may still be of service to it.

B. Pasternak

Irina and a friend brought the letter to the Central Committee building on the Old Square that night. They asked a guard smoking in the shadows of the entryway where they could hand in a letter for Khrushchev.

"Who is it from?" asked the guard.

"Pasternak," replied Irina.

The guard took the letter.

At noon the following day, the virulence of the offensive reached something of a climax inside Cinema House, a classic piece of constructivist architecture near the writers' union. About eight hundred writers from the Moscow branch of the union crowded into the main theater to discuss the single agenda item—"the conduct of B. Pasternak." The meeting was designed to rubber-stamp Pasternak's expulsion from the Union of Soviet Writers and, in the wake of Semichastny's speech, echo his call for Pasternak's expulsion to the West. Attendance was mandatory and the brave simply called in sick. There was already a heaving, moblike atmosphere when Sergei Smirnov opened the meeting. Smirnov spoke at great length and recapped the usual charges against Pasternak: remoteness from the people, the mediocre prose of his shocking novel, and his treachery in colluding with foreigners. "He sent the manuscript to the Italian publisher Feltrinelli, who is a renegade and a deserter from the progressive camp, and you know that there is no worse enemy than the renegade and that the renegade nurses an especially strong hatred for the thing that he has betrayed." At times Smirnov's blustering indignation stretched to the almost comic: "A Nobel Prize went to the fascist-inclined French writer Camus, who is very little known in France and who is morally the kind of person that no decent person would ever sit by."

Murmurs of approval rippled through the crowd and some chorused: "Shame!"

The speech's defining element was not the outrage but the undercurrents of jealousy and long-standing resentment that surfaced in Smirnov's mocking tone and his attempt to imitate Pasternak's way of talking. The myth of Pasternak was fostered by his small group of friends, Smirnov said, and it was one "of an entirely apolitical poet, a child in politics, who understands nothing and is locked away in his castle of 'pure art' where he turns out his talented works. . . . From this coterie, this narrow circle around Pasternak we have heard 'oohs' and 'ahs' about his talent and his greatness in literature. Let us not hide the fact that there have been people among Pasternak's friends who have stated at meetings that when Pasternak's name is spoken, people should stand."

The meeting ran for five hours, and Smirnov was merely the first of fourteen speakers. And they included some surprising names. When Yevtushenko saw that the poet Boris Slutsky, who had solicited Pasternak's opinion on his verse earlier that summer, was scheduled to speak, he warned him to be careful, fearing he would defend Pasternak, rile the crowd, and hurt himself.

"Don't worry," Slutsky replied. "I shall know how to make my point."

Slutsky had only recently been admitted to the Union of Soviet Writers, and he felt that his budding career would be ruined if he didn't speak out against Pasternak. He kept his speech short and avoided the violent language of some of the other speakers. "A poet's obligation is to seek the recognition of his own people, not of his enemies," he said. "This year's Nobel Prize winner could almost be called the winner of the Nobel Prize against Communism. It is a disgrace for a man who has grown up in our country to bear such a title."

In private, Slutsky was angry with Pasternak. He felt he had damaged the possibilities for the "young literature" emerging after Stalin's death. Over time he was haunted by his participation. "That I spoke against Pasternak is my shame," he said years later.

The chairman of the meeting, Smirnov, also said that the "blot" on himself for his attack could "never be washed away." But in a bitter exchange of letters with Yevtushenko in the 1980s, another speaker, Vladimir Soloukhin, said that Pasternak's supporters, who remained silent, were as culpable as those who spoke against him. Yevtushenko, who attended the meeting, was approached about speaking, but refused.

"Let's agree that all of us, all 14 people, were cowards, time-servers, lickspittles, traitors and bastards who will never 'clear themselves,'" wrote Soloukhin. He asked where Pasternak's friends were, among the hundreds in the room. "Why did they keep silent? Not a single sound, not a single move. Why? Not a single exclamation or remark or word in defense of the poet."

Yevtushenko replied that "for 30 years, this sin of yours, Vladimir Alexeyevich, has lain safely hidden. . . .

"But glasnost, like spring waters, has dissolved the shroud of secrecy and your old guilt comes to light like the arm of a murdered child emerges from the snow when it begins to melt," Yevtushenko continued. "I have never considered my refusal as heroism. However, is there no difference between direct participation in a crime and refusal to participate?"

Most of the speakers, in contrast to Slutsky, wielded the knife with striking vehemence. Korneli Zelinsky, the literary scholar who taught at the Gorky Literary Institute, was once a friend of Pasternak's, but his speech was "particularly vile." At Pasternak's request, he had chaired one of his recitals at the Polytechnic Museum in 1932 and had written about Pasternak's work over the years, generally favorably. He had described Pasternak as a "dacha-dweller of genius" and said some of the poems in the collection *Second Birth* would "always remain in Russian poetry . . . as masterpieces of intimate lyric poetry." After the war, Zelinsky attended one of the first readings of *Doctor Zhivago* at the dacha in Peredelkino.

Zelinsky told the audience that he had gone through the novel the previous year with "a fine-tooth comb." He had been involved in the negotiations that led to a contract in early 1957 to bring out an abridged version of the book in the Soviet Union. And Zelinsky had expressed some mild concerns about the novel's remoteness from contemporary themes in the summer of 1958 in an interview with Radio Warsaw. Perhaps it was his involvement with Pasternak's work that led him to speak with such venom.

"I was left with a feeling of great heaviness after reading" *Doctor Zhivago,* Zelinsky told the audience. "I felt as though I had been literally spat upon. The whole of my life seemed to be defiled in the novel. . . . I have no wish to spell out all the evil-smelling nastiness which leaves such a bad taste. It was very strange for me to see Pasternak, the poet and artist, sink to such a level. But what we have subsequently learned has revealed in full the underlying truth, that terrible traitorous philosophy and that pervasive taint of treachery.

"You ought to know, comrades, that Pasternak's name in the West where I have just been is now synonymous with war. Pasternak is a standard-bearer of the cold war. It is not mere chance that the most reactionary, monarchistic, rabid circles have battened upon his name. . . . I repeat that Pasternak's name spells war. It heralds the cold war."

After Zelinsky spoke, he approached Konstantin Paustovsky, one of the grand old men of Russian letters, who turned away in disgust and refused to shake his hand.

Smirnov moved to end the meeting with thirteen more writers waiting in the wings to speak. The crowd was exhausted. After a show of hands, Smirnov announced that the resolution was adopted unanimously. "Not true! Not unanimously! I voted against!" shouted a woman who pushed her way to the front of the crowd as others headed for the exits. The lone dissenter, a Gulag survivor, was Anna Alliluyeva, Stalin's sister-in-law.

The pillorying of Pasternak was front-page news around the world. Correspondents in Moscow reported in detail on the media campaign, the expulsion from the Union of Soviet Writers, the acceptance and rejection of the Nobel Prize, and the threat of exile. Editorialists weighed in on the startling virulence of the assault on a solitary writer. In an editorial headlined "Pasternak and the Pygmies," *The New York Times* declared, "In the fury, venom and intensity of this reaction there is much that is illuminating. Superficially the Soviet leaders are strong. At their command are hydrogen bombs and intercontinental ballistic missiles, large armies and fleets of mighty bombers and warships. Against them is one elderly man who is completely helpless before the physical power of the Kremlin. Yet such is the moral authority of Pasternak, so vividly does he symbolize the conscience of an outraged Russia striking back at its tormentors, that it is the men in the Kremlin who tremble."

In the *St. Louis Post-Dispatch,* the cartoonist Bill Mauldin created a Pulitzer Prize–winning image of Pasternak as a ragged Gulag prisoner wearing a ball and chain and chopping wood in the snow with another inmate. The caption read: "I won the Nobel Prize for Literature. What was your crime?"

The French newspaper *Dimanche* described the literary crisis as "an intellectual Budapest" for Khrushchev.

The Swedes issued their own rebuke. On October 27, the Lenin Peace Prize was presented in Stockholm to the poet Artur Lundkvist. Three members of the Swedish Academy who had been scheduled to attend, including Österling, boycotted the event. A string quartet that was booked to perform refused to play, and a florist sent wilting flowers in protest.

Bewilderment at the treatment of Pasternak only increased when three Soviet scientists won the Nobel Prize for Physics. The award was celebrated in Moscow as a national achievement; Western correspondents were invited to meet two of the winners at the Russian Academy of Sciences, where they discussed their research into atomic particles—and their hobbies and home life. The Soviet press was forced into some contortions in logic to explain the contrasting coverage of the different Nobel Prizes, often on the same pages. *Pravda* explained that while the award in science illustrated "the recognition by the Swedish Academy of Sciences of the major merits of Russian and Soviet scientists . . . the award of this prize for literature was prompted entirely for political motives." Bourgeois scientists "were capable of objectivity," the newspaper concluded, but the assessment of literary works is "entirely under the influence of the ideology of the dominant class."

Feltrinelli was in Hamburg when the loud disparagement of his writer began, and he immediately began to use his contacts in publishing to rally writers in defense of Pasternak. Literary societies from Mexico to India issued statements as the drama unfolded. A group of prominent writers, including T. S. Eliot, Stephen Spender, Somerset Maugham, E. M. Forster, Graham Greene, J. B. Priestley, Rebecca West, Bertrand Russell, and Aldous Huxley, sent a telegram to the Union of Soviet Writers to protest. "We are profoundly anxious about the state of one of the world's great poets and writers, Boris Pasternak. We consider his novel, *Doctor Zhivago,* a moving personal testimony and not a political document. We appeal to you in the name of the great Russian literary tradition for which you stand not to dishonor it by victimizing a writer revered throughout the whole civilized world." PEN, the international association of writers, sent its own message, saying the organization was "very distressed by rumors concerning Pasternak" and demanded protection for the poet by maintaining the conditions for creative freedom. "Writers throughout the world are thinking of him fraternally."

Radio Liberation solicited messages of support for broadcast from Upton Sinclair, Isaac Bashevis Singer, William Carlos Williams, Lewis Mumford, Pearl Buck, and Gore Vidal, among others. Ernest Hemingway said he would give Pasternak a house if he was expelled. "I want to create for him the conditions he needs to carry on with his writing," said Hemingway. "I can understand how divided Boris must be in his own mind right now. I know how deeply, with all his heart, he is attached to Russia. For a genius such as Pasternak, separation from his country would be a tragedy. But if he comes to us we shall not disappoint him. I shall do everything in my modest power to save this genius for the world. I think of Pasternak every day."

The controversy reinvigorated sales of the novel across Europe, and in the United States, where it was published in September, the novel finally hit the top of *The New York Times* bestseller list, dislodging *Lolita*. The book had already sold seventy thousand copies in the United States in its first six weeks. "That is fantastic," his publisher Kurt Wolff wrote. The Nobel controversy boosted sales of an already successful book to rare heights. "You have moved beyond the history of literature into the history of mankind," Wolff concluded in a letter to Pasternak toward the end of the year. "Your name has become a household word throughout the world."

The U.S. secretary of state John Foster Dulles told reporters that Pasternak's refusal of the Nobel Prize was forced on the writer by the Soviet authorities. "The system of international communism," he said, "insists on conformity not only in deed but in thought. Anything a little out of line, they try to stamp out."

The U.S. embassy in Moscow cautioned the State Department against official involvement, and senior officials in Washington said relatively little; instead they relished what they saw as a propaganda coup for the West that was entirely manufactured in Moscow. At a meeting of Dulles's senior staff, he was told that "the communists' treatment of Pasternak is one of their worst blunders. It is on par in terms of embarrassment and damage to them with the brutality in Hungary." Dulles told his staff to explore the possibility of covertly subsidizing publication of the novel in the Far East and the Middle East; presumably he knew that his brother, the head of the CIA, had already organized a Russian edition as they both served on the Operations Control Board. State Department officials were told to coordinate their publication efforts with the "other agency," government-speak for the CIA.

Dulles told his senior staff that he hadn't had a chance to read the book but "supposed he would have to do so." He asked if the novel was damaging to the Communist cause. Abbott Washburn, deputy director of the United States Information Agency, said, "It was because it reveals the stifling of an individual under the oppressive communist system and that the very suppression of the book shows that the communist leaders regard it as injurious." Others at the meeting argued that *Doctor Zhivago* was not particularly anti-Communist but "that the treatment received by the author was the real pay dirt for us."

At first, the CIA also concluded that it should not overplay its hand. Director Allen Dulles said agency assets, including Radio Liberation, should give "maximum factual play" to the Nobel Award "without any propagandistic commentary." Dulles also said the agency should use every opportunity to have Soviet citizens read the novel.

For some within the CIA, Pasternak's plight was another reminder of the West's inability to affect events inside the Soviet Union and Eastern Europe. "Reactions of revulsion and shock cannot conceal from Free World consciousness the sense of its own impotence to further the cause of liberalization within the Bloc," stated an agency memo sent to Dulles. "Any further attempt on our part to portray the personal ordeal of Pasternak as a triumph of freedom will only, as in the case of Hungary, heighten the tragic irony which informs it."

Dulles was not persuaded. At a meeting of the National Security Council's Operations Control Board a few days later, there was "considerable discussion of the actions which the U.S. has taken and might take to exploit" the Zhivago affair. Earlier, some on Dulles's staff had recommended that CIA assets should be used to "sparkplug" anti-Soviet coverage, and encourage the "leftist press and writers" in the West to express their outrage.

The sound of Western consternation was nothing new in Moscow. Much more troubling for the Soviet Union than the statements of "bourgeois writers" and American officials such as John Foster Dulles was the damage to its reputation among friends and allies, and in parts of the world where it expected a sympathetic hearing.

In Lebanon, the affair was front-page news, and the CIA noted approvingly that in a front-page editorial the newspaper *Al-Binaa* concluded that "free thought and dialectical materialism do not go together." In Morocco, the daily *Al-Alam,* which was rarely critical of the Soviet Union, said, whatever the Soviet Union accuses the West of in the future, it "will never be able to deny its suppression of Pasternak." *The Times* of Karachi described the treatment of the writer as "despicable."

The Brazilian writer Jorge Amado said the expulsion of Pasternak from the writers' union demonstrated that it was still controlled by elements from Stalin's time. The Brazilian paper

Boris Pasternak in 1940. He had survived Stalin's purges and had become disillusioned with the Soviet state.

ABOVE: Boris Pasternak *(left)* and Kornei Chukovsky *(center)*, the critic and children's book writer, at the Tenth Komsomol Conference in 1936. The two were lifelong neighbors in Peredelkino, the writer's colony outside Moscow.

BELOW: The poet Anna Akhmatova with Pasternak in 1946, shortly after Pasternak began writing *Doctor Zhivago*. The two writers were the outstanding, surviving poets of their generation, and devoted friends, but Akhmatova was ambivalent about Pasternak's novel.

Olga Ivinskaya, who met Pasternak in 1946, became his lover and literary agent and was the inspiration, in part, for the character Lara in *Doctor Zhivago*.

Olga Ivinskaya, from a medallion made several years before she met Pasternak

Giangiacomo Feltrinelli first published *Doctor Zhivago* in translation in 1957 and defied both the Italian Communist Party and the Kremlin, which wanted to suppress the novel.

Alexei Surkov, the poet and Soviet literary bureaucrat who attempted to block publication of *Doctor Zhivago* in the West and nursed a deep enmity toward Pasternak

The New York publisher Felix Morrow, who was hired by the CIA to secretly produce a Russian-language edition of *Doctor Zhivago*. Morrow and the agency clashed during the operation.

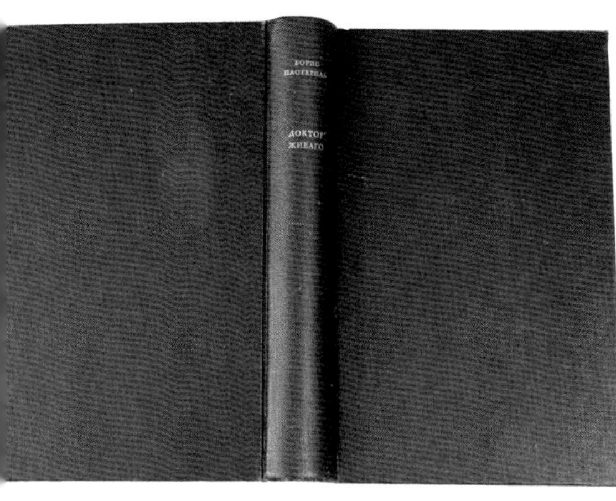

The blue-linen case for the CIA's hardcover edition of *Doctor Zhivago,* which was printed in The Hague by the Dutch publishing house Mouton & Co. A package of 365 copies was sent to Belgium and distributed at the 1958 World's Fair in Brussels.

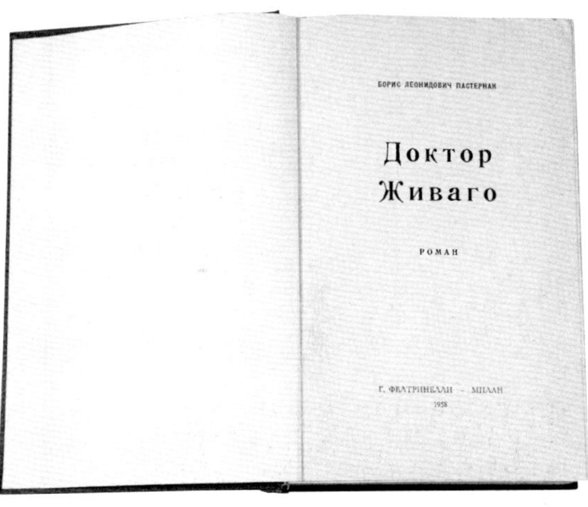

The title page of the CIA's hardcover edition of *Doctor Zhivago* raised suspicions. It acknowledged the copyright of "G. Feltrinelli–Milan," but the name of the publisher was not correctly transcribed into Russian. The use of the writer's full name, Boris Leonidovich Pasternak, also suggested a foreign origin: Russians would not use the patronymic on a title page.

The title page of a 1959 miniature paperback edition of *Doctor Zhivago*. About 10,000 copies were printed at CIA headquarters. A copy is held at the in-house CIA museum in Langley, Virginia.

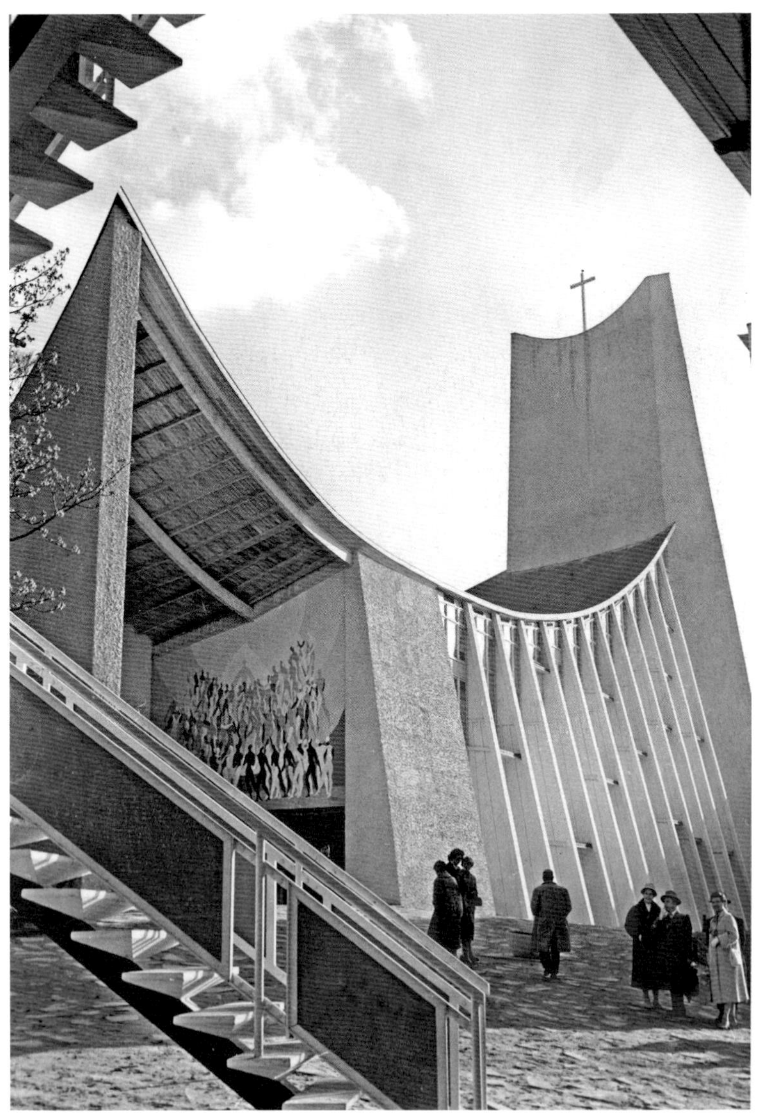

Copies of *Doctor Zhivago* were handed to Soviet visitors from a small hidden library inside the Vatican Pavilion at the 1958 Brussels World's Fair.

Anders Österling was the secretary of the Swedish Academy when it chose Boris Pasternak for the 1958 the Nobel Prize in Literature. Pasternak was forced to turn the prize down after officials in Moscow attacked the Academy's decision as an anti-Soviet provocation.

Pasternak near his home in the countryside outside Moscow, shortly after he learned that he had won the Nobel Prize in Literature

A view of the dacha in the village of Peredelkino, outside Moscow, where Boris Pasternak lived and wrote for several decades. The photo was taken the day after Pasternak's death on May 30, 1960.

Boris Pasternak reads telegrams of congratulations after winning the Nobel Prize in Literature. At right is his wife, Zinaida, and at left is his friend Nina Tabidze, the widow of the Georgian poet Titsian Tabidze, who was killed in the purges.

Olga Ivinskaya and her daughter, Irina, with Pasternak.
They formed a second family for the poet.

The 1958 Pulitzer Prize–winning cartoon by Bill Mauldin. The original caption: "I won the Nobel Prize for literature. What was your crime?"

United Press International

Accompanied by Russian Ambassador Mikhail Menshikov (left), Anastas I. Mikoyan, 63, Deputy Premier of the Soviet Union, looks at volumes in the window of the Reprint Book Shop at 1102-A New York ave. nw., while walking in Washington's business district yesterday. He appears not to notice the red-lettered sign advertising "Dr. Zhivago," the Nobel-prize-winning novel by Russian author Boris Pasternak. The novel, politically embarrassing to the Communists, was not published in the Soviet Union. Another picture and a story of the tour appear on Page B3.

The front page of *The Washington Post* featured senior Soviet official Anastas Mikoyan staring at a bookstore window full of copies of *Doctor Zhivago* during a visit to Washington, D.C., in January 1959.

The casket of Boris Pasternak is carried out of his dacha in Peredelkino.

Pasternak's wife, Zinaida *(foreground, extreme right),* looks down on the body of her husband, while Pasternak's lover, Olga Ivinskaya *(extreme left),* cries. Behind Zinaida, holding her at the waist, is her and Pasternak's son, Leonid.

Boris Pasternak looks out from the upstairs study of his dacha in Peredelkino, 1958.

Última Hora, which had supported good relations with the Soviet Union, called the affair "cultural terrorism."

The Irish playwright Sean O'Casey wrote to *Literaturnaya Gazeta* to protest the decision of the Union of Soviet Writers. "As a friend of your magnificent land since 1917, I would plead for the withdrawal of this expulsion order," he said. "Every artist is something of an anarchist, as Bernard Shaw tells us in one of his prefaces, and the artist should be forgiven many things."

The Icelandic novelist Halldór Laxness, a Nobel laureate and the chairman of the Iceland-Soviet Friendship Society, sent a telegram to Khrushchev: "I implore you as level-headed statesman to use your influence mitigating malicious onslaughts of sectarian intolerance upon an old meritorious Russian poet Boris Pasternak. Why light-heartedly arouse the wrath of the world's poets, writers, intellectuals and socialists against the Soviet Union in this matter? Kindly spare friends of the Soviet Union an incomprehensible and most unworthy spectacle."

"Iceland?" said Pasternak when he learned of the telegram, "Iceland, but if China intervened it would help?"

In fact, the case was drawing major attention in Asia, particularly in India, a nonaligned country that nonetheless had strong ties with the Soviet Union. Prime Minister Jawaharlal Nehru had visited the Soviet Union in 1955 and Khrushchev had traveled to India the following year. The treatment of Pasternak infuriated leading writers in India, including some prominent Communists. And concern about his plight culminated at a press conference in New Delhi when Nehru said Indian opinion had been pained by the daily abuse. "A noted writer, even if he expresses an opinion opposed to the dominating opinion, according to us should be respected and it should be given free play," he told reporters.

The Soviet Union's cultural diplomacy was also being damaged. The Norwegian press demanded that the government abrogate a recently signed cultural-exchange program. Swedish officials threatened to postpone indefinitely a youth-exchange program. Twenty-eight Austrian writers said in an open letter that all future cultural and scientific exchanges should be conditional on Pasternak's complete rehabilitation as a citizen and a writer.

The international backlash was unwelcome and the Kremlin

wanted a way out of the crisis. After receiving Pasternak's letter, Khrushchev ordered a halt. "Enough. He's admitted his mistakes. Stop it." The terms were left to the bureaucracy.

While the writers were fulminating at Cinema House, Polikarpov began maneuvering to end the affair. Khesin, the man who had cold-shouldered Ivinskaya the day before the meeting, phoned her at her mother's apartment, where she had gone to try to get some sleep. (Ivinskaya's movements were clearly being monitored.) Khesin oozed a fake friendliness. "Olga Vsevolodovna, my dear, you're a good girl. They have received the letter from Boris Leonidovich and everything will be all right, just be patient. What I have to say is that we must see you straight away."

Ivinskaya was irritated by the approach, and told Khesin she didn't want to have anything to do with him. Polikarpov came on the line. "We must see you," he said. "We'll drive over to Sobinov Street now, you put on a coat and come down, and we'll go together to Peredelkino. We must bring Boris Leonidovich to Moscow, to the Central Committee, as soon as possible."

Ivinskaya told her daughter to go ahead to alert Pasternak. It seemed to Ivinskaya that if Polikarpov was in such a hurry and willing to go to Peredelkino to fetch Pasternak, it could only mean that Khrushchev would meet the writer. A black government Zil pulled up outside Ivinskaya's mother's apartment building, and Polikarpov and Khesin were inside. The sedan traveled in the middle lane reserved on Moscow streets for select government cars and whisked them to Peredelkino ahead of Irina.

Pasternak was now emotional and fragile, subject to severe mood swings and very much caged in his dacha. Telegrams from well-wishers in the West were piling up on his desk, but at home he felt increasingly isolated and people he thought of as friends were shunning him. When the sculptor Zoya Maslenikova visited Pasternak that Friday around lunchtime, he broke down and wept, his head on the table; the prompt for his tears was a telegram that contained a line from one of his *Zhivago* poems: "To see no distance is lonely."

As Ivinskaya rode with the two men toward Peredelkino, Khesin whispered to her that it was he who had sent Gringolts to her. Ivinskaya gasped at how easily she had been manipulated into getting Pasternak to write a letter to Khrushchev. And now Polikarpov, turning around to face her from the front seat, wanted more. "We're now relying entirely on you," he said. When they arrived in the village, there were already a number of official cars near Pasternak's house, with other officials from the writers' union. Irina, when she arrived, was asked to go to the dacha and get Pasternak; Ivinskaya would not risk meeting Pasternak's wife, but Zinaida tolerated her daughter. Zinaida was frightened by the official hubbub, but Pasternak emerged with a strange cheerfulness. As he got into Polikarpov and Khesin's car, he started to complain that he wasn't wearing a suitable pair of trousers because he, too, concluded that he was to meet Khrushchev. "I'm going to show them," he blustered. "I'll make such a fuss and tell them everything I think—everything." He joked all the way into town, and the mood "was one of almost hysterical gaiety."

At Polikarpov's request, Ivinskaya brought Pasternak to her apartment for a short interlude before they went over to the Central Committee building. When they arrived at the latter, Pasternak went up to the guard and told him he was expected but had no identification except his writers' union card—"the membership card of this union of yours which you've just thrown me out of." And then he continued to be preoccupied with his trousers. "It's all right, it's all right," said the guard, "it doesn't matter, it's quite all right."

There was no meeting with Khrushchev. Pasternak was ushered into a room with Polikarpov, who had freshened up and was acting as if he had been sitting at his desk all day. He rose to his feet and "in a voice befitting a town crier" announced that Pasternak would be allowed "to remain in the Motherland."

But Polikarpov said Pasternak would have to make peace with the Soviet people. "There is nothing we can do at the moment to calm the anger," said Polikarpov. He noted that the following day's issue of *Literaturnaya Gazeta* would include a sampling of this anger.

This was not the meeting Pasternak expected and he erupted in fury. "Aren't you ashamed, Dmitri Alexeyevich? What do you mean 'anger'? You have your human side, I can see, but why do you come out with these stock phrases? 'The people! The people!'—as though it were something you could just produce from your own trouser pockets. You know perfectly well that you really shouldn't use the word 'people' at all."

Polikarpov sucked in his breath to contain himself; the crisis had to be ended and he needed Pasternak's acquiescence. "Now look here, Boris Leonidovich, the whole business is over so let's make things up, and everything will soon be all right again.

"Goodness me, old fellow, what a mess you've landed us in," he continued, coming round to pat Pasternak on the shoulder.

Pasternak recoiled from the intimacy and the reference to an "old fellow."

"Will you kindly drop that tone? You cannot talk to me like that," he said.

"Really now," Polikarpov continued, "here you go sticking a knife in the country's back, and we have to patch it all up."

Pasternak had had it with the accusations of treachery. "I will ask you to take those words back. I do not wish to speak to you anymore."

He headed for the door.

Polikarpov was aghast. "Stop him, stop him, Olga Vsevolodovna."

Ivinskaya, sensing Polikarpov's weakness, told him, "You must take your words back!"

"I do, I do," mumbled Polikarpov.

Pasternak stayed, and the conversation continued in a more civil tone. Polikarpov suggested he would be in touch soon with a plan and quietly told Ivinskaya as she left that another public letter from Pasternak might be necessary.

Pasternak was pleased with his performance. "They are not people but machines," he said. "See how terrible they are, these walls here, and everyone inside them is like an automaton. . . . But all the same I gave them something to worry about—they got what they deserved."

In the car, on the way back to Peredelkino, Pasternak loudly replayed the whole conversation with Polikarpov, ignoring Ivinskaya's warning that the chauffeur was certain to report back on everything that was said.

In a lull, Irina recited some lines from Pasternak's epic poem "Lieutenant Schmidt":

In vain, in years of turmoil,
One seeks a happy ending—
Some are fated to kill—and repent—
While others go to Golgotha . . .
I suppose you never flinch
From wiping out a man.
Ah well, martyrs to your dogma,
You too are victims of the times . . .
I know the stake at which
I'll die will be the boundary mark
Between two different epochs,
And I rejoice at being so elect.

Pasternak fell silent. A very long Friday had come to an end.

Chapter 13

"I am lost like a beast in an enclosure."

The wrath of the people appeared under the headline "Rage and Indignation: Soviet People Condemn B. Pasternak's Behavior" in *Literaturnaya Gazeta*. Twenty-two letters were spread out over much of a broadsheet page under subheads such as "Beautiful Is Our Reality," "The Word of a Worker," and "Paid Calumny." The excavator operator F. Vasiltsev wondered who this Pasternak was. "I have never heard of him before and I have never read any of his books," he wrote. "This is not a writer but a White Guardist." R. Kasimov, an oil worker, also asked: "Who is Pasternak?" and then dismissed his work as "aesthetic verse in obscure language incomprehensible to the people."

Lydia Chukovskaya assumed that the letters were the creations of the editors, and she said she could just imagine "a wench from the editorial board" dictating their content. This assessment was unfair; the letters were written by real people, even though some variation on the words "I have not read *Doctor Zhivago* but . . ." appeared in a number of missives and led to much amused mocking among those who sympathized with Pasternak. The newspaper was indeed inundated with letters, about 423 in all between October 25 and December 1, and a clear majority reflected the genuine response of Soviet readers. They had, unsurprisingly, absorbed the unrelenting message of the previous days that Pasternak was a money-grubbing traitor who had stigmatized the revolution and the Soviet Union. This, many readers felt, was not only grievously insulting, but an attack on their achievement in building Soviet society. "The revolution remained central to these people's consciousness and socioethical order, the sacred foundation of a mental universe," said one historian, "and their reaction to the Pasternak affair was above all a defense against any attempt, real or imaginary, to undermine this intellectual cornerstone of their existence."

American psychologists who were visiting the Soviet Union during the attacks on Pasternak found some sympathy for him and demand for the novel, but such sentiments were far from universal. "There was also substantial evidence that many, perhaps the majority, of students in the literary, historical and philosophical faculties of Moscow and Leningrad higher-educational institutions accepted the official line condemning Pasternak as a traitor to Russia," they reported in a summary of their visit. "Acceptance of the official point of view seems to have been based, in part, upon resentment of what was felt to have been exploitation in the West of the Pasternak matter in the interests of anti-Russian propaganda."

At the height of the Nobel crisis, Pasternak was also getting fifty to seventy letters a day, both from Soviet citizens and from abroad. Most offered support—albeit anonymously from his fellow countrymen. Even among the letters to *Novy Mir* there were about 10 percent, mostly from young people, who backed Pasternak's right to publish *Doctor Zhivago* or their right to read the novel. There is some evidence that the editors of *Novy Mir* forwarded letters defending Pasternak to the KGB.

There were also letters that wounded Pasternak. He singled out one that was addressed "To Pasternak from Judas: 'I only betrayed Jesus, but you—you betrayed the whole of Russia.'"

For a time, all of Pasternak's mail was blocked. At his meeting with Polikarpov, Pasternak had demanded that letters and parcels be allowed through, and the following morning the postwoman brought two bags full. The German journalist Gerd Ruge estimated that in all Pasternak received between twenty thousand and thirty thousand letters after the award of the Nobel Prize. His delight in this correspondence, even though it soaked up his time, was expressed in the light poem "God's World":

I return with a bundle of letters
To the house where my joy will prevail.

The letters broke his isolation, reconnected him with old friends in the West, and forged new literary bonds with writers such as T. S. Eliot, Thomas Merton, and Albert Camus. "The great and undeserved happiness bestowed on me at the end of my life is to be in touch with many honorable people in the widest and far world and to engage with them in spontaneous, spiritual and important conversations," he told one correspondent in 1959. He stayed up until two or three in the morning answering these letters, using his dictionaries to help him respond in multiple languages. "I'm troubled by the volume of it and the compulsion to answer it all," he said. There were moments, as he put it in one poem, when he felt he would like to "merge into privacy, like landscape into fog."

He was troubled, too, by the desire of Western admirers to resurrect and publish many of his old poems, work that he felt was often best forgotten. "It is an unspeakable grief and pain for me to be reminded again and again of those scarce grains of life and truth, interspersed with an immensity of dead, schematic nonsense and nonexistent stuff," he told one translator. "I wonder [at] your . . . attempt to rescue the things deservedly doomed to ruin and oblivion." Nor was he happy with some overelaborate interpretations of the novel in the West. He rejected a proposal by Kurt Wolff to publish a collection of critical essays to be called *Monument to Zhivago.* "Didn't the doctor have enough trouble?" Pasternak asked Wolff in a letter. "There can only be one monument: a new book. And I am the only one who can do that."

Along with the appearance of the letters in *Literaturnaya Gazeta,* the Soviet news agency Tass reported on November 1 that should Pasternak wish "to leave the Soviet Union permanently, the Socialist regime and people he has slandered in his anti-Soviet work, *Doctor Zhivago,* will not raise any obstacles.

He can leave the Soviet Union and experience personally 'all the fascinations of the capitalist paradise.' "

Pasternak's wife told a reporter from United Press International the following day that Pasternak was not feeling well and must rest. She said expulsion from the Soviet Union would be the worst thing that could happen to him. "I am going to cook for him as well as I can, and we shall live very quietly here for one year or longer—with no visits or interviews." Like Emma Ernestovna, the housekeeper of Viktor Komarovsky in *Doctor Zhivago,* Zinaida saw herself the "matron of his quiet seclusion," who "managed his household inaudibly, and invisibly, and he repaid her with chivalrous gratitude, natural in such a gentleman."

On November 4, Polikarpov phoned Ivinskaya's apartment while Pasternak was visiting. "We must ask Boris Leonidovich to write an open letter to the people," he informed her. The letter to Khrushchev was insufficient as a public apology. Pasternak immediately began to craft another attempt. It echoed his earlier statements that he always felt the award of the Nobel would be a matter of pride for the Soviet people. When Ivinskaya brought a draft to Polikarpov, he rejected it and said he and Ivinskaya would have to fashion a more acceptable version. "We 'worked' on it like a pair of professional counterfeiters," said Ivinskaya. When she showed the rewritten version of the letter to Pasternak, he "simply waved his hand. He was tired. He just wanted an end to the whole abnormal situation."

The letter, addressed to the editors of *Pravda,* was published on November 6. Pasternak said he voluntarily rejected the Nobel Prize when he saw "the scope of the political campaign around my novel, and realized that this award was a political step, which had now led to monstrous consequences." He said he regretted that he had not heeded the warning from the editors of *Novy Mir* about *Doctor Zhivago.* And Pasternak said he could not accept erroneous interpretations of the novel, including the assertion that the October Revolution was an illegitimate event. Such claims, he wrote (or rather Polikarpov wrote), have been "carried to absurdity. . . .

"In the course of this tempestuous week," the letter continued,

"I have not been persecuted, I have not risked either my life or my freedom, I have risked absolutely nothing."

The letter concluded with "I believe that I shall find the strength to restore my good name and the confidence of my comrades."

Exhaustion and concern for Ivinskaya combined to give the authorities the concession they wanted even though most careful readers of the letter knew it was not from Pasternak's hand. The repeated assertion that he was acting voluntarily stretched the credulity of even *Pravda* readers. But the fact that he signed any letter of contrition disappointed some Russians. In Ryazan, a schoolteacher named Aleksandr Solzhenitsyn "writhed with shame for him"—that he would "demean himself by pleading with the government."

Anna Akhmatova dismissed Pasternak's ordeal as inconsequential compared to what she and Zoshchenko had suffered when they were thrown out of the Union of Soviet Writers in Stalin's time. Pasternak and his family were left untouched in his fine house, she remarked. "The story of Boris is—a battle of butterflies," she told Chukovskaya. Some long-standing tension between Akhmatova and Pasternak had begun to surface. The Leningrad poet smarted from what she felt was Pasternak's lack of homage to her art; she was irritated by his manner, but still loved him and craved his admiration. Akhmatova continued to believe that *Doctor Zhivago* was a bad novel "except for the landscapes," and that Pasternak was too self-satisfied with his martyrdom and his fame. Later in the year, when the two met at a birthday party in Peredelkino, Akhmatova commented, "Boris spoke the whole time only about himself, about the letters he was receiving. . . . Then for a long time, in a totally boring way, he played the coquette when they asked him to read. After I read, he asked me, shouting across the table: 'What do you do with your poetry? Pass it around to your friends?' "

Akhmatova recalled visiting the composer Dmitri Shostakovich at his summer home in Komarovo outside Leningrad. "I looked at him and thought: he carries his fame like a hunchback, used to it from birth. But Boris—like a crown which just fell down over his eyes, and he shoves it back in place with his elbow."

The *Pravda* letter was a tactical retreat; Pasternak still had to support two households. The authorities in return for Pasternak's signature agreed to restore his and Ivinskaya's ability to earn a living through translation work; Polikarpov also said that a second edition of Pasternak's translation of *Faust* would be published. He lied. That winter, Pasternak was unable to earn any money. His translation of *Maria Stuart* by Juliusz Słowacki, which was about to be published, was suspended; the production of Shakespeare and Schiller plays that he had translated was stopped; and no new translation work was commissioned. In January he wrote to the Soviet copyright agency to ask what had happened to payments he was scheduled to receive and he also wrote to Khrushchev to complain that he couldn't even participate in the "harmless profession" of translation. He even suggested to the copyright agency that it could get his royalties in exchange for fees owed to Western writers who were published in the Soviet Union but not paid, such as Hemingway. The Soviet Union did not pay for the Western books it translated and published until 1967, when it entered into an international copyright agreement.

On paper, Pasternak was a wealthy man. Feltrinelli had been depositing payments from publishers around the world into a Swiss bank account, and both the CIA and the Kremlin speculated that Pasternak was already a millionaire. Accessing some of that money would bring relief, but also more heartache and tragedy. Pasternak realized his wealth was a poisoned chalice and that if he sought permission to transfer it to Moscow, he would face "the perpetual accusation of treacherously living off foreign capital." He did tell his publisher in February to disburse $112,000 in gifts of various sizes to his friends, translators, and family in the West. But initially he expressed some indifference about his fortune, telling Feltrinelli, "The fact that I am completely lacking in curiosity regarding the various details and how much it all amounts to must not amaze or hurt you."

The pinch of no income eventually began to hurt. "Their desire to drown me is so great I can see nothing but this desire," Pasternak said. And he expressed bewilderment at his predicament. "Have I really done insufficient in this life not to have at seventy the possibility of feeding my family?" He began to borrow money, first from his housekeeper and then friends. In late December he asked Valeria Prishvina, the widow of the writer Mikhail Prishvin, if he could borrow 3,000 rubles, about $300, until the end of 1959. Early in January, he borrowed 5,000 rubles from Kornei Chukovsky, who presumed it was for Ivinskaya. His neighbor found Pasternak older. "His cheeks are sunken but no matter: he's full of life." Chukovsky told him he hadn't slept in three months because of what Pasternak had endured. "Well, I'm sleeping fine," Pasternak responded.

He told Ivinskaya the following month, "We must put our financial affairs, both yours and mine, in order." Pasternak asked Gerd Ruge, the German correspondent, if he could get him some cash that would be paid back from the money held in the West by Feltrinelli. Ruge gathered about $8,000 worth of rubles at the West German embassy from Russians of ethnic German origin who had been granted permission to emigrate but could take no money with them. Ruge took their cash in exchange for the payment of deutsche marks when they reached Germany. The German journalist handed Ivinskaya's daughter a package of cash when the two brushed by each other at the metro station Oktyabrskaya in a prearranged piece of amateur spycraft.

Pasternak seemed to realize the danger Ivinskaya and her family faced when he involved them in these secretive efforts to get money. He alerted his French translator, Jacqueline de Proyart, that if he wrote to her and told her he had scarlet fever, it meant that Ivinskaya had been arrested and she should raise the alarm in the West.

In April, Pasternak asked Polikarpov if he could get permission to receive money held by his Norwegian publishers, and he offered to donate part of the royalties to a fund for writers in need. "You know that as of this moment, I have not received one single penny of what is owed to me in royalties from the foreign editions of my novel," Pasternak said.

The authorities, unmoved, warned him not to accept any money held in Western banks, and forced him to sign a letter renouncing the funds. When Ivinskaya complained that Pasternak and she had nothing to live on, Polikarpov replied ambiguously, "It wouldn't be so bad if they even brought you your money in a sack as long as Pasternak quiets down."

Feltrinelli also sent in seven or eight packages, or "rolls" (*Brötchen*) as they called them, amounting to about 100,000 rubles with another German journalist, Heinz Schewe, who had become friends with Pasternak and Ivinskaya and worked for *Die Welt*. At the end of 1959, Pasternak asked Feltrinelli to turn over $100,000 to D'Angelo, who had written to the author to tell him he could purchase rubles in the West and safely smuggle the cash into the Soviet Union.

The average annual income of a Soviet citizen at this time was about 12,000 rubles. Under the official exchange rate, which bore no relation to the black market, one dollar in early 1959 would buy ten rubles. This money smuggling was all well-intentioned but reckless. Pasternak and his circle were still being watched, as were all foreigners in touch with him. Pasternak's Western friends, riven by their own interests and jealousies, wanted to please him. The KGB was monitoring the various streams of cash, and biding its time.

In 1959, Pasternak was caught in another imbroglio, partly of his own making—a bitter business dispute between Feltrinelli and Jacqueline de Proyart. A Radcliffe College graduate who had traveled to Moscow in late 1956 to perfect her Russian at Moscow State University, de Proyart happened to read a manuscript copy of *Doctor Zhivago*, and some Russian friends brought her to see Pasternak on the evening of January 1, 1957. Pasternak had invited them to share leftovers from the New Year's feast; earlier he had had dinner with Akhmatova, Voznesensky, the Neigauzes, and Ariadna Efron, among other friends. Pasternak was thrilled at the presence of a young Frenchwoman—de Proyart was just shy of thirty—and the evening stretched out pleasantly. Pasternak talked about Paris, which he had visited in 1935 for the Congress of Writers in Defense of Culture; about Stalin and the Leader's wife; and about Mandelstam.

The conversation turned to *Doctor Zhivago*. Pasternak asked his guests if they had detected the influence of any Russian writers on his novel. "Leo Tolstoy," said someone, but it was not the answer Pasternak was looking for. He turned to de Proyart, who risked, "Chekhov."

"Magnificent!" cried Pasternak. "You've guessed correctly."

It seemed to de Proyart that Pasternak's willingness to trust her turned on that single answer. They met several more times in January and February. Pasternak showed her his contract with Feltrinelli, and de Proyart expressed reservations about allowing such a young publisher, who didn't speak Russian, to control the novel's destiny. Pasternak gave de Proyart a handwritten literary power of attorney—a decision that could only bewilder and infuriate Feltrinelli.

De Proyart would eventually attempt to assert control over any Russian edition of *Doctor Zhivago,* the publication of some of Pasternak's earlier works, and, armed with a fresh letter from Pasternak, the management of all of his royalties. Feltrinelli felt betrayed. "To find myself bereft of your trust, of the support of your authority, is an unexpected surprise, and an extremely painful one." Pasternak envisioned de Proyart as an aesthetic companion to Feltrinelli's publishing acumen, but the two despised each other and much of 1959 was spent in painful correspondence, disentangling the mess. "I have confused the issue beyond measure," he told them in a joint letter. "Forgive me, therefore, both of you." The confusion was compounded by the difficulty of getting letters in and out of Peredelkino. To discuss publishing and financial matters both Pasternak and his closest Western friends often used trusted couriers to communicate, and letters often took weeks or months to reach their destination. "Conducting business, making decisions, and coming to agreement by means of a mail service that is so uncertain, slow and ill disposed, over such distances, with such tight deadlines—it is a torment, an unsolvable problem, a wretched misfortune," Pasternak wrote.

The novel was the subject of continued attention and acclaim in the West. The premier American critic Edmund Wilson wrote a long and glowing review in *The New Yorker* in November, although he was unhappy with the quality of the translation into English: "*Doctor Zhivago* will, I believe, come to stand as one of the great events in man's literary and moral history. Nobody could have written it in a totalitarian state and turned it loose on the world who did not have the courage of genius."

When Anastas Mikoyan, the first deputy chairman of the Soviet Council of Ministers, visited the United States in early 1959, he went out for a sightseeing stroll and was famously photographed outside a bookstore window full of copies of *Doctor Zhivago*. He gazed into the window as if a little perplexed. Later, outside the venue where a private steak dinner was hosted by the Motion Picture Association, Mikoyan was confronted by protesters carrying placards that read: "Suffering from delusions about Communism? Consult Dr. Zhivago."

By March 1959, 850,000 copies of the novel had been sold in the United States. The *Sunday Times* in London declared *Doctor Zhivago* the novel of the year. When an Uruguayan journalist visited Pasternak, he told his Soviet minder, "Pasternak is so fashionable in Uruguay that girls from aristocratic families believe it is a must and good manners to have copies of *Doctor Zhivago* in your hand when you go out to parties." At an anti-Communist rally held by Roman Catholic youth in Vienna, a massive photograph of Pasternak was raised above the speakers' platform. *The New York Times* reported that "a photomontage made [Pasternak] appear to be standing behind barbed wire. From a distance he seemed to be wearing a crown of thorns."

Not everyone regarded Pasternak as a religious hero, and one of the strongest objections to *Doctor Zhivago* came from David Ben-Gurion, the Israeli prime minister, who was appalled by the novel's position on assimilation and said it was "one of the most despicable books about Jews ever written by a man of Jewish origin." He added that it was "a pity that such a book came from the pen of a man who had the courage to defy his own government."

The Nobel awards ceremony took place on December 10, 1958, at Stockholm Concert Hall, which was packed with two thousand dignitaries, including Gustaf VI, the Swedish king, and the Soviet ambassador. The Soviet science laureates, along with the other winners, sat in a row of plush red chairs; Igor Tamm, wearing a broad grin, bowed so deeply before the king that his medal almost fell off. Toward the end of the ceremony, Österling simply noted of Pasternak that "the laureate has, as is known, announced that he does not wish to accept the prize. This renunciation in no way changes the validity of the distinction. It remains only for the Swedish Academy to state with regret that it was not possible for the acceptance to take place." The audience listened in complete silence.

In the weeks after the *Pravda* letter, Pasternak was circumspect with journalists, and the public hysteria of late October and early November began to fade. "Tempest not yet over do not grieve be firm and quiet. Tired loving believing in the future," Pasternak said in a telegram to his sisters in mid-November. He was worn out. The following day he wrote to a cousin, "It would be best of all to die right now, but probably I shall not lay hands on myself."

His spirit slowly rekindled, however, inflamed by the pettiness of the authorities and disgust at the continuing abuse of old foes like Surkov. At the Congress of Writers in December, Surkov spoke of Pasternak's "putrid internal émigré position" and said he was an "apostate our righteous wrath has driven from the honorable family of Soviet writers." Surkov also was forced to admit that Pasternak's expulsion from the writers' union had "disoriented progressive writers and put in their hearts some doubt about the rightness of our decision."

In a draft letter to the Central Committee, which was obtained by the KGB, Pasternak railed against the "supreme power": "I realize that I can't demand anything, that I have no rights, that I can be crushed like a small insect. . . . I was so stupid to expect generosity after those two letters."

His anger rising, Pasternak told the British journalist Alan Moray Williams in January 1959, "The technocrats want writers to be a sort of power for them. They want us to produce work which can be used for all kinds of social purposes, like so many radioactive isotopes. . . . The Union of Soviet Writers would like me to go on my knees to them—but they will never make me." He told another journalist that "in every generation there has to be some fool who will speak the truth as he sees it."

In a letter to Feltrinelli, he displayed some of his old heightened vigor, describing his life as "distressing, deadly dangerous, but full of significance and responsibility, dizzyingly enthralling, and worthy of being accepted and lived in glad and grateful obedience to God."

Pasternak was also enervated by strains in his relationship with Ivinskaya. He had talked about making a break with his wife and spending the winter in Tarusa, about ninety miles south of Moscow, with his lover. The writer Konstantin Paustovsky had offered them his home. Ivinskaya more than ever wanted to marry. But Pasternak changed his mind at the last minute. He said he didn't want to hurt people who "wanted only to preserve the appearance of the life they were used to." He told Ivinskaya that she was his "right hand" and he was entirely with her.

"What more do you need?" he asked.

"I was very angry indeed," recalled Ivinskaya. "I felt intuitively that I needed the protection of Pasternak's name more than anyone else." She stormed back to Moscow.

In the following days, Pasternak wrote several poems, including one called "The Nobel Prize." It began:

I am lost like a beast in an enclosure
Somewhere are people, freedom, and light,
Behind me is the noise of pursuit,
And there is no way out.

Pasternak showed it to Chukovsky, who thought it was a mood piece, written on impulse. Pasternak gave a copy of it to Anthony Brown, a correspondent for the *Daily Mail* who visited him for an interview on January 30. When it was published, "The Nobel Prize" created another global sensation. The *Daily Mail* declared that "Pasternak is an outcast" under the headline "Pasternak Surprise: His Agony Revealed in 'The Nobel Prize.'"

"I am a white cormorant," Pasternak told the journalist. "As you know, Mr. Brown, there are only black cormorants. I am an oddity, an individual in a society which is not meant for the unit but for the masses."

Pasternak said he asked the journalist to give the poem to Jacqueline de Proyart, and never intended it for publication. He complained to other reporters who visited him on February 10, his birthday. "The poem should not have been published," he told one correspondent. "It makes me look like a young girl who is admiring herself in the mirror. Besides, the translation is bad." Pasternak said the poem was written in a pessimistic mood, which had passed. His wife was furious. "How many times did I tell you that you should not trust reporters?" she asked. "If this is going to continue, I'm leaving you."

Pasternak protested a little too much about Brown's betrayal—perhaps in deference to the hidden microphones. In early 1959 he could no longer legitimately claim to be unaware of the consequences of passing his writing to unknown foreigners. To hand over such a personal and polemical piece of work so soon after the Nobel Prize trouble was perhaps foolish, but it was characteristically defiant. "Only a madman would do such a thing," commented Chukovsky, "and I'm not sure there isn't a glint of madness in his eyes."

Chapter 14

"A college weekend with Russians"

In the West, there was no longer any doubt that Pasternak's renunciation of the Nobel Prize, and the letters of apology to Khrushchev and *Pravda,* were coerced. The authorities reacted with predictable fury to the *Daily Mail* article. Polikarpov told Ivinskaya that Pasternak was to cut off all contact with the foreign press. The writer was also "advised" to get out of Moscow during a visit by British prime minister Harold Macmillan so the inevitable retinue of reporters would not make their way to Peredelkino.

In the face of Ivinskaya's outrage, Pasternak took up an invitation to visit Nina Tabidze in Tbilisi with Zinaida. Ivinskaya took off for Leningrad "in a cold fury."

Georgia was a wonderful escape. Tabidze's house looked out over the city with views of the distant Daryal Gorge and Mount Kazbek. Tabidze told Pasternak that he was the third disgraced Russian poet, after Pushkin and Lermontov, to be sheltered by Georgia. She prepared a private room for him. Pasternak spent his days reading Proust, thinking about a possible new work to be set, in part, in Georgia, and walking the cold, cobblestone streets of the Old Town. In the evening, actors and writers crowded into Tabidze's apartment to eat and drink with Pasternak.

The painter Lado Gudiashvili held a reception in his honor, despite official warnings that Pasternak was not to be celebrated in any way. The poet recited by candlelight, amid the artist's vivid, colorful works, which crowded the walls. Pasternak inscribed Gudiashvili's scrapbook with lines from the poem "After the Storm":

The artist's hand is more powerful still.
It washes all the dust and dirt away
So life, reality, the simple truth
Come freshly colored from his dye works.

Pasternak wrote frequently to Ivinskaya and spoke of the need to move beyond the "scares and scandals." "I really should draw in my horns, calm down and write for the future." He reproached himself for involving Ivinskaya so deeply "in all these terrible affairs."

"I am casting a large shadow on you and putting you in awful danger," he wrote. "It's unmanly and contemptible." He doted on her in his fashion: "Olyusha, my precious girl, I give you a big kiss. I am bound to you by life, by the sun shining through my window, by a feeling of remorse and sadness, by a feeling of guilt (oh, not toward you of course, but toward everyone), by the knowledge of my weakness and the inadequacy of everything I have done so far, by my certainty of the need to bend every effort and move mountains if I am not to let down my friends and prove an imposter. . . . I hold you to me terribly, terribly tight and almost faint from tenderness, and almost cry."

He was also a little smitten with Gudiashvili's nineteen-year-old daughter, Chukurtma, a dark-haired ballet student. Pasternak fell to his knees and read her his poetry, and she went out walking with him, taking him to the excavation of a tenth-century site outside Tbilisi; Pasternak considered writing a novel about geologists discovering their links to early Christianity in Georgia. Lado Gudiashvili thought his daughter, prone to depression, bloomed under the poet's attention. In a letter to Chukurtma after he returned to Moscow, Pasternak told her that she had moved him. "I don't want to talk nonsense to you, don't want to offend your seriousness or my life with something ridiculous or inappropriate, but I have to tell you this. If by the time I die you have not forgotten me, and you, somehow, will still be in need of me, remember that I counted you among my very best friends and gave you the right to mourn for me and to think of me as someone very close."

The trip also brought a reminder of the state's cruelty. The elderly Georgian poet Galaktion Tabidze, a cousin of Nina's murdered husband who had survived Stalin's purges, was pressured by the authorities to write a letter to the newspaper condemning Pasternak. His mental health was already fragile, and Tabidze found the latest official harassment unbearable. He jumped to his death from a hospital window.

On March 14, shortly after he returned to Russia, Pasternak was hauled into Moscow for a meeting with the chief prosecutor of the Soviet Union, Roman Rudenko, who had also led the Soviet prosecution team at the Nuremberg trials of the leading Nazi war criminals. After the appearance of the poem "Nobel Prize," Rudenko recommended that Pasternak be stripped of his citizenship and deported, but the presidium of the Supreme Soviet of the USSR, which had the power to do so, did not approve the measure.

Rudenko was, however, authorized to interrogate the writer. He accused Pasternak of "double-dealing" when he turned over his poem to Brown. He threatened Pasternak with a charge of treason. Pasternak said it was an act of "fatal carelessness," but said he never intended the poem to be published, according to Rudenko's report of the interrogation, which was countersigned by Pasternak. "I denounce those actions of mine and I am well aware that I may be criminally liable in accordance with the law," Pasternak admitted, according to the report. Rudenko told his colleagues that Pasternak "behaved like a coward."

Pasternak's own report to Ivinskaya was somewhat different. "Do you know I've been talking to a man without a neck?" Pasternak told her that Rudenko had asked him to sign a statement saying he would not meet foreigners, but he had refused.

"Cordon me off and don't let foreigners through, if you want," said Pasternak, "but all I can say in writing is that I've read your piece of paper. I can't make any promises." No further action was taken by Rudenko. The state appeared unwilling to draw further attention to Pasternak by openly persecuting him. In England, Isaiah Berlin thought that Pasternak seemed "like Tolstoy in 1903 or so, when all the disseminators of his gospel were punished by the government but the old man himself was too eminent & odd to be touched by the police."

When he got home, Pasternak nonetheless put up signs in English, French, and German on his front and side doors in Peredelkino. They stated: "Pasternak does not receive. He is forbidden to receive foreigners." Zinaida also continued to insist that he not admit foreigners. "You have to stop receiving that trash," she told him, "or else they will cross the threshold of this house over my dead body."

The signs were routinely taken as souvenirs, and the message varied: "Journalists and others, please go away. I am busy." When the journalist Patricia Blake visited him on Easter, Pasternak spoke to her on the top step of his porch and did not invite her in. "Please forgive me for my terrible rudeness," he said, explaining that he was in serious trouble and banned from meeting foreigners. Although Blake found him "astonishingly young for a man of sixty-nine, she was shocked by the immense weariness in his face, in his whole bearing." When she left the dacha, plainclothes policemen followed her back to the train station. The Swedish professor Nils Åke Nilsson didn't make it out of the station before the police told him to return to Moscow. The enforced isolation extended to warnings that Pasternak should not attend public events in Moscow. His friends shrank to a small circle, and the close monitoring continued; the KGB recorded the names of the guests who attended his sixty-ninth-birthday party at the dacha.

The CIA's efforts to exploit *Doctor Zhivago* were re-energized by the Nobel crisis. The agency continued to try to get its dwindling supply of Russian-language copies of *Doctor Zhivago* into the Soviet Union, and it also purchased copies of the English edition for distribution. At first, the agency gave the novel only to non-Americans who were traveling to the Soviet Union, preferably by air rather than train because it calculated that fewer of those passengers would be thoroughly searched. If stopped and checked, visitors carrying the novel were instructed to say they purchased it from a Russian émigré or it was obtained at the Brussels Fair so that the smuggling effort could not be linked to the U.S. government.

As the storm over the Nobel Prize abated, the CIA decided that other parts of the U.S. government, as well as American travelers, could openly participate in the novel's dissemination. The agency calculated that the original rationale for secrecy—to avoid the "possibility of personal reprisal against Pasternak"—was no longer an issue.

"The worldwide discussion of the book and Pasternak's own personal statements have shown that his personal position has not become worse," a CIA memo concluded. "In other words, an all-out overt exploitation of *Dr. Zhivago* would not harm Pasternak more than he has already harmed himself." Shortly afterward, the Soviet Russia Division said it was forwarding by sea freight a batch of copies of the University of Michigan edition of *Doctor Zhivago* so that American travelers in Europe could also carry it into the Soviet Union: "It would be quite natural for an American who speaks or reads Russian to be carrying and reading the book, which has been number one on the bestseller list for the past three months."

The CIA also provided elaborate guidelines for its agents to encourage tourists to talk about literature and *Doctor Zhivago* with Soviet citizens they might meet.

"We feel that *Dr. Zhivago* is an excellent springboard for conversations with Soviets on the general theme of 'Communism versus Freedom of Expression,'" the head of the Soviet Russia Division, John Maury, wrote in a memo in April 1959. "Travelers should be prepared to discuss with their Soviet contacts not only the basic theme of the book itself—a cry for the freedom and dignity of the individual—but also the plight of the individual in the communist society. The whole Pasternak affair is indeed a tragic but classic example of the system of thought control which the party has always used to maintain its position of power over the intellectual. Like jamming, censorship, and the party's ideological decrees for writers and artists, the banning of this book is another example of the means which the regime must use to control the Soviet mind. It is a reflection of the *Nekulturnost*, the intellectual barbarity, and the cultural sterility which are features of the closed society."

The memo went on to say that Americans and other visitors could raise doubts about the tenets of socialist realism: "Perhaps a good opening to such conversations is to ask the Soviet interlocutor about the latest developments in Soviet drama, poetry, art, etc. A sympathetic but curious attitude towards the innovations and trends in the Soviet artistic world will usually set a friendly tone for the conversation. After discussing the latest artistic developments, a Westerner can inquire about what makes the works of Soviet writers such as Sholokhov, Pasternak, Margarita Aliger, Fedin . . . as great as they are. After discussing the works of these writers he can ask what limits the party has placed upon artistic works."

Maury then suggests that the tourist "can point out that a true artist must be free to speak of the ideals as well as the iniquities of any society, to criticize capitalism or communism, in short to say what he believes to be true. A number of American and European writers such as Steinbeck, John Dos Passos, Upton Sinclair, Sinclair Lewis, Sartre, Camus and others have criticized as well as defended various aspects of life in their home countries."

Agency officials congratulated themselves that "in one form or another, including full-length and condensed books and serials in indigenous languages, this book has been spread throughout the world, with assistance from this agency in a number of areas where interest might not normally be great." (Unfortunately, CIA documents provide no further detail on these efforts.) The CIA also considered publishing an anthology of Pasternak's works, including a pirated, Russian-language edition of his *Essay in Autobiography.* This had recently been published in translation in France, and the agency obtained the Russian-language manuscript from which the French translation was made.

In the end, the CIA just went forward with another edition of *Doctor Zhivago*. As early as August 1958, even before the publication of the first Russian-language edition of *Doctor Zhivago*, the CIA began to consider a miniature, paperback edition to be printed on "bible-stock" or similar lightweight paper. Such an edition had the obvious benefit of being "more easily concealed and infiltrated" than either the Mouton or University of Michigan editions. During the height of the Nobel crisis, officials at the agency also considered an abridged edition of the novel that could be handed out to Soviet sailors or even ballooned into East Germany. In November 1958, the Soviet Russia Division began to firm up plans for its miniature edition. In a memo to the acting deputy director for Plans, the chief of the Soviet Russia Division said he believed that there was "tremendous demand on the part of students and intellectuals to obtain copies of this book." The agency reported that Soviet customs officials were instructed to search tourist baggage "for this particularly hot item." In fact, in late 1958, the Soviet Union reinstituted searches of tourist luggage, which it had abandoned after the death of Stalin. One of the seized Mouton copies of the CIA edition of *Doctor Zhivago* was turned over in 1959 to the closed special collections section of Moscow's V. I. Lenin State Library, where top party officials and approved researchers could read banned publications. Books designated for the shelves in this area of the library were affixed with one or two purple hexagonal stamps, the marks of the censor. Different censors had different numbers; *Doctor Zhivago* was stamped once with "124"—a designation that should have allowed some people to read it. But the novel was kept under strict KGB embargo and was off-limits even to favored academics, according to a former librarian in the special collections section.

The CIA had its own press in Washington to print miniature books, and over the course of the Cold War printed a small library of literature—books that would fit "inside a man's suit or trouser pocket." Officials reviewed all the difficulties with the Mouton edition published in the Netherlands, and argued against any outside involvement in a new printing. "In view of the security, legal and technical problems involved, it is recommended that a black miniature edition of *Dr. Zhivago* be published at headquarters using the first Feltrinelli text and attributing it to a fictitious publisher."

By July, at least nine thousand copies of a miniature edition of *Doctor Zhivago* had been printed "in a one and two volume series," the latter presumably to make it not so thick, and easier to split up and hide. "The miniature edition was produced at headquarters from the original Russian language text of the Mouton edition," the agency reported in an internal memo. The CIA attempted to create the illusion that this edition of the novel was published in Paris by ascribing publication to a fictitious entity that was called the Société d'Edition et d'Impression Mondiale. Some of these copies were subsequently distributed by the NTS (National Alliance of Russian Solidarists), the militant Russian émigré group in Germany, another measure to hide the CIA's involvement, although the agency's released records don't mention the organization.

At a press conference in The Hague on November 4, 1958, Yevgeni Garanin, a member of the executive board of the NTS, said his group was planning to print a special bible-stock edition of the novel. Garanin said the NTS had obtained a copy of *Doctor Zhivago* at the Vatican pavilion, but no decisions had been taken on the size of the print run or where the novel would be printed. He said the group planned to distribute copies among sailors and visitors from Russia. A new, unsigned foreword was written by Boris Filippov, a Washington, D.C., resident and prominent Russian émigré who had previously edited *Grani,* the NTS journal; Filippov claimed in correspondence with a colleague that he had "released" this edition of *Zhivago.* Without mentioning the CIA by name, he complained that his introduction was "so maliciously and ignorantly mutilated by the man who gave money for the edition that I removed my name from the edition and the article."

CIA records state that the miniature books were passed out by "agents who [had] contact with Soviet tourists and officials in the West." Two thousand copies of this edition were set aside for dissemination to Soviet and East European students at the 1959 World Festival of Youth and Students for Peace and Friendship, which would be held in Vienna.

The festival, which was sponsored by Communist youth organizations, took place between July 26 and August 4. The Kremlin spent millions of dollars on these events, and the Vienna festival was supervised personally by Alexander Shelepin, the head of the KGB. Until 1958, when he moved to the Lubyanka, Shelepin was the vice president of the International Union of Students, a prime mover behind the festival. After becoming head of the KGB, Shelepin kept his position at the International Union of Students for another year so he could supervise events in Vienna, which attracted thousands of young people from across the world. The Soviet Union underwrote the attendance of delegates from the developing world. Because it was the first such festival held in the West, it was also the target of efforts covertly orchestrated by the CIA to disrupt the proceedings—or as the agency's young provocateurs preferred to call the jamboree, "a tool for the advancement of world communism." Half of the Northern Hemisphere was Communist and the superpowers increasingly fought for the allegiance of Latin Americans, Africans, and Asians.

The CIA created another front organization, the Independent Service for Information (ISI) in Cambridge, Massachusetts, to recruit American students to disrupt the festival. The ISI was headed by Gloria Steinem, a recent graduate, who was made aware of the CIA's role when she asked about the organization's funding. When the CIA's involvement was revealed in 1967, Steinem said she found the CIA officers with whom she worked "liberal and farsighted and open to an exchange of ideas. I never felt I was being dictated to at all. . . .

"The CIA was the only one with enough guts and foresight to see that youth and student affairs were important," said Steinem, who said no member of the ISI delegation passed information to the agency. "They wanted to do what we wanted to do—present a healthy, diverse view of the United States."

The ISI set up a news bureau to feed information to Western correspondents who were refused entry to the festival and smuggled copies of an unsanctioned newspaper into event venues. Newspapers published in several languages were brought in at night and placed in the toilets. The festival grounds were guarded by a security force that checked credentials and patrolled for interlopers. Hotel porters were paid to slip newspapers under the doors of senior officials attending the festival.

Much of the group's activities took the form of student high jinks. Zbigniew Brzezinski, later President Jimmy Carter's national security adviser, tried to sow discord by bumping into

Russian delegates and then in a thick Polish accent telling them in Russian, "Out of my way, Russian pig!" Brzezinski, Walter Pincus—later a national security correspondent at *The Washington Post*—and one of Brzezinski's students at Harvard hid on a rooftop over Vienna's Rathausplatz just as the festival's closing ceremony was about to begin below. The three men hung Hungarian and Algerian flags with the centers cut out in a somewhat strained attempt to equate communism with colonialism and express solidarity with the movements against both. They also hung two white bedsheets with the words *Peace* and *Freedom* spelled vertically and in German. The three used a plank to escape onto another rooftop and away from the festival's security personnel, who dimmed the lights over the square and raced toward the roof to tear down the flags and banners. Pincus later described the ISI's shenanigans in Vienna as "a college weekend with Russians." At the time, however, it all seemed very important. "I suppose this was my small world equivalent of going off to join the Spanish Revolution," Steinem told her aunt and uncle in a letter.

There was a significant effort to distribute books in Vienna—about 30,000 in fourteen languages, including *1984, Animal Farm, The God That Failed,* and *Doctor Zhivago.* The goal was "to expose delegates from the Soviet orbit to revisionist writing" and to "supply the delegates from uncommitted areas with exposés of ideas competing with Communism." The books were handed out from kiosks and sold at discounted prices at bookstores around town. Young activists from the West noted that these locations "were under observation by communist agents." The scrutiny in and around the festival grounds was so intense that teams of young people followed sightseeing delegates so they could hand out books at locations such as museums where the minders were not able to exercise as much control. Alexei Adzhubei, Khrushchev's son-in-law and the editor of *Izvestiya,* as well as the Soviet ambassador to Austria, "complained bitterly" about ISI's projects in Vienna.

Plans for a Vienna book program were created by Samuel Walker, the former editor of the CIA-funded Free Europe Press, and C. D. Jackson, a Time-Life executive who previously had served as an adviser to the Eisenhower administration on psychological warfare. Walker, with the blessing of the "friends," as he called the CIA, set up a dummy company in New York, the Publications Development Corporation, to target the Vienna youth festival with books. Overall responsibility for getting books into the hands of the delegates was mostly left to Austrian allies of the effort. When one of Jackson's European partners, Klaus Dohrn, a Time-Life executive in Zurich, worried that "special efforts . . . will have to be made to secure the original Russian text of Dr. Zhivago," Jackson replied: "Don't worry about the 'Dr. Zhivago' text. We have the authentic one, and that is the one that will be used."

Apart from a Russian edition, plans also called for *Doctor Zhivago* to be distributed in Polish, German, Czech, Hungarian, and Chinese at the festival.

The novel had been published in Taiwan in Chinese in 1958 and serialized in Chinese by two newspapers in Hong Kong late the same year. Reaction to the novel in the Chinese press was hostile and in the periodical *World Literature,* Zang Kejia, the managing secretary of the Chinese Writers Association, said *Doctor Zhivago* was an ulcer on the Soviet Union. At the Vienna festival, the four-hundred-strong Chinese delegation was even more cocooned than their Eastern European comrades; delegates were instructed not to communicate with the Westerners they encountered, even the waiters who served their meals. And a report by a group of Polish anti-festival activists found the Chinese, unlike other delegations from Communist countries, to be "absolutely uncommunicative." The Free Europe Committee flew in fifty copies of *Doctor Zhivago* from Hong Kong for distribution.

The New York Times reported that some members of the Soviet delegation "evinced a great curiosity about Mr. Pasternak's novel, which is available here." Occasionally it was not only available but unavoidable. The Soviet delegation of students and performers arrived in a sweltering Vienna from Budapest on forty buses; among the Soviet visitors was the young ballet dancer Rudolf Nureyev. Crowds of Russian émigrés swarmed the Soviet convoy when it entered the city and tossed copies of the CIA miniature edition of *Doctor Zhivago* through the open windows of the buses.

Pasternak's novel was the book most in demand among many of the delegations, and copies of it and other novels were handed out in bags from Vienna department stores to disguise the contents; in the darkness of movie theaters; and at a changing roster of pickup points, the locations of which were circulated by word of mouth. For the trip home, delegates tucked books inside camping equipment, stage sets, film cans, and other hiding places.

None of the secret police accompanying the delegations were fooled. When the Polish students were set to return home, one of the group's leaders warned there would be a thorough search at the border, and it was best to turn in any illicit books before departure. When he got almost no response, he compromised and said, "Only *Dr. Zhivago* should be given up."

One Soviet visitor recalled returning to his bus and finding the cabin covered with pocket editions of *Doctor Zhivago*. "None of us, of course, had read the book but we feared it," he said. Soviet students were watched by the KGB, who fooled no one when they described themselves as "researchers." The Soviet "researchers" proved more tolerant than might have been expected. "Take it, read it," they said, "but by no means bring it home."

In the summer of 1959, Pasternak began work on a drama to be called *The Blind Beauty*. "I want to re-create a whole historical era, the nineteenth century in Russia with its main event, the liberation of the serfs," he told one visitor. "We have, of course, many works about that time, but there is no modern treatment of it. I want to write something panoramic, like Gogol's *Dead Souls*." He envisioned the drama as an ambitious trilogy with the first two parts taking place on a country estate in the 1840s and then the 1860s before the action shifts to Saint Petersburg in the 1880s. The trilogy includes a serf who loses her sight, but the blind beauty is Russia, a country "oblivious for so long of its own beauty, of its own destinies."

"I don't know whether I'll ever finish it," Pasternak told a visitor. "But I know that when I complete a line that sounds exactly right, I am better able to love those who love me and to understand those who don't."

Pasternak began to put aside his massive correspondence to focus on this "happy endeavor," his enthusiasm for the subject rising as he delved into the research and writing. "I have been eagerly zealous at my new work of late," he told his sister in July. He told a correspondent in Paris, "Since the time when I first lukewarmly toyed with the idea of the play, it has turned from an idle whim or trial shot into a cherished ambition, it has become a passion." He began to read scenes out loud to Ivinskaya, who found the language colorful and every word alive. She felt that the play would "be a work just as bound up with his life and artistic nature as the novel was."

Some of the official hostility in Moscow began to ease that summer. At the Third Congress of Soviet Writers in May, Khrushchev suggested that writers should keep their feuds in-house and not trouble—or embarrass—the government. Pasternak was not mentioned and of course did not attend, but Khrushchev was bothered by the Zhivago affair. Smarting from the global reaction to the campaign against Pasternak, he asked his son-in-law, Alexei Adzhubei, to read *Doctor Zhivago* and report back. According to *The New York Times,* Adzhubei said that while the novel "is not a book that would cause a good Young Communist to toss his cap in the air . . . it is not a book that would touch off counterrevolution." Adzhubei concluded that with the removal of a mere three hundred or four hundred words, *Doctor Zhivago* could have been published. Khrushchev exploded, and had Surkov removed as secretary of the Union of Soviet Writers; one report said he grabbed Surkov by the collar and shook him furiously.

In a speech to the Third Congress, Khrushchev told the delegates, "You may say: 'Criticize us, control us; if a work is incorrect, do not print it.' But you know that it is not easy to decide right away what to print and what not to print. The easiest thing would be to print nothing, then there would be no mistakes. . . . But it would be stupidity. Therefore, Comrades, do not burden the government with the solution of such questions, decide them for yourselves in a comradely fashion." Later in the year, the Union of Soviet Writers suggested that Pasternak could apply to be reinstated, but he rejected the approach. "They all showed themselves up at that time," he said, "and now they think that everything can be forgotten."

Pasternak began to venture out in public in Moscow, and his first appearance, to attend a concert of the New York Philharmonic conducted by Leonard Bernstein, drew press notice. The Philharmonic was playing in Moscow, Leningrad, and Kiev—the first major concert tour by an American organization after the signing in 1958 of the United States–Soviet Union Cultural Exchange Agreement. Bernstein was a sensation, bringing audiences to their feet, although some Communist critics were unhappy with what they saw as his attempt to lift the Iron Curtain in music. As well as American compositions, he played works by Igor Stravinsky that had never been played in the Soviet Union. Before pieces, Bernstein also spoke directly to the audience, and Soviet listeners were completely unused to that kind of engagement with a conductor. Before playing Stravinsky's *Rite of Spring,* he said the composer "created a revolution before your own revolution. Music has never been the same since that performance." *The New York Times* noted that "when the savage rhythms and weird melodies had reached their climax, there was a moment of breathless silence and then a great explosion of wild cheering."

While in Leningrad, Bernstein got Pasternak's address and invited him to the final Moscow concert on September 11. Pasternak responded in a letter with two postscripts in which he accepted the invitation but went back and forth on an invitation to Bernstein and his wife to visit him in Peredelkino on the day before the concert. His changes of mind may have reflected Zinaida's objections before he finally defied her and asked them to come in the final postscript. When Bernstein and his wife arrived they were initially left outside in the pouring rain while Pasternak and his wife had a lengthy argument. The guests, upon being admitted, were told that the family squabble was about what door they should enter; they evidently never suspected that Pasternak's wife despised the thought of foreign visitors.

Bernstein and his wife ate with Pasternak, and the conductor found him "both a saint and a *galant.*" Bernstein reported that they talked for hours about art and music and the "artist's view of history" before later correcting himself and noting that the conversation was "in fact virtually monologues by him on aesthetic matters." When Bernstein complained about his difficulties with the minister of culture, Pasternak replied, "What have ministers got to do with it?"

"The Artist communes with God," he told the American, "and God puts on various performances so that he can have something to write about. This can be a farce, as in your case; or it can be a tragedy—but that is a secondary matter."

Moscow Conservatory's Great Hall was packed with much of the intelligentsia. Pasternak attended with his wife and "every eye in the hall seemed to focus on the two people . . . there was a subdued buzzing in the hall as people motioned to one another and stared.

"The tension, almost unbearable in its intensity, was broken suddenly when Mr. Bernstein appeared on stage, followed by a tremendous cheer. Some of those present, perhaps including Mr. Bernstein, were sure that at least part of the enthusiastic greeting was meant to be shared by Mr. Pasternak."

Pasternak visited Bernstein backstage and the two men shared a bear hug. "You have taken us up to heaven," said Pasternak. "Now we must return to earth."

Chapter 15

"An unbearably blue sky"

Pasternak turned seventy on February 10, 1960. When he arrived at Ivinskaya's to celebrate, he was red-faced from the piercing wind; there were frost flowers on the windows and snow fluttered in the air. Pasternak warmed his stomach with cognac and settled in with the assembled company, including the German journalist Heinz Schewe. Ivinskaya served roast chicken with homemade cabbage salad, and the meal was washed down with more cognac and two bottles of Georgian red wine. Pasternak was happy and loquacious. He spoke at length about a number of German writers. There were lots of presents, and notes of congratulations from around the world. Pasternak's sisters sent a telegram. An alarm clock in a leather case came from Prime Minister Nehru. The owner of a gas station in Marburg mailed him earthenware pots.

"How late everything has come for me," he told Ivinskaya. "If only we could live forever like this."

Pasternak had 109 days.

Late the previous year, he had written to a Western correspondent, "A short time ago I began to notice now and then a disturbance at the left side of my breast. This is allied to my heart—I am telling no one about it as, if I do mention it, I shall have to give up my habitual daily routine. My wife, relatives, friends will stand over me. Doctors, sanatoriums, hospitals crush out life before one is yet dead. The slavery of compassion begins." Earlier that winter, Katya Krasheninnikova, one of his young devotees, visited Pasternak. He told her he had lung cancer, and one or two years to live. He asked her to tell no one but to go to communion with him.

On his birthday, Pasternak still appeared vigorous; he hid the sometimes sharp pain in his chest. But in letters to distant friends, there were hints of an end foreseen, a summing up. "Some benign forces have brought me close to that world where there are no circles, no fidelity to youthful reminiscences, no distaff points of view," he told Chukurtma Gudiashvili, the young Georgian ballerina, "a world which the artist prepares himself all his life to enter, and to which he is born only after death, a world of posthumous existence for those forces and ideas for which you have found expression."

Among his more exotic valedictory thoughts was that Feltrinelli should buy his body from the Soviet Union, bury him in Milan, and have Ivinskaya watch over his tomb. His lover began to notice that his strength was ebbing. He would tire while working on commissioned translations and seemed less buoyant during their walks. She was frightened by a grayness that had begun to creep into his complexion.

At Easter, a German admirer, Renate Schweitzer, came to visit. The two had shared an intimate correspondence since Schweitzer, a poet who worked as a masseuse, first wrote to him in early 1958. She was entranced by a newspaper photo of Pasternak and then by the Russia of Pasternak's *Zhivago*. Schweitzer was a thunderstruck fan, and Pasternak was somehow transported by this epistolary relationship to the Germany of his student days in Marburg. Schweitzer became so moved by the confessional, tender tone in Pasternak's letters—in one he ruminated on his complicated life with Zinaida and Olga—that she considered trying to become a Soviet citizen and moving to Peredelkino. Pasternak preferred her as a creature of their correspondence and was ambivalent about the visit, particularly because he was feeling so poorly.

At the dacha, where she ate Easter dinner with the Pasternaks and their guests, Schweitzer noted the pallor in Pasternak's face and how little he ate. She also visited Ivinskaya with Pasternak, and emboldened by alcohol and in front of her hostess, she kissed her hero with more ardor than affection. She asked the unamused Ivinskaya if she could "have him for a week."

After walking Schweitzer to the train station, Pasternak complained that his coat was "so heavy." He also felt compelled to ask for Ivinskaya's forgiveness, but she was more troubled by his overwrought state—sobbing, on his knees—than the brazen kisses with Schweitzer. Later that week, he also told Nina Tabidze that he thought he had lung cancer but swore her to secrecy. As the pain in his chest became more pronounced, he wondered to Ivinskaya if he was "falling ill as a punishment for what I did to you over Renate."

The following week, Pasternak began to keep a journal on his health, scribbling notes in pencil on loose sheets of paper. "I have heart complaints, pain in the back. I think I've overtaxed myself during Easter. Can hardly stay on my legs. Tiring to stand at my writing desk. Had to stop writing the play. The left arm feels dull. Have to lie down." He sent Ivinskaya a note that he would have to stay in bed for a few days. "I give you a big kiss. Everything will be alright."

On the twenty-third, he surprised Ivinskaya when she saw him approaching her on the road, carrying his old suitcase. He was expecting money from Feltrinelli to be brought to him by Schewe or an Italian courier. He looked "pale and haggard, a sick man."

"I know you love me, I have faith in it, and our only strength is in this," he told her. "Do not make any changes in our life, I beg you."

They never spoke again.

On the twenty-fifth, Pasternak was examined by a doctor, who diagnosed angina and recommended complete bed rest. Pasternak was unconvinced. "I find it hard to imagine that such a constant pain, as firmly embedded as a splinter, should be due only to something wrong with my heart, very overtired and in need of attention as it is."

Two days later, Pasternak felt better and the results of a cardiogram were encouraging. "It will all pass," Pasternak wrote in his journal.

At the end of April, Pasternak was struggling to get up the stairs to his study, and a bed was made for him in the music room downstairs. He told Ivinskaya not to make any attempt to come to see him. "The waves of alarm set off by it would impinge on me and at the moment with my heart in this condition, it would kill me," he told her in a note. "Z in her foolishness would not have the wit to spare me. I have already taken soundings on the subject." He told her not to get upset, that they had come through worse things. But he was now in some physical distress. "The effect on my heart of the slightest movement is instantaneous and horribly painful," he told her. "All I can do that is relatively painless is lie flat on my back."

On May 1, Pasternak was visited by Katya Krasheninnikova, the young woman with whom he wanted to have communion at the church. "I'm dying," he told her. Pasternak asked her to go through the sacrament of confession with him; he read the prayers aloud with his eyes closed, his face serene. Pasternak asked Krasheninnikova to open the door so his wife could hear and then loudly complained that Zinaida refused to call a priest or organize a church burial. Krasheninnikova said she passed Pasternak's confession on to her own priest, and he said the prayer of absolution. "That's how they used to do it in the camps," she later told Pasternak's son.

A few days later, Pasternak again thought he felt better. He got out of bed, but after washing his hair he suddenly felt very unwell. He continued to advise Ivinskaya that the condition was temporary and counseled her to be patient. "If I were really near death, I should insist that you be called over here to see me," he told her in another note. "But thank goodness this turns out to be unnecessary. The fact that everything, by the looks of it, will perhaps go on again as before seems to me so undeserved, fabulous, incredible!!!"

On the night of May 7, Pasternak suffered a heart attack. The USSR Literary Fund Hospital dispatched Dr. Anna Golodets and several nurses to provide care for him around the clock. Golodets found her patient battling a high temperature and severe lung congestion. She thought the low, slanting bed set up downstairs had to be very uncomfortable, but she found Pasternak uncomplaining and determined to hide the extent of his disease from his loved ones. He liked the window open during the day; outside, his garden was in full bloom.

Marina Rassokhina, the youngest nurse at just sixteen, delivered updates to Ivinskaya and sometimes spent the night with her. She relayed to Ivinskaya how Pasternak, without his false teeth, felt unbearably ugly. "Olyusha won't love me anymore," he told the nurse. "I look such a fright now." He was frustrated that he couldn't shave but allowed his son Leonid to do it for him. One of the other nurses, Marfa Kuzminichna, who had served at the front during the war, admired Pasternak's courage as death neared. "I already feel the breath of the other world on me," he told her. He spoke about his "double life" and asked her not to condemn him. He didn't entirely lose his sense of humor. As the nurses prepared for a blood transfusion, he told them they looked like "Tibetan lamas at their altars."

In mid-May, Pasternak was examined by four doctors, who diagnosed a heart attack and stomach cancer. Pasternak was given a series of injections that led to some hallucinations. He thought he spoke to the writer Leonid Leonov about *Faust* and was very upset when he learned that event had not happened. An oxygen tent seemed to ease his breathing and reduce the nightmares.

Zinaida sent a telegram to Oxford, assuring his sisters that he was being treated by Moscow's best doctors. She was draining her savings to pay for some of the care. Western correspondents in the capital tried to obtain antibiotics for him through their embassies.

By now the foreign press was at the gates of the dacha seeking updates in what became a round-the-clock death watch. There were concerned visitors—Akhmatova, the Ivanovs, the Neigauzes, among others—but Pasternak declined to see them. He told them he loved them, was comforted they were nearby, but said the Pasternak they knew was gone. The patient only wanted his wife or his son Leonid, or the nurses, in his sickroom. He didn't even like to see doctors without being freshly shaved with his false teeth in. Silence enveloped the house, and Zinaida, monosyllabic and unsentimental, managed the daily routine, helped by Pasternak's brother, Alexander, and his wife, who had moved out to Peredelkino to assist.

Zinaida several times offered to allow Ivinskaya to see Pasternak and to leave the house while she visited. Over the previous year, she was tormented by gossip about the affair with "that lady," which grew to humiliating proportions because of Pasternak's fame. Pasternak said he couldn't bear to see Zinaida "in tears" because of all the whispers. Zina, he said, is "for me like my own daughter, like my youngest child. I love her as her dead mother would."

Pasternak was adamant that his lover should not come over. Instead, she came to the gate of the dacha weeping and Pasternak's brother would speak to her. Zinaida thought it was "monstrous" that Pasternak would not see her. She wondered if her husband was disappointed in Ivinskaya, and if the relationship had soured. Pasternak's notes to Ivinskaya suggest not. He simply could not bear the stress and the pitched emotion of an Ivinskaya visit. He did not want her to see him in his reduced state, and he did not wish to foist all the drama of a visit on his family. He was too decorous, and his lives with these two women were, for him, distinctly separate. It wasn't who Pasternak loved, but how he wanted to die that kept Ivinskaya hovering near the dacha gate and Zinaida nursing his dying body.

In late May, a portable X-ray machine was brought to the house and it showed cancer in both lungs that was metastasizing to other major organs. There was no hope of recovery. Pasternak asked to see his sister Lydia. Alexander sent a telegram to England: "SITUATION HOPELESS COME IF YOU CAN." Despite pleas directly to Khrushchev, Lydia spent a week in London waiting for the Soviet authorities to make a decision; by the time they issued a visa it was too late.

On the twenty-seventh, Pasternak's pulse dropped, but the doctors worked to revive him. Opening his eyes again, he told them he had felt so good while asleep and now his worries were back. He was still feeling low, and unusually blunt, when he spoke to his son Yevgeni later that day.

"How unnatural everything is. Last night I suddenly felt so

good, but it proved to be bad and dangerous. With quick injections they tried to bring me back and they did.

"And now, just five minutes ago, I started calling the doctor myself, but it proved to be nonsense, gas. On the whole, I feel everything is steeped in shit. They said I had to eat to make my stomach work. But that's painful. And it's the same in literature, recognition, which is no recognition at all, but obscurity. It would seem I was already buried once, and for good; enough. No memories. Relationships with people all ruined in different ways. All fragmentary, no unbroken memories. Everything is steeped in shit. And not only we, but everywhere, the whole world. My whole life has been a single-handed fight against the ruling banality, for the human talent, free and playing."

By the evening of the thirtieth, it was clear to the doctors that death was imminent. Zinaida went in to see Pasternak. "I have loved life and you very much," he said, his voice momentarily strong, "but I am leaving without any regrets. Around us there is too much banality, not only around us, but in the whole world, I simply cannot reconcile myself to it."

His sons followed at about 11:00 p.m. "Borenka, Lydia will soon be here, she's on her way," Yevgeni told his father. "Hold on for a while."

"Lydia, that's good," said Pasternak.

He asked everyone but his sons to leave the room. He told them to stay aloof from that part of his legacy that lay abroad—the novel, and the money, and all the attendant complications. Lydia, he said, would manage it.

Pasternak's breathing became more and more labored. The nurses brought in the oxygen tent. He whispered to Marfa Kuzminichna: "Don't forget to open the window tomorrow."

At 11:20 p.m. on May 30, Pasternak died.

Zinaida and the housekeeper washed and dressed the body. The family stayed up through much of the night.

At 6:00 a.m., on the road near Pasternak's dacha, Ivinskaya saw Kuzminichna coming off duty, her head bowed. She knew without asking that Pasternak was dead and stumbled, crying and unannounced, into the big house: "And now you can let me in, now you don't have to fear me anymore."

Nobody bothered her. She found her way to the body. "Borya was lying there still warm, and his hands were soft. He lay in a small room, with the morning light on him. There were shadows across the floor, and his face was still alive—not at all inert."

She summoned his voice and could hear him recite "August," one of the *Zhivago* poems.

Farewell, azure of Transfiguration,
Farewell the Second Savior's gold.
Ease with a woman's last caress
The bitterness of my fatal hour.

Farewell, years fallen out of time!
Farewell, woman: to an abyss
Of humiliations you threw down
The challenge! I am your battlefield.

Farewell, the sweep of outspread wings,
The willful stubbornness of flight,
And the image of the world revealed in words,
And the work of creation, and working miracles.

Word spread through the village. Lydia Chukovskaya told her father, whose hands began to tremble. He sobbed without tears.

"The weather has been unbelievably beautiful: hot and stable," Chukovsky wrote in his diary later that day. "The apple and cherry trees are in bloom. I've never seen so many butterflies, birds, bees and flowers. I spend entire days out on the balcony. Every hour there's a miracle, every hour something new, while he, the singer of all these clouds, trees and pathways . . . is now lying in state on a pitiful folding bed, deaf and blind, destitute, and we shall never again hear his impetuous, explosive bass."

The Soviet press did not report Pasternak's death, although it was front-page news around the world. Prime ministers, queens, and ordinary people sent their condolences. In Milan, Feltrinelli said in a statement, "The death of Pasternak is a blow as hard as losing a best friend. He was the personification of my nonconformist ideals combined with wisdom and profound culture."

In Moscow, there was silence. Finally, on June 1, a small notice appeared on the bottom of the back page of a minor publication *Literatura i Zhizn* (Literature and Life): "The board of the Literary Fund of the USSR announces the death of the writer and member of Litfond, Pasternak, Boris Leonidovich, which took place May 30 in the seventy-first year of his life after a severe and lengthy illness, and expresses its condolences to the family of the deceased."

There was not even the standard expression of regret in this final attempt at insult. A writer as prominent as Pasternak would normally be memorialized with numerous obituaries in all the leading dailies as well as an appreciation signed by many of his fellow writers in *Literaturnaya Gazeta*. Pasternak was still a pariah worthy of only one run-on sentence, and the Central Committee in an internal memo said that the snub "was welcomed by representatives of the artistic intelligentsia." On June 2, the literary newspaper reprinted the perfunctory notice from *Literatura i Zhizn* and gave it the same small play at the bottom of the back page. But on the same page was a large article about the Czech poet Vítězslav Nezval under the headline "A Magician of Poetry." For some readers, the juxtaposition was no coincidence but the sly tribute of some unknown editor.

There were other notices about Pasternak's death, handwritten and taped to the wall near the ticket office in Moscow's Kiev Station, where the suburban trains departed for Peredelkino. "At three o'clock on the afternoon of Thursday June 2, the last leave-taking of Boris Leonidovich Pasternak, the greatest poet of present-day Russia, will take place." Other versions of this message appeared in different locations around the city. When they were torn down by the police, new ones took their place.

The afternoon of the funeral was another in what had been a series of hot days, and one with an "unbearably blue sky." The apple and lilac trees in Pasternak's garden were ablaze with pink and white and purple blossoms, and underfoot there was a carpet of wildflowers peeking out from the freshly cut pine boughs that had been laid to protect the young grass.

When the American journalist Priscilla Johnson caught the train around 1:00 p.m., it was clear that many of the passengers, wearing black and carrying sprigs of lilac, were on their way to the funeral. And when the train pulled into Peredelkino, it emptied out, disgorging passengers who seemed to her to be either very young or very old. The authorities described them as "mostly intelligentsia" and young people, students from the Institute of Literature and Moscow State University. They formed a loose procession to the dacha. The police were stationed at all the intersections, and they told those who arrived by car, including the foreign press, that they would have to park and walk the last part of the way.

The authorities hoped to manage the funeral, and how it was seen by the world. On the eve of the burial, the local Communist Party chief had provided a tour of the village for foreign correspondents, including the cemetery, where a freshly dug grave stood in the shade of three tall pine trees and within sight of Pasternak's dacha. It was a cemetery of competing ideas: crosses or red stars marked the different graves. "Pasternak will be buried in the best site in the graveyard," the functionary boasted.

Representatives of the USSR Literary Fund had visited the family after Pasternak's death and said they would pay for the burial and help manage the logistics. The KGB set up temporary headquarters in a local office, and agents were sent out to mingle with the crowd and record who attended. Word had already spread among members of the Moscow branch of the Union of Soviet Writers that they should not attend, and in the days before the funeral some writers had snuck in and out through the backyard to pay their respects without being seen by the ubiquitous informers.

Only a few writers were willing to risk the wrath of the authorities by attending the funeral. When the playwright Alexander Shtein was asked why he didn't go to the funeral, he replied, "I don't take part in anti-government demonstrations."

The curtains were drawn in the house of Pasternak's neighbor Konstantin Fedin, Surkov's successor as secretary of the writers' union. Fedin was ill, but his absence was taken as an affront. Two mourners clashed by Pasternak's coffin over Fedin's failure to attend. One had claimed that Fedin was so sick he didn't know about Pasternak's death. Another had angrily retorted: "He can see perfectly well from his windows what is going on here."

The novelist Veniamin Kaverin was so incensed he later wrote to Fedin. "Who can forget the senseless and tragic affair of Pasternak's novel—an affair which did so much damage to our country? Your part in this business went so far that you even felt compelled to pretend you had not heard of the death of the poet who was your friend and lived next door to you for 23 years. Perhaps you could see nothing from your window as people came in their thousands to take their leave of him, and as he was carried in his coffin past your house."

The garden quickly filled to overflowing. Western newsmen stood on boxes by the dacha gates; some climbed into the trees to get a better view. The mourners waited silently to enter the house by the side door and file by the body before exiting out the front door. Pasternak was dressed in his father's dark gray suit and a white shirt. "He could have been lying in a field, rather than in his own living room, for the coffin was banked with wild flowers, with cherry and apple blossoms, as well as red tulips and branches of lilac." The flowers became more and more heaped as mourners left their own sprays. A group of women dressed in black—sometimes including Zinaida and Yevgenia, Pasternak's first wife—stood at the head of the coffin.

The journalist Priscilla Johnson was shocked when she saw the body, "for the face had lost all of its squareness and strength." Veniamin Kaverin thought that Pasternak's familiar face was now "sculpted in white immobility," and he detected what he thought was "a tiny smile lingering on the left corner of his mouth." The body had been embalmed on May 31 after the artist Yuri Vasilyev had made a death mask. On June 1, a local priest held a private requiem service in the dacha for the family and some close friends.

When Johnson asked Pasternak's sister-in-law if the burial would be preceded by a service in the nearby fifteenth-century Russian Orthodox Church of the Transfiguration, she looked the American up and down. "You," she said, "are very naïve."

Ivinskaya passed by the body, unable to linger because of the stream of people behind her. "Inside people were still taking leave of my beloved, who lay there quite impassive now, indifferent to them all, while I sat by the door so long forbidden to me." She was approached by Konstantin Paustovsky, the eighty-year-old dean of Soviet letters, and Ivinskaya began to cry as he bent down to speak to her. Paustovsky must have imagined that she was unable to enter the house because of her complicated situation. "I want to go past the coffin with you," he said, taking Ivinskaya by the elbow.

Paustovsky remarked on what "an authentic event the funeral was—an expression of what people really felt." He said one was bound to recall "the funeral of Pushkin and the Tsar's courtiers—their miserable hypocrisy and false pride."

The secret police moved among the crowd, eavesdropping or taking photographs. They were unmistakable to many of the mourners and the "sole alien element in the crowd which, with all its diversity, was united in its shared feeling."

"How many were there altogether?" Pasternak's old friend Alexander Gladkov wondered. "Two or three thousand, or four? It was hard to say but it was certainly a matter of several thousand." Western correspondents placed the number at a more conservative one thousand and the authorities counted five hundred. Even a crowd of a few hundred was remarkable. Gladkov had worried that the funeral would turn out to be "rather poorly attended and pathetic."

"Who could have expected so many when nobody *had* to come just for form's sake, by way of duty, as is so often the case," Gladkov marveled. "For everybody present, it was a day of enormous importance—and this fact itself turned it into another triumph for Pasternak."

People ran into old friends in the front garden—comrades, in some cases, from the camps. Gladkov met two former inmates he had known and not seen in years. It seemed entirely natural to meet again at this moment, and Gladkov recalled Pasternak's lines from "Soul":

My soul, you are in mourning
For all those close to me
Turned into a burial vault
For all my martyred friends.

Around the back of the dacha, people sat on the grass as some of Russia's finest pianists played on an old upright, the notes wafting through the open windows of the music room. Stanislav Neigauz, Andrei Volkonsky, Maria Yudina, and Svyatoslav Richter took turns, performing slow dirges and some of the melodies Pasternak loved, particularly those by Chopin.

Shortly after 4:00 p.m. Richter ended the music with a rendition of Chopin's "Marche Funèbre." The family asked those still inside the house to move into the front garden so they could have a last moment alone with the deceased. Ivinskaya, outside by the front porch, strained to see inside, at one point climbing up on a bench and looking through a window. One observer thought that "in her humiliated position, she looked overwhelmingly beautiful."

After a short period, Zinaida, dressed in black, her hair highlighted with henna, stepped onto the front porch. It was time for the funeral procession.

The mounds of flowers from around the coffin were passed through the windows to the crowd. The organizers from Litfond had driven up a blue minibus to carry the coffin quickly and ahead of the mourners to the grave, where the casket was to be hastily buried. The pallbearers, including Pasternak's two sons, refused to put the body in the vehicle. The open coffin was hoisted on their shoulders, and the crowd parted as they set off, through the garden, right on Pavlenko, and along "the melancholy dirt road" which "bitterly threw up dust" as the crowd made its way to the cemetery.

The young writers Andrei Sinyavsky and Yuli Daniel, both disciples of Pasternak, followed with the coffin lid. In the Russian tradition, it would not be screwed on until the moment just before interment. The pallbearers, at the head of the throng, walked with such haste that the body appeared to be bobbing on an ocean of humanity. Young men stepped out of the crowd to assist in carrying the coffin when the pallbearers appeared to tire.

Some of those in attendance took a shortcut across the newly plowed field in front of Pasternak's dacha. It led directly down to the cemetery, which stood on a small hillside near the brightly colored cupolas of the local church. The graveyard was already crowded when the procession with the coffin arrived. When the pallbearers reached the edge of the grave, they raised the casket high above the crowd just for a moment before placing it on the ground.

"For the last time, I saw the face, gaunt and magnificent, of Boris Leonidovich Pasternak," recalled Gladkov.

The philosopher Valentin Asmus, a professor at Moscow State University and an old friend of Pasternak's, stepped forward. A young boy leaned in to Priscilla Johnson and told her who he was. "Non-party," he added.

"We have come to bid farewell to one of the greatest of Russian writers and poets, a man endowed with all the talents, including even music. One might accept or reject his opinions but as long as Russian poetry plays a role on this earth, Boris Leonidovich Pasternak will stand among the greatest.

"His disagreement with our present day was not with a regime or a state. He wanted a society of a higher order. He never believed in resisting evil with force, and that was his mistake.

"I never talked with a man who demanded so much, so unsparingly, of himself. There were but few who could equal him in the honesty of his convictions. He was a democrat in the true sense of the word, one who knew how to criticize his friends of the pen. He will forever remain as an example, as one who defended his convictions before his contemporaries, being firmly convinced that he was right. He had the ability to express humanity in the highest terms.

"He lived a long life. But it passed so quickly, he was still so young and he had so much left to write. His name will go down forever as one of the very finest."

The actor Nikolai Golubentsov then recited Pasternak's poem "O Had I Known" from the 1932 collection *Second Birth*.

A slave is sent to the arena
When feeling has produced a line
Then breathing soil and fate take over
And art has done and must resign.

A young man, nervous and stammering, read "Hamlet" from the *Zhivago* cycle of poems. The poem, like the novel, had never been published in the Soviet Union but still "a thousand pairs of lips began to move in silent unison" and a charge seemed to course through the crowd. Someone shouted, "Thank you in the name of the working man. We waited for your book. Unfortunately, for reasons that are well known, it did not appear. But you lifted the name of writer higher than anyone."

The officials from Litfond, sensing the hostile murmur of the crowd, moved to bring the funeral to an end. Someone began to carry the lid toward the coffin. The closest mourners bent over the body to kiss Pasternak farewell. Among the last was Ivinskaya, crying uncontrollably. At certain points during the graveside ceremony, she and Zinaida were just steps away from one another at the head of the coffin. Zinaida was irritated that Ivinskaya and her daughter had pushed their way to the front. As Ivinskaya said her farewell, Zinaida "stood smoking by a fence, not 20 feet from the coffin . . . and throwing baleful glances now and then at the man whose body was about to be lowered into the grave."

Spontaneous shouts continued from the crowd.

"God marks the path of the elect with thorns, and Pasternak was picked out and marked by God!"

"Glory to Pasternak!"

"The poet was killed!" someone cried, and the crowd responded, "Shame! Shame! Shame!"

One of the Litfond officials yelled, "The meeting is over; there will be no more speeches!"

A copy of a prayer for the dead was placed on Pasternak's forehead by his longtime housekeeper, and the lid was hammered shut. There were more cries as the coffin was lowered and the first thuds of dirt hit the wood—"faint, muffled and terrifying."

The sky clouded over. Most of the crowd quickly dispersed but about fifty young people stayed at the grave, reciting Pasternak's poetry. They were still there when the sun began to set—"the voice now of one, now another, rising and falling in an eloquent singsong." The KGB decided not to interfere, but the Central Committee later told the Ministry of Culture and the Union of Soviet Writers to pay attention to the education of students because "some of them (and their number is trifling) have been poisoned with unhealthy, oppositional ideas and are trying to position Pasternak as a great artist and writer who was not understood by his epoch."

Through the long, exhausting day, Lydia Chukovskaya, despite her sorrow, had a "strange feeling of triumph, of victory.

"The victory of what? I don't know. Maybe of his poetry. Of Russian poetry?" she wondered. "Of our unbreakable bond with him?"

Chapter 16

"It's too late for me to express regret that
the book wasn't published."

Ivinskaya was arrested in Peredelkino on August 16. It was dusk, and she was drinking tea with her mother and stepfather when several men came through the garden gate. "You were expecting us to come, of course, weren't you?" said one of the KGB officers, pink-faced and smiling with satisfaction. "You didn't imagine, did you, that your criminal activities would go unpunished?"

Over the previous eighteen months, the secret police had been watching various foreigners bring money into the country for Pasternak—and Ivinskaya was charged with illegal currency trading. While her arrest was at first kept secret, the authorities eventually decided to scapegoat her in a crude attempt to somehow reclaim the early Pasternak, not the author of *Doctor Zhivago,* as a great Soviet writer. Pasternak, according to Surkov, had been misled by an "adventuress who got him to write *Doctor Zhivago* and then to send it abroad, so that she could enrich herself."

In the last year of his life, Pasternak was a rich man, but control of his fortune lay frustratingly beyond his reach. He authorized Feltrinelli to give $100,000 from his royalties to D'Angelo after the Italian had written to Pasternak to tell him he had "reliable" friends who could carry cash into the Soviet Union.

Pasternak was wary at first: "Olyusha, where should we leave all that money?"

"Well, in that suitcase over there!" replied Ivinskaya.

Feltrinelli transferred the money to D'Angelo from an account in the tax haven of Liechtenstein in March 1960. D'Angelo immediately began purchasing rubles in Western Europe and then arranging for Italian friends to smuggle the currency into the Soviet Union and pass it secretly to Pasternak via Ivinskaya or her daughter. D'Angelo described himself as "running" an "operation" with his own security protocols.

The Italian, however, was no match for the KGB.

The secret police watched as Giuseppe Garritano, a Moscow correspondent for the Italian Communist newspaper *L'Unità*, arranged the transfer of a large sum of rubles that D'Angelo had purchased. In March 1960, Garritano's wife, Mirella, called Ivinskaya's city apartment, which was almost certainly bugged and under close surveillance, and asked her to come to the post office and collect some books for Pasternak. Ivinskaya was laid up with a sprained leg and Pasternak was reluctant to meet an unknown foreigner. They agreed to send Ivinskaya's daughter, Irina, who took her younger brother with her. They were handed a shabby black suitcase and when it was opened back in the apartment, Ivinskaya and Pasternak "gasped with astonishment: instead of books, it contained bundles of Soviet banknotes in wrappers, all neatly stacked together, row upon row of them."

Pasternak gave Ivinskaya one bundle and took the suitcase to Peredelkino.

The Italians agreed to take back some documents to Feltrinelli. Garritano and his wife lost the papers while vacationing in the Caucasus, including a signed instruction that gave Ivinskaya control over Pasternak's royalties. When she noticed the papers were gone, Mirella Garritano thought the documents might have fallen out of her bag during a rainstorm. Her husband suspected they were being watched and the documents were stolen when she put her bag down at a party. In August, Ivinskaya separately forwarded to Feltrinelli a power of attorney that Pasternak had signed in December 1956 and gave her "power to carry out all tasks related to the publication of the novel *Doctor Zhivago*."

But this did not provide any broad authority to manage his posthumous affairs.

The Garritanos' carelessness made for a very complicating loss. Pasternak left no will, and often unseemly struggles for control over various parts of his legacy began almost immediately after his death and were litigated by friends and family well into the 1990s.

In late 1959, Feltrinelli had sent Pasternak a new contract, which gave the Milan publisher control over the film rights for *Doctor Zhivago,* Pasternak's other writings, and also sidelined de Proyart as the author's second legally sanctioned adviser in the West. Hesitant about offending his French friend, Pasternak procrastinated for several months. Pressed by both Ivinskaya and the German journalist Heinz Schewe, Feltrinelli's trusted courier to Moscow, Pasternak eventually signed the contract in April 1960.

In the week after the funeral, Ivinskaya wrote to Feltrinelli and after mentioning her "terrible sorrow" told him that they urgently had to talk about practical matters. "In April, when Boris wanted to dedicate himself exclusively to his drama and already felt weak, he wrote me a power of attorney for you," she said, referring to the material she had entrusted to the Garritanos. "It says that he wishes my signature to be as valid as his own whether it concerns financial agreements or any other sort of document." She wrote that D'Angelo's friends would pass it along. She also promised to support Feltrinelli in any conflict with Pasternak's family, including his sisters in England. "The Pasternak family has no claim to the publishing rights," Ivinskaya wrote. "The last power of attorney is the agreement I just informed you about."

Feltrinelli wrote back to Ivinskaya to tell her that he thought D'Angelo's methods "were too dangerous" and she should trust only the German correspondent. In his own effort at spycraft, Feltrinelli enclosed half of a thousand-lira banknote and told Ivinskaya that in the absence of Schewe she should deal with the person who could produce the other half of the bill. Ivinskaya thought the banknote was something out of a "bad thriller," and she would pay a steep price for possessing it.

Ivinskaya said she hadn't had a "quiet moment" since she learned the documents were gone and feared what would happen if they fell into the wrong hands. "My dear, dear Giangiacomo. Let's hope that the most horrible thing will not happen and that I will keep my liberty, for as long as it takes."

Following the death of the author, Feltrinelli hoped that Ivinskaya could continue to entrust him with Pasternak's affairs. The publisher had no previous contact with Pasternak's wife and children, and his adviser Schewe was predisposed to Ivinskaya, not the widow, Zinaida. "I will always make sure that a substantial part of the profits is left for you and Irina," Feltrinelli promised Ivinskaya. He also told her that his contracts with Pasternak "must never end up in the hands of the authorities or the Pasternak family."

Excluding Pasternak's family was a venal suggestion, and one that would be exploited by the Soviet Union. But it didn't entirely reflect Feltrinelli's position. He accepted Ivinskaya as Pasternak's executor but told her "not to get involved in a battle in Moscow" and to be "generous with money matters," for there could be "dangerous enemies."

Unaware of Feltrinelli's misgivings, D'Angelo continued with his own plans. In July, he gave a second, large installment of cash to another Italian couple, the Benedettis, who drove to Moscow from Berlin in a Volkswagen Beetle. The money was hidden in the paneling of the car. When they arrived in Moscow, the couple carried the cash to Ivinskaya's apartment in a large rucksack. The Benedettis brought in 500,000 rubles, which was worth about $125,000 at the official exchange rate, but could be acquired for much less, about $50,000, on the gray market in Western Europe.

Ivinskaya tried to refuse the money after her daughter sensed the danger in accepting it. But the Benedettis had come too far not to complete their mission. "You have no right to refuse it," they said. "This is a personal debt." Ivinskaya's caution was short-lived. She bought a motorcycle for her son and, on the day of her arrest, a polished wardrobe, part of a shopping spree certain to draw attention to a woman with no visible income. Some of the hasty spending may have been caused by a currency reform that would have required Soviet citizens to turn in old rubles for new by the end of the year. The Pasternaks were also involved in some head-turning spending. In April, shortly before his death, Pasternak bought a new car, a Volga, for 45,000 rubles, a strikingly big-ticket cash purchase for an author who had ostensibly lost a great deal of income after the Nobel Prize controversy.

The KGB began to pressure Ivinskaya almost immediately after Pasternak's funeral. She was visited by a "thick-set man with black eyes" who produced the red identity card of a KGB agent and demanded the manuscript of Pasternak's work in progress, *The Blind Beauty*. Ivinskaya was told that unless she produced the original copy she would be "taken to a place that will certainly be more traumatic." Ivinskaya handed it over, but soon after arranged for Schewe to get another copy of the play out of the country. Feltrinelli promised not to publish it without Ivinskaya's permission.

The secret police also began to isolate Ivinskaya's family. Irina was engaged to a French student, Georges Nivat. But before the August 20 wedding he fell ill with a mysterious illness. He was hospitalized after he broke out in blisters over much of his body and started running a high temperature. He recovered but his visa was not renewed and he was forced to fly home to France on August 10. All pleas on his behalf, including directly to Khrushchev from the French ambassador to the Soviet Union, were ignored. In retrospect, Irina considered the possibility that Nivat's contagious disease and hospitalization were not accidental, but organized to stop the marriage.

Day-to-day harassment of Ivinskaya and her family was stepped up. "Strange groups of young people" hung around outside the Moscow apartment, and when Olga and her daughter went out they were shadowed by men who made no effort to hide themselves—repeating a tactic from the days of the Nobel Prize controversy.

On August 16, the day of Ivinskaya's arrest, her rental home in Peredelkino and her apartment in Moscow were searched—as were the homes of some of her friends. She had hidden the remaining money as well as some of Pasternak's papers in a suitcase in a neighbor's house, where it was found. Pasternak's house was also searched by two agents, who said they were acting on information from Ivinskaya that Pasternak had received one hundred pairs of boots and fifty coats from abroad, as well as cash. The lead about the clothing was patently false, and it's doubtful there was any such "tip" from Ivinskaya. The search was probably focused on finding money and documents.

Sandwiched between two agents, Ivinskaya was driven to the Lubyanka—KGB headquarters—where she had been held in 1949.

"I was overcome by a peculiar feeling of indifference," she recalled. "Now that Borya was in his grave, perhaps it was just as well that I had been plucked out of the hopeless dead-end of my existence."

The twenty-two-year-old Irina was arrested on September 5. She was interrogated every day but never for more than two hours. "After all, you are a teeny-weeny criminal," her investigator said.

Feltrinelli learned of Ivinskaya's arrest in early September. "We have read all of your letters at once, as soon as we came home from vacation, and are absolutely appalled," he wrote to Schewe. "The sequence of events—with the culmination in your last letter—is truly awful. This, unfortunately, is due to the carelessness and temporary mistrust in us of our lady friend who, against all cautions and warnings, took advantage of the other party whose goals are very shady." He was apparently referring to D'Angelo's couriers.

"As for D'Angelo, I am really in the dark," he continued. "We are dealing here either with a provocateur or an idiot."

At first the mother and daughter were held in secret; there was no announcement of their arrest. D'Angelo and his wife visited Moscow in September, unaware of what had happened. They checked in at the Hotel Ukraine, the Stalinist skyscraper near their old apartment by the Moscow River. When he called Ivinskaya, a strange female voice answered and said she wasn't home. The following day when D'Angelo called back, someone that he believed to be Irina told him, "Mom's on vacation in the south and she won't be back until the end of the month."

"Well, maybe we could get together with just you and Mitya," said D'Angelo.

The fake Irina eventually agreed that they could come over, but when they did, only Mitya, Ivinskaya's son, was at home. He said his sister was really sorry but "she had to leave rather suddenly.

She had a chance to get a ride with friends who are driving to the south and she wants to go visit our mother."

The boy seemed nervous and uncomfortable. The conversation was being monitored. D'Angelo and his wife withdrew.

At the Lubyanka, Ivinskaya was again subjected to daily interrogations. At one point, she was questioned by Vadim Tikunov, the deputy chairman of the KGB, whose involvement signaled the importance the authorities attached to the case. Ivinskaya described him as consisting of three spheres: "his backside, his belly and his head."

When Ivinskaya was brought before Tikunov, a copy of *Doctor Zhivago* lay on his desk, along with some of Pasternak's letters to her.

"You disguised it very well," he said, "but we know perfectly well that the novel was written not by Pasternak but by you. Look, he says so himself."

Tikunov quoted from one of Pasternak's letters to Ivinskaya: "It was you who did it all, Olyusha! Nobody knows that it was you who did it all—you guided my hand and stood behind me, all of it I owe to you."

"You have probably never loved a woman," said Ivinskaya, "so you don't know what it means, and the sort of things people think and write at such a time."

Ivinskaya was indicted on November 10, 1960.

The trial began and ended on December 7, a day of driving sleet. Ivinskaya and her daughter were brought to Moscow City Court on Kalanchevskaya Street in Black Marias. They were overjoyed to see each other and "could not stop talking."

There were no witnesses, family, or press in the courtroom—only the judge, lawyers, court staff, and investigators. Some of Irina's friends had learned of the trial, probably from the defense attorneys, and they stood at the gates of the courthouse to wave to the women as they were driven in.

The prosecutor told the court that the correspondence between Ivinskaya and Feltrinelli convinced him that the novel was sent abroad by Olga, although Pasternak had also "sold himself to the Western warmongers." The prosecutor said he was uncertain who had actually written the novel—Pasternak or Ivinskaya—but the point was moot as the charges were limited to currency smuggling and trading. The half of Feltrinelli's thousand-lira note was produced in court, and the roster of couriers was detailed along with the amounts of money they smuggled in.

Ivinskaya's lawyers argued that Ivinskaya and her daughter had smuggled nothing and had never exchanged foreign currency for rubles. Moreover, they said, Feltrinelli and his emissaries were following Pasternak's instructions. And the lawyers questioned why couriers who were under surveillance were never arrested.

There was never any doubt about the verdict, but when the length of the sentence was announced, there was utter bewilderment at its severity—eight years forced labor for Ivinskaya, three years for Irina.

In January, the two women were sent by train to a camp in Taishet, Siberia, nearly three thousand miles east of Moscow. The nearest city was Krasnoyarsk. Surrounded by common criminals and nuns who sang about Christ, they were kept in cages inside the train coaches on the journey east. The cold was terrible and Irina was wearing only a light spring coat. The final leg of the trip was a forced walk at night in temperatures of minus twenty-five degrees Celsius. Ivinskaya found it "unbearable for Muscovites like [her and Irina] who were quite unused to such bitter cold."

The regime at the camp, a facility for women convicted of political offenses, proved not to be too harsh. The barracks were warm, there was a *banya* (sauna), and parcels from Moscow arrived without difficulty. Olga and Irina were nicknamed the "Pasternachkis" by the other inmates. But their stay was short-lived. While they were being transported to the camp in Taishet, the Gulag—the system of forced-labor camps that began under Stalin—was officially abolished. After several weeks, the women were sent back west to Potma—the camp where Ivinskaya had served her time between 1950 and 1953 and part of the penitentiary system.

Word about the arrest and trial seeped out slowly. At first a number of Western writers and academics, including Graham Greene, François Mauriac, Arthur M. Schlesinger Jr., and Bertrand Russell, wrote quiet appeals to the Soviet authorities, which were ignored. Russell, an elderly philosopher who had campaigned hard for unilateral nuclear disarmament, told Khrushchev in a letter that the Soviet persecution of Olga and Irina "was the sort of thing that made my campaign for better relations with Russia extremely difficult."

The news broke publicly January 18. *The New York Times* described the sentence as a "pure act of revenge" against "Boris Pasternak's close collaborator and intimate friend, who inspired the novel 'Doctor Zhivago' and served as the model for its heroine, Larisa."

Radio Moscow responded on January 21. The English-language broadcast described the smuggling of cash and quoted from Feltrinelli's letter in July in which he asked Ivinskaya not to let his contracts with Pasternak fall into the hands of the authorities or the Pasternak family. The report said that Ivinskaya had confessed, and it ended with an arch commentary that recalled Hamlet's description of his mother: "Frailty, thy name is woman!" A week later the international broadcaster followed up and recapped the prosecution in a long commentary in Italian: "The dream of fantastic riches impelled her to crime and she began to trade Pasternak's name, wholesale and retail. The more the author's health declined, the greater grew the trade; even death did not stop business."

The report went on to detail what it described as "a whole conspiratorial system, similar to those usually described in thrillers. They had everything: a code language, clandestine meetings, aliases and even identification codes: an Italian currency note cut in half was used as identification token."

The broadcast concluded that "the last page of this sordid history is closed: the Moscow City Court, on behalf of millions of Soviet citizens whose land has been besmirched by these dregs of society, bought with dollars, lire, francs and marks, has pronounced sentence."

In the West, the story was far from over. The prosecution of Ivinskaya was seen as a continuation of the Nobel campaign against Pasternak. "People in the West will be justified in asking what one can expect, on the level of relations between states, from a regime which displays so little courage and generosity toward its own citizens and so little respect for the great culture of which—in many ways—it is the custodian," wrote the retired American diplomat George Kennan in a letter to *The New York Times*. *The Times* of London concluded that the "radio statement is much too vindictive in its wording and too melodramatic to be swallowed whole."

The basis of the Soviet case against Ivinskaya was challenged. Feltrinelli released a statement on January 28: "As Boris Pasternak's publisher I have preferred hitherto to refrain from making any statement, because I maintain that controversy in this matter does not help the persons involved in the case—not even the late author's family. So gross, however, are the inaccuracies reported by the most varied sources that it is my duty to state today a fact of which I am personally aware.

"I myself know that the 100,000 dollars, converted entirely or in part into rubles and transmitted to Moscow, came from funds at the disposal of Boris Pasternak in the West. The amount in question was withdrawn on a written order in the author's own hand, dated 6th December 1959."

Feltrinelli said the order arrived in the West in March 1960.

"In conclusion, it is my opinion that Olga Ivinskaya is not responsible either for the transfer of the sum or for its eventual destination. In the first place, the transfer order was given, I repeat, by Pasternak himself; secondly, it was Pasternak himself who wished that the sum converted into rubles should be sent, without distinction, either to himself or to Mrs. Ivinskaya.

"Nor can one rule out that the wish of the author was, in fact to consider Olga Ivinskaya as his heiress. I trust therefore that the Soviet judicial authorities will take into account the circumstances which I have related, which are all confirmed by irrefutable documents."

D'Angelo also published a series of articles that included the text from Pasternak's letters to him and contained "irrefutable proof to the effect that it was the author himself who requested and received the money." And Nivat told reporters in Paris, "Knowing the ties between Boris Pasternak and Madame Ivinskaya, I know that she would never have undertaken anything without his initiative." Through a friend Nivat asked Queen Elisabeth of Belgium, who in 1958 was the first royal to visit the

Soviet Union, to intervene. "Had Boris Pasternak, whom I loved as a father, still lived, this would not have happened," he wrote.

Surkov entered the fight with an interview in the French Communist daily, *L'Humanité*. He expressed surprise that he was getting letters from writers such as Graham Greene. "What, you intervene and demand the liberation of rogues of whom you know nothing? Now this is really a question of an illegal currency deal and is not connected with Pasternak, who was a great poet. His family, it must be said, has nothing to do with this sordid story. All these rumors offend the writer's memory. If people abroad wish to respect his memory then they should not stir up mud around him, just because among his friends there was an adventuress."

Surkov also wrote to David Carver, the general secretary of International PEN, to say that Ivinskaya "advertised her intimacy with Pasternak" and "despite her advanced age (48) did not stop to have many parallel and frequent intimate relations with other men."

The following month, Surkov and Alexei Adzhubei visited Britain. They brought with them what they called documentary evidence proving Ivinskaya's guilt, including photographs of bundles of rubles; a photograph of the now-famous half of Feltrinelli's thousand-lira note; a letter from Feltrinelli to Ivinskaya; and a copy of a handwritten statement Ivinskaya gave to the KGB.

"We have brought documents and letters which will give you absolute evidence that she was mixed up in some very dirty business, which could only harm Mr. Pasternak's name," said Adzhubei at a press conference in London.

The Soviet officials in London had little understanding of how Ivinskaya's alleged confession would be read in the West: "Everything in the accusation is the essential truth," she wrote. "For my part, I dispute none of it. (Perhaps with the exception of details about which I myself may have become confused owing to my nervous condition.) On the other hand, I wish to thank the interrogator for his tact and correctness, not only in connection with me, but also with my archives, which have been carefully sorted, part of them returned to me, part delivered to the [literary archive], and nothing which I wanted to preserve destroyed."

Adzhubei demanded that British newspapers publish the documents "without comment whatsoever" and accused the British press of censorship when editors told him that this was not how journalism in the West was practiced. The British press also pointed out that none of this material had been published in the Soviet Union and noted that the case against Ivinskaya had been subject to an almost total news blackout.

Surkov persisted in his efforts to cast Pasternak as a great poet who was exploited in his old age by Ivinskaya. And the state began to publish some of Pasternak's work but not, of course, *Doctor Zhivago*. A literary committee "was formed a month after the poet's death to arrange for the publication of his work of which all Russians are very fond," Surkov announced. It was a mixed group of friends and family, including Vsevolod Ivanov, Ehrenburg, Zinaida and Pasternak's sons, as well as some officials. Several months later, Surkov made a selection of Pasternak's poetry for a collection to be published by Goslit, the state publishing house. Some of Pasternak's family and friends objected to the choice of poems and the slimness of the volume, but Zinaida Pasternak was happy to see anything published and get some income. "I don't care how it looks," she said, "as long as they put it out quickly."

Zinaida was left in poor straits in the wake of Pasternak's death. She spent a good deal of money on specialist care in the weeks before his death, and had no way to access the royalties that sat in bank accounts in the West. She suggested that the Soviet government repatriate and take all of the royalties if they would just give her a pension. "I'm a pauper," she complained to Chukovsky.

In August 1961, she asked Surkov if the family could transfer royalties held abroad for Pasternak's poems and other works, but not from *Doctor Zhivago,* which they would reject for "moral reasons." Surkov supported an effort to help her, noting in a memo to his colleagues that "she has practically no means of subsistence" and "has always been and is loyal to the Soviet power." She "never approved" of Pasternak's novel, he added.

Polikarpov, the Central Committee bureaucrat in charge of cultural matters, rejected any attempt to withdraw money from accounts held abroad, arguing that it could lead to "yet another anti-Soviet campaign in the reactionary press."

"It seems appropriate to stop discussing this issue," he wrote.

In 1966, a number of writers and artists wrote to the Politburo to ask for a pension for Zinaida, who had suffered a series of heart attacks since her husband's death. Polikarpov blocked it, apparently because he "had a longstanding dislike for Zinaida . . . who he viewed as overly blunt and lacking in cultural refinement."

Zinaida never saw a ruble and died on June 28, 1966. She was buried next to her husband. Zinaida and Pasternak's son, Leonid, died ten years later of a heart attack while sitting in his car near Manège Square in central Moscow. He was only thirty-eight.

The money continued to pile up in Western Europe. In 1964, Feltrinelli sold the film rights to *Zhivago* to Metro-Goldwyn-Mayer for $450,000. Feltrinelli insisted that the screenplay not misrepresent or distort "the author's ideas in a way that might lead to their being attributed with a meaning and a political orientation that was not in conformity" with his intentions. In Hollywood, this was dismissed as posturing, and the film's producer, Carlo Ponti, thought that Feltrinelli "didn't give a damn, all he wanted was the money." The film, starring Omar Sharif as Zhivago and Julie Christie as Lara, was directed by David Lean, and key scenes were shot in Spain and Finland. The movie was a major hit, and introduced vast numbers of people who had never read the novel to the story of *Doctor Zhivago*. The movie was banned in the Soviet Union. The Soviet Foreign Ministry protested to the United States embassy when American diplomats held private showings of *Doctor Zhivago* in their apartments. The ministry labeled the screenings "frankly provocative" and said the movie, like the book, "falsified Soviet history and the life of the Soviet people."

The film, like most adaptations, was not entirely faithful to the novel, and was criticized for its naïve rendering of history and its melodrama. But like the novel, the film had a huge impact on popular culture. Omar Sharif as Zhivago and Julie Christie as Lara are still remembered in those roles, the cinematography was breathtaking, and the music of "Lara's Theme" by Maurice Jarre remains instantly familiar. Adjusted for inflation, *Doctor Zhivago* is one of the highest-grossing movies of all time.

One Russian reader of *Doctor Zhivago* who changed his mind about the novel was Khrushchev. The Soviet leader was ousted in October 1964 by his colleagues, including Vladimir Semichastny, the former youth leader who compared Pasternak to a pig and had since risen to become chairman of the KGB. In retirement, Khrushchev's son gave him a typewritten, samizdat copy, and he took a long time to read it. "We shouldn't have banned it," he said. "I should have read it myself. There's nothing anti-Soviet in it."

In his memoirs, Khrushchev reflected, "In connection with *Doctor Zhivago,* some might say it's too late for me to express regret that the book wasn't published. Yes, maybe it is too late. But better late than never."

In October 1965, Mikhail Sholokhov, the candidate long favored by the Kremlin, won the Nobel Prize in Literature. The Swedish Academy said the award was "for the artistic power and integrity with which, in his epic of the Don, he had given expression to a historic phase in the life of the Russian people."

Sholokhov proved to be an ungracious winner. "I am the first Russian writer, the first Soviet writer to win the Nobel Prize," he told a press conference in Moscow. "It is natural that I should feel proud. It did come rather late, however."

Pasternak, he said, "was just an internal émigré" and "I am not going to change my opinion of Pasternak just because he's dead."

Sholokhov did change his opinion of the academy, which he had said was "not objective in its judgment of an individual author's worth" when Pasternak won the prize. But in 1965, he "gratefully" accepted the honor.

In Moscow, too, the academy was no longer depicted as a stooge of the West. "The fact that this bright talent has received the world's recognition is estimated by Soviet writers as a victory of Soviet literature," said Leonid Leonov, a Union of Soviet Writers official. "This is the rehabilitation of the Nobel Prize itself as an objective and noble recognition of literary talent."

The Swedish Academy's rehabilitation did not last very long. In 1970, Aleksandr Solzhenitsyn, who had chronicled life in the

Gulag, was awarded the Nobel Prize. Then, the Union of Soviet Writers said that "it is deplorable that the Nobel committee allowed itself to be drawn into an unseemly game that was not started in the interests of the development of the spiritual values and traditions of literature but was prompted by speculative political consideration."

Ivinskaya was released from prison in late 1964; Irina had been released two years earlier, also after serving half her sentence. While at the camp in Potma, Ivinskaya had written to Khrushchev to plead for clemency, particularly for her daughter, whom she described as "dying slowly right in front of my eyes." In June 1961, *The New York Times* reported that Ivinskaya and her daughter were seriously ill and hospitalized. Irina was reported to have a stomach ulcer.

"I am not saying that I am not guilty because I believe Pasternak was guilty," wrote Ivinskaya at the start of the letter, dated March 10, 1961. Nor did she blame Pasternak, although she was frank in her descriptions of his involvement in the effort to bring in his royalties. "One cannot just present [Pasternak] as an innocent lamb," she said, stating the plainest of facts. "This does not deceive anyone and neither does my 'criminal case.'"

In the long, rambling letter that sprawled over sixteen handwritten pages, Ivinskaya argued that the case against her was flawed, if not ludicrous. And she expressed disbelief that her daughter, "this girl," was imprisoned—"and for what? Just for holding the suitcase . . . ?"

Ivinskaya said she only learned at KGB headquarters that the receipt of money from abroad—even though such transactions weren't particularly appealing—had damaged the state. She noted, as had her defense lawyers and Pasternak's defenders in the West, that the author had received royalties from abroad for some time and the money helped support Pasternak and his family. Ivinskaya mentioned the Pasternak family's purchase of a new car. "It was impossible not to know the money came from abroad," she wrote.

"I shared Pasternak's life for 14 years and in most cases I shared not his royalties but all his misfortunes and the vicissitudes of his fate and very often in contrast to my beliefs," she continued. "But

I loved him and I did my best as my friends joked to shield him with my 'broad back.' And he believed that I was his closest and dearest person, the person whom he needed most."

She noted—as she would later in her memoir—that she intervened with D'Angelo to delay publication of *Doctor Zhivago* and that the Central Committee had asked her to stop Pasternak from meeting foreigners. In that, she had an even sterner ally in Zinaida Pasternak.

Ivinskaya concluded that Pasternak would "turn in his coffin if he found out the terrible end of my life was caused by him.

"Please return me and my daughter to life. I promise I will live the rest of my life so that it will be good for my country."

The letter was accompanied by a report from the camp commander on the "characteristics of the detainee." Ivinskaya was described as conscientious, modest, and polite, and it was noted that she "correctly understands" the politics of the Communist Party and the Soviet government. But the commander added that "she feels her conviction was wrong, that she was convicted for a crime she did not commit."

Tendentious excerpts from Ivinskaya's letter to Khrushchev were published in a Moscow newspaper in 1997 when Ivinskaya's heirs were in a dispute with the State Archives of Literature and Art over some of Pasternak's papers. The article, employing selective quotes, attempted to smear Ivinskaya as a KGB informer. The complete letter was not published. Unfortunately, the effort to damage Ivinskaya's reputation largely succeeded, as the article's allegation was uncritically reproduced in the Western press. A reading of the full letter, which is available in the State Archive of the Russian Federation in Moscow, simply doesn't support the label of informer. The KGB, in its own secret assessment, described Ivinskaya as anti-Soviet. The letter is the plea of a desperate woman who tried to ingratiate herself to the Soviet leader—as did countless other inmates who sought mercy from the Kremlin.

After her release, Ivinskaya resumed her career as a literary translator and started writing about her life. Her memoirs were taken out of the Soviet Union in 1976 by Yevtushenko and published under the title *A Captive of Time: My Years with Paster-*

nak. She died in 1995 at the age of eighty-three. Her daughter, Irina Yemelyanova, lives in Paris and has published two memoirs of her own.

Sergio D'Angelo lives in Viterbo, Italy, and continues to write about the Zhivago affair and charm guests as easily as he did Pasternak. He unsuccessfully sued Feltrinelli for half of Pasternak's royalties in the 1960s. He believed he had a claim to the money because of a note Pasternak had written, asking that D'Angelo be rewarded. D'Angelo had hoped to use the royalties to establish a literary prize in Pasternak's name that would be "awarded to writers who have championed the cause of freedom." The court battle was protracted and D'Angelo finally abandoned his appeal of a lower-court ruling. The English translation of his memoir is available online.

In 1966, the Pasternak family, with the support of the Soviet authorities, began to negotiate a settlement with Feltrinelli over the royalties and the transfer of Pasternak's money to the Soviet Union. "It seems to me that the time has come for frankness and loyalty, all the more fitting by way of a tribute to the memory of the late Poet," Feltrinelli wrote to Alexander Volchkov, the president of the College of International Jurists in Moscow, and the Pasternak family's representative. "The time is therefore ripe, in my opinion, for all of us to take a more open and straightforward step forward, including those who at the time showed no mercy to the noble figure of the late Poet."

A deal took several years to reach—so long that the Soviets, on their visits to Milan, "learned to wind spaghetti around their forks," in the words of Feltrinelli's son. Schewe reported that Ivinskaya was "bellicose and uncompromising as ever" and reluctant to share the estate, although she had no legal standing to challenge any agreement. She received the equivalent of $24,000 in rubles in acknowledgment of her role as Pasternak's "faithful companion" when a final settlement was reached in 1970.

By that year, Feltrinelli's political passions were beginning to consume him. After he broke with the Italian Communist Party, he felt like he "no longer believed in anything. No type of commitment either ideological or political." But two visits to Cuba in 1964 and 1965, and long discussions with Fidel Castro, whose memoirs he hoped to publish, had a rejuvenating effect on Feltrinelli. Here was a political experiment he could admire. The Cold War adversaries seemed hopelessly corrupt to him as the 1960s progressed—the Americans were killing in Vietnam and Soviet tanks were smothering the Prague Spring. In Italy, Feltrinelli feared a Fascist coup. The publisher gradually and then completely immersed himself in a radical, anti-imperialist struggle, and his views hardened to the point that he advocated "the use of systematic and progressive counter-violence" to ensure the success of the Italian working class. For the Italian secret services, he was fast becoming an enemy of the state. When bombs exploded in Milan at the Banca Nazionale dell'Agricultura, killing sixteen and injuring eighty-four, Feltrinelli's name was floated as a suspect by the police. He could have fought the accusation, but instead went underground—seeking "untraceability," as he called it. "It is the only condition that allows me to serve the cause of socialism," he said in a letter to his staff. He moved from place to place between Italy, Switzerland, France, and Austria. He assumed new identities. He was unsuited to a life on the run and seemed increasingly haggard and disoriented. "He's lost," his wife, Inge Schönthal Feltrinelli, wrote in her diary. When she met him in Innsbruck in April 1970, she failed to recognize him. "He looked like a tramp." A year later, when the Bolivian consul in Hamburg—a regime thug—was assassinated, the gun was traced to Feltrinelli. He was not involved in the conspiracy but probably met the assassin through his Latin American contacts and gave her the gun—a .38 Colt Cobra—on the Côte d'Azur. There was now no way back. He was a revolutionary outlaw. He wrote a long letter to the Red Brigades, a violent Marxist-Leninist paramilitary group, suggesting that they work together on "a political, strategic and tactical platform." Later in 1971, he wrote a new manifesto, *Class Struggle or Class War?*—a call for the revolutionary movement to confront, wear down, and disarm the political and military power of its adversary.

On March 15, 1972, the body of a man was found under a high-voltage electricity pylon in a suburb of Milan. It was Feltrinelli. He was killed when the bomb he and some co-conspirators planned to use to cause a power cut went off prematurely. "Did the explosion happen because of a sharp movement up on the crossbar (the fabric of the pocket pressing against the timer, the pin making contact) or did someone set the time with minutes instead of hours?" Feltrinelli's son Carlo asked in his memoir of his father. "The answer might close the story, but it would not resolve what really matters."

In 1988 and 1989, as he rode the subway in Moscow, the journalist David Remnick was arrested by an incredible sight: "ordinary people reading Pasternak in their sky-blue copies of *Novy Mir*." The intelligentsia had long since read *Doctor Zhivago* and the other banned works of seven decades of censorship. Now it was the turn of ordinary people to experience the excitement of what for so long had been forbidden.

Official attitudes toward Pasternak began to soften in the early 1980s—before the reformist Mikhail Gorbachev became the Soviet leader and his policy of glasnost allowed the publication of banned works. Pasternak's former protégés, including the poets Voznesensky and Yevtushenko, began to agitate for the publication of *Doctor Zhivago*. Voznesensky described publication as a litmus test of the times, an act necessary to lance the past. "It will be a triumph over the witch hunt against anti-Sovietism," he said.

"You destroy the black magic myth," he continued. "The lie against Pasternak will be dead. It will be a revolution."

The magazine *Ogonyok* (Little Flame) published some short excerpts from *Doctor Zhivago* in December 1987. From January to April 1988, *Novy Mir*, the journal that first rejected *Doctor Zhivago*, serialized the novel and Soviet readers could finally and openly read Pasternak's work in full. A first legal Russian edition appeared the following year and the copyright line read: "Giangiacomo Feltrinelli Editore Milano."

At the V. I. Lenin State Library, which was later renamed the Russian State Library, a copy of the CIA edition of *Doctor Zhivago* that had been hidden away since 1959 was transferred out of the Spetskhran (Special Collections) and made available to the public, albeit on a controlled basis because the edition is considered very precious. In libraries across Russia, thousands of titles and "a wealth of noncommunist philosophy, political science, history, and economics and the treasure trove of Russian émigré memoirs and literature" emerged from the hidden stacks.

Olga Carlisle, who had interviewed Pasternak shortly before his death, was in Moscow at the time *Doctor Zhivago* began to appear. On a spring evening on Gorky Street, she and a friend saw a line of two or three hundred people. Carlisle's companion, a Muscovite, joined the queue out of habit before knowing what was for sale, an old Soviet instinct in case some rare consumer good or food had made it to the threadbare shelves of the city's stores. The line ended at a bookstore and the crowd, they soon learned, was expecting a shipment of copies of *Doctor Zhivago* the following morning.

Also in 1989, the Swedish Academy invited Yevgeny Pasternak, who along with his wife, Yelena, had become the tireless compiler and editor of Boris Pasternak's complete works, to come to Stockholm. In a brief ceremony in the academy's great hall on December 9, Sture Allén, the permanent secretary, read the telegrams Pasternak had sent accepting and then rejecting the Nobel Prize in October 1958. Yevgeny was overcome with emotion when he stepped forward and on behalf of his father accepted the gold medal for the 1958 Nobel Prize in Literature.

Afterword

"A successful stunt, don't you think?" said the Dutch intelligence officer C. C. (Kees) van den Heuvel, who worked with the CIA on the first printing of *Doctor Zhivago*.

There was something of the caper about the Zhivago operation and, more generally, the books program. Émigrés, priests, athletes, students, businessmen, tourists, soldiers, musicians, and diplomats—they all carried books across the Iron Curtain and into the Soviet Union. Books were sent to Russian prisoners of war in Afghanistan, foisted on Russian truck drivers in Iran, and offered to Russian sailors in the Canary Islands, as well being pressed into the hands of visitors to the Vatican pavilion in Brussels and the World Youth Festival in Vienna.

The Zhivago operation left such an impression on CIA officer Walter Cini and his Dutch colleague Joop van der Wilden that they were still talking about it in the 1990s, and discussing the possibility of opening a museum dedicated to Pasternak. The CIA had genuinely lofty ambitions for the vast library of books it spirited east. In one of its only claims for its covert intellectual campaign ever made public, the agency said the books program was "demonstrably effective" and "can inferentially be said to influence attitudes and reinforce predispositions toward intellectual and cultural freedom, and dissatisfaction with its absence."

Even after many of the agency's activities in the cultural Cold War were disclosed in the press in the late 1960s, forcing the agency to halt some of its political warfare operations, the secret distribution of books remained largely unexposed and continued until late 1991. From the birth of the books program in the 1950s until the fall of the USSR, the CIA distributed 10 million books and periodicals in Eastern Europe and the Soviet Union. Either CIA funds went to small publishers who smuggled books or the agency ran its own one-off operations, as in the case of *Doctor Zhivago.* In the program's final years, when Gorbachev was in power, at least 165,000 books were sent to the Soviet Union annually. Not just fiction was smuggled in pockets and suitcases, but "dictionaries and books on language, art and architecture, religion and philosophy, economics, management, and farming, history and memoirs, and catalogues."

Some of this extraordinary story has come out, piecemeal, in revelations by former employees of CIA-sponsored organizations and in the work of scholars such as Alfred A. Reisch, who have put together a history of the programs in Eastern Europe from records in universities and private hands. "Millions of people," he concluded, "were affected one way or another by the book project without ever hearing about its existence." For these individuals, the books program meant a well-thumbed piece of literature or history received in secret from a trusted friend and, in turn, passed on to another.

Much of the official record of this effort, including all the files of the Bedford Publishing Company, which targeted the Soviet Union, remains classified. There are reasons to fear that some of the agency's—and the public's—rich inheritance no longer exists. A former CIA officer told the authors that the agency for a long time had kept a collection of its miniature bible-stock publications, but many of the books were destroyed to make room for other material.

The battle over the publication of *Doctor Zhivago* was one of the first efforts by the CIA to leverage books as instruments of political warfare. Those words can seem distasteful and cynical, and critics of the CIA's role in the cultural Cold War view the agency's secrecy as inherently immoral and corrupting. But the CIA and its contractors were certain of the nobility of their efforts, and that in the face of an authoritarian power with its own propaganda machine, a resort to secrecy was unavoidable. All these years later, in an age of terror, drones, and targeted killing, the CIA's faith—and the Soviet Union's faith—in the power of literature to transform society seem almost quaint.

The global standing of the Soviet Union was bruised by its treatment of Pasternak. "We caused much harm to the Soviet Union," wrote Khrushchev, who said he was "truly sorry for the way [he] behaved toward Pasternak." Khrushchev was a virtual prisoner in his own home when he dictated his memoirs, and in an irony that would surely have brought a small smile to Pasternak's face, he allowed the tapes to be spirited out of the Soviet Union and published in the West.

It was a path that many others, following Pasternak's example, would take. He became a model for a line of courageous Soviet writers who followed his example of publishing abroad. Aleksandr Solzhenitsyn may be the most prominent example. Their number also included Sinyavsky and Daniel, the two young men who carried the lid of Pasternak's coffin, and another Russian Nobel Prize winner, the poet Joseph Brodsky.

In the wake of Pasternak's death, a new community emerged that strived for the same "intellectual and artistic emancipation as the dead poet had," wrote the historian Vladislav Zubok. "And they viewed themselves as the descendants of the great cultural and moral tradition that Pasternak, his protagonist Yuri Zhivago, and his milieu embodied. Thus, they were Zhivago's children, in a spiritual sense."

Brodsky said that, beginning with *Doctor Zhivago,* Pasternak caused a wave of conversions to Russian Orthodoxy, especially among the Jewish intelligentsia. "If you belong to Russian culture and you think in its categories, you know perfectly well that this culture is nursed by Orthodoxy," he said. "That's why you turn to the Orthodox Church. Let alone that it is a form of opposition."

Pasternak's grave became a pilgrimage site, a place to pay homage "to all hunted and tormented poets," as one poet described his visits to Peredelkino in the 1970s. The young people who stayed late reciting Pasternak's poetry on the day of his burial kept coming back, and year after year, new faces and generations continued to recite the lines from his poem "Hamlet":

Yet the order of the acts is planned
And the end of the way inescapable.
I am alone; all drowns in the Pharisees' hypocrisy.
To live your life is not as simple as to cross a field.

Acknowledgments

We have been helped by many very generous people who made this book possible. Thank you.

Paul Koedijk introduced us and started our conversation about *Doctor Zhivago,* exchanges that led to our decision to write this book together. Raphael Sagalyn, our literary agent, shepherded us into the world of publishing. Kris Puopolo, our editor, believed in this story from the first moment.

We thank Sonny Mehta, the editor in chief of Knopf Doubleday, and Dan Frank, the editorial director of Pantheon Books, for taking us into the same house that published *Doctor Zhivago* in the United States in 1958; Daniel Meyer of Doubleday; and Ellie Steel and Matthew Broughton at Harvill Secker in London.

Ken Kalfus, Patrick Farrelly, Kate O'Callaghan, and Paul Koedijk gave us early and important feedback.

We want to single out Natasha Abbakumova of *The Washington Post*'s Moscow bureau, whose assistance was extraordinary.

A number of people were critical to our understanding of this story. Carlo Feltrinelli and Inge Schönthal-Feltrinelli at *Doctor Zhivago*'s first home in Milan; Sergio D'Angelo in Viterbo; the late Yevgeni Pasternak; Natalya Pasternak, Yelena Chukovskaya, and Dmitri Chukovsky in Moscow; Irina Kozovoi (Yemelyanova) and Jacqueline de Proyart in Paris (1998); Roman Bernaut and Alexis Bernaut in Reclos, France; Gerd Ruge in Munich; and Megan Morrow in San Francisco.

We are grateful for the support of Joe Lambert, Mary Wilson, Bruce Barkan, Debbie Lebo, Marie Harf, and Preston Golson at the CIA, and we thank all the officers who served in the CIA's Historical Collections Division. After being greeted with a polite no when we first asked about the agency's *Zhivago* papers, Bruce van Vorst, former CIA officer and journalist, helped through various intermediaries to bring our project to the attention of the right people at the agency. Former CIA officers Burton Gerber and Benjamin Fischer provided insights along the way. We were also helped by Dirk Engelen, in-house historian at the Dutch intelligence services, the AIVD, formerly the BVD. The assistance of the late BVD officer C. C. (Kees) van den Heuvel was invaluable as was that of former MI6 officer Rachel van der Wilden, the widow of BVD officer Joop van der Wilden. Other former CIA officers who assisted us did not wish to be identified.

We have been aided by librarians and researchers across the United States and Europe. Our thanks to: Ron Basich, who conducted research at the Hoover Institution Archives; Janet Crayne and Kate Hutchens at the University of Michigan Library; Valoise Armstrong at the Dwight D. Eisenhower Presidential Museum and Library; David A. Langbart and Miriam Kleiman at the National Archives in College Park, Maryland; Tanya Chebotarev at Columbia University's Bakhmeteff Archive; Koos Couvée Jr., who conducted research at the National Archives in London; Jan Paul Hinrichs, Joke Bakker, Bryan Beemer at Leiden University Library; Willeke Tijssen at the International Institute of Social History in Amsterdam; Professor Gustaaf Janssens at the Archive of the Royal Palace in Brussels; Patricia Quaghebeur of the KADOC (Documentation and Research Centre for Religion, Culture and Society) in Leuven, Belgium; Johanna Couvée for research in the academic libraries in Brussels; Delfina Boero, Paola Pellegatta, Vladimir Kolupaev at the Fondazione Russia Christiana, Villa Ambiveri in Seriate, Italy; Lars Rydquist at the Nobel Library; Magnus Ljunggren in Stockholm; Elisabet Lind for her warm hospitality in Stockholm; Linda Örtenblad, Odd Zschiedrich, and Ulrika Kjellin for their support at the Swedish Academy; the staff of the State Archive of the Russian Federation (GARF); Yelena Makareki at the Russian State Library in Moscow; Anne Qureshi at the Frankfurter Buchmesse; and Rainer Laabs at Axel Springer AG Unternehmensarchiv in Berlin.

We would like to say thank you to Svetlana Prudnikova, Volodya Alexandrov, Maria Lipman, and Anna Masterova in Moscow; Shannon Smiley in Berlin; Leigh Turner in London; Theo Maarten van Lint at Oxford University; Pieter Claerhout in Ghent; Maghiel van Crevel and Jinhua Wu at Leiden University, and Mark Gamsa at Tel Aviv University.

In the United States, we would like to acknowledge the help of Denise Donegan, Max Frankel, Edward Lozansky, Gene Sosin, Gloria Donen Sosin, Manon van der Water, Jim Critchlow, Alan Wald, Anton

Troianovski, Jack Masey, Ulf and Ingrid Roeller, Ansgar Graw, and the Isaac Patch family.

In the Netherlands, the late Peter de Ridder was welcoming and helpful. We are grateful to his family and, in particular, his son, Rob de Ridder. We want to thank the late Cornelius van Schooneveld; Dorothy van Schooneveld; Barbara and Edward van der Beek; and the Starink family. Thanks to Roelf van Til for bringing Couvée's articles about the Zhivago story to a broad Dutch audience on public television in January 1999, and to Bart Jan Spruyt for the introduction to Kees van den Heuvel. Also our thanks to: Brigitte Soethout; Michel Kerres and Edith Loozen; Igor Cornelissen; Rob Hartmans; Elisabeth Spanjer; Kitty van Densen; Han Vermeulen; and Dick Coutinho.

Peter Finn writes: It has been a privilege to work for the Graham family for eighteen years: I would like to thank Don Graham and Katherine Weymouth for the wonderful professional home they created. Editors at *The Washington Post* allowed me to take a leave of absence to work on this book. Thanks to Marty Baron, Kevin Merida, Cameron Barr, Anne Kornblut, and Jason Ukman. I've worked with many great editors and reporters over the years, including my colleagues in the National Security group, but I am especially grateful to Joby Warrick, David Hoffman, Scott Higham, Jean Mack, Walter Pincus, Robert Kaiser, Anup Kaphle, and Julie Tate for their help and encouragement on this book.

I spent my leave at the Woodrow Wilson International Center for Scholars, a wonderful institution that allows the time to think and write. I'm grateful to Peter Reid for getting me in the door, and to the center's leaders and staff, including Jane Harman, Michael Van Dusen, Robert Litwak, Blair Ruble, Christian Osterman, William Pomeranz, Alison Lyalikov, Janet Spikes, Michelle Kamalich, and Dagne Gizaw. Also thanks to my fellow visiting scholars at the Wilson International Center: Jack Hamilton, Steve Lee Myers, Mark Mazetti, Michael Adler, and Ilan Greenberg. I'm very grateful for A. Ross Johnson's continuing interest in this project. I was fortunate to be able to work with two wonderful Wilson International Center interns, Chandler Grigg and Emily Olsen, who conducted research at the National Archives and the Library of Congress.

I would like to acknowledge the support of Walter and Stephanie Dorman; John and Sheila Haverkampf; Barry Baskind and Eileen FitzGerald; Joseph FitzGerald Jr.; and the late Joseph and Deirdre FitzGerald.

In Ireland, I want to thank my brothers Greg and Bill, and their families. It's a great regret that my parents, Bill and Pat, didn't live to read this book. Also, a tip of the hat to old friends: Jeremy and Mary Crean, and Ronan and Grainne Farrell.

Thanks to Rachel, Liam, David, and Ria Finn, who watched this book take shape with pride and patience. Nora FitzGerald is a partner in everything. (Love you!)

Petra Couvée writes: In Moscow I was fortunate to enjoy the encouragement of Thymen Kouwenaar, cultural counselor at the Embassy of the Kingdom of the Netherlands, and the intelligent support of Menno Kraan. The Netherlands Institute in Saint Petersburg provided all sorts of general and technical support. I would like to thank Mila Chevalier, Anna Vyborova, Aai Prins, and Gerard van der Wardt at the Netherlands Institute, Saint Petersburg; my Russian colleagues, especially Vladimir Belousov, at the Lomonosov State University in Moscow, and Irina Mikhailova at the State University of Saint Petersburg; and all my Russian students. Thanks to the Dutch Language Union (Nederlandse Taalunie), Ingrid Degraeve, and my colleagues and students at the 2013 summer course in Zeist for granting me a leave to finalize the book.

I am continuously grateful to my family and my friends Manon van der Water, Harco Alkema, Kees de Kock, Arie van der Ent, Maarten Mous, Nony Verschoor; Maghiel van Crevel, for being illuminating; and Henk Maier for literature and lifelong loving loyalty. My parents, Koos Couvée Sr. and Paula van Rossen, for being together and each for their own part an inspiration.

A Note on Sources

We have been interested in the Zhivago story for a number of years. Petra Couvée, who now teaches at Saint Petersburg State University, first wrote in 1999 about the role of Dutch intelligence, the BVD, in the secret publication of *Doctor Zhivago*. One of the BVD's former senior officers, Kees van den Heuvel, after consulting with his former agency colleagues, told Couvée that the BVD helped arrange a printing of the novel in The Hague at the request of the CIA. This admission was the first semi-official acknowledgment of CIA involvement. Couvée's findings were published in the Amsterdam literary magazine *De Parelduiker* (The Pearl Diver). Peter Finn wrote about the theory that the CIA sought to win the Nobel Prize for Pasternak in *The Washington Post* in 2007 when he was the newspaper's Moscow bureau chief. That story led us to start communicating about the Zhivago affair after we were introduced by the Dutch Cold War historian and journalist Paul Koedijk.

Eventually we began to consider writing a new history of *Doctor Zhivago* in the Cold War. We believed this book could not be written unless we were able to clarify exactly what the CIA did or did not do. The CIA had never acknowledged its role in the secret publication of *Doctor Zhivago*. In 2007, Peter Finn told Yevgeni Pasternak, Boris Pasternak's son, that he would attempt to obtain any CIA records about the operation. Yevgeni Pasternak was skeptical. He did not live to see the release of any material and, in any case, regarded the whole CIA connection as a distressing and "cheap sensation," as he told Finn. His father would no doubt have agreed. Pasternak was unhappy about the exploitation of his novel for Cold War propaganda purposes. He never knew about the CIA's involvement in the secret printing of the novel in Russian; he had reason to believe that it was the work of Russian émigrés, though he knew well that they operated in a murky world that sometimes involved Western intelligence services.

Finn asked the CIA to release any documents that it had on the printing of *Doctor Zhivago*. The first request was made to the agency's public affairs office in 2009. We finally obtained the documents in August 2012. The CIA released approximately 135 previously classified internal documents about its involvement in the printing of two Russian-language editions of the book, the hardback edition distributed in Brussels and a paperback edition printed at CIA headquarters the following year. The CIA's own historians found and reviewed the agency's documentation and shepherded the internal declassification process. We were able to review these documents before their public release. The CIA placed no conditions on our use of these documents and did not review any section of this book.

The documents reveal a series of blunders that nearly derailed the first printing of the book and led the CIA to make the second printing of the paperback edition an entirely black operation. The CIA plans to publish these documents itself and post them on its website. There are undoubtedly still classified documents in the possession of the CIA that bear on the subject, but a U.S. official said the vast majority of the documents that were found in an internal search of agency records have now been released and those withheld will not affect public understanding of the agency's operations regarding *Doctor Zhivago*. A number of documents that were referenced in the released material but were not found are presumed to have been lost, the official said. The CIA did redact most names and those of some allies and institutions in its documents, but through other sources it was possible to identify key actors in the drama. Still secret is the name of the original source who provided the manuscript to the British. The endnotes for chapters 8 and 9 provide details on the reasoning behind all deductions we have made. We hope this release will prompt the CIA to declassify more material on the Cultural Cold War it waged against the Soviet Union, including on the vast books program it underwrote for several decades.

A wealth of new material has appeared since the fall of the Soviet Union, including the Kremlin's own files and a rich array of memoirs and letters. The authors have drawn on Soviet documents in the State Archive of the Russian Federation (GARF), and the files of the Central Committee of the Communist Party of the Soviet Union, which were published in Moscow in 2001 as *"A za mnoyu shum pogoni . . ." Boris Pasternak i Vlast' Dokumenty: 1956–1972.* (Behind Me the Noise of Pursuit: Boris Pasternak and Power. Documents 1956–1972) (referred to in the notes as *Pasternak i Vlast'*). The Soviet documents in *Pasternak i Vlast'* are not available in English, but they have been published in French as *Le Dossier de l'affaire Pasternak, Archives du Comité central et du Politburo.*

Almost all of Pasternak's writing, including prose, poems, autobiographical sketches, correspondence, and biographical essays by family and friends, some of it never published in English, can be found in an eleven-volume collection edited by Yevgeni and Yelena Pasternak, his son and daughter-in-law: *Polnoe Sobranie Sochinenii, s prilozheniyami, v odinnadtsati tomakh* (Complete Collected Works with Appendices, in 11 Volumes). Volume 11, "Boris Pasternak remembered by his contemporaries," is a collection of memoirs and excerpts from memoirs; for this reason we cite the authors of these memoirs when referencing *Polnoe Sobranie Sochinenii* in the bibliography. In the notes and bibliography,we have directed readers to an English translation of material cited, when available, and to English-language books or articles.

The correspondence of Boris Pasternak and Giangiacomo Feltrinelli has been published by Yelena and Yevgeni Pasternak in *Kontinent,* 2001, nos. 107 and 108, and can be read in English in *Feltrinelli: A Story of Riches, Revolution and Violent Death,* Carlo Feltrinelli's memoir of his father, and in Paolo Mancosu, *Inside the Zhivago Storm: The Editorial Adventures of Pasternak's Masterpiece.*

We have also been able to interview a number of participants and contemporaneous witnesses in the drama, and some of their relatives or descendants, including Yevgeni Pasternak, Carlo Feltrinelli, Sergio D'Angelo, Andrei Voznesensky, Irina Yemelyanova, Yelena Chukovskaya, Dmitri Chukovsky, Gerd Ruge, Max Frankel, Walter Pincus, Roman Bernaut, Peter de Ridder, Rachel van der Wilden, Kees van den Heuvel, Cornelis H. van Schooneveld, and Jacqueline de Proyart. Some of these interviews took place before we planned on writing this book when we were working on shorter articles about various aspects of the Zhivago Affair.

We have also drawn on the great number of memoirs of the era, many of which appeared after the fall of the Soviet Union. Carlo Feltrinelli allowed us to hold and peruse the *Doctor Zhivago* manuscript carried out by D'Angelo—a visceral and electrifying moment for us. Megan Morrow, the daughter of the New York publisher Felix Morrow, gave us the relevant portions of her father's still-sealed oral history, which describes his work for the CIA on *Doctor Zhivago;* his oral testimony is held at Columbia University. Peter de Ridder, one of Mouton's publishers, gave his consent to the General Intelligence and Security Service

(AIVD), the successor to the BVD, to turn over any files they held on him to us. We received the files in September 2009; the documents simply record his travel to the Soviet Union and Eastern Europe as a representative of Mouton.

We have consulted archives and personal papers in Russia, the United States, Italy, the United Kingdom, the Netherlands, Germany, Belgium, and Sweden. They are listed in detail in the bibliography. All newspapers, magazines, and journals consulted are cited in the endnotes.

Notes

Prologue

3 **The Italian was in Peredelkino to charm a poet**: The description of May 20, 1956, and D'Angelo's meeting with Pasternak, including direct quotes, comes from D'Angelo's memoir *Delo Pasternaka* (The Pasternak Affair); interviews with D'Angelo in Moscow in September 2007 and in Viterbo, Italy, in May 2012; and numerous email exchanges between the authors and D'Angelo. D'Angelo also provided the authors with an unpublished English-language version of *Delo Pasternaka*. D'Angelo's book can be read in English at his website: http://www.pasternakbydangelo.com. D'Angelo acknowledges that in his memoirs he got the date wrong of the Radio Moscow broadcast about *Doctor Zhivago*, placing it in May, not April. He insists that the May 20 date is correct.

4 **the women wore kerchiefs**: "Boris Pasternak: The Art of Fiction No. 25," interview by Olga Carlisle, *The Paris Review* 24 (1960): 61–66.

4 **village lore**: Lobov and Vasilyeva, "Peredelkino: Skazanie o pisatel'skom gorodke."

4 **"Entrapping writers within a cocoon of comforts"**: Carlisle, *Under a New Sky*, 13.

5 **"The production of souls"**: K. Zelinsky, "Odna vstrecha u M. Gor'kogo. Zapis' iz dnevnika" (A meeting at M. Gorky's. Entry from the diary), *Voprosy literatury* 5 (1991), 166; Ruder, *Making History for Stalin*, 44.

5 **an Arab *and* his horse**: Tsvetaeva, *Art in the Light of Conscience*, 22.

5 **"half closing his slanted brown eyes"**: "Boris Pasternak: The Art of Fiction No. 25," interview by Olga Carlisle, *The Paris Review* 24 (1960): 61–66.

6 **"like speaking to the victims of shipwreck"**: Berlin, *Personal Impressions*, 230.

6 **"like a melting glacier it grew up"**: Boris Pasternak, *Safe Conduct*, 71.

6 **"He always spoke with his peculiar brand of vitality"**: Berlin, *Personal Impressions*, 220.

8 **"Publication abroad would expose me"**: Boris Pasternak, *Family Correspondence*, 376.

8 **the side gate between their gardens**: Shentalinsky, *The KGB's Literary Archive,* 145.

8 **"To me a finished literary work is like weapon"**: Ibid., 141.

9 **Pasternak remembered Pilnyak**: Berlin, *Personal Impressions,* 225.

9 **"Is it really you?"**: Shentalinsky, *The KGB's Literary Archive,* 139.

9 **"to have paper"**: Ibid., 156.

9 **All of Pilnyak's works**: Ibid., 157.

10 **24,138,799 copies of "politically damaging" works**: Westerman, *Engineers of the Soul,* 188.

10 **"It was awful"**: Zinaida Pasternak, *Vospominaniya,* in Boris Pasternak, *Vtoroe Rozhdenie,* 293.

10 **"somnambulistic quality"**: Chukovsky, *Diary,* December 10, 1931, 262.

10 **"My final happiness and madness"**: Boris Pasternak, letter to Olga Freidenberg, January 24, 1947, in Boris Pasternak and Olga Freidenberg, *Correspondence,* 263.

11 **"zoological apostasy"**: *Novy Mir* (New World) board to Pasternak, September 1956 letter published in *Literaturnaya Gazeta* (Literary Gazette) October 25, 1958. See Conquest, *Courage of Genius,* Appendix II, 136–63.

11 **The manuscript "should be given to anyone who asks for it"**: Ivinskaya, *A Captive of Time,* 195.

12 **"Don't yell at me"**: Conquest, *Courage of Genius,* 37–38.

12 **"a vast white expanse"** "Boris Pasternak: The Art of Fiction No. 25," interview by Olga Carlisle, *The Paris Review* 24 (1960): 61–66.

12 **The manuscript was nearly 800 closely typed pages**: This figure is corrected from earlier editions. See Paulo Mancosu's Nov 5, 2014 blogpost at www.zhivagostorm.org. The original manuscript obtained by D'Angelo is held at La Biblioteca della Fondazione Giangiacomo Feltrinelli, Milan.

13 **"You are hereby invited to my execution"**: D'Angelo, *Delo Pasternaka,* 13.

14 **nearly 1,500 writers in the Soviet Union were executed or died in labor camps**: Shentalinsky, *The KGB's Literary Archive,* 6.

14 **"Art belongs to the people"**: Garrard and Garrard, *Inside the Soviet Writers' Union,* 27.

15 **"irretrievably second-rate"**: Caute, *Politics and the Novel During the Cold War,* 150.

15 **In the Obozerka forced-labor camp**: Gladkov, *Meetings with Pasternak,* 172.

15 **"the skies were deeper"**: Victor Frank, "The Meddlesome Poet: Boris Pasternak's Rise to Greatness," *The Dublin Review* (Spring 1958): 52.

16 **"fidelity to poetic truth"**: Fyodor Dostoevsky, *Dnevnik Pisatelya* (A Writer's Diary), quoted in Wachtel, *An Obsession with History,* 13.

16 **"deadening and merciless"**: Boris Pasternak, *Doctor Zhivago* (2010), 360.

16 **It was said that British intelligence**: Felix Morrow letter to Carl R. Proffer, October 20, 1980, in University of Michigan Special Collections

Library: Box 7 of the Ardis Collection Records, Folder heading Ardis Author/Name Files—Morrow, Felix.

17 **Some of Pasternak's French friends believed**: Boris Pasternak, *Lettres à mes amies françaises (1956–1960)*, 41.

17 **a theory that has periodically resurfaced**: Dutch intelligence officials believed the target of the printing for the CIA was the Nobel Prize. C. C. van den Heuvel, interview by Petra Couvée, February 22, 1999. See also Chris Vos, *De Geheime Dienst: verhalen over de BVD* (The Secret Service: Stories about the BVD). The Russian author Ivan Tolstoy most recently gave currency to this thesis in *Otmytyi roman Pasternaka, "Doctor Zhivago" mezhdu KGB i TsRU* (Pasternak's Laundered Novel: Between the KGB and the CIA). For the Malta story see "A Footnote to the Zhivago Affair, or Ann Arbor's Strange Connections with Russian Literature," in Carl R. Proffer, *The Widows of Russia*.

17 **the printing was the work of Russian émigrés**: The Stanford University scholar Lazar Fleishman made this argument in *Vstrecha russkoi emigratsii s "Doktorom Zhivago": Boris Pasternak i "kholodnaya voina."*

Chapter 1

19 **Bullets cracked**: Alexander Pasternak, *A Vanished Present*, 204.

20 **"the scream of wheeling swifts"**: Ibid., 205.

20 **"the air drained clear"**: Ibid., 206.

20 ***kibitka***: Boris Pasternak, "Lyudi i polozheniya" (People and Circumstances), in Boris Pasternak, *Polnoe Sobranie Sochinenii*, vol. 3, 328.

20 **"Just imagine when an ocean of blood"**: Barnes, *Boris Pasternak*, vol. 1, 224; Konstantin Loks, "Povest' ob odnom desyatiletii 1907–1917" (Tale of a Decade 1907–1917) in Boris Pasternak, *Polnoe Sobranie Sochinenii*, vol. 11, 56.

21 **"overwhelmed" and "intoxicated"**: Josephine Pasternak, *Tightrope Walking*, 82.

21 **"I watched a meeting last night"**: This quote up to "the roof over the whole of Russia has been torn off" from Boris Pasternak, *Doctor Zhivago* (2010), 128.

21 **"What magnificent surgery"**: Ibid., 173.

21 **"the abolition of all exploitation"**: Smith, *The Russian Revolution*, 40.

21 **"First, the ideas of general improvement"**: Boris Pasternak, *Doctor Zhivago* (2010), 303.

22 **"I grant you're all bright lights"**: Ibid., 304.

22 **"a man of a dreamy, gentle disposition"**: Mark, *The Family Pasternak*, 110.

23 **"one of those he had described"**: Boris Pasternak, *I Remember*, 67.

23 **"I have observed art and important people"**: Barnes, *Boris Pasternak*,vol.

1, 20; Boris Pasternak letter to M. A. Froman, June 17, 1927, in Boris Pasternak, *Polnoe Sobranie Sochinenii,* vol. 8, 42.

23 **"Mother was music"**: Mark, *The Family Pasternak,* 111.

23 **"craving for improvisation"**: Boris Pasternak, *I Remember,* 38.

24 **his natural talents**: Barnes, *Boris Pasternak,* vol. 1, 82; Alexander Pasternak, *Vanished Present,* 135.

24 **"I despised everything uncreative"**: Boris Pasternak, *I Remember,* 40.

24 **a "tipsy society"**: Boris Pasternak, *Safe Conduct,* 23.

24 **"They did not suspect"**: Barnes, *Boris Pasternak,* vol. 1, 94; Konstantin Loks, "Povest' ob odnom desyatiletii 1907–1917" (Tale of a Decade 1907-1917), in Boris Pasternak, *Polnoe Sobranie Sochinenii,* vol. 11, 37.

24 **"spoke in a toneless voice"**: Tsvetaeva, *Art in the Light of Conscience,* 22.

25 **"not of this world"**: Boris Pasternak and Olga Freidenberg, *Correspondence,* 3.

25 **"Borya did all the talking as usual"**: Ibid., 10.

25 **"Just try to live normally"**: Barnes, *Boris Pasternak,* vol. 1, 140; Boris Pasternak letter to A. Stikh, July 4/17 and June 29/July 11, 1912, in Boris Pasternak, *Polnoe Sobranie Sochinenii,* vol. 7, 125.

25 **"God, how successful my trip"**: Boris Pasternak letter to A. Stikh, June 29/July 11, 1912, in *Boris Pasternak, Polnoe Sobranie Sochinenii,* vol. 7, 122.

25 **"wrote poetry not as a rare exception"**: Boris Pasternak, *I Remember,* 76.

25 **"a tuning-up"**: Andrei Sinyavsky, "Boris Pasternak" (1965) in Davie and Livingstone, *Pasternak: Modern Judgments,* 157.

26 **"The relationship remained platonic"**: Christopher Barnes, "Notes on Pasternak" in Fleishman, *Boris Pasternak and His Times,* 402.

26 **"no poet since Pushkin"**: Fleishman, *Boris Pasternak: The Poet and His Politics,* 109.

26 **"why listen to such nonsense?"**: "O, kak ona byla smela" (Oh, How Bold She Was) in Yevgeni Pasternak, *Ponyatoe i obretyonnoe, stat'i i vospominaniya,* 517.

26 **"It is like a conversation with you"**: Barnes, *Boris Pasternak,* vol. 1, 299; Boris Pasternak letter to Yevgenia Lurye, December 22, 1921, in Boris Pasternak, *Polnoe Sobranie Sochinenii,* vol. 7, 376–77.

26 **"Zhenya and Borya"**: "O, kak ona byla smela" (Oh, How Bold She Was) in Yevgeni Pasternak, *Ponyatoe i obretyonnoe, stat'i i vospominaniya,* 520.

27 **"Hemmed in on all sides by noise"**: Yevgeni Pasternak, *Boris Pasternak: The Tragic Years,* 12.

27 **"a man with inarguably more talent"**: "O, kak ona byla smela" (Oh, How Bold She Was) in Yevgeni Pasternak, *Ponyatoe i obretyonnoe, stat'i i vospominaniya,* 511.

27 **Zinaida was born in Saint Petersburg**: Zinaida Pasternak, *Vospominaniya,* in Boris Pasternak, *Vtoroe Rozhdenie,* 237–44.

27 **"I've shown myself unworthy"**: Boris Pasternak letter to parents and sisters, March 8, 1931, in Boris Pasternak, *Family Correspondence,* 195.
28 **Do not fret, do not cry, do not tax**: Translated by Raissa Bobrova. In Boris Pasternak, *Poems,* 167.
28 **"beauty is the mark of true feelings"**: Boris Pasternak letter to Jacqueline de Proyart, August 20, 1959, in Boris Pasternak, *Lettres à mes amies françaises (1956–1960),* 194–95.
28 **"painfully awkward"**: Zinaida Pasternak, *Vospominaniya,* in Boris Pasternak, *Vtoroe Rozhdenie,* 273–74.
28 **"I begged her to understand"**: Boris Pasternak, letter to Josephine Pasternak, February 11, 1932, in Boris Pasternak, *Family Correspondence,* 207.
28 **he gave long, tearful accounts**: Gerstein, *Moscow Memoirs,* 32.
28 **"It was around midnight"**: Boris Pasternak letter to Josephine Pasternak, February 11, 1932, in Boris Pasternak, *Family Correspondence,* 209.
29 **"In this state of bliss"**: Ibid.
29 **"Well, are you satisfied?"**: Ibid.
29 **"is much cleverer"**: Boris Pasternak, letter to parents and sisters, November 24, 1932, in Boris Pasternak, *Family Correspondence,* 230.
29 **"continued loving my father"**: "O, kak ona byla smela" (Oh, How Bold She Was) in Yevgeni Pasternak, *Ponyatoe i obretyonnoe, stat'i i vospominaniya,* 511.

Chapter 2

31 **devastating and prolonged civil war**: Alexander Pasternak, *Vanished Present,* 194; Barnes, *Boris Pasternak,* vol. 1, 244, 274, and 276.
31 **"Pasternak is uneasy in Berlin"**: Shklovsky, *Zoo, or Letters Not About Love,* 63.
32 **"Amidst Moscow streets"**: Boris Pasternak and Olga Freidenberg, *Correspondence,* page xviii.
32 **Berlin said Pasternak**: Berlin, *Personal Impressions,* 222.
32 **"Come to your senses"**: Boris Pasternak, *Doctor Zhivago* (2010), 110.
32 **"late accretion"**: Isaiah Berlin, letter to Edmund Wilson, December 23, 1958, in Berlin, *Enlightening: Letters 1946–1960,* 668.
32 **"My family was interested in music and art"**: Jhan Robbins, "Boris Pasternak's Last Message to the World," *This Week,* August 7, 1960.
32 **"last gamble of some croaking publisher"**: Tsvetaeva, *Art in the Light of Conscience,* 21.
33 **"To read Pasternak's verse"**: Osip Mandelstam, *Critical Prose and Letters,* 168.
33 **"in a downpour"**: Tsvetaeva, *Art in the Light of Conscience,* 22.

33 **"What century is it outside?"**: Lydia Pasternak Slater, "About These Poems," in Boris Pasternak, *Poems of Boris Pasternak,* 35.
33 **"hothouse aristocrat"**: Barnes, *Boris Pasternak,* vol. 1, 286.
34 **"It is silly, absurd, stupid"**: Trotsky, *Literature and Revolution,* 31.
34 **"Trotsky was no liberal"**: Service, *Trotsky,* 315.
34 **Pasternak was recovering**: Accounts of the meeting in Vil'mont, *O Borise Pasternake, vospominaniya i mysli,* 93–95; and Boris Pasternak, letter to V. F. Bryusov, August 15, 1922, in Boris Pasternak, *Polnoe Sobranie Sochinenii,* vol. 7, 398.
35 **"one remarkable feature"**: Nadezhda Mandelstam, *Hope Against Hope,* 161.
35 **black funeral carriage**: Montefiore, *Stalin,* 108.
35 **Pasternak was agitated**: Yevgeni Pasternak, *Sushchestvovan'ya tkan' skvoznaya, Boris Pasternak. perepiska s Yev. Pasternak,* 379.
36 **"suffered from a serious mental illness"**: Montefiore, *Stalin,* 12.
36 **For the evening at Voroshilov's**: Ibid., 3–22; Chuev, *Molotov Remembers,* 172–75.
37 **"On the evening before"**: Boris Pasternak's message to Stalin in *Literaturnaya Gazeta,* November 17, 1932.
37 **"From that moment onwards"**: Gerstein, *Moscow Memoirs,* 348.
38 **passionate, opinionated**: Akhmatova, *My Half-Century,* 85.
38 **We live, deaf to the land beneath us**: Nadezhda Mandelstam, *Hope Against Hope,* 13.
38 **In the version**: Shentalinsky, *The KGB's Literary Archive,* 172.
39 **"I didn't hear this"**: Ivinskaya, *A Captive of Time,* 61.
39 **playing the ukulele**: Akhmatova, *My Half-Century,* 101.
39 **Mandelstam thought he was doomed**: Shentalinsky, *The KGB's Literary Archive,* 175.
39 **"ideological food"**: Cohen, *Bukharin and the Bolshevik Revolution,* 238.
39 **"Pasternak is completely bewildered by Mandelstam's arrest"**: Bukharin, letter to Stalin, June 1934, in Russian State Archive of Socio-Political History. Col. : 558, I.: 11, F.: 709, S.: 167.
40 **"Isolate but preserve"**: Shentalinsky, *The KGB's Literary Archive,* 182.
40 **"If I were a poet and a poet friend of mine were in trouble"**: There are at least eleven versions of this conversation, according to Benedikt Sarnov in *Stalin and the Writers.* We have relied on the account of Nadezhda Mandelstam, Osip's widow, who spoke directly with Pasternak about it, albeit sometime after the phone call. See Nadezhda Mandelstam, *Hope Against Hope,* 146–48. We however translate the word *master,* which was used by Nadezhda Mandelstam in the Russian version of her memoir, as "master" rather than "genius."
41 **"He was quite right to say"**: Nadezhda Mandelstam, *Hope Against Hope,* 149.
41 **"Like many other people in our country"**: Ibid., 148.

41 **"something to say"**: Berlin, *Personal Impressions,* 223.

42 **"The immense talent of B. L. Pasternak"**: De Mallac, *Boris Pasternak,* 145.

42 **"Your lines about him"**: Clark et al., *Soviet Power and Culture: A History in Documents,* 322–23.

43 **"I am never sure where modesty ends"**: Gladkov, *Meetings with Pasternak,* 119.

43 **"a sincere and one of the most intense"**: Ivinskaya, *A Captive of Time,* 81.

43 **"Koba, why is my death necessary for you?"**: Service, *Stalin,* 592.

43 **Stalin personally signed**: Conquest, *Stalin: Breaker of Nations,* 203.

44 **Anatoli Tarasenkov, an editor of the journal *Znamya***: Anatoli Tarasenkov, "Pasternak, Chernovye zapisi [Pasternak, Draft Notes], 1934–1939," in Boris Pasternak, *Polnoe Sobranie Sochinenii,* vol. 11, 178–79.

44 **"My soul has never recovered from the trauma"**: Boris Pasternak and Olga Freidenberg, *Correspondence,* 175.

44 **"Everything snapped inside me"**: Ivinskaya, *A Captive of Time,* 81.

44 **"No forces will convince me"**: Barnes, *Boris Pasternak,* vol. 2, 138.

45 **In the 1937 file**: Eduard Shneiderman, "Benedikt Livshits: Arest, sledstvie, rasstrel" (Benedikt Livshits: Arrest, Investigation, Execution), *Zvezda* (Star) 1, (1996): 115.

45 **"I don't give them life"**: Barnes, *Boris Pasternak,* vol. 2, 148.

45 **"In those awful bloody years"**: Ibid., 144.

45 **"He seemed afraid"**: Berlin, *Personal Impressions,* 226.

45 **"Why, for example, did Stalin"**: Ehrenburg, *Post-War Years,* 277.

46 **"consumed in their flames"**: Gladkov, *Meetings with Pasternak,* 127.

46 **"My health is very poor"**: Shentalinsky, *The KGB's Literary Archive,* 192.

46 **"The only person"**: Nadezhda Mandelstam, *Hope Against Hope,* 132.

Chapter 3

47 **he hoped his prose would be worthy**: Boris Pasternak, letter to Nina Tabidze, January 24, 1946, in Boris Pasternak, *Polnoe Sobranie Sochinenii,* vol. 9, 438.

47 **large numbers of receipts**: Yevgeni Pasternak, *Boris Pasternak: The Tragic Years,* 178.

47 **"He was too great"**: Boris Pasternak, *Letters to Georgian Friends,* 151.

48 **he turned to look at Nina Tabidze**: Nina Tabidze, "Raduga na rassvete" (Rainbow at Dawn), in *Boris Pasternak, Polnoe Sobranie Sochinenii,* vol. 11, 333.

48 **"what it can be, real prose"**: Boris Pasternak, letter to E. D. Romanova, December 23, 1959, quoted in Ivinskaya, *A Captive of Time,* 186.

48 **"major works of literature exist"**: Gladkov, *Meetings with Pasternak,* 87.
48 **"I shall bid goodbye"**: Barnes, *Boris Pasternak,* vol. 1, 268.
48 **He told Tsvetaeva**: Ibid., 269.
48 **"dreamy, boring and tendentiously virtuous"**: Ibid.
48 **"Still in his high school years"**: Boris Pasternak, *Doctor Zhivago* (2010), 58.
48 **"his usual sense of acute dissatisfaction"**: Gladkov, *Meetings with Pasternak,* 113.
49 **General Alexander Gorbatov invited**: Tamara Ivanova, "Boris Leonidovich Pasternak," in Boris Pasternak, *Polnoe Sobranie Sochinenii,* vol. 11, 281.
49 **"I am reading Simonov"**: Gladkov, *Meetings with Pasternak,* 115.
49 **"the constant, nagging sense of being an imposter"**: Ibid., 87.
49 **"Shakespeare, the old man of Chistopol"**: Barnes, *Boris Pasternak,* vol. 2, 213.
49 **Mandelstam, who had once warned**: Akhmatova, *My Half-Century,* 99.
50 **"I want your poetry"**: Osip Mandelstam, *Critical Prose and Letters,* 562.
50 **"burn with shame"**: Boris Pasternak, letter to sisters, end of December 1945, in Boris Pasternak, *Family Correspondence,* 365.
50 **"profound inner change"**: Gladkov, *Meetings with Pasternak,* 124.
50 **The first recorded mention**: Boris Pasternak, letter to Nadezhda Mandelstam, in Boris Pasternak, *Polnoe Sobranie Sochinenii,* vol. 9, 421.
50 **Pasternak said he was working on a novel**: Gladkov, *Meetings with Pasternak,* 125.
50 **"I have started on this"**: Boris Pasternak, letter to sisters, end of December 1945, in Boris Pasternak, *Family Correspondence,* 370.
50 **"I am in the same high spirits"**: Boris Pasternak, letter to Olga Freidenberg, February 24, 1946, in Boris Pasternak and Olga Freidenberg, *Correspondence,* 251.
50 **days and weeks were whistling**: Yevgeni Pasternak, *Boris Pasternak: The Tragic Years,* 162.
50 **"I wrote it with great ease"**: De Mallac, *Boris Pasternak,* 181.
51 **"You see it in the concert halls"**: Boris Pasternak, letter to sisters, end of December 1945, in Boris Pasternak, *Family Correspondence,* 368.
51 **One acquaintance suggested**: Barnes, *Boris Pasternak,* vol. 2, 252.
51 **Pasternak arrived late**: Yevgeni Pasternak, *Boris Pasternak: The Tragic Years,* 163.
51 **"An Evening of Poetry"**: Max Hayward, introduction to Gladkov, *Meetings with Pasternak,* 20–24; De Mallac, *Boris Pasternak,* 194.
52 **"Who organized that standing ovation?"**: Nadezhda Mandelstam, *Hope Abandoned,* 375.
52 **Death to Fascism!**: Dalos, *The Guest from the Future,* 54.

52 **One Western reporter in Moscow**: Gerd Ruge, "Conversations in Moscow," *Encounter* 11, no. 4 (October 1958): 20–31.

52 **"in order to understand a figure"**: Dalos, *The Guest from the Future,* 95.

53 **"a KGB man"**: Testimony of Yuri Krotkov, aka George Karlin, before the U.S. Senate subcommittee to investigate the administration of the Internal Security Act. November 13, Committee on the Judiciary, Karlin Testimony, at 171, U.S. Government Printing Office, pt. 3 (1969).

53 **" 'They,' as I noticed"**: Nadezhda Mandelstam, *Hope Abandoned,* 594–95.

53 **"he worked heart and soul"**: Dalos, *The Guest from the Future,* 95.

53 **"hated him"**: Ivinskaya, *A Captive of Time,* 205.

53 **"Yes, really, don't be surprised"**: Valentin Berestov, "Srazu posle voiny" (Right After the War), in Boris Pasternak, *Polnoe Sobranie Sochinenii,* vol. 11, 485.

53 **He called it an epic**: Boris Pasternak, letter to Olga Freidenberg, October 5, 1946, in Boris Pasternak and Olga Freidenberg, *Correspondence,* 253.

54 **"on a knife-edge"**: Boris Pasternak, letter to Lydia Pasternak Slater, June 26, 1946, in Boris Pasternak, *Family Correspondence,* 373.

54 **"writes all kind of cock and bull stories"**: Transcript of Orgburo meeting in Moscow, August 9, 1946, in Clark et al., *Soviet Culture and Power,* 412.

54 **"vapid, content-less and vulgar things"**: Resolution published in *Pravda* on August 21, 1946, in Ibid., 421.

55 **a colossal boozer**: Service, *Stalin,* 437–38.

55 **"sycophantic contributions from the floor"**: Dalos, *The Guest from the Future,* 56.

55 **"Anna Akhmatova's subject-matter"**: Ibid., 56–57.

55 **She rued**: Boris Pasternak and Olga Freidenberg, *Correspondence,* 252–53.

55 **"Praising American Democracy"**: Conquest, *Stalin,* 277.

55 **"not one of us"**: Hingley, *Pasternak,* 166.

56 **"Yes, yes, [out of touch with] the people"**: Barnes, *Boris Pasternak,* vol. 2, 233.

56 **"For all the charm of certain passages"**: Chukovsky, *Diary,* September 10, 1946, 359.

56 **"it is a failure of genius"**: Mikhail Polivanov, "Tainaya Svoboda" (Silent Freedom), in Boris Pasternak, *Polnoe Sobranie Sochinenii,* vol. 11, 471.

56 **slackened**: Pasternak used this word in a letter to one reader. See Barnes, *Boris Pasternak,* vol. 2, 296.

56 **"an effort in the novel"**: Boris Pasternak, "Three Letters," *Encounter* 15, no. 2 (August 1960): 3–6.

57 **"gobbled down"**: Tamara Ivanova, "Boris Leonidovich Pasternak," in Boris Pasternak, *Polnoe Sobranie Sochinenii,* vol. 11, 285.

57 **"heard Russia"**: Emma Gerstein, commentary on *Doctor Zhivago,* Boris Pasternak, *Polnoe Sobranie Sochinenii,* vol. 4, 653.

57 **"a spring of pristine"**: Yevgeni Pasternak, *Boris Pasternak: The Tragic Years,* 181.

57 **Pasternak arrived with the pages**: Muravina, *Vstrechi s Pasternakom,* 46–52.

57 **Pasternak told the Gulag survivor**: Varlam Shalamov, "Pasternak," in Boris Pasternak, *Polnoe Sobranie Sochinenii,* vol. 11, 645–46.

58 **the home of the pianist Maria Yudina**: For descriptions of this evening see Ivinskaya, *A Captive of Time,* 182; Chukovskaya, "Otryvki iz dnevnika" (Diary fragments), in Boris Pasternak, *Polnoe Sobranie Sochinenii,* vol. 11, 407–8; and Yelena Berkovskaya, "Mal'chiki i devochki 40-kh godov" (Boys and Girls of the 1940s), in ibid., 540–41.

58 **looking forward to the reading**: Maria Yudina, in A. M. Kuznetsova, "'Vysokii stoikii dukh': Perepiska Borisa Pasternaka i Marii Yudinoi" ("High Resilient Spirit": Correspondence of Boris Pasternak and Maria Yudina), *Novy Mir,* no. 2 (1990): 171.

59 **"And he began to recite from memory"**: Ehrenburg, *Post-War Years,* 165.

59 **Fadeyev was well-disposed**: Gladkov, *Meetings with Pasternak,* 75.

59 **"Alexander Alexandrovich has rehabilitated himself"**: Ivinskaya, *A Captive of Time,* 141.

59 **"Mass Grave"**: Nikolai Lyubimov, *Boris Pasternak iz knigi "Neuvyadaemyi tsvet"* (Boris Pasternak from the book "The Unfading Blossom"), in Boris Pasternak, *Polnoe Sobranie Sochinenii,* vol. 11, 620.

59 **below a call for Pasternak's isolation and ruin**: See Max Hayward's notes in Gladkov, *Meetings with Pasternak,* 188.

59 **"With all its dishonesty"**: Ibid., 132.

59 **"At least they are not going to let me starve"**: Ibid.

60 **"Who would bear the phony greatness"**: Vladimir Markov, "An Unnoticed Aspect of Pasternak's Translations," *Slavic Review* 20, no. 3 (October 1961): 503–8.

60 **"I started to work again"**: Gladkov, *Meetings with Pasternak,* 136–37.

60 **"I write no protests"**: Boris Pasternak, lettter to Olga Freidenberg, March 26, 1947, Boris Pasternak and Olga Freidenberg, *Correspondence,* 269.

Chapter 4

61 **"My wife's passionate love of work"**: Boris Pasternak, letter to Renate Schweitzer, quoted in Ivinskaya, *A Captive of Time,* 185.

61 **"big hands"**: Interview with Lyusya Popova, *Komsomol'skaya Pravda,* August 19, 1999.

61 **"a divided family"**: Quotes up to "Her present condition" from Boris Pasternak, letter to parents, October 1, 1937, in Boris Pasternak, *Family Correspondence,* 321–22.

61 **made it hard to carry the pregnancy**: Zinaida Pasternak, *Vospominaniya,* in Boris Pasternak, *Vtoroe Rozhdenie,* 295.

61 **Zinaida had little interest**: Barnes, *Boris Pasternak,* vol. 2, 27.

62 **"a dragon on eight feet"**: Feinstein, *Anna of All the Russias,* 242.

62 **the previously active seventeen-year-old**: Barnes, *Boris Pasternak,* vol. 2, 189.

62 **"as a matchbox"**: Zinaida Pasternak, *Vospominaniya,* in Boris Pasternak, *Vtoroe Rozhdenie,* 330.

62 **"fulfill my duty as a wife"**: Ibid., 340.

62 **"Boris Leonidovich, let me introduce"**: The descriptions of Ivinskaya's meeting and subsequent romance with Pasternak in this chapter, and the dialogue between the two, are all from Ivinskaya's memoir, *A Captive of Time,* unless another source is cited.

63 **"few women who have had an affair with me"**: Boris Pasternak, letter to Nina Tabidze, September 30, 1953, in Boris Pasternak, *Letters to Georgian Friends,* 154.

63 **Pasternak was known for his flings**: Vyacheslav Ivanov, "Perevyornutoe nebo. Zapisi o Pasternake" (The Upturned Sky. Notes on Pasternak), *Zvezda* 8 (August 2009): 107.

63 **Zinaida said that after the war**: Zinaida Pasternak, *Vospominaniya,* in Boris Pasternak, *Vtoroe Rozhdenie,* 344.

63 **"Poor Mama mourned"**: Yemelyanova, *Legendy Potapovskogo pereulka,* 16.

64 **treated his birthdays as days of mourning**: Voznesensky, *An Arrow in the Wall,* 270.

65 **"faces could be seen side by side"**: Lydia Chukovskaya, "Otryvki iz dnevnika" (Diary fragments), January 6, 1948, in *Boris Pasternak, Polnoe Sobranie Sochinenii,* vol. 11, 426.

65 **"pretty but slightly fading blonde"**: Emma Gerstein, "O Pasternake i ob Anne Akhmatovoi" (About Pasternak and Anna Akhmatova), in Boris Pasternak, *Polnoe Sobranie Sochinenii,* vol. 11, 392.

65 **"a beauty"**: Yevgeni Yevtushenko, "Bog stanovitsya chelovekom" (God Becomes Man), in Boris Pasternak, *Polnoe Sobranie Sochinenii,* vol. 11, 721.

65 **Zinaida found out about the affair**: Zinaida Pasternak, *Vospominaniya,* in Boris Pasternak, *Vtoroe Rozhdenie,* 340–42.

65 **tried to poison herself**: Yemelyanova, *Legendy Potapovskogo pereulka,* 21.

65 **"formed a deep new attachment"**: Boris Pasternak, letter to Olga Freidenberg, August 7, 1949, in Boris Pasternak and Olga Freidenberg, *Correspondence,* 292.

66 **He imagined at one point**: Interview with Lyusya Popova, *Komsomol'skaya Pravda,* August 19, 1999.

66 **nominated Pasternak for the Nobel Prize**: Pamela Davidson, "C. M. Bowra's 'Overestimation' of Pasternak and the Genesis of *Doctor Zhivago,*" in Fleishman, *The Life of Boris Pasternak's Doctor Zhivago,* 42.

66 **"the greatest of Russian poets"**: Conquest, *Courage of Genius,* 86.

66 **"It appears to us beyond all doubt"**: International Conference of Professors of English, The National Archives, London, 1950, FO 954/881.

67 **"Leave him, he's a cloud dweller"**: Livanov, *Mezhdu dvumya Zhivago, vospominaniya i vpechatleniya, p'esy,* 177.

67 **Nearly a dozen uniformed agents**: Ivinskaya, *A Captive of Time,* 86. Some authors have suggested that Ivinskaya was arrested because of a fraud investigation into an editor she worked under and have also suggested that she might have been involved. There is no evidence for such claims. The almost exclusive focus of her long interrogations was Pasternak, and she was not charged with any kind of fraud but with a political crime.

67 **she was strip-searched**: For the detention at the Lubyanka, see ibid., 91–110, unless another source is cited.

68 **known to unroll a bloodstained carpet**: Montefiore, *Stalin,* 539.

68 **The KGB's accounting**: Yemelyanova, *Pasternak i Ivinskaya: provoda pod tokom,* 97–107.

71 **"Everything is finished"**: Ivinskaya, *A Captive of Time,* 86.

71 **"About the gown with the tassels"**: Lydia Chukovskaya, *Zapiski ob Anne Akhmatovoi,* vol. 2,173.

72 **"I have pondered for a long time"**: Nikiforov letter, in Ivinskaya, *A Captive of Time,* 113–14. Ivinskaya said she forgave him, and her mother helped him to find English lessons when he was released and returned to Moscow. Nikiforov's real name was Yepishkin. A former merchant and therefore suspect, he took his wife's name after he returned to Russia from Australia following the 1917 Revolution.

73 **"Here Borya's and my child"**: One biographer has cast doubt on whether Ivinskaya was pregnant. The tempestuous nature of the romance, and the fact that the couple appeared to have broken and repaired their relations several times, makes it plausible that Pasternak and Ivinskaya were again intimate before her arrest—as does his persistent unhappiness with aspects of his home life. A prison document cited by Ivinskaya's daughter, Irina, in her book does not conclusively confirm a pregnancy, but it does support her mother's account. A doctor's note stated that Ivinskaya was in the prison clinic "due to bleeding from womb" and that the arrested person said she was pregnant. (See Yemelyanova, *Pasternak i Ivinskaya: provoda pod tokom* 103.) There is no further medical documentation in the public record.

73 **"I have told [Zinaida]"**: Account of Lyusya Popova, in Ivinskaya, *A Captive of Time,* 107–8.

Chapter 5

75 **"with a miscellany of mortals"**: Boris Pasternak, letter to Olga Freidenberg, January 20, 1953, in Boris Pasternak and Olga Friedenberg, *Correspondence,* 309.

75 **"Lord, I thank you"**: Boris Pasternak, letter to Nina Tabidze, January 17, 1953, in Boris Pasternak, *Letters to Georgian Friends,* 149–59.

75 **Pasternak suffered constantly from toothache**: Zinaida Pasternak, *Vospominaniya,* in Boris Pasternak, *Vtoroe Rozhdenie,* 347.

75 **a new "distinguished" look**: Lydia Chukovskaya, *Zapiski ob Anne Akhmatovoi,* vol. 2, 57.

76 **"It's the disease of our time"**: Boris Pasternak, *Doctor Zhivago* (2010), 430.

76 **"My dear Olya, my joy!"**: Ivinskaya, *A Captive of Time,* 118.

76 **"Without him my children"**: Ibid., 119.

76 **"I am burying myself in work"**: Boris Pasternak, letter to Olga Freidenberg, December 9, 1949, in Boris Pasternak and Olga Freidenberg, *Correspondence,* 298.

76 **"When they print it"**: Barnes, *Boris Pasternak,* vol. 2, 273.

76 **Lydia Chukovskaya wrote to him**: Lydia Chukovskaya, letter to Boris Pasternak, August 28, 1952, in Lydia Chukovskaya, *Sochineniya,* vol. 2, 438–39.

77 **Often attending were Boris Livanov**: Voznesensky, *An Arrow in the Wall,* 258–61.

77 **Krotkov was present**: Testimony of Yuri Krotkov, aka George Karlin, before the U.S. Senate subcommittee to investigate the administration of the Internal Security Act. November 3, Committee on the Judiciary, Karlin Testimony, at 6, U.S. Government Printing Office, pt. 1 (1969).

77 **a stew made of game**: Olga Carlisle described a typical meal in "Boris Pasternak: The Art of Fiction No. 25," interview by Olga Carlisle, *The Paris Review* 24 (1960): 61–66.

77 **"Of those who have read"**: Boris Pasternak, letter to S. I. and M. N. Chikovani, June 14, 1952, in Boris Pasternak, *Letters to Georgian Friends,* 142–43.

78 **Vovsi confessed to being the inspiration**: Brent and Naumov, *Stalin's Last Crime,* 212.

78 **"I am now happy and free"**: Boris Pasternak, letter to V. F. Asmus, March 3, 1953, in Boris Pasternak, *Selected Writings and Letters,* 409.

78 **her sons loved Stalin**: Barnes, *Boris Pasternak,* vol. 2, 10.

78 **the killer of the intelligentsia**: Zinaida Pasternak, *Vospominaniya*, in Boris Pasternak, *Vtoroe Rozhdenie*, 351.

79 **"mixture of candor"**: Ivinskaya, *A Captive of Time*, 24.

79 **"turned into a palace"**: Boris Pasternak, letter to Olga Freidenberg, July 12, 1954, in Boris Pasternak and Olga Freidenberg, *Correspondence*, 328.

79 **She put a large bed**: Ivinskaya, *A Captive of Time*, 37.

79 **a ritual of lunch**: Matthews, *Stalin's Children*, 157.

80 **"her debauchery, irresponsibility"**: For Chukovskaya's and Adol'f-Nadezhdina's accounts of this dispute see Lydia Chukovskaya, *Zapiski ob Anne Akhmatovoi* vol. 2, 658–61; and Adol'f-Nadezhdina, letter to Chukovskaya in Mansurov, *Lara Moego Romana*, 266–68.

80 **"I've never heard of such a thing"**: Reeder, *Anna Akhmatova*, 357.

81 **"painful moral trauma"**: Yesipov, *Shalamov*, 226–29.

81 **"Pasternak was her bet"**: Varlam Shalamov, letter to Nadezhda Mandelstam, September 1965, in http://shalamov.ru/library/24/36.html.

81 **And everything looks real enough**: Frankel, *Novy Mir: A Case Study*, 22.

81 **"a writer is not an apparatus"**: Ibid., 30.

81 **"A new age is beginning"**: Chukovsky, *Diary*, entry October 20, 1953, 379.

81 **"It is anticipated that the novel"**: Yevgeni Pasternak, *Boris Pasternak: The Tragic Years*, 207.

81 **"manically unfree man"**: Boris Pasternak, letter to Olga Freidenberg, March 20, 1954, in Boris Pasternak and Olga Freidenberg, *Correspondence*, 320.

82 **"The party has always reminded"**: Quoting Surkov. See "The Official Intervention in the Literary Battle," *Soviet Studies* 6, no. 2 (October 1954): 179–86.

82 **"rich and indolent"**: Ruge, *Pasternak: A Pictorial Biography*, 90–91.

82 **"I personally do not keep heirlooms"**: Boris Pasternak and Olga Freidenberg, *Correspondence*, xii.

83 **Pasternak as half ill, half detained**: Lydia Chukovskaya, *Zapiski ob Anne Akhmatovoi*, vol. 2, 105.

83 **"her lips pursed"**: Voznesensky, *An Arrow in the Wall*, 260.

83 **"Surely Brecht realizes"**: Barnes, *Boris Pasternak*, vol. 2, 296; Ruge, *Pasternak: A Pictorial Biography*, 88–89.

83 **"heavy and complicated passages"**: Barnes, *Boris Pasternak*, vol. 2, 298.

83 **"You mark my words"**: Ivinskaya, *A Captive of Time*, 195.

83 **"You cannot imagine"**: Boris Pasternak, letter to Nina Tabidze in Zubok, *Zhivago's Children*, 1.

Chapter 6

85 **His entrepreneurial ancestors**: For family background, see Carlo Feltrinelli, *Feltrinelli,* 1–36.
86 **"he was just as prepared to abandon"**: Ibid., 65.
87 **a mass movement**: De Grand, *The Italian Left in the Twentieth Century,* 100.
87 **the feminist Unione Donne Italiane**: Ibid.
87 **"little big world"**: Calvino, *Hermit in Paris,* 128.
87 **"I learned to control"**: Carlo Feltrinelli, *Feltrinelli,* 52.
87 **"We had dreams"**: Anna Del Bo Boffino, *L'Unità,* March 1992, quoted in Carlo Feltrinelli, *Feltrinelli,* 45.
87 **"Muscovite Pasionaria"**: Carlo Feltrinelli, *Feltrinelli,* 38.
87 **"a portrait of Stalin among the old masters"**: Ibid, 55.
88 **"little university of Marxism"**: Ibid., 61.
88 **"the Jaguar"**: Ibid., 78.
88 **"mass arrests and deportation"**: Taubman, *Khrushchev,* 271.
89 **the delegates in the great hall of the Kremlin**: Medvedev, *Khrushchev,* 86–88.
89 **D'Angelo called Milan**: D'Angelo, *Delo Pasternaka,* 5–6.
89 **"Not to publish a novel like this"**: Carlo Feltrinelli, *Feltrinelli,* 101.
89 **"What kind of nonsense is that?"**: Vyacheslav Ivanov in *Zvezda* 1 (2010): 152.
90 **"This may put an end to the poetry volume!"**: Ivinskaya, *A Captive of Time,* 197.
90 **"Quite recently I have completed my main"**: Yevgeni Pasternak, *Boris Pasternak: The Tragic Years,* 215.
91 **"How can anyone love his country so little?"**: Ivinskaya, *A Captive of Time,* 201.
91 **"If its publication here"**: Carlo Feltrinelli, *Feltrinelli,* 102–3.
92 **In a long memo, Serov informed**: Ibid., 103–5.
92 **The book was described as a hostile attack**: August 31, 1956, note of the deputy foreign minister, and appendix with Central Committee's culture department report in Afiani and Tomilina, *Boris Pasternak i Vlast',* 63.
92 **talked openly at their workplace**: D'Angelo, *Delo Pasternaka,* 13.
93 **she would show the novel to Vyacheslav Molotov**: Ivinskaya, *A Captive of Time,* 200.
93 **"She relieves me from the vexing negotiations"**: Boris Pasternak, letter to Lydia Pasternak Slater, November 1, 1957, in Boris Pasternak, *Family Correspondence,* 389.
93 **not the informer some would label her**: In 1997, the Russian newspaper *Moskovsky Komsomolets* published a number of quotations from a letter Ivinskaya wrote to Soviet leader Nikita Khrushchev on March 10,

1961, from a labor camp in Siberia where she had been re-imprisoned. (See also Alessandra Stanley, "Model for Dr. Zhivago's Lara Betrayed Pasternak to KGB," *The New York Times,* September 27, 1997.) Selective quotation from the letter, which was not published in full, led to charges that Ivinskaya was a KGB informer. Ivinskaya, to bolster her plea for mercy, told Khrushchev that she had tried to cancel Pasternak's meetings with foreigners and had worked with the Central Committee to prevent publication in the West of *Doctor Zhivago.* She said Pasternak was not an "innocent lamb" in all that happened. Read in full, Ivinskaya's letter is the desperate cry of a mother and breadwinner (Her own mother was still alive.) There is nothing in it that would justify labeling her a KGB informer (See afterword for a fuller treatment). And in fact much of her dealing with the Soviet authorities was at Pasternak's urging. The KGB may have regarded her as malleable but did not see her as reliable. (See next note.) The full letter is available at Gosudarstvennyi arkhiv Rossiiskoi Federatsii (State Archive of the Russian Federation) Col.: 8131, I.: 31, F.: 89398, S.: 51–58. The authors also have a copy.

93 **"very anti-Soviet"**: KGB to the Council of Ministers, memo on Pasternak's connections with Soviet and foreign individuals, February 16, 1959, in Afiani and Tomilina, *Boris Pasternak i Vlast',* 181.

93 **"we must get the manuscript back"**: Ivinskaya, *A Captive of Time,* 219.

93 **Polikarpov was known in the literary community**: Benedikt Sarnov, "Tragicheskaya figura" (A Tragic Figure), in *Lekhaim* (October 2003), http://www.lechaim.ru/ARHIV/138/sarnov.htm; Yevtushenko, *Shestidesantnik, memuarnaya proza,* 162–92.

94 **Kotov's proposal was absurd**: D'Angelo, *Delo Pasternaka,* 31.

94 **"this great [publication] battle will be won by you"**: Varlam Shalamov, letter to Boris Pasternak, August 12, 1956, in http://shalamov.ru/library/24/1.html.

94 **gave her a copy of his manuscript to read**: Boris Pasternak, letter to Hélène Peltier, September 14, 1956, in Boris Pasternak, *Lettres à mes amies françaises (1956–1960),* 58.

94 **"If ever you receive a letter"**: The scrap of paper is held at La Biblioteca della Fondazione Giangiacomo Feltrinelli, Milan.

95 **"it was important—more than important"**: Berlin, *Personal Impressions,* 227.

95 **Zinaida believed that their son Leonid**: Boris Pasternak, letter to sisters, August 14, 1956, Boris Pasternak, *Family Correspondence,* 380.

96 **Yevgeni, was prevented**: Mikhail Polivanov, "Tainaya Svoboda" (Silent Freedom), in Boris Pasternak, *Polnoe Sobranie Sochinenii,* vol. 11, 469.

96 **Pasternak was incensed**: Berlin, *Personal Impressions,* 229.

96 **"chose open-eyed"**: Isaiah Berlin, letter to David Astor, October 27, 1958, in Berlin, *Enlightening: Letters, 1946–1960,* 652–53.

96 **"You may not even like it"**: Boris Pasternak, letter to sisters, August 14, 1956, in Boris Pasternak, *Family Correspondence,* 380.
96 **"tall, mustachioed, hugely impressive"**: Patricia Blake, introduction to Hayward, *Writers in Russia, 1917–1978,* xlvii.
96 **The KGB referred to him contemptuously as a "White émigré"**: KGB to the Council of Ministers, memo on Pasternak's connections with Soviet and foreign individuals, February 18, 1959, Afiani and Tomilina, *Boris Pasternak i Vlast',* 183.
97 **"he's too jealous of my position"**: Patricia Blake, introduction to Hayward, *Writers in Russia, 1917–1978,* l.
97 **"His verse is convex"**: Barnes, *Boris Pasternak,* vol. 1, 308.
97 **"Doctor Zhivago is a sorry thing"**: Boyd, *Vladimir Nabokov: The American Years,* 372.
97 **Pasternak's mistress must have written it**: Schiff, *Vera (Mrs. Vladimir Nabokov),* 243.
97 **Katkov promised Pasternak with a kiss**: Patricia Blake, introduction to Hayward, *Writers in Russia, 1917–1978,* l.
97 **taught himself Hungarian in six weeks**: Ibid., xlix.
97 **"going over everything for accuracy"**: Ibid., li.
97 **"obviously wished to be a martyr"**: Isaiah Berlin, letter to James Joll, November 25, 1958, in Berlin, *Enlightening: Letters, 1946–1960,* 658.

Chapter 7

99 **"The thing that has disturbed us"**: The letter was published in *Literaturnaya Gazeta* (Literary Gazette) on October 25, 1958. It is reproduced in full in Conquest, *Courage of Genius,* Appendix II, 136–63.
100 **"Dear friends, oh, how hopelessly ordinary"**: Boris Pasternak, *Doctor Zhivago* (2010), 429.
100 **"most heretical insinuation"**: Barnes, *Boris Pasternak,*vol. 2, 316.
100 **"brilliant, extremely egocentric"**: Chukovsky, *Diary,* entry September 1, 1956, 408.
100 **"I have also asked Konstantin Aleksandrovich"**: Tamara Ivanova, "Boris Leonidovich Pasternak," in Boris Pasternak, *Polnoe Sobranie Sochinenii,* vol. 11, 286–87.
100 **He asked Fedin not to mention the rejection**: Yevgeni Pasternak, *Boris Pasternak: The Tragic Years,* 221.
101 **"composed very courteously and gently"**: Barnes, *Boris Pasternak,* vol. 2, 317.
101 **D'Angelo and his wife visited**: D'Angelo, *Delo Pasternaka,* 23.
101 **his arrest and torture**: Urban, *Moscow and the Italian Communist Party,* 139.

101 **"The issue with Pasternak's manuscript"**: October 24, 1956, note of the department of the Central Committee of the Communist Party of the Soviet Union for relations with foreign Communist parties, in Afiani and Tomilina, *Pasternak i Vlast'*, 71.

101 **pressure divided editors**: Mancosu, *Inside the Zhivago Storm*, 44; Valerio Riva, "La vera storia del dottor Zivago" (The true story of Dr. Zhivago), *Corriere della Sera*, cultural supplement, January 14, 1987, in Carlo Feltrinelli, *Feltrinelli*, 108.

102 **Khrushchev would eventually argue**: McLean and Vickery, *The Year of Protest 1956*, 25.

102 **a quarter of a million rank-and-file members abandoned the movement**: De Grand, *The Italian Left in the Twentieth Century*, 125.

102 **"a strong plea for socialist democracy"**: Carlo Feltrinelli, *Feltrinelli*, 89.

102 **"the loss of small fringe groups"**: Giorgio Amendola, quoted in ibid., 94.

102 **"brought luster to the party"**: Ibid., 95.

104 **"phantasmagoria"**: Puzikov, *Budni i prazdniki*, 202.

104 **"He assures me"**: D'Angelo, *Delo Pasternaka*, 75.

104 **"His is a perfect portrayal"**: Carlo Feltrinelli, *Feltrinelli*, 110–11.

104 **"Here in Russia, the novel will never appear"**: Ibid., 112.

105 **"seldom, periodically and only faintly shared"**: Boris Pasternak, letter to Andrei Sinyavsky, June 29, 1957, in Boris Pasternak, *Polnoe Sobranie Sochinenii*, vol. 10, 235.

105 **Khrushchev spoke for nearly two hours**: Taubman, *Khrushchev*, 307–8.

105 **"a broad intricate story"**: Conquest, *Courage of Genius*, 54.

106 **"choice of stories in the first issue"**: August 30, 1957, and September 18, 1957, Central Committee culture department notes on *Opinie*, in Afiani and Tomilina, *Pasternak i Vlast'*, 81–82 and 83–84.

106 **there was a blonde in an hour before**: Zinaida Pasternak, *Vospominaniya*, in Boris Pasternak, *Vtoroe Rozhdenie*, 364.

106 **Khrushchev himself**: D'Angelo, *Delo Pasternaka*, 95.

106 **"a selection of the most unacceptable parts"**: Boris Pasternak, letter to Nina Tabidze, August 21, 1957, in Boris Pasternak, *Polnoe Sobranie Sochinenii*, vol. 10, 249–50.

106 **"the consequences it could have on me"**: Boris Pasternak, letter to Pietro Zveteremich, July 1957, in Valerio Riva, *Corriere della Sera*, January 14, 1987.

107 **Letters to his sister Lydia**: Boris Pasternak, *Family Correspondence*, 388. One of the letters is quoted in a KGB memo, February 18, 1959, in Afiani and Tomilina, *Pasternak i Vlast'*, 184.

107 **"with the spontaneity of a child"**: Ivinskaya, *A Captive of Time*, 216. Ivinskaya mistakes the date of this meeting by a year in her memoirs, placing it in 1958.

107 **"We all left beaten"**: Alexander Puzikov in Boris Pasternak, *Polnoe Sobranie Sochinenii*, vol. 10, 249; and Puzikov, *Budni i prazdniki*, 206.

107 **a "'37 type of meeting"**: Boris Pasternak, letter to Nina Tabidze, August 21, 1957, in Yevgeni Pasternak, *Boris Pasternak: The Tragic Years*, 228–29.

107 **"People who are morally scrupulous"**: Ibid.

108 **"very unpleasant consequences"**: D'Angelo, *Delo Pasternaka*, 90.

108 **"I have started rewriting"**: Carlo Feltrinelli, *Feltrinelli*, 114.

108 **"If you're here to advise me"**: D'Angelo, *Delo Pasternaka*, 90–91.

109 **He angrily waved Pasternak's telegram**: Carlo Feltrinelli, *Feltrinelli*, 115.

109 **"It does not matter what might happen"**: Miriam H. Berlin, "A Visit to Pasternak," *The American Scholar* 52, no. 2 (Summer 1983): 327–35.

109 **"Vittorio, tell Feltrinelli"**: Carlo Feltrinelli, *Feltrinelli*, 113.

109 **"To look at him, Pasternak might have been"**: Yevtushenko, *A Precocious Autobiography*, 104.

109 **Pasternak and Yevtushenko drank and talked**: Yevtushenko, *Shestidesantnik, memuarnaya proza*, 386.

110 **Soviet trade representatives in Paris and London**: The International Book Association to the Central Committee of the Communist Party of the Soviet Union, note, October 3, 1957, in Afiani and Tomilina, *Pasternak i Vlast'*, 84–85.

110 **The Soviet embassy in London**: Philip de Zulueta, British Foreign Office, letter to British ambassador in Moscow, titled "Vetting and Translation of Dr. Zhivago," March 8, 1958, in the National Archives, London. Prime Minister's file. Classmark, PREM 11/2504.

110 **"the atmosphere created around the book"**: Carlo Feltrinelli, *Feltrinelli*, 116.

110 **Zveteremich was handed a typewritten letter**: D'Angelo, *Delo Pasternaka*, 98.

111 **"A brawl, I can truly say"**: Mancosu, *Inside the Zhivago Storm*, 76.

111 **"P. asks you not to pay any heed to this"**: Carlo Feltrinelli, *Feltrinelli*, 116.

111 **"I became convinced"**: Mancosu, *Inside the Zhivago Storm*, 241.

111 **"In order to avoid any further tension"**: Ibid., 117.

111 **"I know how such letters are written"**: November 16, 1957, note for the Central Committee of the CPSU, in Afiani and Tomilina, *Pasternak i Vlast'*, 86.

111 **"free publisher in a free country"**: Giangiacomo Feltrinelli quoted indirectly in "Pubblicato in URSS il libro di Borghese sulla 'X Mas' mentre si proibisce la stampa dell'ultimo romanza di Pasternàk" (Borges Book Will Be Published in the USSR by Christmas while Pasternak's Last Novel Remains Banned), *Corrispondenza Socialista*, October 27, 1957.

112 **"a hyena dipped in syrup"**: Carlo Feltrinelli, *Feltrinelli*, 116.

112 **"The Cold War is beginning to involve literature"**: Gino Pagliarani, "Boris Pasternak e la cortina di ferro" (Boris Pasternak and the Iron Curtain), *L'Unità*, October 22, 1957, in Conquest, *Courage of Genius*, 66.

112 **"I have seen my friends"**: Alexei Surkov, *Mladost*, October 2, 1957, in ibid., 67.

112 **"*Time* and *Newsweek*"**: Mancosu, *Inside the Zhivago Storm*, 91.

112 **He told him he was "stunned"**: November 16, 1957, letter of Boris Pasternak attached to note for the Central Committee of the CPSU, in Afiani and Tomilina, *Pasternak i Vlast'*, 86.

112 **I can find no words**: Carlo Feltrinelli, *Feltrinelli*, 118–19.

112 **printed on November 15, 1957**: Information on the novel's first printing and appearance in bookstores from Carlo Feltrinelli, email correspondence.

113 **"You look for a political libel and find a work of art"**: Giorgio Zampa, "Si cerca il libello politico e si trova un'opera d'arte," review of *Doctor Zhivago*, *Corriere della Sera*, November 22, 1957.

Chapter 8

115 **in the form of two rolls of film**: CIA, Dispatch to Chief, WE [Western Europe], "Transmittal of Film of Pasternak Book," January 2, 1958. The name of the sender in the January 2, 1958, document, as well as the source of the film, has been redacted. It is standard CIA practice not to reveal liaison relationships with allied intelligence services even in documents that are more than fifty years old. It is nonetheless clear from the January 2, 1958, document that the film came from London. The document states that the provider of the film also wished to know what plans the CIA had so that it could synchronize its efforts with the agency. The provider could only have been MI6. Moreover, a U.S. official speaking on background to one of the authors confirmed that the source of the manuscript was Great Britain. A spokesman for the British government when contacted by the authors said that after MI6's official history was published in 2010 a decision was made not to open the archives again.

115 **In a memo to Frank Wisner**: CIA, Memorandum for Deputy Director (Plans) from Chief, SR Division, "Request for Authorization to Obligate up to [redacted] from AEDINOSAUR," July 9, 1958.

116 **an assistant naval attaché in Moscow**: Trento, *The Secret History of the CIA*, 497, note 4. Maury's name, like others, is redacted in the CIA documents, but he has been identified as the chief, Soviet Russia Division, in numerous books, and former CIA officials confirmed his identity in interviews with the authors.

116 **"He considered the Soviet regime"**: Chavchavadze, *Crown and Trenchcoats*, 224.

116 **"Our specialty was the *charochka*"**: Ibid.

116 **"asked that it not be done in the U.S."**: CIA, Memorandum for PP Notes,

"Publication of Pasternak's Dr. Zhivago," September 8, 1958. A British request not to publish in the United States is apparent from subsequent CIA actions and concerns, and it is explicitly mentioned in this memo, although references to the British, as noted earlier, are redacted.

116 **"should be published in a maximum number"**: CIA, Memorandum, "Pasternak's Dr. Zhivago," December 12, 1957. This memo was likely written by the Psychological and Paramilitary Staff.

117 **gave the CIA exclusive control**: CIA, Memorandum for the Record, "Exploitation of Dr. Zhivago," March 27, 1959. This memo does not date the OCB guidelines. Librarians at the Eisenhower Presidential Library could find no record of the directive to the CIA, presumably because it was verbal. On November 7, 1958, in a single sentence, the minutes of an OCB meeting, which was attended by DCI Allen Dulles, recorded: "Discussed and noted actions being taken with respect to the Pasternak case." Eisenhower Presidential Library. White House Office, Office of the Special Assistant for National Security Affairs: Records, OCB series, Administration subseries, Box 4: OCB Minutes of Meetings 1958 (6).

117 **"could incrementally over time"**: Meyer, *Facing Reality,* 114.

118 **"appeared natural and right"**: Wilford, *The Mighty Wurlitzer,* 147.

118 **the Cold War was also cultural**: For full treatments of the Cultural Cold War, and contrasting views on the merit and efficacy of CIA operations, see Saunders, *The Cultural Cold War,* and Wilford, *The Mighty Wurlitzer.*

118 **"manifest diversity and differences of view"**: Michael Warner, "Sophisticated Spies: CIA Links to Liberal Anti-communists, 1947–1967," *Journal of Intelligence and Counterintelligence* 9, no. 4 (1996): 425–33.

118 **"became one of the world's largest grant-making institutions"**: Ibid.

119 **"centralized snooping," as Truman called it**: Jeffreys-Jones, *The CIA and American Democracy,* 35.

119 **the CIA's general counsel was uncertain**: Thorne et al., *Foreign Relations of the United States, 1945–1950,* 622.

119 **"do things that very much needed to be done"**: Gaddis, *George F. Kennan,* 317.

119 **"The Inauguration of Organized Political Warfare"**: Emergence of the Intelligence Establishment, 668–72.

120 **He had served for six months in Bucharest**: Thomas, *The Very Best Men,* 21–23.

120 **"The OSS operative was 'brutally shocked'"**: Dobbs, *Six Months in 1945,* 14.

120 **Wisner divided his planned clandestine activity**: Thorne et al., *Foreign Relations of the United States, 1945–1950,* 730–31.

120 **There were 302 CIA staffers**: U.S. Senate, *Final Report of the Select Committee to Study Government Operations with Respect to Intelligence Activities,* book 1, 107.

120 **"the atmosphere of an order of Knights Templar"**: Colby and Forbath, *Honorable Men,* 73.

120 **"boyishly charming, cool but coiled"**: Tom Braden, "I'm Glad the CIA Is Immoral," *The Saturday Evening Post,* May 20, 1967.

120 **that "added dimension"**: Winks, *Cloak & Gown,* 54.

121 **"under an appropriate pseudonym"**: Cord Meyer, letter to Robie Macauley, September 19, 1996, Cord Meyer Papers, box 1, folder 8, Manuscript Division, Library of Congress.

121 **wrote his novel *Partisans***: Saunders, *The Cultural Cold War,* 246.

121 **"I went down to Washington"**: Meyer, *Facing Reality,* 63–64.

121 **Members included Dwight D. Eisenhower**: Saunders, *The Cultural Cold War,* 131; and Wilford, *The Mighty Wurlitzer,* 31.

121 **about 12 percent of the FEC budget**: Johnson, *Radio Free Europe and Radio Liberty,* 15.

122 **the CIA routed through a Wall Street bank**: Wilford, *The Mighty Wurlitzer,* 31.

122 **enjoyed a good deal of autonomy**: See Meyer, *Facing Reality,* 115. This is also A. Ross Johnson's thesis.

123 **"a single stoker or sweeper"**: Critchlow, *Radio Hole-in-the-Head,* 15.

123 **The KGB called Munich**: Ibid., 87.

123 **About one-third of the urban adult population**: Johnson, *Radio Free Europe and Radio Liberty,* 184.

123 **"the mighty non-military force"**: Solzhenitsyn, *The Mortal Danger,* 129.

123 **In 1958, the Soviet Union was spending**: Simo Mikkonen, "Stealing the Monopoly of Knowledge? Soviet Reactions to U.S. Cold War Broadcasting," *Kritika: Explorations in Russian and Eurasian History* 11, no. 4 (2010): 771–805.

123 **"A new wind is blowing"**: "Propaganda: Winds of Freedom," *Time,* August 27, 1951.

123 **the FEC launched 600,000 balloons**: Hixon, *Parting the Curtain,* 65–66.

124 **The Czechoslovakian air force tried to shoot down**: Reisch, *Hot Books in the Cold War,* 10.

124 **"an extremely worrisome violation of airspace sovereignty"**: Johnson, *Radio Free Europe and Radio Liberty,* 72.

124 **"Let's do it," he said**: John P. Matthews, "The West's Secret Marshall Plan for the Mind," *Journal of Intelligence and Counterintelligence* 16, no. 3 (2003): 409–27.

125 **"There should be no total attacks on communism"**: Reisch, *Hot Boots in the Cold War,* 15.

125 **"We are swallowing them passionately"**: Alfred A. Reisch, "The Reception and Impact of Western and Polish Émigré Books and Periodicals in Communist-Ruled Poland Between July 1, 1956 and June 30, 1973," *American Diplomacy,* November 2012, http//www.unc.edu/depts/diplomat/item/2012/0712/comm/reisch_reception.html.

125 **"Your priceless publications"**: Reisch, *Hot Books in the Cold War,* 251.
125 **"Through our book program we hoped to fill"**: Patch, *Closing the Circle,* 255–62.
126 **on the shelves at Stockmann**: Burton Gerber, former CIA station chief in Moscow, interview by Finn, in Washington, D.C., November 20, 2012.
126 **Members of the Moscow Philharmonic**: Ludmilla Thorne, letter, *The New Yorker,* November 21, 2005, 10.
126 **in food cans and Tampax boxes**: Reisch, *Hot Books in the Cold War,* 515.
126 **"the main wellspring of hostile sentiments"**: Mark Kramer, introduction to ibid., xxiii.
126 **"the CIA has stood foursquare"**: Richard Elman, "The Aesthetics of the CIA," Richard Elman Papers, box 1 (1992 accession), "Writings—Essays," Special Collections Research Center, Syracuse University Library.
126 **"get books published or distributed abroad"**: Chief of Covert Action, CIA, in U.S. Senate, *Final Report of the Select Committee to Study Governmental Operations with Respect to Intelligence Activities,* book 1, 192–95.
127 ***The Penkovsky Papers,* published by Doubleday**: John M. Crewdson and Joseph B. Treaster, "The CIA's 3-Decade Effort to Mold the World's Views," *The New York Times,* December 25, 1977.
127 **"Books are the most important and most powerful weapons"**: Garrand and Garrand, *Inside the Soviet Writers' Union,* 42.

Chapter 9

129 **Katkov told an American diplomat**: American Consul General in Munich to the Department of State, Foreign Service Dispatch, March 7, 1958, Department of State Central File, 1955–59, 961.63: "Censorship in the USSR," The National Archives, College Park, Maryland.
130 **"Don't let the opportunity pass"**: Boris Pasternak, letter to Jacqueline de Proyart, January 7, 1958, in Boris Pasternak, *Lettres à mes amies françaises (1956–1960),* 81.
130 **Pasternak knew that Mouton**: Yevgeni Pasternak, "Perepiska Borisa Pasternaka s Elen Pel't'e-Zamoiskoi" (Pasternak–Hélène Peltier-Zamoiska Correspondence), *Znamya* 1 (1997): 118.
130 **code-named AEDINOSAUR**: CIA, Memorandum, October 29, 1957.
130 **The letters AE designated**: A former CIA officer who discussed the agency and its practices on condition of anonymity, interview by Finn.
130 **"we'll do it black"**: CIA, "Notes on PASTERNAK'S novel, Dr. Zhivago," January 13, 1958.

131 **about 18 million visitors**: Pluvinge, *Expo 58: Between Utopia and Reality*, 11.

131 **Belgium issued 16,000 visas**: Travel by Soviet Officials to Belgium, RG 59, 1955–59, 033.6155, National Archives, College Park, MD.

131 **"This book has great propaganda value"**: CIA, Memorandum for SR Division Branch Chiefs, "Availability of Dr. Zhivago in English," April 24, 1958.

132 **"Stalinophobia—abhorrence at Stalinism"**: Les Evans, introduction to Cannon, *The Struggle for Socialism*, 14.

132 **"organized anti-Communism had become"**: Jason Epstein, "The CIA and the Intellectuals," *The New York Review of Books*, April 20, 1967.

132 **a "contract consultant" for the CIA**: Saunders, *The Cultural Cold War*, 157.

132 **negotiated directly**: Ibid., 443, note 4.

132 **"You can't expel me; I'll live and die in the movement!"**: Wald, *The New York Intellectuals*, 287.

132 **Morrow was a charming, brilliant man**: Alan M. Wald, who interviewed Morrow several times, phone conversation with Finn, November 12, 2012.

133 **a bottle of whiskey and a box of chocolates**: Excerpt from the oral history of Felix Morrow, Oral History Project, Columbia University. (The full transcript remains sealed but Morrow's daughter allowed us to read and paraphrase the section dealing with his work for the CIA.)

133 **"make arrangements with anti-Stalinist trade unionists"**: Felix Morrow, letter to Carl Proffer, October 6, 1980, in Correspondence of Felix Morrow and Carl and Ellendea Proffer, University of Michigan Special Collections Library, Ann Arbor, Box 7 of the Ardis Collection Records, Folder heading Ardis Author/Name Files—Morrow, Felix. Morrow's name is redacted throughout the CIA documents, but he had written of his role in a series of letters to Carl Proffer of Ardis Publishers in 1980 and 1986. Morrow also described it in his oral history (see note above, chap. 9).

133 **"an astonishing and attractive task"**: Ibid.

133 **"probably warranted in view of the time factor"**: CIA, Contact Report, June 20, 1958.

133 **On June 23, 1958, Morrow signed a contract**: CIA, Memorandum for the Record, June 20, 1958.

133 **Morrow was provided with a manuscript copy**: CIA, copy of contract, June 19, 1958.

133 **The agency wanted a "major literary figure" to write a preface**: CIA, Soviet Russia Division Memorandum, "Background Information and Outstanding Problems on the Publication of *Doctor Zhivago*," June 26, 1958.

134 **"credentialed Russian scholars"**: Felix Morrow, letter to Carl Prof-

fer, October 6, 1980, in Correspondence of Felix Morrow and Carl and Ellendea Proffer, University of Michigan Special Collections Library, Ann Arbor, Box 7 of the Ardis Collection Records, Folder heading Ardis Author/Name Files—Morrow, Felix.

134 **reproductions for the CIA were prepared by Rausen Bros.**: Felix Morrow, letter to Ellendea Proffer, November 4, 1986, in Correspondence of Felix Morrow and Carl and Ellendea Proffer, University of Michigan Special Collections Library, Ann Arbor.

134 **"I can publish anywhere else I please"**: CIA, letter, July 7, 1958. The University of Michigan is also redacted but it is clear from Morrow's testimony, other CIA documents, and subsequent events.

134 **University of Michigan Press was planning to publish**: CIA, Memorandum for the Record, "AEDINOSAUR Meeting of July 17, 1958," July 17, 1958.

134 **Morrow gave a copy of the manuscript**: Excerpt from oral history of Felix Morrow (see note above).

135 **"the CIA's interest in the book"**: CIA, Memorandum for the Record, "AEDINOSAUR—Recent Developments," July 28, 1958.

135 **the Soviet Russia Division representative argued**: CIA, Memorandum for the Record, "AEDINOSAUR—Events of 15–20 August."

135 **meet with Harlan Hatcher**: CIA, "Report of Trip to [the University of Michigan] Regarding Publication of *Doctor Zhivago*," September 2, 1958. The name of the university president is redacted, as is the name of Fred Wieck, the editorial director of the University of Michigan Press. Morrow wrote in his letter to Proffer that the "CIA sent one emissary after another to Wieck and Hatcher."

135 **a series of temporary buildings**: Burton Gerber, former CIA station chief in Moscow, interview by Finn, in Washington, D.C., November 20, 2012.

136 **agreed to hold off**: CIA, Memorandum for Chief, Soviet Russia Division from Commercial Staff, "Chronology of AEDINOSAUR," October 14, 1958.

136 **"It is our desire that it be made completely clear"**: CIA, Memorandum for the Record, September 10, 1958.

136 **following reports of a possible publication**: CIA, Telex, February 24, 1958; CIA, Memorandum, February 28, 1958; CIA, Memorandum for the Record, March 3, 1958.

136 **Rumors of a Mouton edition**: Mancosu, *Inside the Zhivago Story*, 112–13.

137 **CIA subsidies in 1958**: Bob de Graaff and Cees Wiebes, "Intelligence and the Cold War Behind the Dikes: The Relationship between the American and Dutch Intelligence Communities, 1946–1994," in Jeffreys-Jones and Andrew, *Eternal Vigilance? 50 years of the CIA*, 46.

137 **The Soviet Russia Division decided**: CIA, Memorandum for the Record,

"AEDINOSAUR—Recent Developments," July 28, 1958. Any reference to Mouton and the BVD is redacted in the July 28 memo and most other CIA memos, but it is clear from subsequent events and other CIA documents that this is the track the agency pursued. In a November 28, 1958, memo for the acting deputy director of Plans, Mouton is described as having agreed to conditions laid down by the CIA, among them that the agency would obtain the first one thousand copies off the press.

137 **On August 1, the reproduction proofs**: CIA, Memorandum for Acting Deputy Director (Plans) from the Acting Chief, Soviet Russia Division, "Publication of the Russian edition of Dr. Zhivago," November 25, 1958.

137 **The BVD decided not to deal directly with Mouton**: Details about BVD involvement are based on interviews with Kees van den Heuvel from 1999 to 2000 in Leidschendam, the Netherlands; Rachel van der Wilden, widow of BVD officer Joop van der Wilden, in The Hague, August 16, 2012; Barbara and Edward van der Beek, children of Rudy van der Beek, January 14, 2012, in Voorburg, the Netherlands; correspondence with the retired in-house historian of the BVD, Dirk Engelen (email February 9, 2010); and discussions with the Cold War historian Paul Koedijk over the last years. See also Petra Couvée, "Leemten in het lot. Hoe Dokter Zjivago gedrukt werd in Nederland" (Fateful Gaps. How Doctor Zhivago Was Printed in the Netherlands), *De Parelduiker* 2 (1998): 28–37; Petra Couvée, "Een geslaagde stunt, Operatie Zjivago, de ontknoping" (A Successful Stunt. Operation Zhivago, Dénouement) in *De Parelduiker* 1 (1999): 63–70; and Vos, *De Geheime Dienst*.

137 **The three men spoke for twenty minutes**: Peter de Ridder, interview by Couvée in Lisse, the Netherlands, October 2008.

137 **he told a newspaper reporter**: Peter de Ridder, "Geheimzinnige uitgave van Pasternak. Door Russen verbannen roman in Nederland—clandestien?—gedrukt?" (Mysterious Edition of Pasternak. Novel Banned by Russians in the Netherlands—Secretly?—Printed?), *Haagsche Post*, October 4, 1958, 5–6.

138 **"I felt the book needed to be published"**: Peter de Ridder, interviews in Lisse, the Netherlands, by Couvée on August 13, 1997, and by Finn and Couvée on July 29, 2008.

138 **In the first week of September**: CIA, Memorandum for PP Notes, "Publication of Pasternak's Dr. Zhivago," September 8, 1958.

138 **The books, wrapped up in brown paper**: Rachel van der Wilden, widow of Joop van der Wilden and herself a former MI6 officer, interview by Couvée in The Hague, August 16, 2012. Joop van der Wilden kept one of the books, still wrapped in brown paper and dated September 6. Rachel van der Wilden still has this copy. The CIA memo above of November 25, 1958, also states that the novel was printed in "early September."

138 **Two hundred copies were sent to headquarters**: CIA, Memorandum for

Chief, PRD, "Distribution of Russian Copies of Dr. Zhivago," October 31, 1958.

138 **Sputnik satellites, rows of agricultural machinery**: For descriptions of the Expo, see *The New York Times,* April 27, 1958, and May 11, 1958; *The Washington Post,* May 25, 26, and 27, 1958.

139 **"Socialist economic principles will guarantee"**: Pluvinge, *Expo 58: Between Utopia and Reality,* 93.

139 **"from what we know about Soviet plans"**: Rydell, *World of Fairs,* 200.

139 **"heavy, belabored and fatiguing propaganda"**: Ibid., 197.

140 **he chose Abraham Lincoln**: Tour guide Betty Rose to William Buell, office memorandum, Travel by Soviet Officials to Belgium, RG 59, 1955–59, 033.6155, National Archives, College Park, MD.; "2 Red Leaders Visit U.S. Pavilion at Fair," *The Washington Post,* July 5, 1958.

140 **"These are all lies"**: Boris Agapov, "Poezdka v Bryussel'" (A Trip to Brussels), *Novy Mir* (January 1959): 162.

141 **"the leading, privileged classes"**: Joos, *Deelneming van de H. Stoel aan de algemene Wereldtentoonstelling van Brussel 1958,* 627.

141 **provided one of the few accounts of how Soviet visitors were greeted**: Boris Agapov, "Poezdka v Bryussel'" (A Trip to Brussels), *Novy Mir* (January 1959): 155–59.

142 **"Is it true that *Doctor Zhivago* appeared in the original?"**: Kozovoi, *Poet v katastrofe,* 250.

142 **"This phase can be considered"**: CIA, Memorandum for the Record, "Status of AEDINOSAUR as of 9 September 1958," September 9, 1958.

142 **"In appreciation of your courage"**: Rachel van der Wilden, who has the inscribed copy of *Doctor Zhivago,* interview by Couvée in The Hague, August 16, 2012.

142 **"I have just seen"**: Mancosu, *Inside the Zhivago Story,* 131–36.

142 ***Der Spiegel* in Germany followed up**: *Der Spiegel,* October 29, 1958, 63–64.

143 **Pasternak apparently read the *Spiegel* article**: Boris Pasternak, letter to Valeria Prishvina, December 12, 1958, in Boris Pasternak, *Polnoe Sobranie Sochinenii,* vol. 10, 408.

143 **"during the closing days of the Brussels Fair"**: Lewis Nichols, "In and Out of Books," *The New York Times,* November 2, 1958.

143 **"only owing to a deplorable misunderstanding"**: One such ad appeared in *The New York Times Book Review,* January 22, 1959, 22.

144 **"a gift of copies of *Doctor Zhivago* reached our residence"**: Draft of statement made by Antoine Ilc of the organization Pro Russia Cristiana, at a press conference in the Foyer Oriental Chrétien, Brussels, November 10, 1958. Life with God Papers, folder I. 6. 3, Fondazione Russia Cristiana, Seriate, Italy.

144 **"That quaint workshop of amateur subversion"**: Quincy (pseudonym), *National Review Bulletin,* November 15, 1958.

144 **an "indemnity obligation" to print another five thousand**: Cornelius van Schooneveld, letter to Roman Jakobson, November 11, 1958, in the C. H. van Schooneveld Collection, University of Leiden, the Netherlands.

144 **imposed special controls**: CIA, Memorandum, November 21, 1958.

144 **"the 12 or 14 reviewers"**: *The New York Times*, November 2, 1958.

144 **"abounds with errata"**: Carlo Feltrinelli, *Feltrinelli*, 155.

144 **the Mouton edition printed for the CIA**: Mancosu, *Inside the Zhivago Story*, 165–66; Couvée, *De Parelduiker* 2 [1998], 28–37.

144 **"This is almost another text, not the one I wrote"**: Boris Pasternak, letter to Jacqueline de Proyart, March 30, 1959, in Boris Pasternak, *Lettres à mes amies françaises (1956–1960)*, 152. (Proyart eventually did edit and publish a corrected version with the University of Michigan Press.)

144 **"It is our duty to inform you"**: Giangiacomo Feltrinelli, letter to the University of Michigan Press, October 8, 1958, in University of Michigan Press Papers, University of Michigan Special Collections Library, Ann Arbor, Box 1, folder entitled University of Michigan Press Pasternak Records—Dr. Zhivago—Pre-Publication Records—Copyright Negotiations.

144 **"We would be interested to know"**: Fred Wieck, letter to Giangiacomo Feltrinelli Editore, October 20, 1958, in University of Michigan Press Papers, University of Michigan Special Collections Papers, Ann Arbor.

145 **"we witness the amazing spectacle"**: Kurt Wolff, letter to Harlan Hatcher, November 13, 1958, in University of Michigan Press Papers, University of Michigan Special Collections Library, Ann Arbor.

145 **"You can see, therefore, why we resent your indictment"**: Harlan Hatcher, letter to Kurt Wolff, November 21, 1958, in University of Michigan Press Papers, University of Michigan Special Collections Library, Ann Arbor.

145 **"fully worth trouble in view obvious effect on Soviets"**: CIA, Cable from Director, November 5, 1958.

145 **"based on the CIA proof":** Paulo Mancosu reached the same conclusion about the first Michigan edition by a different route. See *Inside the Zhivago Storm*, chapter 2

145 **"Their reported price on the black market"**: "From the Other Shore," *Encounter* 11, no. 6 (December 1958): 94.

Chapter 10

147 **a dozen friends**: Max Frankel, interview by Finn in New York City, March 5, 2013.

147 **"This book is the product of an incredible time"**: Frankel, *The Times of My Life*, 169.

147 **he wanted "more than anything"—the Nobel Prize**: Blokh, *Sovetskii Soyuz v Inter'ere Nobelevskikh premii,* 407, note 11. The remark was made by Akhmatova in 1962 to a Swedish academic.

147 **"You will think me immodest"**: Max Frankel, "Author Hoped for Prize," *The New York Times,* October 25, 1958.

148 **"the most outstanding work of an idealistic nature"**: Espmark, *The Nobel Prize in Literature,* 1.

148 **"to work for the purity, vigor and majesty of the Swedish Language"**: Svensén, *The Swedish Academy and the Nobel Prize in Literature,* 44.

148 **214,599.40 Swedish kronor**: *Haagsche Courant,* October 11, 1958.

148 **described the writer as often inaccessible**: Kjell Strömberg, The 1958 Prize in the Nobel Prize Library: Pasternak, page 375.

149 **"to be placed side by side"**: Boris Pasternak, letter to Olga Freidenberg, November 12, 1954, Boris Pasternak and Olga Freidenberg, *Correspondence,* 336.

149 **"If, as some people think"**: Boris Pasternak, letter to Lydia Pasternak Slater, December 18, 1957, in Boris Pasternak, *Family Correspondence,* 391.

149 **"modeled on *War and Peace*"**: Renato Poggioli, letter to the Swedish Academy, January 20, 1958, in Pasternak file, Archive of the Swedish Academy.

149 **"fresh, innovative, difficult style"**: Ernest Simmons, letter to the Swedish Academy, January 14, 1958, in Pasternak file, Archive of the Swedish Academy.

149 **"In a world where great poetry"**: Harry Levin, letter to the Swedish Academy, January 15, 1958, in Pasternak file, Archive of the Swedish Academy.

150 **"A strong patriotic accent comes through"**: Quoted in Kjell Strömberg, The 1958 Prize in the Nobel Prize Library: Pasternak, page 375.

150 **The articles were translated for the Central Committee**: November 1957 translations in Afiani and Tomilina, *Pasternak i Vlast',* 101–4.

150 **Polikarpov even suggested in one note**: February 20, 1958, note of the Department of Culture of the Central Committee, in Afiani and Tomilina, *Pasternak i Vlast',* 101–5.

151 **"halfway through the twentieth century"**: Calvino, *Why Read the Classics?,* 185.

151 **"as odd as an Aztec temple"**: Victor Frank, "A Russian Hamlet," *The Dublin Review* (Autumn 1958): 212.

151 **"in an openly censored form"**: Boris Pasternak, letter to Yelena Blaginina, December 16, 1957, in Yevgeni Pasternak, *Boris Pasternak: The Tragic Years,* 230–31.

152 **efforts "to canonize" Pasternak's works**: *Literaturnaya Gazeta,* November 28, 1957.

152 **"The reviews were enthusiastic"**: Pyotr Suvchinsky, letter to Boris Pasternak, January 28, 1958, in Kozovoi, *Poet v katastrofe,* 219–20.

152 **"I deplore the fuss now being made about my book"**: Gerd Ruge, "A Visit to Pasternak," *Encounter* 10, no. 3 (March 1958): 22–25. Ruge visited Pasternak for the first time in late 1957. See also Ruge, *Pasternak: A Pictorial Biography,* 96–101.

152 **"unworthy of a bed in the Kremlin Hospital"**: Chukovsky, *Diary,* entry February 1, 1958.

152 **"scorned by one and all"**: Ibid., entry February 3, 1958.

153 **He blew kisses**: Ibid., entry February 7, 1958.

153 **"More and more does fate carry me off"**: Boris Pasternak, letter to G. V. Bebutov, May 24, 1958, in Boris Pasternak, *Letters to Georgian Friends,* 170.

153 **"My first impression"**: Lydia Chukovskaya, "Otryvki iz dnevnika" (Diary fragments), entry April 22, 1958, in Boris Pasternak, *Polnoe Sobranie Sochinenii,* vol. 11, 433.

153 **"he also looks the genius"**: Kornei Chukovsky, *Diary,* entry April 22, 1958, 431.

153 **"It is the most important novel"**: Kurt Wolff, letter to Boris Pasternak, February 12, 1958, in Wolff, *A Portrait in Essays and Letters,* 176–77.

154 **he burst into tears**: Hingley, *Pasternak,* 235.

154 **He wrote to de Proyart**: Boris Pasternak, letter to Jacqueline de Proyart, July 9, 1958, in Boris Pasternak, *Lettres à mes amies françaises (1956–1960),* 102.

154 **"I would be nothing without 19th century Russia"**: Albert Camus, letter to Boris Pasternak, June 9, 1958, in *Canadian Slavonic Papers/Revue Canadienne Des Slavistes* 22, no. 2 (June 1980): 276–78.

154 **"To those who are familiar with Soviet novels"**: *The New York Times,* September 7, 1958.

154 **"this book has come to us"**: *Frankfurter Allgemeine Zeitung,* October 4, 1958, in Sieburg, *Zur Literatur 1957–1963,* 92.

154 **"If it were written by a Russian émigré"**: Orville Prescott, "Books of the Times," *The New York Times,* September 5, 1958.

155 **"In your bourgeois society"**: R. H. S. Crossman, "London Diary," *New Statesman,* November 29, 1958.

155 **One writer from Vilnius**: Chukovsky, *Diary,* entry April 22, 1958, 431.

155 **go to Baku**: Ivinskaya, *A Captive of Time,* 214.

156 **"Wanting justice to be served"**: Markov to the Central Committee, note, April 7, 1958, in Afiani and Tomilina *Pasternak i Vlast',* 136.

156 **"a man of immense talent"**: Werth, *Russia under Khrushchev,* 237.

157 **"I would vote against Sholokhov"**: Espmark, *The Nobel Prize in Literature,* 106–7.

157 **The academy shortlisted three**: Pasternak file, Archive of the Swedish Academy.

157 **"impossible for the bourgeois media to make a scandal"**: October 10,

1958, note for the Central Committee, in Afiani and Tomilina, *Pasternak i Vlast'*, 139.

158 **he told Österling that the prize could be awarded**: Blokh, *Sovetskii Soyuz v Inter'ere Nobelevskikh premii*, 406–7.

158 **Pasternak mistakenly believed**: Boris Pasternak, letter to Hélène Peltier, July 30, 1958, in Boris Pasternak, *Lettres à mes amies françaises (1956–1960)*, 111.

158 **"no hesitation about receiving the prize"**: De Mallac, *Boris Pasternak*, 225.

158 **"In this era of world wars"**: Nils Åke Nilsson, "Pasternak: We Are the Guests of Existence," *The Reporter*, November 27, 1958.

158 **"I wish this could happen in a year's time"**: Boris Pasternak, letter to Lydia Pasternak Slater, August 14, 1958, in Boris Pasternak, *Family Correspondence*, 402.

158 **"He several times referred"**: Hingley, *Pasternak*, 235.

159 **"will turn the reading into a riot"**: Chukovsky, *Diary*, entry June 14, 1958, 433.

159 **"an anti-Soviet novel"**: Ivinskaya, *A Captive of Time*, 219.

159 **contradicted what Mesterton and Nilsson**: Pasternak file, Archive of the Swedish Academy.

160 **"It is indeed a great achievement"**: Ibid.

Chapter 11

161 **"To receive this prize fills me"**: Max Frankel, "Soviet's Writers Assail Pasternak," *The New York Times*, October 26, 1958.

161 **Zinaida was shocked and upset**: Zinaida Pasternak, *Vospominaniya*, in Boris Pasternak, *Vtoroe Rozhdenie*, 368.

161 **Ivanova was thrilled**: Tamara Ivanova, "Boris Leonidovich Pasternak," in Boris Pasternak, *Polnoe Sobranie Sochinenii*, vol. 11, 289.

162 **"I know Pasternak as a true poet"**: UPI, October 23, 1958.

162 **Fedin ignored her**: Zinaida Pasternak, *Vospominaniya*, in Boris Pasternak, *Vtoroe Rozhdenie*, 369.

162 **"I'm not going to congratulate you"**: Kornei Chukovsky, *Diary*, entry October 27, 1958, 435.

162 **"They can do whatever they want with me"**: Dmitri Polikarpov, note to Mikhail Suslov, October 24, 1958, in Afiani and Tomilina, *Pasternak i Vlast'*, 146–47.

163 **"Do what seems right to you"**: Tamara Ivanova, "Boris Leonidovich Pasternak," in Boris Pasternak, *Polnoe Sobranie Sochinenii*, vol. 11, 290.

163 **He told them he wouldn't be taking Zinaida**: Yelena Chukovskaya,

"Nobelevskaya premiya" (The Nobel Prize), in Boris Pasternak, *Polnoe Sobranie Sochinenii,* vol. 11, 738–39.

164 **He was diagnosed with a possible stroke**: Tamara Ivanova, "Boris Leonidovich Pasternak," in Boris Pasternak, *Polnoe Sobranie Sochinenii,* vol. 11, 290–91.

164 **"face grew dark"**: Chukovsky, *Diary,* entry October 27, 1958, 435.

164 **"had been amputated"**: Tamara Ivanova, "Boris Leonidovich Pasternak," in Boris Pasternak, *Polnoe Sobranie Sochinenii,* vol. 11, 291–92.

164 **"There would be no mercy"**: Chukovsky, *Diary,* entry October 27, 1958, 435.

164 **Pasternak asked Tamara**: Tamara Ivanova, "Boris Leonidovich Pasternak," in Boris Pasternak, *Polnoe Sobranie Sochinenii,* vol. 11, 291–92.

164 **Dear Yekaterina Alekseyevna**: Boris Pasternak, letter to Yekaterina Furtseva, October 24, 1958, in ibid., vol. 10, 398.

165 **Radio Liberation announced**: UPI, October 23, 1958.

165 **"You and those who made this decision"**: October 26, 1958, instructions to the Soviet embassy in Sweden, in Afiani and Tomilina, *Pasternak i Vlast',* 147–49; Pasternak file, Archive of the Swedish Academy.

166 **By 6:00 a.m. people were lining up**: Michel Tatu, "En dépit des attaques du congrès des écrivains Russes, <<L'Affaire Pasternak>> semble terminée" (Despite attacks at the Congress of Russian Writers, "The Pasternak Affair" Seems to Have Reached an End), *Le Monde,* December 11, 1958.

166 **a circulation of 880,000**: Kozlov, *The Readers of Novyi Mir,* 112.

166 **"The internal emigrant Zhivago"**: Editorial, *Literaturnaya Gazeta,* October 25, 1958. See Conquest, *Courage of Genius,* Appendix II, 136–63, for a full translation of the editorial.

167 **Three students in Leningrad**: Kozlov, *The Readers of Novyi Mir,* 128.

167 **Only 110 of about 300 Literary Institute students**: Yemelyanova, *Legendy Potapovskogo pereulka,* 106–7.

167 **"reaching for a sack of dollars"**: Ivinskaya, *A Captive of Time,* 224.

167 **about forty-five writers**: October 28, 1958, note for the Central Committee, in Afiani and Tomilina, *Pasternak i Vlast',* 155.

168 **he was away at a sanitarium**: Polikarpov memo, October 28, 1958, in ibid., 157.

168 **"moral support"**: *Le Monde,* October 26 and 27, 1958.

168 **"Zaslavsky has acted only as a scandal monger"**: Kozlov, *The Readers of the Novyi Mir,* 128.

169 **Zaslavsky began his career as a provocateur**: Kemp-Welsh, *Stalin and the Literary Intelligentsia,* 63.

169 **"an especially sinister nuance"**: Fleishman, *Boris Pasternak: The Poet and his Politics,* 289.

169 **"Reactionary Propaganda Uproar"**: *Pravda,* October 26, 1958. See Con-

quest, *Courage of Genius,* Appendix III, 164–72, for a full translation of the article.

169 **"The radio, from 5 in the morning"**: Kadare, *Le Crépuscule des dieux de la steppe,* 138.

169 **"Everybody listened in silence"**: Gladkov, *Meetings with Pasternak,* 166.

170 **"it was in fact all very painful"**: Ivinskaya, *A Captive of Time,* 225.

170 **"Really now"**: Ibid., 226.

170 **called Pasternak his teacher**: Gladkov, *Meetings with Pasternak,* 167.

171 **"I now take it on myself"**: Ivinskaya, *A Captive of Time,* 230.

171 **"Why? The most terrible thing is"**: Vitale, *Shklovsky: Witness to an Era,* 29–30.

171 **"gripped by the sickening, clammy feeling"**: Gladkov, *Meetings with Pasternak,* 167.

172 **"I still believe even after all this noise"**: Boris Pasternak, letter to the board of the Union of Soviet Writers, October 27, 1958, in Afiani and Tomilina, *Pasternak i Vlast',* 153.

172 **"with the cold eyes of a dutiful clerk"**: Vyacheslav Ivanov, *Zvezda,* 2 (2010): 113.

172 **Pasternak's letter was read**: Polikarpov report to the Central Committee, October 28, 1958, in ibid., 157.

172 **"put a bullet through a traitor's head"**: Ivinskaya, *A Captive of Time,* 272.

173 **"harsh, very direct, hostile"**: Konstantin Vanshenkin, "Kak isklyuchali Pasternaka" (How Pasternak Was Expelled), in Boris Pasternak, *Polnoe Sobranie Sochinenii,* vol. 11, 740–47.

173 **She recalled in her diary**: Lydia Chukovskaya, *Zapiski ob Anne Akhmatovoi,* vol. 2, 311.

173 **Chukovsky had recently set up the translators' section**: Dmitri Chukovsky, interview by Finn and Couvée, in Moscow, May 2012.

174 **a long, formal resolution stated**: Tass, October 28, 1958. See full resolution in Conquest, *Courage of Genius,* Appendix IV, 173–75.

174 **"Good day to you, microphone"**: Ivinskaya, *A Captive of Time,* 233.

175 **she expected to hear someone shout stop**: Lydia Chukovskaya, *Zapiski ob Anne Akhmatovoi,* vol. 2, 316–19.

175 **"I cannot stand this business anymore"**: Ivinskaya, *A Captive of Time,* 233–36.

176 **"willing to write any letter"**: Fedin, letter to Polikarpov, October 28, 1958, in Afiani and Tomilina, *Pasternak i Vlast',* 160.

177 **"Of course, they won't harm you"**: Yevgeni Pasternak, "Poslednie gody" (The last years), in Boris Pasternak, *Polnoe Sobranie Sochinenii,* vol. 11, 684.

177 **It was only the third time**: "Three Rejections of Nobel Prizes Preceded Pasternak's," *The New York Times,* October 31, 1958.

177 **"I made the decision quite alone"**: Conquest, *Courage of Genius,* 93.
177 **"My father was unrecognizable"**: Yevgeni Pasternak, *Boris Pasternak: The Tragic Years,* 237.
177 **"silly ideas into his head"**: Ivinskaya, *A Captive of Time,* 236.
178 **"This is an even dirtier provocation"**: "Judgment on Pasternak: The All-Moscow Meeting of Writers, Oct. 31,1958, Stenographic Report," *Survey* (July 1966): 134–63.

Chapter 12

179 **"We'll find a place where it fits"**: Semichastny, *Bespokoynoe serdtse,* 72–74.
179 **before twelve thousand young people**: Max Frankel, "Young Communist Head Insists Writer Go to 'Capitalist Paradise,'" *The New York Times,* October 30, 1958.
179 **"As the Russian proverb goes"**: *Komsomol'skaya Pravda,* October 30, 1958. For the full passage on Boris Pasternak, see Conquest, *Courage of Genius,* Appendix V, 176–77.
180 **"Not in my life"**: Zinaida Pasternak, *Vospominaniya,* in Boris Pasternak, *Vtoroe Rozhdenie,* 372–73.
181 **"I must have the work-a-day life"**: Ivinskaya, *A Captive of Time,* 238.
181 **"What are we to do?"**: Ibid.
181 **the house in Peredelkino would be sacked**: Ibid., 240.
181 **a group of local thugs**: Gladkov, *Meetings with Pasternak,* 168.
181 **After Semichastny's speech**: British Embassy in Moscow to the Foreign Office, confidential memo, December 8, 1958, in Nobel Prize for Boris Pasternak Classmark FO 371/135422, National Archives, London.
182 **a letter couldn't hurt**: Yemelyanova, *Pasternak i Ivinskaya: provoda pod tokom,* 212.
182 **"with whom will I be expelled"**: Vyacheslav Ivanov, *Zvezda,* 2 (2010): 120.
183 **"Who is it from"**: Yemelyanova, *Legendy Potapovskogo pereulka* (Legends of Potapov Street), 136–37.
183 **"He sent the manuscript to the Italian publisher"**: "Judgment on Pasternak: The All-Moscow Meeting of Writers, October 31, 1958, Stenographic Report," *Survey* (July 1966): 134–63.
184 **"to imitate Pasternak's way of talking"**: Ivinskaya, *A Captive of Time,* 260.
184 **"Don't worry"**: Ibid., 261.
184 **"young literature"**: Vyacheslav Ivanov, *Zvezda,* 2 (2010): 119.
184 **"That I spoke against Pasternak"**: Lipkin, *Kvadriga,* 510–11.
185 **"Let's agree that all of us"**: Vladimir Soloukhin, "Time to Settle Accounts," *Sovetskaya Kul'tura* (Soviet Culture), October 6, 1988.

185 **"for 30 years, this sin of yours"**: Yevgeny Yevtushenko, "Execution by One's Own Conscience," *Sovetskaya Kul'tura* (Soviet Culture), October 13, 1988.

185 **"particularly vile"**: Kornei Chukovsky, *Dnevnik*, entry January 14, 1967, 518.

185 **"dacha-dweller of genius"**: De Mallac, *Boris Pasternak*, 161.

185 **"always remain in Russian poetry"**: Ibid., 130.

186 **"he approached Konstantin Paustovsky"**: Chukovsky, *Dnevnik*, entry December 6, 1965.

186 **"Not true! Not unanimously!"**: Konstantin Vanshenkin, "Kak isklyuchali Pasternaka" (How Pasternak was expelled), in Boris Pasternak, *Polnoe Sobranie Sochinenii*, vol. 11, 747.

186 **"In the fury, venom and intensity"**: "Pasternak and the Pygmies," *The New York Times*, October 27, 1958.

187 **"an intellectual Budapest"**: "Pasternak Fate Studied," *The Washington Post*, November 3, 1958.

187 **Three members of the Swedish Academy**: British embassy in Stockholm to the Foreign Office, confidential memorandum, Nobel Prize for Boris Pasternak Classmark FO 371/135422, National Archives, London.

187 **Western correspondents were invited**: Max Frankel, "Young Communist Head Insists Writer Go to 'Capitalist Paradise,'" *The New York Times*, October 30, 1958.

187 **"the recognition by the Swedish Academy"**: *Pravda*, October 29, 1958. See Conquest, *Courage of Genius*, 81.

187 **Feltrinelli was in Hamburg**: Carlo Feltrinelli and Inge Schönthal-Feltrinelli, interview by Finn and Couvée, in Milan, June 2, 2012.

188 **"We are profoundly anxious"**: Conquest, *Courage of Genius*, 97.

188 **"I want to create for him the conditions"**: Ivinskaya, *A Captive of Time*, 276.

188 **"That is fantastic"**: Kurt Wolff, letter to Boris Pasternak, October 25, 1958, in Wolff, *A Portrait in Essays and Letters*, 180.

188 **"You have moved beyond"**: Kurt Wolff, letter to Boris Pasternak, December 14, 1958, in ibid., 181.

189 **"The system of international communism"**: Associated Press, October 29, 1958.

189 **"the communists' treatment of Pasternak"**: Notes from Meeting, November 4, 1958, Albert Washburn Papers, box 16. Eisenhower Presidential Library.

189 **should give "maximum factual play" to the Nobel**: CIA, Classified Message from the Director, October 24, 1958.

190 **"Reactions of revulsion and shock"**: CIA, Memorandum for Director of Central Intelligence, October 30, 1958.

190 **"considerable discussion"**: CIA, Memorandum for the Record, November 5, 1958.

190 **should be used to "sparkplug" anti-Soviet coverage**: CIA, Classified Message to the Director, October 28, 1958.

190 **"free thought and dialectical materialism"**: CIA, Current Intelligence Weekly Review, November 6, 1958.

190 **Jorge Amado said the expulsion**: Conquest, *Courage of Genius*, 99.

190 **The Brazilian paper *Última Hora***: CIA, Current Intelligence Weekly Review, November 6, 1958.

190 **"As a friend of your magnificent land"**: Sean O'Casey, letter to O. Prudkov, November 7, 1958, in O'Casey, *The Letters of Sean O'Casey*, vol. 3, 645.

191 **The Icelandic novelist Halldór Laxness**: British embassy in Reykjavik, memo to Foreign Office, October 31, 1958, Nobel Prize for Boris Pasternak. Classmark FO 371/135422, National Archives, London.

191 **"Iceland?"**: Associated Press, May 31, 1959.

191 **pained by the daily abuse**: "Nehru Regrets Soviet Stand," *The New York Times*. November 8, 1958.

191 **"A noted writer"**: Conquest, *Courage of Genius*, 100.

191 **The Soviet Union's cultural diplomacy**: CIA, Current Intelligence Weekly Review, November 6, 1958.

191 **"Enough. He's admitted his mistakes"**: Sergei Khrushchev, *Khrushchev on Khrushchev*, 209.

192 **"Olga Vsevolodovna, my dear"**: Ivinskaya, *A Captive of Time*, 262. (The interactions with Polikarpov and his meeting with Boris Pasternak on October 31 are all from Ivinskaya, 262–68, unless there is another citation.)

192 **he broke down and wept**: Maslenikova, *Portret Borisa Pasternaka*, 118.

Chapter 13

197 **"Rage and Indignation"**: "Gnev i vozmushchenie. Sovetskie lyudi osuzhdayut deistviya B. Pasternaka" (Rage and Indignation: Soviet People Condemn B. Pasternak's Behavior), *Literaturnaya Gazeta*, November 1, 1958.

197 **"a wench from the editorial board"**: Lydia Chukovskaya, *Zapiski ob Anne Akhmatovoi*, vol. 2, 331.

197 **The newspaper was indeed inundated**: Kozlov, *The Readers of Novyi Mir*, 116.

198 **"The revolution remained central"**: Ibid., 125.

198 **"There was also substantial evidence"**: Barghoorn, *The Soviet Cultural Offensive*, 156.

198 **the editors of *Novy Mir* forwarded letters**: Kozlov, *The Readers of Novyi Mir*, 126.

198 **"To Pasternak from Judas"**: Reference in Boris Pasternak, letter to O. Goncharyov, February 18, 1959, in Boris Pasternak, *Polnoe Sobranie Sochinenii*, vol. 10, 430.

198 **The German journalist Gerd Ruge**: Ivinskaya, *A Captive of Time*, 275.

199 **"The great and undeserved happiness"**: Boris Pasternak, letter to N. B. Sologub, July 29, 1959, in Boris Pasternak, *Polnoe Sobranie Sochinenii*, vol. 10, 509.

199 **He stayed up until two**: Zinaida Pasternak, *Vospominaniya*, in Boris Pasternak, *Vtoroe Rozhdenie*, 375.

199 **"I'm troubled by the volume of it"**: "Boris Pasternak, The Art of Fiction No. 25," interview by Olga Carlisle, *The Paris Review* 24 (1960): 61–66.

199 **"merge into privacy"**: Gladkov, *Meetings with Pasternak*, 171.

199 **"It is an unspeakable grief"**: Boris Pasternak, letter to George Reavy, December 10, 1959, in "Nine Letters of Boris Pasternak," *Harvard Library Bulletin* 15, no. 4 (October 1967): 327.

199 **"Didn't the doctor have enough trouble?"**: Boris Pasternak, letter to Kurt Wolff, May 12, 1959, in Lang, *Boris Pasternak–Kurt Wolff*, 105.

199 **Tass reported**: Reuters, November 1, 1958.

200 **"I am going to cook for him"**: UPI, November 2, 1958.

200 **"matron of his quiet seclusion"**: Boris Pasternak, *Doctor Zhivago* (2010), 39.

200 **"like a pair of professional counterfeiters"**: Ivinskaya, *A Captive of Time*, 278.

200 **"the scope of the political campaign"**: *Pravda*, November 6, 1958. See Conquest, *Courage of Genius*, Appendix VII, 180–81.

201 **Solzhenitsyn "writhed with shame for him"**: Solzhenitsyn, *The Oak and the Calf*, 292.

201 **"The story of Boris is—a battle of butterflies"**: Reeder, *Anna Akhmatova*, 365.

201 **"Boris spoke the whole time"**: Ibid., 366.

201 **agreed to restore his and Ivinskaya's ability**: Ivinskaya, *A Captive of Time*, 278.

202 **Feltrinelli had been depositing**: Carlo Feltrinelli, *Feltrinelli*, 151.

202 **both the CIA and the Kremlin speculated**: CIA, Memorandum for the Record, April 2, 1959; Central Committee Memo, January 20, 1959, in Afiani and Tomilina, *Pasternak i Vlast'*, 179–80.

202 **"The fact that I am completely lacking in curiosity"**: Carlo Feltrinelli, *Feltrinelli*, 146.

202 **"Their desire to drown me"**: D'Angelo, *Delo Pasternaka*, 143.

202 **"Have I really done insufficient"**: Yevgeni Pasternak, *Boris Pasternak: The Tragic Years*, 228.

202 **first from his housekeeper**: Yemelyanova, *Pasternak i Ivinskaya: provoda pod tokom*, 240.

202 **3,000 rubles**: Boris Pasternak, letter to Valeria Prishvina, December 27,

1958, in note 1 to letter of December 12, 1958, Boris Pasternak, *Polnoe Sobranie Sochinenii,* vol. 10, 409.

203 **"His cheeks are sunken"**: Chukovsky, *Diary,* entry January 7, 1959, 437.

203 **"We must put our financial affairs"**: Boris Pasternak, letter to Olga Ivinskaya, February 24, 1959, in Ivinskaya, *A Captive of Time,* Appendix A, 378.

203 **Ruge gathered about $8,000**: Gerd Ruge, interview by Finn and Couvée, in Munich, May 29, 2012. Ruge was unable to place an exact date on the transfer, but the gathering and transfer of the money was probably in and around March 1959. In a letter to Feltrinelli on February 2, Pasternak asked his publisher to disburse cash gifts to a number of friends, translators, and family in the West. The list of beneficiaries didn't immediately reach Feltrinelli, and Pasternak revised the list in April, adding another $5,000 to the $10,000 to be paid to Ruge. This addition, to clear the debt, was also mentioned in a March 30 letter to Jacqueline de Proyart.

203 **He alerted his French translator**: Boris Pasternak, letter to Jacqueline de Proyart, February 3, 1959, in Boris Pasternak, *Lettres à mes amies françaises (1956–1960),* 141.

203 **Pasternak asked Polikarpov**: Central Committee Memo, April 16, 1959, with attachments, in Afiani and Tomilina, *Pasternak i Vlast',* 251.

203 **"It wouldn't be so bad"**: Ivinskaya, *A Captive of Time,* 337.

204 **"brötchen"**: Giangiacomo Feltrinelli, letter to Heinz Schewe, November 13, 1959, Heinz Schewe Papers, Nachlass Heinz Schewe, Unternehmensarchiv, Axel Springer AB, Berlin.

204 **The average annual earnings**: Barnes, *Boris Pasternak,* vol. 2, 364.

205 **"To find myself bereft of your trust"**: Carlo Feltrinelli, *Feltrinelli,* 149.

205 **"one of the great events"**: Edmund Wilson, "Doctor Life and His Guardian Angel," *The New Yorker,* November 15, 1958, 213–37.

206 **famously photographed**: Photograph captioned "Sightseeing in Washington," *The New York Times,* January 5, 1959.

206 **"Suffering from delusions"**: Barbara Thompson, "Locked-in Guests Dine on Steak with Mikoyan," *The Washington Post,* January 6, 1959.

206 **850,000 copies of the novel**: CIA, Memorandum for the Record, April 2, 1959.

206 **"Pasternak is so fashionable"**: Soviet Ministry of Foreign Affairs memo, February 12, 1959, Afiani and Tomilina, in *Pasternak i Vlast',* 242.

206 **"a photomontage"**: *The New York Times,* March 8, 1959.

206 **"one of the most despicable books about Jews"**: *Haagsche Courant,* February 7, 1959.

206 **bowed so deeply before the king**: "Pasternak Cited at Nobel Session," *The New York Times,* December 11, 1958.

207 **"Tempest not yet over"**: Boris Pasternak, telegram to sisters, November 10, 1958, Boris Pasternak, *Family Correspondence,* 407.

207 **"It would be best of all to die"**: Barnes, *Boris Pasternak,* vol. 2, 352.

207 **"putrid internal émigré position"**: Conquest, *Courage of Genius,* 95.
207 **"disoriented progressive writers"**: CIA, Memo from the Chief, Soviet Russia Division, April 9, 1959.
207 **"I realize that I can't demand anything"**: KGB memo on Pasternak, February 18, 1958.
207 **"like so many radioactive isotopes"**: Conquest, *Courage of Genius,* 96.
207 **"in every generation"**: "Pasternak Stands on 'Zhivago Views,'" *The New York Times,* February 19, 1959.
207 **"distressing, deadly dangerous"**: Carlo Feltrinelli, *Feltrinelli,* 144. (Feltrinelli never received this letter, which was sent to Jacqueline de Proyart, who didn't forward it.)
208 **"What more do you need?"**: Ivinskaya, *A Captive of Time,* 297.
208 **I am lost like a beast in an enclosure**: This is the translation that appeared in the *Daily Mail* on February 12, 1959. Other renderings of the poem into English are slightly different.
208 **"I am a white cormorant"**: Anthony Brown, "Pasternak on My Life Now," *Daily Mail,* February 12, 1959.
208 **"The poem should not have been published"**: February 13, 1959, memo on Western media coverage of Pasternak's birthday [February 10], in Afiani and Tomilina, *Pasternak i Vlast',* 243.

Chapter 14

211 **"in a cold fury"**: Ivinskaya, *A Captive of Time,* 300.
212 **Pasternak inscribed Gudiashvili's scrapbook**: Yevgeni Pasternak, *Boris Pasternak: The Tragic Years,* 240.
212 **"I really should draw in my horns"**: Boris Pasternak, letter to Olga Ivinskaya, February 22, 1959, in Ivinskaya, *A Captive of Time,* Appendix A377.
212 **"Olyusha, my precious girl"**: Boris Pasternak, letter to Olga Ivinskaya, February 28, 1959, in Ivinskaya, *A Captive of Time,* Appendix A 380.
212 **Pasternak fell to his knees**: Bykov, *Boris Pasternak,* 834.
212 **"I don't want to talk nonsense to you"**: Boris Pasternak, letter to Chukurtma Gudiashvili, March 8, 1959, Boris Pasternak, *Polnoe Sobranie Sochinenii,* vol. 10, 439.
213 **was pressured by the authorities**: Barnes, *Boris Pasternak,* vol. 2, 356.
213 **"fatal carelessness"**: Report on the interrogation of B. L Pasternak, March 14, 1959, in Afiani and Tomilina, *Pasternak i Vlast',* 192.
214 **"like Tolstoy in 1903"**: Isaiah Berlin, letter to Edmund Wilson, December 23, 1958, in Berlin, *Enlightening,* 688.
214 **"Pasternak does not receive"**: Ivinskaya, *A Captive of Time,* 294.
214 **"You have to stop receiving that trash"**: Zinaida Pasternak, *Vospominaniya,* in Boris Pasternak, *Vtoroe Rozhdenie,* 378.

214 **"Journalists and others, please go away"**: Conquest, *Courage of Genius*, page 104.

214 **The CIA's efforts**: CIA, Memo to Acting Chief, Soviet Russia Division, November 18, 1958; Memo to the Chief, Psychological and Paramilitary Staff, November 21, 1958; Memo to CIA Director, November 21, 1958; Dispatch from SR Chief, December 17, 1958.

215 **"The worldwide discussion of the book"**: CIA, Memo for the Record, March 27, 1959.

215 **"It would be quite natural for an American"**: CIA, Memo from the Chief, Soviet Russia Division, April 8, 1958.

215 **"We feel that Dr. Zhivago is an excellent springboard"**: CIA, Memo from the Chief, Soviet Russia Division, April 9, 1959.

216 **"in one form or another"**: CIA, Memo for the Record, March 27, 1959.

216 **The CIA also considered publishing an anthology of Pasternak's works**: CIA, Memo for the Office of General Counsel, February 5, 1959.

216 **to be printed on "bible-stock"**: CIA, Memo from the Chief of the Soviet Russia Division, August 9, 1958.

217 **"more easily concealed and infiltrated"**: CIA, Memo for Acting Deputy Director (Plans) from the Acting Chief, SR Division, November 19, 1958.

217 **"ballooned into East Germany"**: CIA, Classified Message to the Director, November 5, 1958.

217 **"particularly hot item"**: CIA, Memo from the Chief of the Soviet Russia Division, December 17, 1959.

217 **the Soviet Union reinstituted searches**: Barghoorn, *The Soviet Cultural Offensive*, 119.

217 **the novel was kept under strict KGB embargo**: Yelena Makareki, former employee of the V. I. Lenin State Library's Special Collections section, interview by Couvée, in Moscow, May 8, 2011.

217 **The CIA had its own press in Washington**: Former CIA Moscow station chief Burton Gerber, interview by Finn, in Washington, D.C., November 20, 2012.

217 **"inside a man's suit or trouser pocket"**: CIA, Memorandum, July 16, 1959.

217 **"In view of the security"**: Memorandum for the Acting Deputy Director (Plans), November 19, 1958.

217 **nine thousand copies of a miniature edition**: CIA, Memorandum, "Publication of the Miniature Edition of *Dr. Zhivago*," July 16, 1959.

218 **Société d'Edition et d'Impression Mondiale**: Copies of the book are held at the CIA museum in Langley, Virginia.

218 **At a press conference in The Hague**: November 4, 1958, editions of the newspapers *Haagsche Courant* and *Vaderland*.

218 **he had "released" this edition of *Zhivago***: Boris Filippov, letter to Gleb Struve, November 24, 1977, quoted in Ivan Tolstoy, *Otmytyi Roman Pasternaka*, 331.

218 **overseen personally by Alexander Shelepin**: Kotek, *Students and the Cold War,* 213.

219 **"a tool for the advancement of world communism"**: Independent Service for Information, *Report on the Vienna Youth Festival,* 19.

219 **"liberal and farsighted and open to an exchange of ideas"**: Robert G. Kaiser, "Work of CIA with Youths at Festivals Is Defended," *The Washington Post,* February 18, 1967.

219 **Newspapers published in several languages were brought in at night**: Walter Pincus, interview by Finn, in Washington, D.C., April 24, 2013.

220 **"Out of my way, Russian pig!"**: Stern, *Gloria Steinem,* 119–20.

220 **"college weekend with Russians"**: Walter Pincus, interview by Finn, in Washington, D.C., April 24, 2013. (Pincus has used this phrase in several different interviews.)

220 **"going off to join the Spanish Revolution"**: Heilbrun, *The Education of a Woman,* 89.

220 **about 30,000 in fourteen languages**: Independent Service for Information, *Report on the Vienna Youth Festival,* 93.

220 **"to expose delegates from the Soviet orbit"**: Youth Festival, Vienna, General Correspondence 1959, C. D. Jackson Papers, Box 115, Folder 4, Eisenhower Presidential Library.

220 **handed out from kiosks**: Reisch, *Hot Books in the Cold War,* 297.

220 **"under observation by communist agents"**: "Final Report of the Activities of the Person-to-Person (Polish) Program at the 7th World Youth Festival," Samuel S. Walker Papers, Box 8, Hoover Institution Archives.

220 **"Complained bitterly" about ISI's projects**: Samuel S. Walker, letter to C. D. Jackson, July 31, 1959, Samuel S. Walker Papers, Box 1, Hoover Institution Archives.

221 **with the blessing**: Samuel S. Walker to C. D. Jackson, status report on Vienna Youth Festival, June 25, 1959, C.D. Jackson Papers, Box 110, Eisenhower Presidential Library.

221 **Overall responsibility for getting books**: Samuel S. Walker, letter to C. D. Jackson, February 2, 1959, C. D. Jackson Papers, Box 115, Folder 5, Eisenhower Presidential Archives.

221 **"special efforts"**: Klaus Dohrn, letter to C. D. Jackson, December 8, 1958, C. D. Jackson Papers, Box 115, Folder 5, Eisenhower Presidential Library.

221 **"Don't worry about the 'Dr. Zhivago' text"**: C. D. Jackson, letter to Klaus Dohrn, January 5, 1959, C. D. Jackson Papers, Box 115, Folder 5, Eisenhower Presidential Library.

221 **distributed in Polish, German, Czech, Hungarian, and Chinese**: "Vienna Youth Festival: Book Program," February 20, 1959, and C. D. Jackson, letter to Fritz Molden, January 5, 1958, C. D. Jackson Papers, Eisenhower Presidential Library; George Trutnovsky, letter to Samuel S.Walker, plus attachment, May 4, 1959, Samuel S. Walker Papers, Box 1, Hoover Institution Archives.

221 **published in Taiwan**: Huang Wei, "*Doctor Zhivago* in China," Ph.D. diss., Jinan University, 2006.

221 **serialized in Chinese by two newspapers in Hong Kong**: CIA, Memo for the Record, "Editions for Dr. Zhivago," March 23, 1959.

221 **an ulcer on the Soviet Union**: Zang Kejia, "Ulcer or Treasure: Why the Nobel Prize Was Awarded to Pasternak," *World Literature* 1 (1959), cited in "*Doctor Zhivago* in China," Ph.D. diss., Huang Wei.

221 **the four-hundred-strong Chinese delegation**: Summary of April 23, 1959, *Volkstimme* article in Samuel S. Walker Papers, Box 8, Hoover Institution Archives.

221 **"absolutely uncommunicative"**: "Final Report of the Activities of the Person-to-Person (Polish) Program at the 7th World Youth Festival," Samuel S. Walker Papers, Box 8, Hoover Institution Archives.

221 **fifty copies of *Doctor Zhivago* from Hong Kong**: George Trutnovsky to Samuel Walker, "Progress Report on Preparations for the World Youth Festival," attachment to letter, May 4, 1959, Samuel S. Walker Papers, Box 1, Hoover Institution Archives.

221 **through the open windows**: Kavanagh, *Nureyev,* 74.

222 **bags from Vienna department stores**: "Final Report of the Activities of the Person-to-Person (Polish) Program at the 7th World Youth Festival," Samuel S. Walker Papers, Box 8, Hoover Institution Archives.

222 **"None of us, of course, had read the book"**: Armen Medvedev, "Tol'ko o kino" (Only on Cinema), Chapter 4, in *Iskusstvo kino* (Cinema Art) 4 (1999): http://kinoart.ru/archive/1999/04/n4-article22.

222 **"I want to re-create a whole historical era"**: "Boris Pasternak: The Art of Fiction No. 25," interview by Olga Carlisle, *The Paris Review* 24 (1960): 61–66.

222 **"I don't know whether I'll ever finish it"**: Jhan Robbins, "Boris Pasternak's Last Message to the World," *This Week* magazine, August 7, 1960.

223 **"I have been eagerly zealous"**: Boris Pasternak, letter to Lydia Pasternak Slater, July 31, 1959, Boris Pasternak, *Family Correspondence,* 412.

223 **"when I first lukewarmly toyed"**: Ivinskaya, *A Captive of Time,* 310.

223 **"not a book that would cause a good Young Communist"**: Harrison E. Salisbury, "Khrushchev's Russia," *The New York Times,* September 14, 1959.

223 **he grabbed Surkov by the collar**: Dewhirst and Farrell, *The Soviet Censorship,* 13.

223 **"'Criticize us, control us'"**: Max Hayward, "The Struggle Goes On," in Brumberg, *Russia under Khrushchev,* 385.

223 **"They all showed themselves up at that time"**: Barnes, *Boris Pasternak,* vol. 2, 366.

224 **Bernstein was a sensation**: For an account of the tour and the meeting with Pasternak, see Burton, *Leonard Bernstein,* 304–10.

224 **they were initially left outside**: Briggs, *Leonard Bernstein: The Man, His Work and His World,* 233–34.
225 **"The Artist communes with God"**: Barnes, *Boris Pasternak,* vol. 2, 366.
225 **"every eye in the hall"**: Hans N. Tuch, "A Nonperson Named Boris Pasternak," *The New York Times,* March 14, 1987.

Chapter 15

227 **Pasternak warmed his stomach with cognac**: Schewe, *Pasternak privat,* 17–18.
227 **"a disturbance at the left side"**: De Mallac, *Boris Pasternak,* 256.
228 **he told her he had lung cancer**: Yekaterina Krasheninnikova, "Krupitsy o Pasternake" (Nuggets on Pasternak), *Novy Mir* 1 (1997): 210.
228 **"Some benign forces have brought me close"**: Barnes, *Boris Pasternak,* vol. 2, 368.
228 **Feltrinelli should buy his body**: Boris Pasternak, letter to Jacqueline de Proyart, November 14, 1959, in Boris Pasternak, *Lettres à mes amies françaises (1956–1960),* 206.
228 **She was frightened by a grayness**: Ivinskaya, *A Captive of Time,* 315.
229 **She was entranced by a newspaper photo**: Schweitzer, *Freundschaft mit Boris Pasternak,* 6.
229 **If she could "have him for a week"**: Maslenikova, *Portret Borisa Pasternaka,* 247.
229 **"so heavy"**: Zinaida Pasternak, *Vospominaniya,* in Boris Pasternak, *Vtoroe Rozhdenie,* 386.
229 **"falling ill as a punishment"**: Ivinskaya, *A Captive of Time,* 317.
229 **a journal on his health**: Boris Pasternak, *Pasternak privat,* 43–46.
229 **"such a constant pain"**: Ivinskaya, *A Captive of Time,* 385. (Notes to Ivinskaya in this period are reproduced in Appendix A of her memoir.)
230 **"I'm dying"**: Yevgeni Pasternak, "Poslednie gody" (The Last Years), in Boris Pasternak, *Polnoe Sobranie Sochinenii,* vol. 11, 710.
230 **Golodets found her patient**: Anna Golodets, "Poslednie dni" (The Last Days), in Boris Pasternak, *Polnoe Sobranie Sochinenii,* vol. 11, 747–62.
231 **"Olyusha won't love me anymore"**: Ivinskaya, *A Captive of Time,* 320.
231 **antibiotics**: Priscilla Johnson, "Death of a Writer," *Harper's* magazine (May 1961): 140–46.
232 **Zinaida several times offered**: Zinaida Pasternak, *Vospominaniya,* in Boris Pasternak, *Vtoroe Rozhdenie,* 388.
232 **tormented by gossip about the affair**: Ibid., 362.
232 **"like my own daughter, like my youngest child"**: Boris Pasternak, letter to Jacqueline de Proyart, September 21, 1959, in Boris Pasternak, *Lettres à mes amies françaises (1956–1960),* 197.

232 **Zinaida thought it was "monstrous"**: Zinaida Pasternak, *Vospominaniya,* in Boris Pasternak, *Vtoroe Rozhdenie,* 388.

232 **"SITUATION HOPELESS"**: Alexander Pasternak, telegram to Lydia Pasternak Slater, May 27, 1960, in Boris Pasternak, *Family Correspondence,* 418.

232 **"How unnatural everything is"**: Yevgeni Pasternak, "Poslednie gody" (Last Years), in Boris Pasternak, *Polnoe Sobranie Sochinenii,* vol. 11, 712.

233 **"I have loved life and you very much"**: Zinaida Pasternak, *Vospominaniya,* in Boris Pasternak, *Vtoroe Rozhdenie,* 391.

233 **"Lydia will soon be here"**: Anna Golodets, "Poslednie dni" (Last Days), in Boris Pasternak, *Polnoe Sobranie Sochinenii,* vol. 11, 761.

233 **"Don't forget to open the window"**: Ivinskaya, *A Captive of Time,* 323.

233 **"And now you can let me in"**: Anna Golodets, "Poslednie dni" (Last Days), in Boris Pasternak, *Polnoe Sobranie Sochinenii,* vol. 11, 762.

233 **"Borya was lying there still warm"**: Ivinskaya, *A Captive of Time,* 324.

234 **Farewell, azure of Transfiguration**: Boris Pasternak, "August," in *Doctor Zhivago* (2010), 478–80.

234 **whose hands began to tremble**: Reeder, *Anna Akhmatova,* 366.

234 **"The weather has been unbelievably beautiful"**: Chukovsky, *Diary,* entry May 31, 1960, 444.

234 **"The death of Pasternak"**: Carlo Feltrinelli, *Feltrinelli,* 177.

235 **the snub**: Central Committee memo on the funeral of Pasternak, June 4, 1960, in Afiani and Tomilina, *Pasternak i Vlast',* 289.

235 **"A Magician of Poetry"**: Dewhirst and Farrell, *The Soviet Censorship,* 61.

235 **"the last leave-taking of Boris Leonidovich Pasternak"**: Priscilla Johnson, "Death of a Writer," *Harper's* (May 1961): 140–46; Ivinskaya, *A Captive of Time,* 326.

235 **"unbearably blue sky"**: Voznesensky, *An Arrow in the Wall,* 285.

235 **The authorities described them as "mostly intelligentsia"**: Central Committee memo on funeral of Pasternak, June 4, 1960, in Afiani and Tomilina, *Pasternak i Vlast',* 287.

236 **"Pasternak will be buried"**: Associated Press, "1,000 at Rites for Pasternak," June 2, 1960.

236 **The KGB set up temporary headquarters**: Krotkov, "Pasternaki" ("The Pasternaks"), *Grani* 63 (1967), 84–90.

236 **snuck in and out**: Kaverin, *Epilog,* 390.

236 **"I don't take part in anti-government demonstrations"**: Chukovsky, *Diary,* entry June 16, 1960, 446.

236 **"Who can forget the senseless and tragic affair"**: Ivinskaya, *A Captive of Time,* 325.

237 **"He could have been lying in a field"**: Priscilla Johnson, "Death of a Writer," *Harper's* (May 1961), 140–46.

238 **"I want to go past the coffin with you"**: Ibid., 328.
238 **"sole alien element"**: Gladkov, *Meetings with Pasternak,* 179.
238 **The authorities counted five hundred**: Central Committee memo on the funeral of Pasternak, June 4, 1960, in Afiani and Tomilina, *Pasternak i Vlast',* 287.
238 **Gladkov recalled Pasternak's lines**: Gladkov, *Meetings with Pasternak,* 176.
239 **"in her humiliated position"**: Orlova, *Memoirs,* 147.
239 **hastily buried**: Kaminskaya, *Final Judgment,* 163.
239 **"the melancholy dirt road"**: Voznesensky, *An Arrow in the Wall,* 286.
240 **"We have come to bid farewell"**: There are slightly different variations of Asmus's eulogy. This is the one recorded by Priscilla Johnson, in "Death of a Writer," *Harper's* (May 1961): 140–46.
240 **A slave is sent to the arena**: "O Had I Known," in Boris Pasternak, *Poems of Boris Pasternak,* 60.
240 **"a thousand pairs of lips"**: Priscilla Johnson, "Death of a Writer," *Harper's* (May 1961): 140–46.
241 **Zinaida was irritated**: Zinaida Pasternak, *Vospominaniya,* in Boris Pasternak, *Vtoroe Rozhdenie,* 396.
241 **"The poet was killed!"**: De Mallac, *Boris Pasternak,* 271.
241 **"The meeting is over"**: Ivinskaya, *A Captive of Time,* 331.
241 **"faint, muffled and terrifying"**: Lydia Chukovskaya, *Zapiski ob Anne Akhmatovoi,* vol. 2, 401.
241 **"the voice now of one"**: Priscilla Johnson, "Death of a Writer," *Harper's* (May 1961): 140–46.
241 **"have been poisoned with unhealthy, oppositional ideas"**: Central Committee memo on the funeral of Pasternak, June 4, 1960, in Afiani and Tomilina, *Pasternak i Vlast',* 289.
242 **"The victory of what?"**: Lydia Chukovskaya, *Zapiski ob Anne Akhmatovoi,* vol. 2, 397.

Chapter 16

243 **"You were expecting us to come"**: Ivinskaya, *A Captive of Time,* 339–40.
243 **"adventuress who got him to write *Doctor Zhivago*"**: Ibid., 340.
243 **"Olyusha, where should we leave all that money?"**: Yemelyanova, *Legendy Potapovskogo pereulka,* 211.
244 **"an account in the tax haven of Liechtenstein"**: D'Angelo, *Delo Pasternaka,* 154.
244 **"running" an "operation"**: Ibid., 162.
244 **a large sum of rubles**: Carlo Feltrinelli, *Feltrinelli,* 191.
244 **"gasped with astonishment"**: Ivinskaya, *A Captive of Time,* 338.

244 **The Italians agreed to take back some documents**: Ibid., 296.

244 **Mirella Garritano thought the documents**: D'Angelo, *Delo Pasternaka,* 201–2.

245 **"power to carry out all tasks"**: Mancosu, *Inside the Zhivago Storm,* 216.

245 **"he wrote me a power of attorney for you"**: Olga Ivinskaya, letter to Giangiacomo Feltrinelli, in Schewe, *Pasternak privat,* 54–57.

245 **D'Angelo's methods "were too dangerous"**: D'Angelo, *Delo Pasternaka,* 183.

245 **"bad thriller"**: Ivinskaya, *A Captive of Time,* 351.

245 **"My dear, dear Giangiacomo"**: Olga Ivinskaya, letter to Giangiacomo Feltrinelli, July 28, 1960, Heinz Schewe Papers, Nachlass Heinz Schewe, Unternehmensarchiv, Axel Springer AB, Berlin.

246 **"Not to get involved in a battle in Moscow"**: Giangiacomo Feltrinelli, letter to Olga Ivinskaya, June 24, 1960, Heinz Schewe Papers, Nachlass Heinz Schewe, Unternehmensarchiv, Axel Springer AB, Berlin.

246 **$125,000 at the official exchange rate**: See "Publisher Backs Pasternak Ally," *The New York Times,* January 28, 1961.

246 **"You have no right to refuse it"**: Ivinskaya, *A Captive of Time,* 338.

246 **bought a motorcycle**: Schewe, *Pasternak privat,* 78.

246 **Pasternak bought a new car**: Zinaida Pasternak, *Vospominaniya,* in Boris Pasternak, *Vtoroe Rozhdenie,* 384.

246 **"thick-set man with black eyes"**: Ivinskaya, *A Captive of Time,* 333.

247 **In retrospect, Irina considered**: Yemelyanova, *Legendy Potapovskogo pereulka,* 209.

247 **searched by two agents**: Zinaida Pasternak, *Vospominaniya,* in Boris Pasternak, *Vtoroe Rozhdenie,* 406–7.

247 **"I was overcome by a peculiar feeling of indifference"**: Ivinskaya, *A Captive of Time,* 342.

248 **"a teeny-weeny criminal"**: Yemelyanova, *Legendy Potapovskogo pereulka,* 232.

248 **"We have read all your letters"**: Giangiacomo Feltrinelli, letter to Heinz Schewe, September 3, 1960, Heinz Schewe Papers, Nachlass Heinz Schewe, Unternehmensarchiv, Axel Springer AB, Berlin.

248 **"Mom's on vacation in the south"**: D'Angelo, *Delo Pasternaka,* 165.

249 **"You disguised it very well"**: Ivinskaya, *A Captive of Time,* 343.

249 **Ivinskaya was indicted on November 10, 1960**: State Archive of the Russian Federation, Col.: 8131, I.: 31, F.: 89398, S.: 35.

249 **"sold himself to the Western warmongers"**: For description of Ivinskaya on trial, see Ivinskaya, *A Captive of Time,* 351–54.

250 **"unbearable for Muscovites"**: Ivinskaya, *A Captive of Time,* 355.

250 **The barracks were warm**: Yemelyanova, *Legendy Potapovskogo pereulka,* 276.

250 **"Pasternachkis"**: Yemelyanova, *Pasternak i Ivinskaya: provoda pod tokom,* 309.

250 **"quiet appeals to the Soviet authorities"**: Conquest, *Courage of Genius,* 108.

250 **"was the sort of thing that made my campaign"**: "Khrushchev Gets Inquiry in Jailing," *The New York Times,* January 20, 1961.

250 **"pure act of revenge"**: Harry Schwartz, "Woman Friend of Pasternak Said to Be Imprisioned by Soviet," *The New York Times,* January 18, 1961.

251 **Radio Moscow responded on January 21**: For full transcript, see Conquest, *Courage of Genius,* Appendix VIII, 182–86.

251 **a long commentary in Italian**: For full transcript, see ibid., Appendix IX, 187–91.

251 **"People in the West will be justified in asking"**: "Pasternak's Collaborator's Arrest," Letters, *The New York Times,* January 26, 1961.

251 **"radio statement is much too vindictive"**: *The Times,* January 23, 1961.

251 **Feltrinelli released a statement on January 28**: Conquest, *Courage of Genius,* 111.

252 **Nivat told reporters in Paris**: W. Granger Blair, "Frenchman, Who Studied in Moscow, Denies Mme. Ivinskaya Accepted Smuggled Foreign Royalties," *The New York Times,* January 25, 1961.

252 **"Had Boris Pasternak, whom I loved as a father, still lived"**: Georges Nivat to Queen Elisabeth of Belgium, letter, January 21, 1960, Archive of the Private Secretariat of Queen Elisabeth, Archive of the Royal Palace, Brussels.

252 **"you intervene and demand the liberation of rogues"**: Conquest, *Courage of Genius,* 116.

253 **"advertised her intimacy with Pasternak"**: Stephen S. Rosenfeld, "Soviet see 'Honest' Pasternak Misled by 'Evil' Woman," *The Washington Post,* October 15, 1961.

253 **"We have brought documents and letters"**: "Russian Backs Jailing," *The New York Times,* February 21, 1961.

253 **"Everything in the accusation is the essential truth"**: Conquest, *Courage of Genius,* 120.

254 **"I don't care how it looks"**: Chukovsky, *Diary,* entry May 1, 1961, 454.

254 **"moral reasons"**: Alexei Surkov, letter to Mikhail Suslov, August 19, 1961, in Afiani and Tomilina, *Pasternak i Vlast',* 289–90.

254 **"yet another anti-Soviet campaign"**: Memo on request of Pasternak's widow, September 20, 1961, in ibid., 291.

254 **"had a longstanding dislike for Zinaida"**: De Mallac, *Boris Pasternak,* 276.

255 **Feltrinelli sold the film rights**: Carlo Feltrinelli, *Feltrinelli,* 196.

255 **"frankly provocative"**: *The New York Times,* April 16, 1977.

255 **"We shouldn't have banned it"**: Taubman, *Khrushchev,* 628.

256 **"some might say it's too late"**: Nikita Khrushchev, *Khrushchev Remembers: The Last Testament,* 77.

256 **"I am the first Russian writer"**: Peter Grose, "Sholokhov Proud of Role as 'Soviet' Nobel Winner," *The New York Times*, December 1, 1965.

256 **"gratefully"**: Tass, October 16, 1965.

256 **"The fact that this bright talent"**: Associated Press, October 15, 1965.

256 **"it is deplorable that the Nobel committee"**: James F. Clarity, "Soviet Writers Union Criticizes Nobel Prize Given Solzhenitsyn," *The New York Times*, October 10, 1970.

257 **"dying slowly right in front of my eyes"**: Olga Ivinskaya to Nikita Khrushchev, letter, March 10, 1961. The full letter is available in the State Archive of the Russian Federation, Col.: 8131, I.: 31, F.: 89398, S.: 51.

257 **Irina was reported to have a stomach ulcer**: "Pasternak Friends Now Seriously Ill," *The New York Times*, June 17, 1961.

257 **"I am not saying that I am not guilty"**: Olga Ivinskaya, letter to Nikita Khrushchev, March 10, 1961, State Archive of the Russian Federation, Col.: 8131, I.: 31, F.: 89398, S.: 51.

258 **"characteristics of the detainee"**: Ibid., S.: 50.

259 **"It seems to me that the time has come for frankness"**: Carlo Feltrinelli, *Feltrinelli*, 198.

259 **"learned to wind spaghetti"**: Ibid., 199.

259 **"bellicose and uncompromising"**: Heinz Schewe, letter to Giangiacomo Feltrinelli, January 27, 1965, Heinz Schewe Papers, Nachlass Heinz Schewe, Unternehmensarchiv, Axel Springer AB, Berlin.

259 **the equivalent of $24,000**: Schewe, *Pasternak privat*, 94.

259 **Pasternak's "faithful companion"**: Feltrinelli press release published in *Corriere della Sera* on March 1, 1970, and cited in D'Angelo, *Delo Pasternaka*, 238.

259 **"no longer believed in anything"**: For an account of Feltrinelli's last years, including all quotations, see Carlo Feltrinelli, *Feltrinelli*, 235–334.

261 **the copyright line read**: Carlo Feltrinelli, *Feltrinelli*, 200.

261 **At the V. I. Lenin State Library**: Yelena Makareki, former employee of the V. I. Lenin State Library's Special Collections section, interview and visit to library by Petra Couvée in Moscow, May 8, 2011.

261 **"a wealth of noncommunist philosophy"**: Zubok, *Zhivago's Children*, 343.

261 **On a spring evening on Gorky Street**: Olga Carlisle, *Under a New Sky*, 74.

262 **overcome with emotion**: Linda Örtenblad, archivist at the Swedish Academy, email message to the authors, March 1, 2013.

Afterword

263 **A successful stunt**: Kees van den Heuvel, interview by Petra Couvée in Leidschendam, February 22, 1999.

263 **Russian prisoners of war in Afghanistan**: Reisch, *Hot Books in the Cold War,* 515.

263 **"a museum dedicated to Pasternak"**: Rachel van der Wilden, interview by Couvée in The Hague, August 16, 2012.

263 **The books program is "demonstrably effective"**: "Foreign Relations of the United States, 1969–1976," *Soviet Union* 12 (January 1969–October 1970): 463.

263 **The CIA distributed 10 million books . . . at least 165,000 books**: "ILC: A Short Description of Its Structure and Activities," George C. Minden Papers, box 3, Hoover Institution Archives.

264 **"dictionaries and books on language"**: Reisch, *Hot Books in the Cold War,* 525.

265 **"We caused much harm"**: Nikita Khrushchev, *Khrushchev Remembers: The Glasnost Tapes,* 196.

265 **They viewed themselves as the descendants**: Zubok, *Zhivago's Children,* 20.

265 **A wave of conversions**: Adam Miknik, 1995 interview by Joseph Brodsky, in *Kniga Interv'yu* (Book of Interviews), 713.

265 **"all hunted and tormented poets"**: Bakhyt Kenzheyev, email message to Couvée, May 10, 2006.

265 **Yet the order of the acts is planned**: Boris Pasternak, "Zhivago's Poems," *Doctor Zhivago* (1958), 467.

Bibliography

ARCHIVES:

UNITED STATES

The National Archives, College Park, Maryland:
General Records of the Department of State, 1955–1959:
Travel by Soviet Officials to Belgium
Awards by Sweden to Citizens of the USSR
Internal Political Affairs of the USSR
Literature in the USSR
Censorship in the USSR
Assistant Secretary of State for Public Affairs, Records Relating to the Brussels Universal and International Exhibition, 1956–1959
Intelligence Reports on the USSR and Eastern Europe, 1942–1974, IR 7871
Eisenhower Presidential Library, Abilene, Kansas:
C. D. Jackson Papers
Abbott Washburn Papers
White House Office, Office of the Special Assistant for National Security Affairs Records, Operations Control Board
Hoover Institution Archives, Stanford, California:
Samuel S. Walker Papers
George C. Minden Papers
University of Michigan Special Collections Library, Ann Arbor:
University of Michigan Press Papers
Correspondence of Felix Morrow and Carl and Ellendea Proffer
University of California, Irvine:
Guy de Mallac Papers
Syracuse University Library, Special Collections Research Center:
Richard Elman Papers
Columbia University, Bakhmetoff Archives of Russian and East European History and Culture:
S. L. Frank Papers

ITALY

La Biblioteca della Fondazione Giangiacomo Feltrinelli, Milan:
Doctor Zhivago manuscript
Pasternak-Feltrinelli correspondence
Fondazione Russia Cristiana, Seriate:
Papers of Life with God organization

RUSSIA

State Archive of the Russian Federation (GARF):
File on Olga Ivinskaya
Russian State Archive of Socio-Political History (RGASPI):
Bukharin-Stalin letter, June 1934

SWEDEN

Archive of the Swedish Academy, Stockholm:
File on Boris Pasternak

UNITED KINGDOM

The National Archives, London:
Foreign Office Files:
Nobel Prize for Boris Pasternak
International Conference of Professors of English
Persia: Persian edition of *Dr. Zhivago*
Prime Minister's Files: Vetting and Translation of *Dr. Zhivago* by Boris Pasternak

BELGIUM

Archive of the Royal Palace, Brussels:
Archive of the Private Secretariat of Queen Elisabeth
Leuven University, Kadoc (Documentation and Research Centre for Religion, Culture and Society):
Jan Joos Papers

NETHERLANDS

University of Leiden:
The C. H. van Schooneveld Collection
The Hague:
Archives of the Dutch intelligence service (AIVD) :
File on Peter de Ridder

The Hague City Archives (Haags gemeente archief):
City maps and real estate records

GERMANY

Unternehmensarchiv Axel Springer AG, Berlin:
Heinz Schewe Papers
Schewe-Feltrinelli correspondence
Pasternak-Feltrinelli correspondence

Afiani, V. Yu, and N. G. Tomilina, eds. *"A za mnoyu shum pogoni . . ." Boris Pasternak i Vlast': Dokumenty 1956–1972* (Behind Me the Noise of Pursuit. Boris Pasternak and Power: Documents 1956–1972). Moscow: Rosspen, 2001.

Akhmatova, Anna. *My Half-Century: Selected Prose*. Evanston, IL: Northwestern University Press, 1997.

Alliluyeva, Svetlana. *Twenty Letters to a Friend*. New York: Harper & Row Publishers, 1967.

Barghoorn, Frederick C. *The Soviet Cultural Offensive: The Role of Cultural Diplomacy in Soviet Foreign Policy*. Princeton, NJ: Princeton University Press, 1960.

Barnes, Christopher. *Boris Pasternak: A Literary Biography*. Vol. 1, *1890–1928*. Cambridge: Cambridge University Press, 1989.

———. *Boris Pasternak: A Literary Biography*. Vol. 2, *1928–1960*. Cambridge: Cambridge University Press, 1998.

Berghahn, Volker R. *America and the Intellectual Cold War in Europe*. Princeton, NJ: Princeton University Press, 2001.

Berlin, Isaiah. *Enlightening: Letters 1946–1960*. London: Chatto & Windus, 2009.

———. *Personal Impressions*. London: Pimlico, 1998.

———. *The Soviet Mind: Russian Culture under Communism*. Washington, DC: Brookings Institution Press, 2004.

Blokh, Abram. *Sovetskii Soyuz v Inter'ere Nobelevskikh premii* (The Soviet Union in the Context of the Nobel Prize). Saint Petersburg: Gumanistika, 2001.

Boyd, Brian. *Vladimir Nabokov: The American Years*. Princeton, NJ: Princeton University Press, 1991.

Brent, Jonathan, and Vladimir P. Naumov. *Stalin's Last Crime: The Plot Against the Jewish Doctors*. New York: HarperCollins, 2003.

Briggs, John. *Leonard Bernstein: The Man, His Work and His World*. Cleveland, OH: The World Publishing Co., 1961.

Brodsky, Iosif (Joseph). *Kniga Interv'yu* (Book of Interviews). Edited by V. Polukhina. Moscow: Zakharov, 2005.

Brumberg, Abraham, ed. *Russia Under Khrushchev*. London: Methuen & Co., 1962.

Burton, Humphrey. *Leonard Bernstein*. New York: Doubleday, 1994.

Bykov, Dmitri. *Boris Pasternak*. Moscow: Molodaya Gvardiya, 2011.

Calvino, Italo. *Hermit in Paris: Autobiographical Writings*. New York: Vintage Books, 2003.

———. *Why Read the Classics?* New York: Pantheon Books, 1999.

Cannon, James. P. *Writings and Speeches, 1945–47: The Struggle for Socialism in the "American Century."* New York: Pathfinder Press, 1977.

Carlisle, Olga Andreyev. *Under a New Sky: A Reunion with Russia*. New York: Ticknor & Fields, 1993.

Caute, David. *Politics and the Novel During the Cold War*. New Brunswick, NJ: Transaction Publishers, 2010.

Chavchavadze, David. *Crowns and Trenchcoats: A Russian Prince in the CIA*. New York: Atlantic International Publications, 1990.

Chuev, Felix. *Molotov Remembers: Inside Kremlin Politics, Conversations with Felix Chuev*. Chicago: Ivan R. Dee, 1993.

Chukovskaya, Lydia. *The Akhmatova Journals*. Vol. 1, *1938–1941*. New York: Farrar Straus and Giroux, 1994.

———. *Iz dnevnika, Vospominaniya* (From the Diary, Memoirs). Moscow: Vremya, 2010.

———. *Zapiski ob Anne Akhmatovoi* (Notes on Anna Akhmatova). 3 vols. Moscow: Soglasie, 1997.

———. *Sochineniya v 2 tomakh* (Works in Two Volumes). Moscow: Gudyal Press, 2000.

Chukovsky, Kornei. *Diary, 1901–1969*. New Haven, CT: Yale University Press, 2005.

———. *Dnevnik, v 3 tomakh* (Diary, in 3 volumes). Moscow: ProzaiK, 2011.

Clark, Katerina, and Evgeny Dobrenko, eds. *Soviet Culture and Power: A History in Documents, 1917–1953*. Compiled by Andrei Artizov and Oleg Naumov. New Haven, CT: Yale University Press, 2007.

Cohen, Stephen. F. *Bukharin and the Bolshevik Revolution*. New York: Alfred A. Knopf, 1973.

Colby, William, and Peter Forbath. *Honorable Men: My Life in the CIA*. New York: Simon and Schuster, 1978.

Coleman, Peter. *The Liberal Conspiracy: The Congress for Cultural Freedom and the Struggle for the Mind of Postwar Europe*. New York: The Free Press, 1989.

Conquest, Robert. *Courage of Genius: The Pasternak Affair*. London: Collins and Harvill Press, 1961.

———. *Stalin: Breaker of Nations*. New York: Penguin Books, 1991.

Critchlow, James. *Radio Hole-in-the-Head: Radio Liberty*. Washington, DC: The American University Press, 1995.

Dalos, György. *The Guest from the Future*. New York: Farrar, Straus and Giroux, 1998.

———. *Olga, Pasternaks letzte Liebe* (Olga, Pasternak's Last Love). Hamburg: Europäische Verlagsantsalt/Rotbuch Verlag, 1999.

D'Angelo, Sergio. *Delo Pasternaka: Vospominaniya Ochevidtsa* (The Pasternak Affair: Memoirs of a Witness). Moscow: Novoe Literaturnoe Obozrenie, 2007.

Davie, Donald, and Angela Livingstone, eds. *Pasternak: Modern Judgments*. London: Macmillan, 1969.

De Grand, Alexander. *The Italian Left in the Twentieth Century: A History of the Socialist and Communist Parties*. Bloomington: Indiana University Press, 1989.

De Mallac, Guy. *Boris Pasternak: His Life and Art*. London: Souvenir Press, 1983.

Dewhirst, Martin, and Robert Farrell, eds. *The Soviet Censorship*. Metuchen, NJ: The Scarecrow Press, 1973.

Dobbs, Michael. *Six Months in 1945*. New York: Alfred A. Knopf, 2012.

Ehrenburg, Ilya. *Post-War Years, 1945–54*. Cleveland, OH: The World Publishing Co., 1967.

Espmark, Kjell. *The Nobel Prize in Literature: A Study of the Criteria Behind the Choices*. Boston: G. K. Hall & Co., 1986.

Feinstein, Elaine. *Anna of All the Russias: The Life of Anna Akhmatova*. London: Weidenfeld & Nicolson, 2005.

Feltrinelli, Carlo. *Feltrinelli: A Story of Riches, Revolution and Violent Death*. Translated by Alistair McEwen. New York: Harcourt, 2001.

Fleishman, Lazar. *Boris Pasternak, The Poet and His Politics*. Cambridge, MA: Harvard University Press, 1990.

———. *Vstrecha russkoi emigratsii s "Doktorom Zhivago": Boris Pasternak i "kholodnaya voina"* (Encounter of the Russian Emigration with *Doctor Zhivago:* Boris Pasternak and "The Cold War"). Stanford Slavic Studies, 2009.

Fleishman, Lazar, ed. *Boris Pasternak and His Times: Selected Papers*. Berkeley: Berkeley Slavic Specialties, 1989.

———, ed. *Eternity's Hostage: Stanford International Conference on Boris Pasternak*. 2 vols. Berkeley: Berkeley Slavic Specialties, 2006.

———, ed. *The Life of Boris Pasternak's Doctor Zhivago*. Berkeley: Berkeley Slavic Specialties, 2009.

Frankel, Edith. *Novy Mir: A Case Study in the Politics of Literature, 1952–1958*. Cambridge: Cambridge University Press, 1981.

Frankel, Max. *The Times of My Life and My Life with The* Times. New York: Random House, 1999.

Gaddis, John Lewis. *George F. Kennan: An American Life*. New York: The Penguin Press, 2011.

Garrand, John, and Carol Garrand. *Inside the Soviet Writers' Union.* New York: The Free Press, 1990.

Gerstein, Emma. *Memuary* (Memoirs). Saint Petersburg: Inapress, 1998.

———. *Moscow Memoirs.* Woodstock, NY, and New York: The Overlook Press, 2004.

Gladkov, Alexander. *Meetings with Pasternak: A Memoir.* New York and London: Harcourt Brace Jovanovich, 1977.

Grose, Peter. *Gentleman Spy: The Life of Allen Dulles.* New York: Houghton Mifflin, 1994.

Hayward, Max. *Writers in Russia, 1917–1978.* Edited and with an introduction by Patricia Blake. San Diego: Harcourt Brace Jovanovich, 1983.

Heilbrun, Carolyn G. *The Education of a Woman: The Life of Gloria Steinem.* New York: Ballantine Books, 1995.

Hingley, Ronald. *Pasternak, a Biography.* New York: Alfred A. Knopf, 1983.

Hinrichs, Jan Paul. *The C. H. van Schooneveld Collection in Leiden University Library.* Leiden: Leiden University Library, 2001.

Hixson, Walter L. *Parting the Curtain: Propaganda, Culture and the Cold War.* New York: St. Martin's Griffin, 1998.

Independent Service for Information. Report on the Vienna Youth Festival (with a foreword by Senator Hubert H. Humphrey). Cambridge, MA: Independent Service for Information, 1960.

Ivinskaya, Olga. *A Captive of Time: My Years with Pasternak.* New York: Doubleday, 1978.

Jeffreys-Jones, Rhodri. *The CIA and American Democracy.* New Haven: Yale University Press, 2003.

Jeffreys-Jones, Rhodri, and Christopher Andrew, eds. *Eternal Vigilance? 50 Years of the CIA.* London and Portland, OR: Frank Cass, 1997.

Johnson, A. Ross. *Radio Free Europe and Radio Liberty: The CIA Years and Beyond.* Washington, DC: Woodrow Wilson Center Press, 2010.

Johnson, Ian. *A Mosque in Munich: Nazis, the CIA, and the Rise of the Muslim Brotherhood in the West.* New York: Houghton Mifflin Harcourt, 2010.

Joos, Jan. *Deelneming van de H. Stoel aan de algemene Wereldtentoonstelling van Brussel 1958* (Participation of the Holy See in the Universal and International Exhibition of Brussels 1958). Brussels: Commissariaat van de Heilige Stoel, 1962.

Kadare, Ismail. *Le Crépuscule des dieux de la steppe* (Twilight of the Steppe Gods). Paris: Fayard, 1981.

Kaminskaya, Dina. *Final Judgment: My Life as a Soviet Defense Attorney.* New York: Simon and Schuster, 1982.

Kavanagh, Julie. *Nureyev.* New York: Pantheon Books, 2007.

Kaverin, Veniamin. *Epilog* (Epilogue). Moscow: Vagrius, 2006.

Kemp-Walsh, Anthony. *Stalin and the Literary Intelligentsia 1928–39.* London: Macmillan, 1991.

Khrushchev, Nikita. *Khrushchev Remembers: The Glasnost Tapes*. New York: Little, Brown, 1990.

———. *Khrushchev Remembers: The Last Testament*. New York: Little, Brown, 1974.

Khrushchev, Sergei. *Khrushchev on Khrushchev*. Boston: Little, Brown, 1990.

Kotek, Joël. *Students and the Cold War*. New York: St. Martin's Press, 1996.

Kozlov, Denis. *The Readers of Novyi Mir: Coming to Terms with the Stalinist Past*. Cambridge, MA: Harvard University Press, 2013.

Kozovoi, Vadim. *Poet v katastrofe* (Poet in the Catastrophe). Moscow: Paris Institut d'Études Slaves, Gnozis, 1994.

Lamphere, Robert J., and Tom Shachtman. *The FBI-KGB War*. Macon, GA: Mercer University Press, 1995.

Lipkin, Semyon. *Kvadriga* (Quadriga). Moscow: Agraf, 1997.

Livanov, Vasili. *Mezhdu dvumya Zhivago, vospominaniya i vpechatleniya, p'esy, Sobranie Sochinenii* (Between Two Zhivagos, Memoirs and Impressions, Plays. Collected Works). Vol. 2. Saint Petersburg: Azbuka, 2010.

Lobov, Lev, and Kira Vasilyeva. "Peredelkino. Skazanie o pisatel'skom gorodke" (Peredelkino: The Tale of a Writers' Village). Moscow, 2011, http://www.peredelkino-land.ru.

Mancosu, Paolo. *Inside the Zhivago Storm: The Editorial Adventures of Pasternak's Masterpiece*. Milan: Fondazione Giangiacomo Feltrinelli, 2013.

Mandelstam, Nadezhda. *Hope Abandoned*. New York: Atheneum, 1974.

———. *Hope Against Hope*. New York: Modern Library, 1999.

Mandelstam, Osip. *Critical Prose and Letters*. Woodstock, NY, and New York: Ardis, 2003.

Mansurov, Boris. *Lara, moego romana, Boris Pasternak i Ol'ga Ivinskaya* (The Lara of My Novel: Boris Pasternak and Olga Ivinskaya). Moscow: Infomedia, 2009.

Mark, Paul J., ed. *The Family Pasternak—Reminiscences, Reports*. Geneva: Éditions Poésie Vivante, 1975.

Masey, Jack, and Conway Lloyd Morgan. *Cold War Confrontations: U.S. Exhibitions and Their Role in the Cultural Cold War*. Zurich: Lars Müller Publishers, 2008.

Maslenikova, Zoya. *Portret Borisa Pasternaka* (Portrait of Boris Pasternak). Moscow: Sovietskaya Rossiya,1990.

Matthews, Owen. *Stalin's Children: Three Generations of Love, War and Survival*. New York: Walker & Co., 2008.

McLean, Hugh, and Walter N. Vickery, eds. *The Year of Protest 1956: An Anthology of Soviet Literary Materials*. New York: Vintage Books, 1961.

Medvedev, Roy. *Khrushchev*. Oxford: Basil Blackwell, 1983.

Merton, Thomas. *The Literary Essays of Thomas Merton*. New York: New Directions, 1985.

Meyer, Cord. *Facing Reality: From World Federation to the CIA*. Lanham, MD: University Press of America, 1980.

Montefiore, Simon Sebag. *Stalin. The Court of the Red Tsar*. New York: Alfred A. Knopf. 2004.

Muravina, Nina. *Vstrechi s Pasternakom* (Meetings with Pasternak). Tenafly, NJ. Ermitazh, 1990.

O'Casey, Sean. *The Letters of Sean O'Casey, 1955–1958*. Edited by David Krause. Washington, DC: The Catholic University of America Press,1989.

Orlova, Raisa. *Memoirs*. New York: Random House, 1983.

Pasternak, Alexander. *A Vanished Present: The Memoirs of Alexander Pasternak*. New York: Harcourt Brace Jovanovich, 1985.

Pasternak, Boris. *Doctor Zhivago*. Translated by Max Hayward and Manya Harari. New York: Pantheon Books, 1958.

———. *Doctor Zhivago*. Translated by Richard Pevear and Larissa Volokhonsky. New York: Pantheon Books, 2010.

———. *Family Correspondence 1921–1960*. Translated by Nicolas Pasternak Slater. Stanford, CA: Hoover Institution Press, 2010.

———. *I Remember: Sketch for an Autobiography*. New York: Pantheon, 1959.

———. *Lettres à mes amies françaises (1956–1960)*. Introduction and notes by Jacqueline de Proyart. Paris: Gallimard, 1994.

———. *Letters to Georgian Friends*. New York: Harcourt, Brace & World, 1967.

———. *Poems*. Moscow: Raduga Publishers, 1990.

———. *Poems of Boris Pasternak*. Trans. Lydia Pasternak Slater. London: Unwin, 1984.

———. *Polnoe Sobranie Sochinenii* (Complete Collected Works). 11 Vols. Edited by Yevgeni and Yelena Pasternak. Moscow: Slovo, 2003–5.

———. *Safe Conduct*. New York: New Directions, 1959.

———. *Vtoroe Rozhdenie. Pis'ma k Z.N. Pasternak. Z.N. Pasternak, Vospominaniya. Sostavlenie i podgotovka teksta, N. Pasternak, M. Feinberg* (Second Birth. Letters to Z. N. Pasternak. Z. N. Pasternak, Memoirs). Edited by N. Pasternak and M. Feinberg. Moscow: Dom-muzei Borisa Pasternaka, 2010.

———. *Selected Writings and Letters*. Moscow: Progress Publishers, 1990.

Pasternak, Boris, and Freidenberg, Olga. *The Correspondence of Boris Pasternak and Olga Freidenberg, 1910–1954*. New York: Harcourt Brace Jovanovich, 1982.

Pasternak, Boris, and Kurt Wolff. *Im Meer der Hingabe: Briefwechsel 1958–1960* (In A Sea of Devotion: Correspondence 1958–1960). Frankfurt am Main: Peter Lang, 2007.

Pasternak, Josephine. *Tightrope Walking: A Memoir by Josephine Pasternak*. Bloomington, IN: Slavica, 2005.

Pasternak, Leonid. *The Memoirs of Leonid Pasternak*. New York: Harcourt Brace Jovanovich, 1985.

Pasternak, (Yevgeni) Evgeny. *Boris Pasternak: The Tragic Years, 1930–1960.* London: Collins Harvill, 1991.

———. *Sushchestvovan'ya tkan' skvoznaya, Boris Pasternak: Perepiska s Yev. Pasternak* (The Transparent Fabric of Being, Boris Pasternak: Correspondence with Yevgeni Pasternak). Moscow: Novoe Literaturnoe Obozrenie, 1998.

———. *Ponyatoe i obretyonnoe, stat'i i vospominaniya* (The Understood and Found, Articles and Memoirs). Moscow: Tri Kvadrata, 2009.

Pasternak, Zinaida. *Vospominaniya.* In Pasternak, Boris. *Vtoroe Rozhdenie.*

Patch, Isaac. *Closing the Circle: A Buckalino Journey Around Our Time.* Self-published.

Pluvinge, Gonzague. *Expo 58: Between Utopia and Reality.* Tielt, Belgium: Lannoo, 2008.

Poretsky, Elizabeth K. *Our Own People: A Memoir of "Ignace Reiss" and His Friends.* Ann Arbor: The University of Michigan Press, 1969.

Proffer, Carl R. *The Widows of Russia.* Ann Arbor: Ardis, 1987.

Puzikov, Alexander. *Budni i prazdniki: Iz zapisok glavnogo redaktora* (Weekdays and Holidays: From the Notes of an Editor-in-Chief). Moscow: Khudozhestvennaya Literatura, 1994.

Reeder, Roberta. *Anna Akhmatova: Poet and Prophet.* New York: St. Martin's Press, 1994.

Reisch, Alfred A. *Hot Books in the Cold War: The CIA-Funded Secret Western Book Distribution Program Behind the Iron Curtain.* Budapest: Central European University Press, 2013.

Richmond, Yale. *Cultural Exchange & The Cold War.* University Park: Pennsylvania State University Press, 2003.

Ruder, Cynthia. *Making History for Stalin. The Story of the Belomor Canal.* Gainesville: University Press of Florida, 1998.

Ruge, Gerd. *Pasternak: A Pictorial Biography.* New York: McGraw-Hill, 1959.

Rydell, Robert R. *World of Fairs.* Chicago: University of Chicago Press, 1993.

Sarnov, Benedikt. *Stalin i pisateli* (Stalin and the Writers). Moscow: Eksmo, 2008.

Saunders, Francis Stonor. *The Cultural Cold War: The CIA and the World of Arts and Letters.* New York: The New Press, 2001.

Schewe, Heinz. *Pasternak privat* (Private Pasternak). Hamburg: Hans Christians Verlag, 1974.

Schiff, Stacy. *Vera (Mrs. Vladimir Nabokov): Portrait of a Marriage.* New York: Random House, 1999.

Schweitzer, Renate. *Freundschaft mit Boris Pasternak* (Friendship with Boris Pasternak). Munich: Verlag Kurt Desch, 1963.

Semichastny, Vladimir. *Bespokoynoe serdtse* (Restless Heart). Moscow: Vagrius, 2002.

Service, Robert. *Stalin: A Biography*. London: Macmillan, 2004.

———. *Trotsky*. Cambridge, MA: The Belknap Press of Harvard University Press, 2009.

Shentalinsky, Vitaly. *The KGB's Literary Archive.* Translated, abridged, and annotated by John Crowfoot. With an introduction by Robert Conquest. London: The Harvill Press, 1995.

Shklovsky, Viktor. *Zoo, or Letters Not About Love*. Ithaca, NY: Cornell University Press, 1971.

Sieburg, Friedrich. *Zur Literatur 1957–1963* (On Literature 1957–1963). Munich: Deutsche Verlags-Anstalt, 1981.

Smith, S. A. *The Russian Revolution: A Very Short Introduction*. Oxford: Oxford University Press, 2002.

Solzhenitsyn, Aleksandr. *The Mortal Danger. How Misconceptions About Russia Imperil America.* New York: HarperCollins, 1986.

———. *The Oak and the Calf*. New York: Harper & Row, 1979.

Sosin, Gene. *Sparks of Liberty: An Insider's Memoir of Radio Liberty*. University Park: Pennsylvania State University Press, 1999.

Stern, Sydney Ladensohn. *Gloria Steinem: Her Passions, Politics and Mystique*. Secaucus, NJ: Birch Lane Press, 1997.

Strömberg, Kjell. Nobel Prize Library. New York: Alexis Gregory, 1971.

Svensén, Bo. *The Swedish Academy and the Nobel Prize in Literature*. Stockholm: Swedish Academy, 2011.

Taubman, William. *Khrushchev: The Man and His Era*. New York: W. W. Norton & Company, 2003.

Thomas, Evan. *The Very Best Men: Four Who Dared: The Early Years of the CIA*. New York: Touchstone, 1995.

Thorne, C. Thomas, Jr., David S. Patterson, and Glenn W. LaFantasie, eds. *Foreign Relations of the United States, 1945–1950: Emergence of the Intelligence Establishment.* Washington, DC: U.S. State Department Office of the Historian / GPO, 1996.

Tolstoy, Ivan. *Doktor Zhivago: novye fakty i nakhodki v Nobelevskom arkhive* (*Doctor Zhivago:* New facts and Finds in the Nobel Archive). Prague: Human Rights Publishers, 2010.

———. *Otmytyi roman Pasternaka, "Doctor Zhivago" mezhdu KGB i TsRU* (Pasternak's Laundered Novel: *Doctor Zhivago* Between the KGB and the CIA). Moscow: Vremya, 2009.

Trento, Joseph J. *The Secret History of the CIA*. New York: Basic Books, 2001.

Trotsky, Leon. *Literature and Revolution*. Chicago: Haymarket Books, 2005.

Tsvetaeva, Marina. *Art in the Light of Conscience: Eight Essays on Poetry*. Translated by Angela Livingstone. Northumberland, UK: Bloodaxe Books, 2010.

U.S. Senate. *Final Report of the Select Committee to Study Governmen-*

tal Operations with Respect to Intelligence Activities. Washington, DC: U.S. Government Printing Office, 1976.

———. *Subcommittee to investigate the administration of the Internal Security Act, Committee on the Judiciary. Karlin Testimony*. Washington, DC: U.S. Government Printing Office, 1969.

Urban, Joan Barth. *Moscow and the Italian Communist Party: From Togliatti to Berlinguer*. Ithaca, NY: Cornell University Press, 1986.

Vil'mont, Nikolai. *O Borise Pasternake, vospominaniya i mysli* (On Boris Pasternak, Memories and Thoughts). Moscow: Sovetskii pisatel', 1989.

Vitale, Serena. *Shklovsky: Witness to an Era*. Champaign, IL: Dalkey Archive Press, 2012.

Vos, Chris. *De Geheime Dienst: Verhalen over de BVD* (The Secret Service: Stories about the BVD). Amsterdam: Boom, 2005.

Voznesensky, Andrei. *An Arrow in the Wall: Selected Poetry and Prose*. New York: Henry Holt, 1978.

Wachtel, Andrew Baruch. *An Obsession with History: Russian Writers Confront the Past*. Stanford, CA: Stanford University Press, 1994.

Wald, Alan M. *The New York Intellectuals: The Rise and Decline of the Anti-Stalinist Left from the 1930s to the 1980s*. Chapel Hill: The University of North Carolina Press, 1987.

Werth, Alexander. *Russia Under Khrushchev*. New York: Hill and Wang, 1961.

Westerman, Frank. *Engineers of the Soul: The Grandiose Propaganda of Stalin's Russia*. New York: The Overlook Press, 2011.

Wilford, Hugh. *The Mighty Wurlitzer: How the CIA Played America*. Cambridge, MA: Harvard University Press, 2008.

Winks, Robin. *Cloak & Gown. Scholars in the Secret War, 1939–1961*. New York: William Morrow, 1987.

Wolff, Kurt. *A Portrait in Essays and Letters*. Edited by Michael Ermarth. Chicago: University of Chicago Press, 1991.

Yemelyanova, Irina. *Legendy Potapovskogo pereulka* (Legends of Potapov Street). Moscow: Ellis Lak, 1997.

———. *Pasternak i Ivinskaya: provoda pod tokom* (Pasternak and Ivinskaya: Live Wires). Moscow: Vagrius, 2006.

Yesipov, Valery. *Shalamov*. Moscow: Molodaya Gvardiya, 2012.

Yevtushenko, Yevgeni. *Shesti-desantnik, memuarnaya proza* (Memoirs). Moscow: Ast Zebra, 2008.

———. *A Precocious Autobiography*. London: Collins and Harvill Press, 1963.

Zubok, Vladislav. *Zhivago's Children: The Last Russian Intelligentsia*. Cambridge, MA: The Belknap Press of Harvard University Press, 2009.

Index

Photographic Credits

Boris Pasternak with books and paintings: ITAR-TASS
Pasternak and Kornei Chukovsky: ITAR-TASS
Anna Akhmatova and Pasternak: ITAR-TASS
Olga Ivinskaya in overcoat: Axel Springer AG, Berlin
Young Olga Ivinskaya, wearing pearls: Irina Ivinskaya
Giangiacomo Feltrinelli: Archivio Giangiacomo Feltrinelli Editore
Alexei Surkov: ITAR-TASS
Felix Morrow: Meghan Morrow
Case of the CIA hardcover edition of Doctor Zhivago: Tim Gressie
Title page of the CIA hardcover edition: Tim Gressie
Title page of the miniature paperback edition: CIA Museum Collection
Vatican Pavilion at the 1958 World's Fair: www.studioclaerhout.be/Gent/Belgium
Anders Österling: Kent Östlund/Scanpix Sweden/Sipa USA
Pasternak near his home in the countryside: AP Photo/Harold K. Milks
Dacha in the village of Peredelkino: AP Photo
Pasternak reads telegrams with wife, Zinaida, friend Nina Tabidze: Bettmann/Corbis
Olga Ivinskaya and her daughter, Irina, with Pasternak: Axel Springer AG, Berlin
Cartoon by Bill Mauldin: © Bill Mauldin, 1958. Courtesy of the Bill Mauldin Estate LLC
Front page of The Washington Post: *The Washington Post;* Bettmann/Corbis
Carrying the casket of Pasternak: Bettmann/Corbis
Pasternak's funeral with wife, Zinaida, and Olga Ivinskaya: Axel Springer AG, Berlin
Boris Pasternak looks out from the upstairs study in his dacha: Bettmann/Corbis

A Note on the Type

The text of this book was composed in Trump Mediaeval, designed by Professor Georg Trump (1896–1985) in the mid-1950s. The roman letterforms are based on classical prototypes, and the italic letterforms are closely related to their roman counterparts. The result is a truly contemporary type, notable for both its legibility and its versatility.

Composed by North Market Street Graphics, Lancaster, Pennsylvania

Printed and bound by Berryville Graphics, Berryville, Virginia

Designed by Iris Weinstein

www.vintage-books.co.uk